AUGUSTINE, RAHNER, AND TRINITARIAN EXEGESIS

T&T Clark Studies in Systematic Theology

Edited by
Ian A. McFarland
Ivor Davidson
Philip G. Ziegler
John Webster†

Volume 42

AUGUSTINE, RAHNER, AND TRINITARIAN EXEGESIS

An Exploration of Augustine's Exegesis of Scripture as a Foundation for Rahner's Trinitarian Project and Rule

Martin E. Robinson

LONDON • NEW YORK • OXFORD • NEW DELHI • SYDNEY

T&T CLARK
Bloomsbury Publishing Plc, 50 Bedford Square, London, WC1B 3DP, UK
Bloomsbury Publishing Inc, 1359 Broadway, New York, NY 10018, USA
Bloomsbury Publishing Ireland, 29 Earlsfort Terrace, Dublin 2, D02 AY28, Ireland

BLOOMSBURY, T&T CLARK and the T&T Clark logo are trademarks of
Bloomsbury Publishing Plc

First published in Great Britain 2024
Paperback edition published 2026

Copyright © Martin E. Robinson, 2024

Martin E. Robinson has asserted his right under the Copyright, Designs and Patents Act, 1988, to be identified as Author of this work.

For legal purposes the Acknowledgments on p. ix constitute an extension of this copyright page.

All rights reserved. No part of this publication may be: i) reproduced or transmitted in any form, electronic or mechanical, including photocopying, recording or by means of any information storage or retrieval system without prior permission in writing from the publishers; or ii) used or reproduced in any way for the training, development or operation of artificial intelligence (AI) technologies, including generative AI technologies. The rights holders expressly reserve this publication from the text and data mining exception as per Article 4(3) of the Digital Single Market Directive (EU) 2019/790.

Bloomsbury Publishing Plc does not have any control over, or responsibility for, any third-party websites referred to or in this book. All internet addresses given in this book were correct at the time of going to press. The author and publisher regret any inconvenience caused if addresses have changed or sites have ceased to exist, but can accept no responsibility for any such changes.

A catalogue record for this book is available from the British Library.

Library of Congress Cataloging-in-Publication Data

Names: Robinson, Martin E., author.
Title: Augustine, Rahner and trinitarian exegesis : an exploration of Augustine's exegesis of Scripture as a foundation for Rahner's trinitarian project and rule / Martin E. Robinson.
Description: [New York] : [T&T Clark], [2024] | Series: T&T Clark studies in systematic theology | Includes bibliographical references and index.
Identifiers: LCCN 2023051372 (print) | LCCN 2023051373 (ebook) | ISBN 9780567714831 (hardback) | ISBN 9780567714862 (paperback) | ISBN 9780567714848 (epub) | ISBN 9780567715678 (pdf)
Subjects: LCSH: Rahner, Karl, 1904-1984. | Trinity–History of doctrines–20th century. | Augustine, of Hippo, Saint, 354-430. | Trinity–History of doctrines–Early church, ca. 30-600. | Bible–Criticism, interpretation, etc.–History–Early church, ca. 30-600. | Catholic Church–Doctrines–History.
Classification: LCC BX4705.R287 R63 2024 (print) | LCC BX4705.R287 (ebook) | DDC 231/.044–dc23/eng/20240322
LC record available at https://lccn.loc.gov/2023051372
LC ebook record available at https://lccn.loc.gov/2023051373

ISBN: HB: 978-0-5677-1483-1
PB: 978-0-5677-1486-2
ePDF: 978-0-5677-1567-8
eBook: 978-0-5677-1484-8

Series: T&T Clark Studies in Systematic Theology, volume 42

Typeset by Newgen KnowledgeWorks Pvt. Ltd., Chennai, India

For product safety related questions contact productsafety@bloomsbury.com.

To find out more about our authors and books visit www.bloomsbury.com and sign up for our newsletters.

CONTENTS

Acknowledgments ix
Abbreviations x

Chapter 1
INTRODUCTION 1
   1. Rahner's Criticisms of the Augustinian Tradition 3
      Religious Piety 3
      Christological Peculiarity 4
      Doctrine of Grace 5
      Doctrine of Creation 6
      De Deo Uno and *De Deo Trino* 7
      The Economy and Scripture 8
      The Old Testament 9
      The Missions and Processions 10
   2. Exegetical Criticisms of Rahner's Solution 11
      The Father–Son Relationship 13
      The Son–Spirit Relationship 14
   3. The Lacunae 15
      Augustine's Exegesis and Rahner's Assessment of the West 15
      A Biblical Defence of Rahner's Rule 18
      Rahner's Rule and Patristic Exegesis 19
   4. The Argument 20

Chapter 2
AUGUSTINE AND THE ECONOMY: SCRIPTURE, *DE DEO UNO* AND
TRINO, CHRISTOLOGY, CREATION, AND PIETY 23
   1. Trinity and Scripture 23
      The Western Tradition and the Separation of Trinity and Scripture 23
      The Biblical Foundations of *Trin.* Book 1 25
      The Biblical Backdrop of the Psychological Analogy 31
   2. *De Deo Uno* and *De Deo Trino* 34
      The Western Tradition and the Separation of the *De Deo Uno* and
         De Deo Trino 34
      Augustine's Integration of the *De Deo Uno* and *De Deo Trino* 35
      The *Inseparabilis Operatio* 37
      God the Father and the Trinity 37
   3. Trinity and Christology 39
      The Western Tradition and the Separation of Trinity and Christology 39

		Augustine's Strategies for Preserving Christological Peculiarity	41
	4.	Trinity and Creation	47
		The Western Tradition and the Separation of Trinity and Creation	47
		John 1:3 and the *Inseparabilis Operatio*	47
		John 1:3 and the Psychological Analogy	48
		Gen 1:26 and the Psychological Analogy	49
		Rom 1:20 and the *Vestigia*	51
		A Trinitarian Reading of Gen 1–3	52
		Augustine and Bonaventure: A Comparison	53
	5.	Trinity and Faith	54
		The Western Tradition and the Separation of Trinity and Faith	54
		The Starting Point of Faith	55
		Praying to the Father and the Trinity	57
		Faith as the End	58
		Faith and the Psychological Analogy	59
	6.	Summary	60

Chapter 3
AUGUSTINE AND THE ECONOMY: THE OLD TESTAMENT, SOTERIOLOGY, AND THE MISSIONS AND PROCESSIONS

			63
	1.	Introduction	63
	2.	Trinity and the Old Testament Theophanies	64
		Rahner on the Trinity and the Old Testament	64
		Augustine's Approach to the Theophanies	66
		Augustine and the Tradition	67
		Augustine's Exegesis	71
	3.	Trinity and Salvation	76
		Rahner on the Trinity and Salvation	76
		The Place of *Trin.* 4 in Augustine's Argument	78
		The Exegetical Backdrop	78
		Mediation, the One, and the Many	80
		Mediation, Christ, and the Devil	81
		The Inadequacy of Philosophy	82
		Conclusion	84
	4.	Trinity, Missions, and Processions	86
		Rahner on the Missions and Processions	86
		Augustine's Definition of "Missions"	88
		The Correspondence of the Son's Mission and Procession	89
		Exegetical Support for the Correspondence of the Son's Mission and Procession	92
		The Correspondence of the Spirit's Mission and Procession	94
		Exegetical Support for the Correspondence of the Spirit's Mission and Procession	96
		Conclusion	99
	5.	Summary	99

Chapter 4
THE FATHER–SON RELATIONSHIP: RAHNER'S RULE, CONTEMPORARY
OBJECTIONS, AND AUGUSTINE'S EXEGESIS 101
  1. Introduction 101
    Rahner and Scripture 101
    Defining Rahner's Rule 102
    Alleged Difficulties for Rahner's Rule 104
    Preview 105
  2. Subordinationism 106
    The Problem of Subordinationism 106
    Augustine's Strategy for Preventing Subordinationism 107
  3. Reversibility and the Transfer of Authority 109
    The Problem of Reversibility and the Transfer of Authority 109
    1 Cor 15:24–28 110
    John 5:22, 5:26, 5:27; Phil 2:9 111
    John 16:15 112
    Dan 7:13–14 114
    Matt 28:18 114
    Summary 115
  4. Reversibility and Mutuality 116
    The Problem of Reversibility and Mutuality 116
    Mutual Glorification 117
    Mutual Knowledge and Revelation 119
    Mutual Love 122
    Mutual Indwelling 125
    Summary 126
  5. Reversibility and Triadic Patterns 127
    The Problem of Reversibility and Triadic Patterns 127
    Son–Father–Spirit Texts 129
    Son–Spirit–Father Texts 132
    Spirit–Son–Father Texts 136
    Summary 140
  6. The Ascension 141
    The Parallel Starting Point 142
    The Parallel End Point 143
  7. Conclusion 144

Chapter 5
THE SON–SPIRIT RELATIONSHIP: RAHNER'S RULE, CONTEMPORARY
OBJECTIONS, AND AUGUSTINE'S EXEGESIS 147
  1. Introduction 147
  2. Alleged Difficulties for Rahner's Rule 149
  3. Proposed Solutions and Their Alleged Difficulties 151
  4. The Virgin Conception 157
  5. The Jordan Baptism 164

6. Ministry	166
7. Resurrection	174
8. Pentecost	177
9. Other Triads	180
Spirit–Son–Father and Son–Spirit–Father Texts	181
Father–Spirit–Son Texts	183
Spirit–Father–Son Texts	188
Summary	190
10. Conclusion	191

Chapter 6
CONCLUSION 193
  1. Research Findings 193
  2. Contributions 196
  3. Recommendations for Future Research 196
  4. Summary 198

Bibliography 199
  1. Primary Literature 199
  2. Secondary Literature 205
Ancient Source Index 213
Scripture Index 221
Subject Index 227

ACKNOWLEDGMENTS

Words cannot express my gratitude to David Höhne, who supervised the dissertation that developed into this book. I'm extremely grateful for the counsel of Mark Earngey, my secondary supervisor, George Athas, Director of Research, and the rest of the Moore Theological College faculty for their encouragement, direction, and wise counsel. This endeavour would not have been possible without the generous support of Moore Theological College, who financed my research, nor would it have been feasible without the generous provision of accommodation from Yagoona and Condell Park Anglican Church for All Nations. I am indebted to both.

I am grateful to my friends in the postgraduate room, Chris Conyers, Kamina Wüst, Jonathan Wu, James Rutherford, and Vivian Cheung, for their feedback, editing help, and moral support, and our much-beloved coffee and lunch breaks. I am also grateful to Luke Tucker and Jonathan Adams, for their help in checking my translations, and to Keith Hill, Mark Woodhouse, and Bronwyn Windsor for their assistance in proofreading. Similarly, I am very thankful to Sophie Beardsworth, Jack Curtin, Sam Augustin and the teams from Bloomsbury and Newgen for their help in getting this book ready for publication, and to Lewis Ayres and Matthew Levering for directing me to these teams. All remaining errors are my own.

I would like to extend my sincere thanks to Neil Ormerod of Sydney College of Divinity for his advice and encouragement along the way. Thanks should also go to the Moore College librarians, Erin Mollenhauer and Rod Benson, for their determination in helping me obtain resources, and to Michael Hauber, Roman Siebenbrock, Benedikt Collinet, Hernán Rojas, Dennis Jowers, Karen Kilby, and Philip Endean for their encouragement and assistance in acquiring resources either unavailable in Australia or inaccessible due to Covid-19 restrictions.

I would be remiss in not mentioning my family, especially my wife, Emma, our parents, Grant, Clare, Peter, and Bronwyn, and our children, Levi, Isaac, and Sophie. Your prayer, encouragement, support, and ability to distract me has kept my spirits and motivation high during this process. I could not have done this without you. Thank you.

Lastly, praise be to the Father, Son, and Holy Spirit, about whom this book is written, and without whose help it could not have been written.

ABBREVIATIONS

All abbreviations follow The SBL Handbook of Style

Ambrose

Fid.	De fide
Spir.	De Spiritu Sancto

Athanasius

C. Ar.	Orationes contra Arianos
C. Gent.	Contra gentes

Augustine

Adim.	Contra Adimantum
Arian.	Contra sermonem Arianorum
Civ.	De civitate Dei
Coll. Max.	Collatio cum Maximino Arianorum episcopo
Conf.	Confessionum libri XIII
Cons.	De consensu evangelistarum
Div. quaest. LXXXIII	De diversis quaestionibus LXXXIII
Doctr. chr.	De doctrina christiana
Enarrat. Ps.	Enarrationes in Psalmos
Enchir.	Enchiridion de fide, spe, et caritate
Ep.	Epistulae
Fund.	Contra epistulam Manichaei quam vocant Fundamenti
C. du. ep. Pelag.	Contra duas epistulas Pelagianorum ad Bonifatium
Exp. Gal.	Expositio in epistulam ad Galatas
Faust.	Contra Faustum
Gen. litt.	De Genesi ad litteram
Grat.	De gratia et libero arbitrio
C. Jul. op. imp.	Contra secundam Juliani responsionem imperfectum opus
C. litt. Petil.	Contra litteras Petiliani
Man.	De moribus Manichaeorum
Maxim.	Contra Maximinum Arianum

Parm.	Contra epistulam Parmeniani
Pecc. merit.	De peccatorum meritis et remissione
Praed.	De praedestinatione sanctorum
Priscill.	Ad Orosium contra Priscillianistas et Origenistas
Quaest. Hept.	Quaestiones in Heptateuchum
Retract.	Retractationum libri II
Serm.	Sermones
Spec.	De scriptura sancta speculum
Serm. Dom.	De sermone Domini in monte
Spir. et litt.	De spirituet littera
Tract. Ep. Jo.	In epistulam Johannis ad Parthos tractatus
Tract. Ev. Jo.	In Evangelium Johannis tractatus
Trin.	De Trinitate

Basil

Eun.	Contra Eunomium

Bonaventure

Brev.	Breviloquium

Clement of Alexandria

Paed.	Paedagogus

Cyril of Alexandria

Ev. Jo.	In Joannis Evangelium

Cyril of Jerusalem

Catech.	Catecheses

Didymus

Trin.	De Trinitate

Epiphanius

Exp. Fid.   Expositio Fide

Gregory of Nyssa

Ep.   Epistulae
Ref. Eun.   Et Refutationem Confessionis Eunomii
Or. cat   Oratio catechetica magna

Hilary

Syn.   De synodis
Trin.   De Trinitate

Irenaeus

Haer.   Adversus haereses

John of Damascus

Exp. Fid.   Expositio Fidei orthodoxae

Justin

Dial.   Dialogus cum Tryphone

Maximus the Confessor

Quaest.   Quaestiones et Dubia

Novatian

Trin.   Liber de Trinitate

Origen

Hom. Gen.	Homiliae in Genesim
Princ.	De principiis (Peri archōn)

Theophilus

Autol.	Ad Autolycum

Tertullian

Prax.	Adversus Praxean

Other Abbreviations

BTT	Bible de tous les Temps. 8 vols. Paris, 1984–8.
BTTS	Bonaventure Text in Translation Series. Saint Bonaventure, 1996–
DS	Denzinger, H., and A. Schönmetzer, eds. Enchiridion Symbolorum, Definitionum et Declarationum de Rebus Fidei et Morum. Rome, 1973.
EAA	Collection des Études Augustiniennes, Série Antiquité. Paris, 1954–
CCSL	Corpus Christianorum: Series latina. Turnhout, 1953–
CSEL	Corpus Scriptorum Ecclesiasticorum Latinorum. Vienna, 1866–
GNO	Gregorii Nysseni Opera. 60 vols. Edited by Wernerus Jaeger. Leiden, 1960–
MiAg	Miscellanea Agostiniana. 2 vols. Rome, 1931–2.
NPNF 1	Nicene and Post-Nicene Fathers, Series 1. Edited by Philip Schaff. 14 vols. London, 1886–9.
PG	Patrologia graeca [= Patrologiae cursus completus: Series graeca]. Edited by J.-P. Migne. 162 vols. Paris, 1857–86.
PL	Patrologia latina [= Patrologiae cursus completus: Series latina]. Edited by J.-P. Migne. 217 vols. Paris, 1844–64.
PLS	Patrologiae cursus completus. Series latina. Supplementum. Edited by J.-P. Migne; A. Hamman. 4 vols. Paris, 1958–74.
RBén	*Revue Bénédictine*
REAug	*Revue des études augustiniennes*
SC	Sources Chrétiennes. Paris: Cerf, 1943–
SPM	Stromata Patristica et Mediaevalia. Utrecht, 1950–

Chapter 1

INTRODUCTION

In his essay *Der Dreifaltige Gott*, Karl Rahner famously asserted "that Christians in all of their orthodox confession of the Trinity are almost merely 'monotheists' in the religious conduct of their lives."[1] According to Rahner, this problem stemmed from the tendency of the Western tradition—beginning with Augustine—to conceive of God speculatively and psychologically to the exclusion of the economy. Rahner insisted that Trinitarian theology must return to a biblical starting point. However, as has often been observed, Rahner largely ignores the Scriptures in *Der Dreifaltige Gott*,[2] as he does in most of his writings on the Trinity.[3] Moreover, in dismissing

---

1. All translations in this book are original, unless indicated otherwise. Karl Rahner, "Der Dreifaltige Gott als Transzendenter Urgrund der Heilsgeschichte," in *Sämtliche Werke*, ed. Peter Walter and Michael Hauber, vol. 22/1b, 32 vols (Freiburg im Brisgau: Herder, 2013), 517: "All das wird indes nicht darüber hinwegtäuschen dürfen, daß die Christen bei all ihrem orthodoxen Bekenntnis zur Dreifaltigkeit in ihrem religiösen Daseinsvollzug beinahe nur 'Monotheisten' sind." *Der Dreifaltige Gott* was an expanded reproduction of Rahner's earlier essay, "Bemerkungen zum Dogmatischen Traktat 'De Trinitate,'" in *Schriften zur Theologie*, vol. 4, 16 vols (Einsiedeln: Benziger, 1960), 103–33.

2. Cf. Thomas F. Torrance, "Toward an Ecumenical Consensus on the Trinity," in *Trinitarian Perspectives: Toward Doctrinal Agreement* (Edinburgh: T&T Clark, 1994), 84; Khaled Anatolios, *Retrieving Nicaea: The Development and Meaning of Trinitarian Doctrine* (Grand Rapids: Baker, 2011), 5; Paul D. Molnar, *Divine Freedom and the Doctrine of the Immanent Trinity: In Dialogue with Karl Barth and Contemporary Theology*, 2nd ed. (New York: T&T Clark, 2017), 376–7.

3. For example, Karl Rahner, "Über den Begriff des Geheimnisses in der Katholischen Theologie," in *Schriften zur Theologie*, vol. 4 (Einsiedeln: Benziger, 1960), 51–99; Rahner, "Bemerkungen Zum Dogmatischen Traktat 'De Trinitate'"; Rahner, "Der Dreifaltige Gott"; Karl Rahner, "Fragen zur Unbegreiflichkeit Gottes nach Thomas von Aquin," in *Sämtliche Werke*, ed. Peter Walter and Michael Hauber, vol. 22/1b, 32 vols (Freiburg im Brisgau: Herder, 2013), 306–19; Karl Rahner, "Über das Geheimnis der Dreifaltigkeit," in *Sämtliche Werke*, ed. Peter Walter and Michael Hauber, vol. 22/2, 32 vols (Freiburg im Brisgau: Herder, 2013), 833–44; Karl Rahner, ed., "Trinität," in *Sacramentum Mundi: Theologisches Lexikon für die Praxis* (Freiburg im Breisgau: Herder, 1969); Karl Rahner, ed., "Trinitätstheologie," in *Sacramentum Mundi: Theologisches Lexikon für die Praxis* (Freiburg im Breisgau: Herder,

much of the tradition as driven by speculation and psychology, Rahner overlooks the varied ways the great theologians of the West—especially Augustine—attend to the Scriptures in their Trinitarian theology.

To overcome the shortcomings of the Western tradition, Rahner proposes his famous *Grundaxiom* or Rule as the solution—that *the economic Trinity is the immanent Trinity and vice versa*.[4] By this, he means to assert that, in the economy of salvation, "what is communicated is precisely the threefold personal God, and likewise the communication (to creatures in free grace), *if* it happens freely, can only happen in the inner-divine manner of the two communications of the divine being from the Father to the Son and Spirit" (emphasis in original).[5] In other words, the relations and τάξις of the economic Trinity truly correspond with and reflect the relations and τάξις of the immanent Trinity. Rahner insists that his rule must do justice both to the "binding data of the official church doctrine of the Trinity" as laid out in the Catholic magisterium and to "the biblical statements concerning the economy of salvation."[6] As might be expected, both Rahner's diagnosis of the Western Trinitarian tradition and his solution have been subject to much scrutiny. In terms of the solution, it is alleged that his description of the Father–Son, Son–Spirit, and (to a lesser degree) Father–Spirit relations in the economy do not always correspond with the Western conception of immanent Trinitarian relations that Rahner affirms. Thus, for Rahner's Rule to hold, it is supposed that he must dispense either with some of the biblical statements concerning the economy of salvation or with his Western conception of the intra-Trinitarian relations.

This book explores the intersection of Augustine's exegesis of the "biblical statements concerning the economy of salvation" with the criticisms levelled both *by* and *at* Rahner. It argues that in Augustine's Trinitarian exegesis, the Augustinian-Western tradition has always had the resources at its disposal to avoid and address the most poignant criticisms levelled both *by* and *at* Rahner. Thus, as Hill mentioned decades ago, "what Rahner so rightly requires of a new

---

1969). A key exception to this is Rahner's "Theos im Neuen Testament," *Bijdragen*, vol. 11, no. 3 (1950): 212–36. This work offers extensive treatment of the word θεος in the New Testament.

4. Rahner, "Der Dreifaltige Gott," 535: "*Die 'ökonomische' Trinität ist die 'immanente' Trinität und umgekehrt.*"

5. Ibid., 553: "Denn eben das Mitgeteilte ist gerade der Dreifaltige persönliche Gott, und ebenso kann die (an die Kreatur in freier Gnade geschehende) Mitteilung, *wenn* sie frei geschieht, nur in der innergöttlichen Weise der zwei Mitteilungen des göttlichen Wesens vom Vater an den Sohn und Geist geschehen."

6. Ibid., 535: "Gelingt es dort nämlich, mit Hilfe dieses Axioms eine Trinitätslehre systematisch zu entwickeln, die *erstens* den wirklich verbindlichen Daten der kirchenamtlichen Trinitätslehre gerecht wird, *zweitens* die biblischen Aussagen über die Heilsökonomie, deren dreifaltige Struktur und über die expliziten biblischen Sätze im Blick auf den Vater, Sohn und Geist unbefangener würdigen kann … *dann* ist dieses Axiom gerechtfertigt."

treatise on the Trinity does not have to be composed from scratch in the Latin tradition; it is nearly all there in Augustine's *De Trinitate*."⁷ This chapter begins by detailing the substance and weaknesses of these criticisms before accounting for the lacunae in the extant literature and previewing the argument to follow in subsequent chapters.

1. Rahner's Criticisms of the Augustinian Tradition

Firstly, we attend to Rahner's criticisms of the Augustinian-Western tradition in the order in which they appear in *Der Dreifaltige Gott*. Rahner's criticisms can be grouped into eight divisions, pertaining to religious piety, Christological peculiarity, the doctrine of grace, the doctrine of creation, the treatises *De Deo uno* and *De Deo trino*, the Old Testament, the Scriptures more generally, and the missions and processions. From these criticisms, Rahner concluded that the major weaknesses in the modern Western doctrine of God ultimately stem back to Augustine's account of the Trinity. To correct this, Rahner insists that we re-moor the doctrine of the Trinity to the Scriptures and the economy of salvation. Surprisingly, Rahner does not tease out precisely *how* attention to the Scriptures avoids these purported weaknesses. Moreover, Rahner overlooks Augustine's important and extensive treatment of "the biblical statements concerning the economy of salvation," especially in books 1–4 of *Trin*.

Religious Piety

As mentioned, Rahner is concerned with the disconnect between the doctrine of the Trinity and religious piety. A Jesuit priest deeply influenced in his religious formation by the spirituality of Ignatius of Loyola, Rahner found the apparent disconnect of theology proper from piety intolerable. As well as describing Christians as "almost merely monotheists" in *Der Dreifaltige Gott*, Rahner asserts that "if one had to eradicate the doctrine of the Trinity as false, the majority of religious literature could remain almost unchanged with this procedure."⁸ The doctrine of the Trinity was not even implicit in the believer's faith in the incarnation, because "theological and religious focus fell only on the fact that 'God' became man, that 'a' divine person (of the Trinity) has assumed flesh, and

---

7. Edmund Hill, "Karl Rahner's 'Remarks on the Dogmatic Treatise *De Trinitate* and St. Augustine,'" *Augustinian Studies*, vol. 2 (1971): 80.
8. Rahner, "Der Dreifaltige Gott," 517. In full, he writes: "All das wird indes nicht darüber hinwegtäuschen dürfen, daß die Christen bei all ihrem orthodoxen Bekenntnis zur Dreifaltigkeit in ihrem religiösen Daseinsvollzug beinahe nur "Monotheisten" sind. Man wird also die Behauptung wagen dürfen, daß, wenn man die Trinitätslehre als falsch ausmerzen müßte, bei dieser Prozedur der Großteil der religiösen Literatur fast unverändert bleiben könnte."

not that this person is precisely the Logos."[9] The evidence for this focus emerges when Christians indiscriminately address their prayers to the three persons of the Trinity or when the Mass is offered to the three.[10] Modern Christians thus "have nothing to do with the mystery of the Trinity except that we know something 'about it' through revelation."[11] While Bonaventure is praised for going against this trend, Augustine is portrayed as the villain:

> Since Augustine, Christian theology has tried to imagine the inner life of God in self-awareness and in love in such a way that a certain foreboding understanding of God's threefold personality results, as it were, an understanding of God's inner life that is quite unrelated to us and to our Christian existence, and is ultimately not very helpful.[12]

According to Rahner, it was Augustine's so-called psychological analogy that drove a wedge between the doctrine of the Trinity and Christian experience of the same God.

Christological Peculiarity

In an earlier work, Rahner wrote at length of the Father's peculiarity as "God"[13] but in *Der Dreifaltige Gott* his focus turns to the hypostatic peculiarity of the Logos. According to Rahner, the tradition since Augustine has ignored the peculiarity of the Logos enfleshed. "It has been more or less a foregone conclusion among theologians since Augustine (contrary to the tradition that preceded him) that each of the divine persons (if only it is freely willed by God) can become man and thus the incarnation of precisely this person can tell us nothing about the

---

9. Ibid.: "Denn wenn von der Menschwerdung Gottes die Rede ist, fällt heutzutage theologisch und religiös der Blick nur auf die Tatsache, daß "Gott" Mensch geworden ist, daß "eine" göttliche Person (der Trinität) Fleisch angenommen hat, nicht aber darauf, daß diese Person eben gerade die des Logos ist."

10. Ibid., 519.

11. Ibid., 523: "wir selbst eigentlich mit dem Geheimnis der Trinität nichts zu tun haben als dies, daß wir etwas 'darüber' durch Offenbarung wissen."

12. Karl Rahner, *Grundkurs des Glaubens: Einführung in den Begriff des Christentums*, eBook (Freiburg im Breisgau: Herder, 1976), 140:

> Wir können wohl auch sagen, daß die großartigen Spekulationen, durch die sich seit Augustinus die christliche Theologie das innere Leben Gottes in Selbstbewußtsein und in Liebe so vorzustellen sucht, daß ein gewisses ahnendes Verständnis der Dreipersönlichkeit Gottes daraus resultiert, ein Verständnis, das ganz unbezüglich zu uns und unserer christlichen Existenz sich gleichsam ein inneres Leben Gottes ausmalt, im letzten Grunde doch nicht sehr hilfreich sind.

13. Rahner, "Theos im Neuen Testament."

peculiar features of *this* person within the Divinity" (emphasis in original).[14] It is not entirely clear why Rahner so regularly blames Augustine for advocating this view that allegedly has "no clear roots in the earlier tradition and still less in Scripture."[15] He never substantiates his claim from Augustine's writings and, according to LaCugna, Anselm of Canterbury was the first to make this claim.[16] In *Der Dreifaltige Gott* and his other Trinitarian writings, Rahner seems unaware of a number of passages in which Augustine explicitly or implicitly affirms the Son's incarnational peculiarity.[17] Furthermore, Rahner never argues his case for incarnational peculiarity directly from the Scriptures despite being convinced of the danger of this line of thought. Nevertheless, Augustine is held the culprit.

According to Rahner, Augustine's alleged move to downplay the Son's hypostatic peculiarity in the incarnation is partially responsible for the isolation of the Trinity and religious piety. He believes that in emphasizing that "God" rather than the Logos became man, the average Christian fails to grasp the peculiarity of the incarnation. They fail to grasp why it was the Logos, rather than the Father or Spirit, who should become man. Therefore, faith in the incarnation has no impact on normal Christian religious activity. For Rahner, this cannot be so. What Jesus does as a man reveals the Logos himself, and the Logos with God is the Logos with us.[18] Average Christians situated in the Augustinian-Western tradition have missed what we might call Rahner's *Christological* Rule, that the economic Logos is the immanent Logos and vice versa.

Doctrine of Grace

Flowing directly from the lack of peculiarity afforded to the Logos in modern Trinitarian theology, Rahner was also concerned with what he perceived to be a

---

14. Rahner, "Der Dreifaltige Gott": "Es ist ja unter den Theologen seit Augustinus (gegen die ihm vorausgehende Tradition) eine mehr oder weniger ausgemachte Sache, daß jede der göttlichen Personen (wenn es von Gott nur frei gewollt werde) Mensch werden könne und somit die Menschwerdung gerade dieser bestimmten Person über die innergöttliche Eigentümlichkeit gerade *dieser* Person nichts aussage."

15. Rahner, "Über den Begriff des Geheimnisses in der Katholischen Theologie," 97; Rahner, "Bemerkungen Zum Dogmatischen Traktat 'De Trinitate,'" 119; Karl Rahner, "Zur Theologie der Menschwerdung," in *Schriften zur Theologie*, vol. 4, 16 vols (Einsiedeln: Benziger, 1960), 139; Karl Rahner, "Dogmatische Fragen zur Osterfrömmigkeit," in *Schriften zur Theologie*, vol. 4, 16 vols (Einsiedeln: Benziger, 1960), 162; Karl Rahner, "Natur und Gnade," in *Schriften zur Theologie*, vol. 4, 16 vols (Einsiedeln: Benziger, 1960), 222–3; Karl Rahner, "Zur Theologie des Symbols," in *Schriften zur Theologie*, vol. 4, 16 vols (Einsiedeln: Benziger, 1960), 292–3.

16. Catherine M. Lacugna, *God for Us: The Trinity and Christian Life* (San Francisco: HarperCollins, 1993), 98–9.

17. These passages will be explored in Chapter 2.

18. Rahner, "Der Dreifaltige Gott," 550–1.

disconnect between the Trinity and soteriology. Like the incarnation, soteriology is said to tell us nothing of the Trinity. This modern construction of the doctrine of grace tells the Christian that grace is merited by Christ, but "this grace of Christ is presented, at best, as the grace of the *Dei-hominis*, not as the grace of the *Verbum incarnatum* as *Logos*."[19] According to Rahner, the isolation of the Trinity and soteriology is exemplified in the famous constitution of Benedict XII over the *Visio beatifica*,[20] where the Trinity remains completely out of consideration and only the "divine essence" (*göttlichen Essenz*) is referenced.[21] Thus, "where the treatise is headed 'De gratia Christi,' the doctrine of grace is in fact monotheistic, not Trinitarian: a participation in the divine *naturae* leads to a blessed vision of the divine *essentiae*."[22] According to Rahner, this is a flow-on effect from the non-peculiarity of the divine persons in the Western tradition and the psychological analogy. While Rahner may have grounds for detecting these weaknesses in Western theology, he overlooks Augustine's significant contributions in books 4 and 13 of *Trin*. At the same time, Rahner does not flesh out *how* attention to "the biblical statements concerning the economy of salvation" can reunite the two doctrines. It is simply assumed that it will.

Doctrine of Creation

Rahner similarly laments the isolation of the doctrine of creation from the doctrine of the Trinity in contemporary theology:

> In the doctrine of creation today (in contrast to the great old theology in Bonaventure) there is hardly a word about the Trinity anymore. It is believed that this silence is also completely legitimate, because the divine works are so "common" to the outside world that the world as creation basically does not bear any real signs of the Triune inner-divine life.[23]

---

19. Rahner, "Der Dreifaltige Gott," 521: "Da aber einmal diese Gnade Christi dann im besten Fall als Gnade 'Dei'-hominis, nicht als Gnade des Verbum incarnatum als Logos."

20. H. Denzinger and A. Schönmetzer, eds., *Enchiridion Symbolorum, Definitionum et Declarationum de Rebus Fidei et Morum*, 35th ed. (Rome, 1973), DS 1000 (hereafter cited as DS).

21. Rahner, "Der Dreifaltige Gott," 521, note (n.) 8.

22. Ibid., 521: "Dementsprechend ist dann auch dort, wo der Traktat mit "De gratia Christi" überschrieben wird, die Gnadenlehre faktisch monotheistisch, nicht trinitarisch: consortium divinae *naturae* bis zur visio beata *essentiae* divinae."

23. Ibid., 521–3:

> In der Schöpfungslehre ist heute (im Unterschied zur alten großen Theologie bei Bonaventura) auch kaum mehr ein Wort über die Trinität zu finden. Man glaubt, daß dieses Schweigen auch völlig legitim sei, weil ja die göttlichen Werke "nach außen" so "gemeinsam" seien, daß die Welt als Schöpfung im Grunde doch keine wirklichen Zeichen des dreifaltig innergöttlichen Lebens an sich tragen könne.

The doctrine of the "vestiges" and the "image of the Trinity" is thought to be nothing but pious speculation, telling us nothing about the Trinity or created reality which we did not know from other sources. Though Rahner does not explicitly lay the blame on Augustine for this, Rahner certainly holds the doctrine of *inseparabilis operatio* responsible for this disconnect and Augustine was the early champion of this doctrine. Moreover, Rahner holds the West's "speculative" and inward-looking doctrine of the Trinity responsible for this disconnect, which implicitly lays the blame on Augustine.[24] Thus, it would not be imprudent to suggest that Rahner ultimately holds Augustine responsible for the isolation of the doctrine of the Trinity from the doctrine of creation. Nevertheless, Rahner offers no worked corrective to the problem he diagnoses. He asserts that the two must be integrated but does not detail what this might look like. Moreover, Rahner overlooks the ways in which Augustine integrates the doctrine of creation with the doctrine of the Trinity in view of "the biblical statements concerning the economy of salvation."

De Deo Uno *and* De Deo Trino

Next, Rahner laments the division of the treatises *De Deo uno* and *De Deo trino* in contemporary theology. According to Rahner, Western emphasis on the psychological analogy and denial of hypostatic peculiarity has produced an inappropriate preferencing of the "One" over the "Three." Though recognizing that the division only took place formally in St. Thomas, he asserts that this division and ranking of the two tracts ultimately arises from the Augustinian-Western conception of the Trinity in contrast to the Greeks, most notably the Cappadocians.[25] Whereas the "biblical" and "Greek" view would have us start with the one unoriginate "God" who is properly known as *Father*, the "Augustinian-Western" tradition begins with the one God, and only afterwards turns to the persons. This ordering results in a treatise that is "philosophically abstract" (*philosophisch-abstrakt*), "absolutely self-contained" (*absolut in sich geschlossene*), and unopen to anything distinct from it.[26] Thus Rahner concludes that the doctrine of the Trinity only gives the impression of being able to make formal assertions about the divine person with the help of the two processions and relations. These assertions deal with a reality centred entirely on itself. Rahner ignores the fact that Augustine, at the very beginning of the "Augustinian-Western" tradition, begins his major treatise on the Trinity with great attention to the coactivity of the three divine persons as presented in "the biblical statements concerning the economy of salvation," especially in books 1–4.

24. Ibid., 523–5.
25. Ibid., 529, n. 14.
26. Ibid., 528–9.

The Economy and Scripture

For Rahner, the speculative, psychological Augustinian-Western conception of the Trinity ultimately cuts the Trinity off from the economy of salvation, and thus Scripture. "It speaks of the necessary metaphysical properties of God, and not very explicitly of God as experienced in salvation history in his free relations with his creation."[27] The "psychological doctrine of the Trinity skips over the economic experience of salvation of the Trinity in favour of an almost gnostic speculation about what happens inside God."[28] Thus, it is unable to do justice to the biblical statements concerning salvation history and its threefold nature, and to the statements concerning the divine persons.[29] According to Rahner, such a trajectory stands in contrast with the more biblical Greeks who understood the Trinity so naturally in terms of the economy of salvation that they could regard their entire theology as a doctrine of the Trinity.[30]

Ironically, even if Rahner's assessment of the Western tradition of his time is correct, Rahner pays less attention to Scripture than the tradition he criticizes. When recapping the second section at the beginning of the third section, Rahner posits that we have "*listened* very carefully and patiently to what Scripture, the history of dogma, and the official doctrine of the church tell us about the Trinity" (emphasis in original).[31] However, the first two sections (like the third) offer no explicit or direct engagement with the Scriptures. In Der Dreifaltige Gott, we are left with nothing except footnotes to the preceding chapters in Mysterium Salutis penned by Schulte (on the Trinitarian mystery in the Old Testament and outside of Christianity)[32] and Schierse (on the revelation of the Trinity in the New Testament),[33] and to Rahner's *Theos im Neuen Testament*.[34] If Der Dreifaltige Gott is supposed to be the showpiece of his thought on the Trinity, and if it is supposed to do "justice to the biblical statements concerning the economy of salvation and its threefold structure," one would expect more than footnotes to exegetical studies. Rahner's account seems as detached from the economy as the tradition

---

27. Ibid., 529: "Man spricht über die notwendigen metaphysischen Eigenschaften Gottes und nicht sehr ausdrücklich über die heilsgeschichtlichen Erfahrungen, die man über die freien Verhaltungen Gottes zu seiner Schöpfung gemacht hat."

28. Rahner, *Grundkurs des Glaubens*, 141: "Die psychologische Trinitätslehre überspringt die heilsökonomische Erfahrung der Trinität zugunsten einer fast gnostisch anmutenden Spekulation darüber."

29. Rahner, "Der Dreifaltige Gott," 535.

30. Ibid., 529, n. 14.

31. Ibid., 596: "Nachdem—gemessen an dem in einem Hand buch möglichen Raum—sehr ausführlich und geduldig *gehört* wurde, was Schrift, Dogmengeschichte und kirchenamtliche Lehre über die Trinität sagen, soll nochmals kurz *gesagt* werden, was man gehört hat."

32. Ibid., 513, n. 1; 533, n. 17; 561, n. 33.

33. Ibid., 513, n. 1; 557, n. 39; 583, n. 13 and 15; 587, n. 20.

34. Rahner, "Über das Geheimnis der Dreifaltigkeit," 580.

he describes. At the same time, Rahner's Trinitarian writings ignore Augustine's pronounced attention to the economy and the Scriptures, especially in the first four books of *Trin*.

The Old Testament

According to Rahner, the modern habit of isolating the doctrine of the Trinity from the Old Testament naturally follows on from the isolation of the Trinity from the economy. Contemporary theologians are said to ignore the Old Testament preparations for the Trinity. With few exceptions (e.g., Schulte), contemporary works on the Trinity exhibit no desire to attribute any positive value to Trinitarian allusions or analogies in the Old Testament.[35] They have become accustomed "to rejecting the opinion of the ancients that there was some kind of faith in the Trinity even before Christ."[36] Rahner insists that "a real, secret prehistory of the revelation of the Trinity in the Old Testament can be understood."[37] In Rahner's view, Augustine's speculative approach to the Trinity has led the Western tradition to isolate the doctrine of the Trinity from the economy of salvation. Thus, it has cut the Trinity off from the Hebrew Scriptures.

Moreover, there is good reason to suppose that Rahner's distaste for Augustine's alleged denial of incarnational peculiarity can be traced to Augustine's interpretation of the theophanies. When insisting that incarnational peculiarity was "practically unanimously held" (*so gut wie einhellig vertreten*) prior to Augustine, Rahner cites Schmaus's *Die psychologische Trinitateslehre*.[38] However, at the location cited, Schmaus says nothing about Augustine's alleged incarnational non-peculiarity. Instead, Schmaus argues that Augustine alters the traditional Christological interpretation of the Old Testament theophanies. According to Schmaus:

> Before Augustine they [the early church fathers] almost without exception [*fast ausnahmslos*] believe that the Son of God appeared in the theophanies of the Old Testament, who for these purposes assumed a perceptible form, while the Father was exalted above such entering into the world.[39]

---

35. Rahner, "Der Dreifaltige Gott," 533.

36. Ibid., 561: "Man hat sich in neuerer Zeit in der Theologie daran gewöhnt, zu einfach und apodiktisch und ohne Unterscheidung die Meinung der Alten abzulehnen, daß es doch auch schon vor Christus in irgendeiner Form einen Glauben an die Trinität gegeben habe."

37. Ibid., 563: "Von da aus ist somit durchaus eine echte geheime Vorgeschichte der Trinitätsoffenbarung im Alten Testament zu verstehen."

38. Rahner, "Zur Theologie des Symbols," 293, n. 12.

39. Michael Schmaus, *Die psychologische Trinitätslehre des heiligen Augustinus* (Münster: Aschendorff, 1927), 20–1: "Trotzdem glauben sie vor Augustinus fast ausnahmslos, in den Theophanien des Alten Testaments sei der Sohn Gottes erschienen, der zu diesen Zwecken eine wahrnehmbare Gestalt angenommen habe, während der Vater über ein solches Eingehen in die Welt erhaben gewesen sei."

In other words, Schmaus asserts that Augustine rejects a kind of *theophanic peculiarity* which holds that the Old Testament theophanies were the exclusive domain of the Son. It is worth noting that Schmaus drew heavily on de Régnon in his discussion of Augustine and the theophanies. De Régnon believed that when Augustine said "that a theophany can take on the role of the Trinity, *personam ipsius Trinitatis*, he is declaring that the Trinity can appear as a single person."[40] Scheffczyk similarly asserted that Augustine's interpretation of the Old Testament theophanies results in a lack of differentiation in the economic Trinity.[41] In the absence of any other evidence, this appears to be the foundation of Rahner's claim that Augustine rejects incarnational peculiarity. It is not entirely clear whether Rahner holds to theophanic peculiarity, an indication that he himself has not managed to integrate the doctrine of the Trinity with the Old Testament. In the essay on Old Testament preparations for the Trinity in *Mysterium Salutis*, an essay twice endorsed by Rahner, Schulte distances himself from the view of the early Greek fathers.[42] However, given Rahner's preference for the theology of the earlier Greek fathers, and the link he seems to draw between incarnational and theophanic non-peculiarity, it seems likely that Rahner would reject Augustine's interpretation of the theophanies in favour of the earlier view. Thus, for Rahner, not only does the tradition ignore the Old Testament; when it does pay heed to the Hebrew Scriptures, it inevitably begets a rejection of incarnational peculiarity.

The Missions and Processions

Finally, Rahner laments the disconnection of the missions and processions in the modern Western tradition from Augustine. He asserts that the doctrine of the missions is at best an afterthought.[43] Rahner believes that if Jesus is not simply God in general but the Son, there must then be

> at least *one* "mission," *one* presence in the world, *one* salvation-economic reality, that is not merely appropriated to a certain divine person but is peculiar to him. Here, we are not only *talking* "about" this certain divine person in the world. Something happens "outside" of the inner-divine life in the world itself, which is not simply an event of the tri-personal God who is effective in the world as

---

40. Theodore de Régnon, *Études de Théologie Positive sur la Sainte Trinité*, vol. 1, 3 vols (Paris: Victor Retaux, 1892), 261–2: "Mais lorsqu'il dit qu'une théophanie peut jouer le rôle de la Trinité, *personam ipsius Trinitatis*, il déclare que la Trinité peut se manifester à la manière d'une personne unique."

41. Leo Scheffczyk, "Lehramtliche Formulierungen und Dogmengeschichte der Trinitätslehre," in *Mysterium salutis*, ed. Johannes Feiner and Magnus Löhrer, vol. 2 (Einsiedeln: Benziger, 1967), 146.

42. Raphael Schulte, "Die Selbstschliessung des Dreifaltigen Gottes," in *Mysterium Salutis*, ed. Johannes Feiner and Magnus Löhrer (Einsiedeln: Benziger, 1967), 64.

43. Rahner, "Der Dreifaltige Gott," 560–1.

the one, but belongs only to the Logos alone, the history of one divine person in contrast to the other divine persons. (emphases in original)[44]

If this were not true, there would no longer be any real connection between "mission" and inner-Trinitarian life.[45] It may have been true that some recent works on the Trinity had disconnected the missions and processions. However, it was not due to a dependence on Augustine that contemporary theology was guilty of what Rahner claimed. Augustine offers exactly what Rahner requires at the end of *Trin.* book 4 and does so with great attention to Scripture. For his part, Rahner does not demonstrate how attention to the Scriptures leads to the reintegration of the missions and processions. As with most of the previous criticisms, Rahner fails to acknowledge the many ways Augustine meets his requirements and surpasses what the Jesuit priest promises in terms of exegetical attention.

2. Exegetical Criticisms of Rahner's Solution

Having considered Rahner's criticisms of the Augustinian-Western tradition, we pivot, next, to the criticisms levelled *at* Rahner's Rule. We will focus specifically on the *exegetical* difficulties associated with his Rule, thus bypassing several of the criticisms levelled at Rahner's Trinitarian thought more broadly. One noteworthy criticism that will be largely circumnavigated pertains to Rahner's use of the *economic/immanent* (or *Ökonomische/immanente*) taxonomy. Such language is commonly said to be "dialectical," "wooden,"[46] insinuating "two Trinities,"[47] and derived from an Hegelian framework—via Johannes August Urlsperger—that seeks "to deny that missions reveal processions."[48] An argument could also be made that this taxonomy fails to take into account the way that the New Testament

---

44. Ibid., 535–7:

> Es gibt also zumindest *eine* "Sendung," *eine* Anwesenheit in der Welt, *eine* heilsökonomische Wirklichkeit, die nicht bloß einer bestimmten göttlichen Person appropriiert wird, sondern ihr eigentümlich ist. Hier wird nicht bloß "über" diese bestimmte göttliche Person in der Welt *geredet*. Hier ereignet sich "außerhalb" des innergöttlichen Lebens in der Welt selbst etwas, was nicht einfach Ereignis des in Wirkursächlichkeitbb in der Welt wirksamen dreipersönlichen Gottes als des einen ist, sondern nur dem Logos allein zukommt, Geschichte einer göttlichen Person im Unterschied zu den anderen göttlichen Personen ist.

45. Ibid., 545.
46. Gilles Emery, *The Trinity: An Introduction to Catholic Doctrine on the Triune God*, trans. Matthew Levering (Washington, DC: CUA, 2011), 178.
47. Bruce D. Marshall, "The Unity of the Triune God: Reviving an Ancient Question," *The Thomist: A Speculative Quarterly Review*, vol. 74, no. 1 (2010): 8.
48. Fred Sanders, *The Triune God* (Grand Rapids: Zondervan Academic, 2016), 148.

presents God as God is, and God as God works in the world, as interwoven, each commenting on the other. To allow greater space for discussion of the exegetical difficulties associated with the Rule, these difficulties will be set aside. The following comments will have to suffice. Firstly, while there may be limitations associated with the *economic/immanent* taxonomy, there are limitations with any taxonomy. An Augustinian articulation of *missions* and *processions* cannot account for God's *ad extra* activity prior to the incarnation, that is, in the Old Testament. While the *economic/immanent* nomenclature will struggle to avoid wooden deployment or an unintended insinuation of two "Trinities," the various English and Latin substitutes (e.g., *evangelical-ontological*; *ad extra/ad intra*; *pro nobis/in se*) find themselves susceptible to the same criticism. LaCugna and Sanders prefer the *theologia/oikonomia* distinction due to its patristic ancestry.[49] However, the authors cited by Lacugna (Theordoret) and Sanders (Athanasius) apply this distinction to the person of Christ, and not the Trinity specifically. As Behr writes, it is doubtful that the patristic usage of these terms corresponds to what we might call the economic Trinity and the immanent Trinity.[50] Secondly, even if the *economic/immanent* taxonomy was coined to separate the *missions* and *processions*, Rahner uses the terms to achieve the opposite. He can hardly be blamed for Urlsperger's Hegelian tendencies. Thirdly, though the New Testament account of the Triune God as God is and God as God works in the world may be interwoven, the reality is that a distinction exists and must exist if we wish to preserve what the Scriptures teach about God's freedom and aseity. Though the *economic/immanent* nomenclature may be awkward and of questionable origin, this does not render contemporary deployment of such language as necessarily obsolete or invalid.

Thus, we now turn to the exegetical difficulties associated with Rahner's Rule. As previously noted, Rahner insists that his rule must do justice both to the magisterium and to Scripture.[51] In doing justice to the magisterium, Rahner upholds the traditional account of the processions of the Son and Spirit and the *Filioque* clause. According to Rahner, "The Spirit proceeds from the Father through (*durch*) the Son,"[52] but this is not a capitulation to the Eastern model of

---

49. Lacugna, *God for Us*, 43, 52; Fred Sanders, *The Image of the Immanent Trinity: Rahner's Rule and the Theological Interpretation of Scripture* (New York: International Academic Publishers, 2004), 3.

50. Behr makes this point with respect to LaCugna. John Behr, *The Nicene Faith* (Crestwood, NY: St Vladimir's Seminary Press, 2004), 7, n. 17.

51. Rahner, "Der Dreifaltige Gott," 535.

52. Ibid., 586. According to DS 1300,

> The Holy Spirit is eternally from the Father and the Son (*ex Patre et Filio*) and has His essence and His subsistent being both from the Father and the Son, and proceeds (*procidit*) from both eternally as from one principle (*principio*) and one spiration. We declare that what the holy doctors and fathers say, namely, that the Holy Spirit proceeds from (*ex*) the Father through (*per*) the Son, tends to this meaning, that by

the Spirit's procession. Rahner has magisterial warrant for this statement in the pronouncements of Florence (DS 1300) and Gregory XIII (DS 1986).[53] Nevertheless, many insist that Rahner's Rule cannot stand if it must do justice both to Scripture and to the magisterium. The reason for this has to do with an alleged incongruity between the economic Father–Son and Son–Spirit relationships (and, to a lesser degree, the Father–Spirit relationship) and their immanent counterpoints. Thus, it is supposed that Rahner's Rule cannot be supported by Scripture.

The Father–Son Relationship

At least five overarching challenges can be discerned with reference to the Father–Son relationship. First, Sanders and Benner suggest that an "even-handed" application of Rahner's Rule to the Son's economic subordination results in the heresy of Subordinationism.[54] Second, it is suggested that texts speaking of the Father's transfer of authority and power to the Son indicate reversibility or interchangeability in the economic Father–Son relationship. From this, it is suggested that Rahner's Rule invariably results in reversibility, interchangeability, or reversed subordination in the immanent Father–Son relationship.[55] Similarly,

> this it is signified that the Son also is the cause (*causum*), according to the Greeks, and according to the Latins, the principle (*principium*) of the subsistence of the Holy Spirit, as is the Father also. And since all that the Father has, the Father himself, in begetting, has given to His only begotten Son, with the exception of Fatherhood, the very fact that the Holy Spirit proceeds from the Son, the Son himself has from the Father eternally, by whom He was begotten also eternally.

In DS 1986, Gregory XIII cites this verbatim.

53. Confusion arises because the Latin word *processio* can be translated as the narrower ἐκπόρευσις or the broader προϊέναι in Greek. While many Eastern orthodox theologians willingly speak of the Spirit's ἐκπόρευσις "through" the Son and his προϊέναι "from" the Son, a problem arises if we speak of the Spirit's ἐκπόρευσις from the Father and the Son as this indicates two sources of the Spirit.

54. Sanders, *The Image of the Immanent Trinity*, 8; Drayton C. Benner, "Augustine and Karl Rahner on the Relationship between the Immanent Trinity and the Economic Trinity," *International Journal of Systematic Theology*, vol. 9, no. 1 (2007): 35.

55. Jürgen Moltmann, *Trinität und Reich Gottes: Zur Gotteslehre* (Munich: Kaiser, 1980), 109–10; Leonardo Boff, *A Santíssima Trindade é a Melhor Comunidade* (Petrópolis: Vozes, 1988), 26; Wolfhart Pannenberg, *Systematic Theology*, trans. Geoffrey W. Bromiley, vol. 1, 3 vols (London: T&T Clark, 1992), 312–3, 325, 330; Millard J. Erickson, *God in Three Persons: A Contemporary Interpretation of the Trinity* (Grand Rapids: Baker, 1995), 331; Sanders, *The Image of the Immanent Trinity*, 168; Royce G. Gruenler, *The Trinity in the Gospel of John: A Thematic Commentary on the Fourth Gospel* (Eugene, OR: Wipf & Stock, 2004), 37; Scott Harrower, *Trinitarian Self and Salvation: An Evangelical Engagement with Rahner's Rule* (Eugene, OR: Wipf & Stock, 2012), 109–14; Matthew L. Tinkham, "Neo-Subordinationism: The Alien Argumentation in the Gender Debate," *Andrews University*

third, texts referring to mutuality in the Father–Son relationship are likewise said to introduce reversibility—even "mutual subordination"—into the immanent Father–Son relationship.[56] Fourth, Bobrinskoy and Harrower suggest that since various biblical texts cite the three divine persons in multiple patterns, applying Rahner's Rule inevitably produces multiple τάξεις in the immanent Trinity, thus again resulting in intra-Trinitarian inversion or reversibility.[57] Fifth, Harrower and Sanders suggest that no immanent analogue can be found for the Son's ascension to the Father, thus undermining the explanatory power of the Rule.[58]

The Son–Spirit Relationship

Similar challenges are levelled at Rahner's Rule with respect to the Son–Spirit relationship. Many refer to Jesus' incarnation, baptism, sending, and empowerment in the Spirit, crucifixion, resurrection, and Pentecostal outpouring of the Spirit as instances in which the economic Son–Spirit relationship is inverted. It is suggested that the Son–Spirit relationship (and, by implication, the Father–Spirit relationship) is also inverted in texts containing all three divine persons where the Spirit is mentioned prior to the Son (and/or the Father).[59] It is then suggested that applying Rahner's Rule to these texts produces results inconsistent with Rahner's Latin Filioquism. While some, like Weinandy, Mühlen, Bourassa, Balthasar, and Congar, have attempted to overcome these difficulties,[60] others, like Jowers and Sanders, have detected potential weaknesses in these proposals. They note that these models either (1) result in multiple τάξεις in the immanent Trinity (Bourassa),[61] (2) require a *Spirituque* or *Patreque* to complement the *Filioque*

Seminary Studies, vol. 55, no. 2 (2017): 269; Jeffrey A. Dukeman, *Mutual Hierarchy: A New Approach to Social Trinitarianism* (Eugene, OR: Wipf & Stock, 2019), 74.

56. Dukeman, *Mutual Hierarchy*, 74; Harrower, *Trinitarian Self and Salvation*, 54, 111; Erickson, *God in Three Persons*, 331.

57. Boris Bobrinskoy, *The Mystery of the Trinity: Trinitarian Experience and Vision in the Biblical and Patristic Tradition*, trans. Anthony P. Gythiel (Crestwood, NY: St Vladimir's Seminary Press, 1999), 65; Harrower, *Trinitarian Self and Salvation*, 158.

58. Harrower, *Trinitarian Self and Salvation*, 115; Scott Harrower, "Bruce Ware's Trinitarian Methodology," in *Trinity without Hierarchy: Reclaiming Nicene Orthodoxy in Evangelical Theology*, ed. Harrower Scott and Michael F. Bird (Kregel: Grand Rapids, 2019), 320–1; Fred Sanders, foreword to *Trinitarian Self and Salvation: An Evangelical Engagement with Rahner's Rule*, by Scott Harrower (Eugene, OR: Wipf & Stock, 2012), xiii; Sanders, *The Triune God*, 112.

59. The Father–Spirit relationship is seldom, if ever, challenged. However, one assumes that if it was challenged, it would be on the basis of triadic texts such as these.

60. For an overview of these proposals, see pages 151–7.

61. Dennis W. Jowers, "A Test of Karl Rahner's Axiom, 'The Economic Trinity *is* the Immanent Trinity and Vice Versa,'" *The Thomist: A Speculative Quarterly Review*, vol. 70, no. 3 (2006): 451–5.

(Weinandy, Mühlen, Balthasar),[62] or (3) lack the necessary criteria to determine which economic events should be seen to correspond with the immanent relations (Congar).[63]

In addition to these alleged difficulties, Harrower argues that applying Rahner's Rule to the "reversals" above threatens the stability of the Trinitarian relations *ad intra*, potentially undermining eternal generation, and perhaps even resulting in pantheism or "ontological morphing."[64] Furthermore, Harrower argues that if the Son's multiple receptions of the Spirit in the narrative of Luke-Acts—at the baptism (Luke 3:21–22) and at Pentecost (Acts 2:33)—are mapped onto the τάξις of the immanent Trinity, "the nature of the relations mean the Son's first reception of the Spirit is not sufficient."[65] It could even mean that the structure of God's "relational life is open to continuous change."[66]

3. The Lacunae

Augustine's Exegesis and Rahner's Assessment of the West

While there is a wealth of literature available on the Trinitarian theology of both Rahner and Augustine, three lacunae remain. Firstly, no one has yet considered how Augustine's attention "to the biblical statements concerning the economy of salvation" intersects with Rahner's assessment of the Augustinian-Western tradition. As Roland Kany observes, "There has been relatively little research into the scriptural interpretation of *De Trinitate*."[67] He notes that none of the major monographs on Augustine's doctrine of the Trinity go into detail on Augustine's use of the Bible, and that the most significant works on Augustine's exegesis only occasionally touch on *Trin*.[68] Likewise, more recent studies on Augustine's

---

62. Jowers argues this explicitly concerning Weinandy and implicitly concerning Mühlen (Jowers, "A Test of Karl Rahner's Axiom," 435–45). In Chapter 5, the case is made that Balthasar's proposal inevitably requires a *Spirituque* clause. Cf. page 156. See, also, Sanders, *The Image of the Immanent Trinity*, 168.

63. Sanders, *The Image of the Immanent Trinity*, 127.

64. Harrower, *Trinitarian Self and Salvation*, 153–4.

65. Ibid., 135.

66. Ibid.

67. Roland Kany, *Augustins Trinitätsdenken: Bilanz, Kritik und Weiterführung der modernen Forschung zu "De trinitate,"* Studien und Texte zu Antike und Christentum/Studies and Texts in Antiquity and Christianity (Tübingen: Mohr, 2007), 190: "Die Schriftauslegung in *De trinitate* ist relativ wenig erforscht."

68. Kany, *Augustins Trinitätsdenken*, 190. For example, Gerhard Strauss, *Schriftgebrauch, Schriftauslegung und Schriftbeweis bei Augustin*, BGBH 1 (Tübingen: Mohr, 1957); Anne-Marie La Bonnardière, *Bible de tous les temps: Saint Augustin et la Bible* (Paris: Beauchesne, 1986); Frederick Van Fleteren, "Principles of Augustine's Hermeneutic: An Overview," in *Augustine: Biblical Exegete*, ed. Frederick Van Fleteren and Joseph C. Schnaubelt

Trinitarian thought have generally tended to offer very little detailed analysis on the bishop's use of Scripture, even those works written by Kany.[69] It is telling that only one of seventeen essays in a recent book titled Le *"De Trinitate" de Saint Augustin: Exégèse, logique et noétique* touches on Augustine's exegesis, the rest focusing on the logic and noetics of the treatise.[70] There are exceptions of course. One thinks of the short studies by Ayres,[71] Pelikan,[72] Barnes,[73] and Studer,[74] and Kloos's monograph on the theophanies.[75] Nevertheless, one would expect more literature given the prominence of *Trin.* and the frequency with which the bishop draws from and quotes Scripture, especially in the first four books. With such little research on Augustine's Trinitarian exegesis, it is not surprising that no one has yet considered how Augustine's exegesis connects with Rahner's assessment of the Augustinian-Western tradition. This book seeks to begin to fill that void.

There are some studies that explicitly set out to challenge Rahner's assessment of Augustine and the Western tradition, most notably those by Hill, Benner,

---

(New York: Peter Lang, 2004), 1–32; Isabelle Bochet, *Le firmament de l'Ecriture: L'herméneutique Augustinienne* (Paris: Institut d'Études Augustiniennes, 2004).

69. We find much less than might be expected in works such as Basil Studer, *Augustins De Trinitate: eine Einführung* (Paderborn: Ferdinand Schöningh, 2005); Luigi Gioia, *The Theological Epistemology of Augustine's De Trinitate* (Oxford: OUP, 2008); Scott A. Dunham, *The Trinity and Creation in Augustine: An Ecological Analysis* (Albany: SUNY Press, 2008); Lewis Ayres, *Augustine and the Trinity* (Cambridge: CUP, 2010); Maarten Wisse, *Trinitarian Theology beyond Participation: Augustine's De Trinitate and Contemporary Theology* (London: Bloomsbury, 2011); Travis E. Ables, *Incarnational Realism: Trinity and the Spirit in Augustine and Barth* (London: Bloomsbury, 2013); John C. Cavadini, *Visioning Augustine* (Oxford: John Wiley & Sons, 2019).

70. In this volume, Boulnois accounts for Augustine's treatment of the theophanies in books 2 and 3. Marie-Odile Boulnois, "Le *De Trinitate* de Saint Augustin: Exégèse, logique et noétique," in *Le "De Trinitate" de Saint Augustin: Exégèse, logique et noétique*, ed. Emmanuel Bermon and Gerald O'Daly (Paris: Institut d'Études Augustiniennes, 2012), 35–66.

71. Lewis Ayres, "Spiritus Amborum: Augustine and Pro-Nicene Pneumatology," *Augustinian Studies*, vol. 39, no. 2 (2008): 207–21.

72. Jaroslav Pelikan, "Canonica Regula: The Trinitarian Hermeneutics of Augustine," in *Collectanea Augustiniana: Augustine: "Second Founder of the Faith*," ed. Joseph C. Schnauabelt and Frederick van Fleteren (New York: Peter Lang, 1990), 329–43.

73. Michel R. Barnes, "Exegesis and Polemic in Augustine's *De Trinitate* I," *Augustinian Studies*, vol. 30 (1999): 43–52; Michel R. Barnes, "The Visible Christ and the Invisible Trinity: Mt. 5:8 in Augustine's Trinitarian Theology of 400," *Modern Theology*, vol. 19, no. 3 (2003): 329–55; Michel R. Barnes, "Augustine's Last Pneumatology," *Augustinian Studies*, vol. 39, no. 2 (2008): 223–34.

74. Basil Studer, "Zur Bedeutung der Heiligen Schrift in Augustin's *De Trinitate*," *Augustinianum*, vol. 42, no. 1 (2002): 127–47.

75. Kari Kloos, *Christ, Creation, and the Vision of God: Augustine's Transformation of Early Christian Theophany Interpretation* (Leiden: Brill, 2011).

and Ormerod. As noted earlier, Hill suggests that Augustine anticipates much of what Rahner requires in a treatise on the Trinity. This does not mean that it could not do with some "pruning" or "amplification" in parts. However, "the basic structure and the basic ideas are all there."[76] These ideas include what Augustine writes concerning the *De Deo uno* and *De Deo trino*, incarnational peculiarity, the missions and processions, and religious piety. Benner adopts a similar argument to Hill, adding that "Rahner's outworking of his fundamental axiom leads him into numerous difficulties that he could have avoided had he adhered to Augustine's view of a close but differentiated relationship between the immanent Trinity and the economic Trinity."[77] These difficulties include "(1) the nature of the Son's subordination to the Father, (2) the relationship between the doctrine of the Trinity and the doctrine of the atonement, (3) the balance in focus on the economic and immanent Trinities, (4) the relationship between the Creator and the creature, and (5) the balance of God's immanence and transcendence."[78] Ormerod criticizes Rahner for ignoring the *Filioque* when advocating the correspondence of the economic and immanent τάξις of the Trinity. This is contrasted with Augustine who starts with Scripture, where the Son speaks of sending the Spirit.[79] It should be noted, however, that these articles do not consider *how* Augustine's exegesis of "the biblical statements concerning the economy of salvation" challenges Rahner's assessment of Augustine. It is simply assumed. This book considers how Augustine's attention to Scripture challenges this assessment.

Other studies attend to the kinds of accusations that Rahner levels at Augustine and the Western tradition, though Rahner himself is less visible. Thinkers and writers such as Bourassa,[80] Bailleux,[81] Arnold,[82] Studer,[83] and

---

76. Hill, "Karl Rahner's 'Remarks on the Dogmatic Treatise *De Trinitate* and St. Augustine,'" 80.

77. Benner, "Augustine and Karl Rahner on the Relationship between the Immanent Trinity and the Economic Trinity," 24.

78. Ibid., 35.

79. Neil Ormerod, "Wrestling with Rahner on the Trinity," *Irish Theological Quarterly*, vol. 68, no. 3 (2003): 213–27.

80. François Bourassa, "Sur le Traité de la Trinité," *Gregorianum*, vol. 47, no. 2 (1966): 254–85; François Bourassa, "Théologie Trinitaire chez Saint Augustin," *Gregorianum*, vol. 58, no. 4 (1977): 675–718; François Bourassa, "Theologie Trinitaire de Saint Augustin," *Gregorianum*, vol. 59, no. 2 (1978): 375–412.

81. Emile Bailleux, "La Sotériologie de Saint Augustin dans le *De Trinitate*," *Mélanges de Science Religieuse*, vol. 23 (1966): 149–73.

82. Johannes Arnold, "Begriff und heilsökonomische Bedeutung der göttlichen Sendungen in Augustinus' *De Trinitate*," *Recherches Augustiniennes et Patristiques*, vol. 25, no. 1 (1991): 3–69.

83. Studer, *Augustins* De Trinitate, 28, 38, 172, 189; Basil Studer "Theologia—Oikonomia: Zu einem traditionellen Thema in Augustins De Trinitate," in *Patrimonium fidei*, ed. Magnus Löhrer and Pius-Ramon Tragan, Studia Anselmiana 124 (Rome: Pontificio Ateneo S. Anselmo, 1997), 575–600.

Anatolios[84] demonstrate the close link between Augustine's account of the Trinity and the economy through the missions and processions. Bailleux especially details the integral function of soteriology in Augustine's Trinitarian thought.[85] With recourse to Augustine, Barnes and Ayres have done much to challenge the East–West/One–Three typology associated with de Régnon and adopted by Rahner.[86] In response to Colin Gunton's critiques of Augustine (many similar to those of Rahner), Bradley Green has demonstrated at length that "there are strengths and insights in Augustine's writings, particularly in *De Trinitate*, which at least partially acquit Augustine from the charges Gunton has levied against him."[87] Nevertheless, for the most part, these studies overlook Augustine's exegesis. In his 2005 monograph, Studer asserts that Scripture is the basis (*grundlage*) for Augustine's doctrine of the Trinity,[88] and yet he only devotes nine of 250 pages (103–10 and 117–18) to Augustine's exegesis. Even if, with Kany, we question the extent to which Scripture *is* ultimately the basis of Augustine's Trinitarian theology, it is difficult to ignore its importance or the frequency with which it appears in his work. Thus, it is still not clear from the extant literature whether, how, or to what extent Augustine's *exegesis* pre-empts and addresses the criticisms levelled at him by Rahner.

A Biblical Defence of Rahner's Rule

A second lacuna pertains to studies on the extent to which the economic τάξις of the divine persons reflects their immanent τάξις. Though many have commented on this issue tangentially (cf. pp. 11–14), to date, only Jowers and Harrower have sought to fill this void directly. In his 2006 monograph, Jowers offers perhaps the most comprehensive refutation of Rahner's Rule to date. Of particular importance, in his fourth chapter he offers the first explicitly exegetical examination of the Rule (also published as an article in *The Thomist*).[89] Jowers argues that "the biblical accounts of Christ's anointing with the Holy Spirit (Matt 3:16, 17; Mark 1:10, 11;

---

84. Anatolios, *Retrieving Nicaea*, 221–31.

85. Bailleux, "La Sotériologie de Saint Augustin dans le *De Trinitate*."

86. Michel Barnes, "De Régnon Reconsidered," *Augustinian Studies*, vol. 26, no. 2 (1995): 51–79; Lewis Ayres, *Nicaea and Its Legacy: An Approach to Fourth-Century Trinitarian Theology* (Oxford: OUP, 2004), 364–81; Ayres, *Augustine and the Trinity*.

87. Bradley G. Green, "The Protomodern Augustine? Colin Gunton and the Failure of Augustine," *International Journal of Systematic Theology*, vol. 9, no. 3 (2007): 341; cf. Bradley G. Green, *Colin Gunton and the Failure of Augustine: The Theology of Colin Gunton in Light of Augustine* (Eugene, OR: Pickwick, 2011).

88. Studer, *Augustins* De Trinitate, 103.

89. Dennis W. Jowers, *The Trinitarian Axiom of Karl Rahner: The Economic Trinity is the Immanent Trinity and Vice Versa* (Lewiston: Edwin Mellen, 2006), 212–41; Dennis W. Jowers, "Test of Rahner's Axiom, The Economic Trinity Is the Immanent Trinity and Vice Versa," *The Thomist: A Speculative Quarterly Review*, vol. 70, no. 3 (2006): 421–55.

Luke 3:22; and John 1:32), when interpreted in accordance with the *Grundaxiom* of Rahner's theology of the Trinity … entail conclusions incompatible with Rahner's orthodox, Latin Trinitarianism."[90] By Rahner's "Latin Trinitarianism" he refers to the Council of Florence which affirms that the Holy Spirit "has His essence and His subsistent being both from the Father and the Son" (DS 1300) and thus "presupposes the personal constitution of the Son."[91] Jowers's study thus exposes a perceived inconsistency in Rahner's theology. The account of the Spirit's descent upon the Son in the economy cannot easily be reconciled with this magisterial statement concerning the immanent procession of the Spirit jointly from the Father and Son. In the only monograph focusing specifically on the exegetical validity of Rahner's Rule, Harrower mounts a similar argument with respect to Luke-Acts, also accounting for the Father–Son relationship. He argues that a strict exegetical application of Rahner's Rule simply cannot be reconciled with the Western understanding of the immanent relations. To date, no one has offered an extended exegetical case in support of Rahner's Rule. Such an offering is the substance of the second half of this book.

Rahner's Rule and Patristic Exegesis

A third lacuna pertains to the intersection of Rahner's Rule and patristic exegesis more specifically. From time to time, historical and systematic theologians have commented that the issues raised by Rahner's Trinitarian theology invites further research into the Trinitarian exegesis of the church fathers. Anatolios comments that Rahner's "identification of the immanent Trinity with the economic Trinity pays little attention to the narrative particularities of the economy."[92] Though recognizing the overall biblical thrust of Rahner's theology, he suggests that "his axiom needs to be more thoroughly integrated with particular details of the scriptural narrative." He then comments that "Rahner's axiom and the complexities of its implementation should make us ask how such complexities were dealt with in the historical construction of the doctrine itself."[93] If Rahner's Rule is truly to do justice "to the biblical statements concerning the economy of salvation," perhaps it needs the assistance of a church father. In the foreword to Harrower's monograph, Sanders likewise writes that theological investigation into the exegetical validity of Rahner's Rule makes one eager "to enlist the advice of superiors like Augustine, Cyril of Alexandria, and Thomas Aquinas, gathered around the text of Scripture and submitting to it as the norm."[94]

To date, no one has considered in detail how Augustine addresses the narrative particularities and exegetical complexities surrounding the degree

---

90. Jowers, *The Trinitarian Axiom of Karl Rahner*, vi; cf. Jowers, "Test of Rahner's Axiom."
91. Jowers, *The Trinitarian Axiom of Karl Rahner*, 227.
92. Anatolios, *Retrieving Nicaea*, 5.
93. Ibid., 5.
94. Sanders, "Foreword," xiii.

of correspondence between the economic and immanent relations. Thus, unsurprisingly, no one has argued that he offers considerable exegetical support for Rahner's Rule. Though a strong case could be made that we should turn to another of the superiors listed earlier, Rahner's project ultimately stems back to his problems with Augustine and the tradition that emerged in his aftermath. Even if we focused on Rahner's problems with Thomas, we would still be dealing with Augustine implicitly. Thus, we turn to Augustine's exegesis.

4. The Argument

Through close and sustained analysis of Augustine's exegesis of the "biblical statements concerning the economy of salvation," this book argues that Augustine's Trinitarian exegesis offers *significant*—though certainly not *inexhaustible*—support for Rahner's Trinitarian project and particularly his *Grundaxiom*. Firstly, Augustine provides weighty, biblically rich, support for Rahner's Trinitarian agenda at exactly those points where Rahner is explicitly critical of the "Augustinian-Western tradition," overcoming various weaknesses detected in the later tradition, and pre-empting many of Rahner's later solutions. Secondly, Augustine offers a reading strategy that addresses the major exegetical difficulties perceived to result from Rahner's Rule. Thus, in Augustine's attention to Scripture, the Augustinian-Western tradition has always had the resources at its disposal to avoid or address the most poignant criticisms levelled *by* and *at* Rahner.

Chapters 2 and 3 attend to the criticisms Rahner levels at Augustine and the Augustinian-Western tradition. Chapter 2 argues that several of the themes emerging in (but not restricted to) *Trin.* book 1 address the weaknesses Rahner discerns in the tradition and pre-empt the solutions Rahner proposes. First and foremost, Augustine attends to "the biblical statements concerning the economy of salvation" from the very beginning of his *magnum opus* on the Trinity. Second, in attending to these narrative particularities, Augustine's account of the Trinity is far less prone to the criticism of separating the *De Deo uno* from the *De Deo trino* than is often suggested and can even be seen to integrate the two. Third, Augustine preserves the Son's incarnational peculiarity (even through his psychological analogy) by attending to Scripture. Fourth, Augustine's doctrine of the Trinity is closely integrated with his doctrine of creation and natural revelation, even with respect to the *vestigia*. Fifth, from start to finish, Augustine's account is designed to integrate the Trinity with the Christian's faith and piety. In each case, it is argued that Augustine pays greater attention to "the biblical statements concerning the economy of salvation" than Rahner does in *Der Dreifaltige Gott*.

Chapter 3 argues that Augustine's attention to "the biblical statements concerning the economy of salvation" in themes emerging in (but, again, not restricted to) books 2–4 of *Trin.* overcomes three further Western shortcomings discerned by Rahner, pre-empting Rahner's solutions. Even if Rahner was correct about the tradition in his time, it was only because that tradition had strayed from Augustine. First, Augustine considers in great detail the narrative particularities of the Old Testament theophanies in his presentation of the Trinity. Second, the bishop integrates the doctrine of the Trinity with the doctrine of grace. Third, Augustine offers a closely tethered account of the missions and processions. From Chapters 2 and 3, we can thus discern eight ways in which Augustine's attention to "the biblical statements concerning the economy of salvation" addresses the alleged weaknesses in the Augustinian-Western tradition, thus pre-empting many of Rahner's positive proposals. Ironically, Augustine provides the attention to the biblical particularities that Rahner promised but failed to deliver.

Chapters 4 and 5 pivot to the criticisms levelled at the exegetical application of Rahner's Rule. For greater exposure to Augustine's exegesis, we also examine his corpus beyond *Trin.*, drawing particularly on his preaching (e.g., *In Iohannis euangelium tractatus CXXIV* and *Sermones*) and anti-Arian writings (e.g., *Conlatio cum Maximino Arrianorum episcopo*, *Contra Maximinum Arrianum* and *Contra sermonem Arrianorum liber unus*). It is argued that Augustine's understanding of the relationship between the missions and processions (as outlined in Chapter 3) functions as a reading strategy through which the Trinitarian dynamics of the economy parallel a Western conception of the immanent Trinitarian relations. In following this strategy, the bishop overcomes several criticisms directed at the Rule.

Chapter 4 turns to the Father–Son relationship. It argues, first, that Augustine's ruled reading of Scripture provides a clear strategy for avoiding ontological Subordinationism when moving from the economic Trinity to the immanent Trinity. Second, it is argued that Augustine's strategy for reading texts speaking of power transfer between the Father and the Son removes the risk of a reversed or inverted Father–Son relationship. A similar argument is offered, third, with texts portraying mutuality between the Father and the Son. Each of these texts can be read in parallel to the Father's eternal generation of the Son. Fourth, Augustine demonstrates that it is possible to read biblical texts mentioning all three divine persons—in this case, those citing the Son prior to the Father—without contradicting the τάξις of the immanent Trinity or reversing the Father–Son relationship. Finally, Augustine offers a strategy—or at the very least, the starting point of a strategy—for discerning a parallel between the ascension and eternal generation. Thus, an eternal analogue is not out of the question.

Chapter 5 explores how Augustine's exegesis addresses the criticisms levelled at Rahner's Rule concerning the Son–Spirit relationship (and to a lesser degree, the Father–Spirit relationship). According to Augustine, the dynamic between the Son and the Spirit in the virgin conception, Jordan baptism, desert temptation, earthly ministry, resurrection, and Pentecostal outpouring mirrors the Son's immanent reception of the Spirit, whom the Father gives to him, both to proceed from him, and to have "without measure" in the fullness of deity. The Son's immanent reception of the Spirit is the eternal analogue to the Son's multiple economic receptions of the Spirit. Moreover, little can be gleaned from the order in which divine persons are mentioned in the various triadic texts. We cannot conclude that these texts reverse the Son–Spirit or Father–Spirit relationships. Thus, an even-handed application of Rahner's Rule does not require a *Spirituque* since the Spirit is given to the Son *as* he is begotten. A *Patreque* is not required since the monarchy of the Father is preserved. As such, the doctrine of eternal generation is not compromised and the risk of multiple τάξεις is likewise avoided. Given the congruity of the economic and immanent Son–Spirit relationship—the economic reflecting and grounded in the immanent—there is no need to fear relational instability, ontological morphing, or pantheism. Hence, Augustine offers a framework that avoids the major obstacles for applying Rahner's Rule to the economic Son–Spirit relationship (and, to a lesser degree, the Father–Spirit relationship). We now turn to Chapter 2 to explore how Augustine's treatment of five themes emerging in book 1 of *Trin.* support and enhance Rahner's agenda.

Chapter 2

AUGUSTINE AND THE ECONOMY: SCRIPTURE, *DE DEO UNO* AND *TRINO*, CHRISTOLOGY, CREATION, AND PIETY

The next two chapters attend to the criticisms Rahner levels at Augustine and the Augustinian-Western tradition. This chapter argues that several motifs first arising in (though not restricted to) book 1 of Augustine's *De Trinitate* address the weaknesses Rahner discerns in the tradition and pre-empt the solutions proposed by the Jesuit priest. These include Augustine's integration of the Trinity with Scripture more generally, his integration of the *De Deo uno* and *De Deo trino*, and his connection of the doctrine of the Trinity with Christology, creation, and faith or piety. Those motifs more specific to books 2–4—the Old Testament, soteriology, and the missions and processions—are left for the next chapter. As each theme is explored we will see, with Hill, that "what Rahner so rightly requires of a new treatise on the Trinity does not have to be composed from scratch in the Latin tradition; it is nearly all there in Augustine's *De Trinitate*."[1] To date, there have been no studies exploring how Augustine's specific attention to "the biblical statements about the economy of salvation, its Triune structure and the explicit biblical sentences with regard to the Father, Son and Spirit"[2] supports and enhances Rahner's thesis. These chapters seek to fill that void.

1. Trinity and Scripture

The Western Tradition and the Separation of Trinity and Scripture

As mentioned in the previous chapter, Rahner argues that many of the problems in Western Christianity stem from the isolation of the doctrine of the Trinity from Scripture and the economy. Specifically, Rahner contests that whereas the

---

1. Hill, "Karl Rahner's 'Remarks on the Dogmatic Treatise *De Trinitate* and St. Augustine,'" 80.
2. Rahner, "Der Dreifaltige Gott," 535: "die biblischen Aussagen über die Heilsökonomie, deren dreifaltige Struktur und über die expliziten biblischen Sätze im Blick auf den Vater, Sohn und Geist."

Greeks, particularly the Cappadocians, had naturally assumed that the Trinity was connected with the economy of salvation, the Augustinian-Western tradition had taken what the Greeks said as assumed, and sought to fill it out by developing Augustine's psychological analogy.[3] As a result, the Western conception of the Trinity had become detached from Scripture and "absolutely contained in itself" (*absolut in sich geschlossene und in ihrer*).[4] According to Rahner, any solution to this detachment would thus need to do justice to "the biblical statements about the economy of salvation."

Rahner was not alone in arguing that Augustine's doctrine of the Trinity was disconnected from the Scriptures and the economy of salvation. Several leading Augustinian scholars and church historians in the century leading up to *Der Dreifaltige Gott* had reached the same conclusion. The titles of the two most influential monographs on Augustine's Trinitarian thought in the century prior to Rahner (Gangauf's *Des Heiligen Augustinus speculative Lehre von Gott dem Dreieinigen* and Schmaus' *Die psychologische Trinitätslehre des heiligen Augustinus*) summarize the general depiction of Augustine's Trinity in this time period: it is speculative and psychological.[5] Schmaus asserted that Augustine's "doctrine of the Trinity had to pay for the gains made in philosophical penetration with a loss of the dynamics of salvation history."[6] With respect to his Trinitarian theology, French historian Theodore de Régnon would describe the bishop as "an eagle soaring in the high regions of speculation" (*un aigle planant dans les hautes régions de la spéculation*).[7] German historian Adolf von Harnack described Augustine's psychological analogy as "incomprehensible" (*Unbegreiflichen*), adding: "This speculation, which tries to construct the most immanent of the immanent Trinities and to sublimate the Trinity into a unity, distances itself from any historical-religious basis and loses itself in paradoxical distinctions and speculations, and yet it is still unable to express clearly its new and valuable idea."[8]

---

3. Ibid., 529, note (n.) 14.

4. Ibid.

5. Theodor Gangauf, *Des Heiligen Augustinus speculative Lehre von Gott dem Dreieinigen* (Augsburg: Schmid, 1865); Schmaus, *Die psychologische Trinitätslehre des heiligen Augustinus*.

6. Michael Schmaus, "Die Spannung von Metaphysik und Heilsgeschicte in der Trinitätslehre Augustins," in *Studia Patristica*, ed. F. L. Cross, vol. 6 (Berlin: Akademie-Verlag, 1962), 511: "Die augustinische Trinitätslehre hat den Fortschritt, welchen sie im Bereiche der philosophischen Durchdringung darstellt, mit dem Verlust heilsgeschichtlicher Dynamik bezahlen müsen."

7. Theodore de Régnon, *Études de Théologie Positive sur la Sainte Trinité*, vol. 3, 3 vols (Paris: Victor Retaux, 1898), 39.

8. Adolf von Harnack, *Lehrbuch der dogmengeschichte*, 3rd ed., vol. 2 (Freiburg im Brisgau: Mohr, 1894), 295: "Diese Speculation, welche die immanenteste unter den immanenten Trinitäten zu construiren und die Dreiheit zur Einheit zu sublimiren versucht, entfernt sich eben damit von jeder geschichtlich-religiösen Grundlage und verliert sich in

In the mid-1960s, Oliver du Roy would write that "Augustine bequeathed to the West a dogmatic scheme of the Trinity which tends to cut it off from the economy of salvation,"[9] the starting point "so well safeguarded in Eastern theology."[10] In the same volume of *Mysterium Salutis* as Rahner's *Der Dreifaltige Gott*, Scheffczyk likewise maintained that the advantages of Augustine's account of the Trinity came at the price of a "renunciation of economic consideration and evaluation of the Trinitarian mystery."[11] However, in each of the works cited earlier, as in Rahner's *Der Dreifaltige Gott*, Augustine's copious attention to Scripture and the economy— especially in *Trin.* books 1–4—remains largely ignored. As will now be shown, even though it may be true that many works on the Trinity in the Western tradition pay little attention to the biblical statements about the economy of salvation, the same cannot be said of Augustine's *Trin.*

The Biblical Foundations of Trin. *Book 1*

From the very beginning of *Trin.*, even a cursory reading reveals that the Bible is foundational for Augustine's Trinitarian theology. According to Augustine, to avoid the errors of those "mocking the starting point of faith [*fidei contemnentes initium*]," it is necessary to start from what God has communicated about himself.[12] This is found in the Scriptures:

> Therefore, in order that the human mind may be cleansed from errors of this kind, Holy Scripture, adapting itself to little ones, has employed words from every class of objects in order that our intellect, as though strengthened by them, might rise as it were gradually to divine and sublime things.[13]

---

paradoxe Distinctionen und Speculationen, während sie ihren neuen und werth vollen Gedanken doch nicht rein auszudrücken vermag."

9. Olivier Du Roy, *L'Intelligence de la Foi en la Trinité selon Saint Augustin* (Paris: Études Augustiniennes, 1966), 460: "Augustin a légué à l'Occident un scheme dogmatique de la Trinité qui tend à couper celle-ci de l'économie du salut."

10. Ibid., 464: "Si la théologie trinitaire augustinienne nous a paru perdre dans une large mesure l'économie si bien sauve gardée dans la théologie orientale, elle a, pour une part, compensé cette perte par sa découverte de l'intériorité subjective."

11. Scheffczyk, "Lehramtliche Formulierungen und Dogmengeschichte der Trinitätslehre," 204: "Bei genauerer Betrachtung zeigt sich ..., daß Augustin die Vorzüge seiner theologischen Erklärung der Trinität um den Preis eines großen Verzichtes erkaufte, nämlich um den Verzicht der ökonomischen Betrachtung und Wertung des Trinitätsgeheimnisses."

12. *Trin.* 1.1.1 (CCSL 50: 27).

13. *Trin.* 1.1.2 (CCSL 50: 28): "Vt ergo ab huiusmodi falsitatibus humanus animus purgaretur, sancta scriptura paruulis congruens nullius generis rerum uerba uitauit ex quibus quasi gradatim ad diuina atque sublimia noster intellectus uelut nutritus assurgeret."

Before accommodating those talkative "reason-mongers" (*rationators*) who reject this starting point, Augustine "must first find out by an appeal to the authority of the Holy Scriptures whether faith is in a position to do so."[14] Such an appeal will lead him to the conviction of his Catholic forefathers, that "the Trinity is the one, only, and true God and how rightly that the Father, the Son, and the Holy Spirit are said to be of one and the same substance or essence."[15] This does not mean that Augustine's attention to Scripture (especially in books 1–4) should be seen as scriptural evidence for Augustine's doctrine of the Trinity.[16] As Kany notes, Augustine's purpose in books 1–4 is not to "provide 'scriptural evidence' of the dogma of the Trinity, but to refute a Subordinationist interpretation of Scripture, to show the necessity of the economy of salvation for the salvation of man and to show the connection between the 'missions' of the Son and the Holy Spirit and inner processions."[17] Nevertheless, the fact that Augustine is compelled to appeal

---

14. *Trin.* 1.2.4 (CCSL 50: 31): "Sed primum secundum auctoritatem scripturarum sanctarum utrum its se fides habeat domstrandum est."

15. *Trin.* 1.2.4 (CCSL 50: 31): "Quapropter adiuuante domino deo nostro suscipiemus et eam ipsam quam flagitant, quantum possumus, reddere rationem, quod trinitas sit *unus et solus* et *uerus deus*, et quam recte pater et filius et spiritus sanctus *unius eiusdem* que *substantiae* uel *essentiae* dicatur."

16. As suggested, for example, by Berthold Altaner and Alfred Stuiber, *Patrologie: Leben, Schriften Und Lehre Der Kirchenväter* (Freiburg im Breisgau: Herder, 1938), 426.

17. Kany, *Augustins Trinitätsdenken*, 182: "Außerdem treten die Bücher I bis IV keinen »Schriftbeweis « für das Trinitätsdogma an, sondern widerlegen eine subordinatianische Schriftauslegung, zeigen die Notwendigkeit der Heilsökonomie für das Heil des Menschen und den Zusammenhang der »Sendungen« des Sohnes und des Heiligen Geistes mit den inneren Hervorgängen."

Barnes has made a strong case that Augustine is demonstrably engaged in refuting Homoian theology from as early as book 1. In 1.6.9, Augustine refers to those "who have affirmed that our Lord Jesus Christ is [1] not God, or is [2] not true God, or is [3] not with the Father the one and only God, or is [4] not truly immortal because he is subject to change" (*Trin.* 1.6.9 (CCSL 50: 37–8)). Barnes has shown from the works of Paladius and Maximinus that the second, third, and fourth affirmations refer to Homoian theology (Barnes, "Exegesis and Polemic in Augustine's *De Trinitate*," 45–7).

In a later study, Barnes also argues that book 1 is polemically charged. Appealing again to Augustine's engagement with Maximinus, he argues that Augustine's discussion of the Old Testament theophanies are designed to combat a false economy of the Trinity (Michel R. Barnes, "Augustine in Contemporary Trinitarian Theology," *Theological Studies*, vol. 56, no. 2 (1995): 247). Importantly, "Anti-Nicenes excluded the Father from Old Testament theophanies so as to argue from these appearances the Son's changeability and materiality" (ibid., 247). Barnes also notes that Augustine is involved in a polemic against many of his theological forebears. He argues that while "the specific passages disputed are determined in response to Homoian polemic, some scriptural passages cited in support of Augustine's position are used because these have an older history, authority, and role in an economic theology of the Trinity" (ibid.). He is particularly thinking of Augustine's treatment of John

to Scripture demonstrates that he views Scripture as foundational to the doctrine of the Trinity, even if his account is not specifically a "grounds up" construction of the doctrine.

In *Trin.* 1.2.4 Augustine goes on to list the economic events that he—and his Catholic forefathers—attend to when "they intend to teach, in accordance with the Scriptures, that the Father, the Son, and the Holy Spirit constitute a divine unity of one and the same substance in an indivisible equality."[18] He writes:

> This same Trinity was not born of the virgin Mary nor crucified and buried under Pontius Pilate, nor rose again on the third day, nor ascended into heaven, but only the Son. Nor did this same Trinity descend upon Jesus in the form of a dove when he was baptized. Nor was this same Trinity at Pentecost, after the Lord's ascension, when a sound came from heaven as if a mighty wind were blowing, settled upon each one of them with parted tongues of fire, but only the Holy Spirit. Nor did this same Trinity say from heaven, "You are my Son," either when Jesus was baptized by John or when the three disciples were with him on the mountain, nor when the voice sounded saying, "I have glorified and I shall glorify again." This was the Word of the Father only, spoken to the Son although the Father, the Son, and the Holy Spirit, as they are inseparable, likewise work inseparably. This is also my faith since it is the Catholic faith.[19]

What Augustine believes is the Catholic faith, but he is ultimately convinced that it is the Catholic faith because it is taught in Scripture. Crucially, the Scriptures take him (with his Catholic forefathers) directly to the economy of salvation: to

---

1:1–3 at 2.2.9, which resembles Tertullian and Hippolytus' "use of the Johannine prologue (but especially John 1:1) as the paradigmatic expression of the economy of the Trinity" (ibid., 248).

18. *Trin.* 1.4.7 (CCSL 50: 34): "hoc intenderunt secundum scripturas docere, quod pater et filius et spiritus sanctus *unius substantiae* inseparabili aequalitate diuinam insinuent unitatem."

19. *Trin.* 1.4.7 (CCSL 50: 35–6):

> Non tamen eandem trinitatem natam *de uirgine Maria et sub Pontio Pilato* crucifixam et sepultam *tertio die resurrexisse* et *in caelum ascendisse*, sed tantummodo filium. Nec eandem trinitatem descendisse *in specie columbae* super Iesum baptizatum aut *die pentecostes post ascensionem domini* sonitu facto *de caelo quasi ferretur flatus uehemens* et linguis diuisis *uelut ignis*, sed tantummodo spiritum sanctum. Nec eandem trinitatem dixisse de caelo: *Tu es filius meus*, siue cum baptizatus est a Iohanne siue in monte quando cum illo erant tres discipuli, aut quando sonuit uox dicens: *Et clarificaui et iterum clarificabo*, sed tantummodo patris uocem fuisse ad filium factam—quamuis pater et filius et spiritus sanctus sicut inseparabiles sunt, ita inseparabiliter operentur. Haec et mea fides est quando haec est catholica fides.

the Christ's virgin birth, baptism, transfiguration, crucifixion, burial, resurrection, and ascension as well as the events of Pentecost.

As the footnotes below indicate, specific attention to the biblical accounts of these events saturate Augustine's discussion throughout the rest of book 1, books 2–4, books 5–15 (to a lesser degree), as well as his various other Trinitarian works.[20] He discusses the incarnation and virgin birth with specific reference to Matt 1:18,[21] Luke 1:35,[22] John 1:14,[23] and Gal 4:4.[24] He refers to the baptism with reference to Matt 3:16–17 (cf. Mark 1:10–11; Luke 3:21–22)[25] and John 1:32–33,[26] the messianic ministry with reference to Luke 4:18,[27] and the death of the Christ with reference to 1 Tim 2:5,[28] Matt

---

20. In particular, *Tract. Ev. Jo.*, *Maxim.*, *Coll. Max.*, *Arian.*, and *sermo* 52 (hereafter *Serm.* 52). While these works may not qualify as strictly "Trinitarian" writings, they reveal a great deal about Augustine's Trinitarian thought and are thus an invaluable resource.

21. *Trin.* 2.5.8 (CCSL 50: 90); 2.5.9 (CCSL 50: 91); *Serm.* 51.6.9 (CCSL 41Aa: 19); *Maxim.* 2.17.2 (CCSL 87A: 606).

22. *Trin.* 2.5.8 (CCSL 50: 89); *Tract. Ev. Jo.* 99.7 (CCSL 36: 586); *Maxim.* 2.17.2 (CCSL 87A: 606).

23. *Trin.* 1.6.9 (CCSL 50: 38); 2.5.9 (CCSL 50: 90–1); 2.6.11 (CCSL 50: 94); 2.7.12 (CCSL 50: 97); 3.proem.3 (CCSL 50: 129); 4.2.4 (CCSL 50: 163); 4.20.27 (CCSL 50: 196); 4.20.28 (CCSL 50: 198); 7.3.4 (CCSL 50: 251–2); 8.1.2 (CCSL 50: 381); 13.9.12 (CCSL 50: 399); 13.17.22 (CCSL 50: 412); 13.19.24 (CCSL 50: 414); 14.18.24 (CCSL 50: 455); 15.11.20 (CCSL 50: 487–8); 15.26.46 (CCSL 50: 526); *Tract. Ev. Jo.* 2.15–16 (CCSL 36: 19); 3.6 (CCSL 36: 23); 10.3 (CCSL 36: 102); 12.10 (CCSL 36: 126); 13.3 (CCSL 36: 131); 13.6 (CCSL 36: 133); 15.6 (CCSL 36: 152); 16.7 (CCSL 36: 169); 18.2 (CCSL 36: 180); 19.15 (CCSL 36: 198); *Arian.* 9.7 (CCSL 87A: 201); 12.9 (CCSL 87A: 208); 27.23 (CCSL 87A: 236); 27.24 (CCSL 87A: 237); *Coll. Max.* 11 (CCSL 87A: 394); 14.5 (CCSL 87A: 410); 15.8 (CCSL 87A: 427); *Maxim.* 2.22.3 (CCSL 87A: 637).

24. *Trin.* 1.6.9 (CCSL 50: 38); 1.7.14 (CCSL 50: 46); 1.11.22 (CCSL 50: 60); 2.5.8 (CCSL 50: 89); 2.5.9 (CCSL 50: 91); 2.7.12 (CCSL 50: 97); 3.proem.3 (CCSL 50: 129); 3.1.4 (CCSL 50:130–1); 4.7.11 (CCSL 50: 175); 4.19.25–4.20.30 (CCSL 50: 193–202); 7.5 (CCSL 50: 276); 15.28.51 (CCSL 50: 534); *Tract. Ev. Jo.* 12.12 (CCSL 36: 127); 28.5 (CCSL 36: 279); 104.2 (CCSL 36: 602); *Serm.* 52.4.9 (CCSL 41Aa: 65); 52.4.11 (CCSL 41Aa: 66); *Arian.* 6.6 (CCSL 87: 192).

25. *Trin.* 2.5.10 (CCSL 50: 93); *Tract. Ev. Jo.* 6.5 (CCSL 36: 56); *Serm.* 52.1 CCSL 41Aa: 58–9).

26. *Tract. Ev. Jo.* 4.12 (CCSL 36: 37); 5.1 (CCSL 36: 41–2); 5.18 (CCSL 36: 51); 6.5 (CCSL 36: 55–6); 6.7 (CCSL 36: 56–7); 7.3 (CCSL 36: 68); 9.13 (CCSL 36: 74); 13.10 (CCSL 36: 136); 14.10 (CCSL 36: 148); 15.3 (CCSL 36: 151).

27. *Trin.* 1.11.22 (CCSL 50: 60); *Tract. Ev. Jo.* 74.3 (CCSL 36: 514); *Coll. Max.* 11 (87A: 393–4); *Arian.* 22.18 (87A: 229).

28. *Trin.* 1.7.14 (CCSL 50: 44); 1.8.16 (CCSL 50: 49); 1.8.17 (CCSL 50: 50); 1.10.20 (CCSL 50: 57); 3.11.26 (CCSL 50: 157); 13.10.13 (CCSL 50: 399); 13.17.22–13.18.23 (CCSL 50: 412–13); 15.25 (CCSL 50: 523); *Tract. Ev. Jo.* 16.6 (CCSL 36: 169); 17.7 (CCSL 36: 174); 80.1 (CCSL 36: 527).

2. Augustine and the Economy—Part 1

26:39,[29] John 3:14,[30] Rom 8:32,[31] Phil 2:8,[32] 1 Cor 2:2,[33] 1 Cor 2:8,[34] Gal 2:20,[35] and Rev 1:7 (cf. Zech 12:10).[36] He discusses the resurrection with reference to Luke 24:26,[37] Luke 24:39,[38] John 20:28,[39] and Phil 2:9[40] and the ascension with reference to John 14–16[41] and John 20:17.[42] The descent of the Spirit is examined with reference to John 14:15–17,[43] John 14:26,[44] John 15:26,[45] John

---

29. *Trin.* 1.11.22 (CCSL 50: 61); *Arian.* 9.7 (CCSL 87A: 200).

30. *Trin.* 3.10.20 (CCSL 50: 148); *Tract. Ev. Jo.* 12.11 (CCSL 36: 126–7).

31. *Trin.* 1.10.21 (CCSL 50: 59); 2.5.9 (CCSL 50: 90); 13.16.21 (CCSL 50: 410); *Tract. Ev. Jo.* 45.12 (CCSL 36: 394).

32. *Trin.* 1.11.22 (CCSL 50: 60); 1.13.29 (CCSL 50: 70); 3.10.20 (CCSL 50: 148); 13.17.22 (CCSL 50: 412); *Tract. Ev. Jo.* 12.6 (CCSL 36: 124); 26.19 (CCSL 36: 269); 47.13 (CCSL 36: 412); 51.3 (CCSL 36: 440); 104.3 (CCSL 36: 602); 119.4 (CCSL 36: 660); *Coll. Max.* 15.2 (CCSL 87A: 421); 15.15 (CCSL 87A: 445); *Arian.* 8.6 (CCSL 87A: 197); 38.34 (CCSL 87A: 255).

33. *Trin.* 1.1.3 (CCSL 50: 30); 1.12.23 (CCSL 50: 62); *Tract. Ev. Jo.* 7.23 (CCSL 36: 81); 98.3 (CCSL 36: 577).

34. *Trin.* 1.13.28 (CCSL 50: 69); *Tract. Ev. Jo.* 17.3 (CCSL 36: 171); *Maxim.* 2.20.3 (CCSL 87A: 623); *Arian.* 8.6 (CCSL 87A: 197).

35. *Trin.* 2.5.9 (CCSL 50: 90); *Tract. Ev. Jo.* 62.4 (CCSL 36: 484); *Maxim.* 2.20.4 (CCSL 87A: 624).

36. *Trin.* 1.13.28 (CCSL 50: 71); 1.13.29 (CCSL 50: 73); *Tract. Ev. Jo.* 3.3 (CCSL 36: 21); 19.16 (CCSL 36: 199); 36.12 (CCSL 36: 331).

37. *Trin.* 2.17.31 (CCSL 50: 121); *Tract. Ev. Jo.* 9.4 (CCSL 36: 92).

38. *Trin.* 4.3.6 (CCSL 50: 168); *Tract. Ev. Jo.* 121.3 (CCSL 36: 666).

39. *Trin.* 4.3.6 (CCSL 50: 168); *Tract. Ev. Jo.* 16.4 (CCSL 36: 167); 66.2 (CCSL 36: 494); 121.5 (CCSL 36: 667–8).

40. *Trin.* 1.13.29 (CCSL 50: 72); *Tract. Ev. Jo.* 10.11 (CCSL 36: 105); 104.3 (CCSL 36: 602); *Maxim.* 2.2 (CCSL 87A: 537).

41. *Trin.* 1.8.18 (CCSL 50: 52–3); *Tract. Ev. Jo.* 69.2 (CCSL 36: 500–1); 71.3 (CCSL 36: 506–7); 72.1 (CCSL 36: 507–8); 73.1–2 (CCSL 36: 509–10); 78.1–3 (CCSL 36: 523–5); 79.1 (CCSL 36: 525–6); 94.6 (CCSL 36: 564); 95.2–3 (CCSL 36: 565–7); 101.1 (CCSL 36: 591); 101.6 (CCSL 36: 593–4) 102.6 (CCSL 36: 597); 103.1–2 (CCSL 36: 598–600); 121.3 (CCSL 36: 665–6); *Coll. Max.* 13 (CCSL 87A: 406); *Maxim.* 2.25 (CCSL 87A: 661).

42. *Trin.* 1.9 (CCSL 50: 54); 2.17.30 (CCSL 50: 120); 4.3.6 (CCSL 50: 168–9); *Tract. Ev. Jo.* 121.3 (CCSL 36: 665–6); *Coll. Max.* 13 (CCSL 87A: 404); 15.16 (CCSL 87A: 557); *Maxim.* 1.7 (CCSL 87A: 507); *Maxim.* 2.16.1 (CCSL 87A: 599).

43. *Trin.* 1.8.18 (CCSL 50: 52); 1.8.19 (CCSL 50: 52); *Tract. Ev. Jo.* 74.1 (CCSL 36: 512); 102.4 (CCSL 36: 597); 103.1 (CCSL 36: 598); *Coll. Max.* 12 (CCSL 87A: 400).

44. *Trin.* 1.12.25 (CCSL 50: 64); 2.5.7 (CCSL 50: 87); 4.20.29 (CCSL 50: 200); 15.26 (CCSL 50: 525); 15.28.51 (CCSL 50: 534); *Tract. Ev. Jo.* 77.2 (CCSL 36: 520); *Serm.* 265A (MiAg 1: 392).

45. *Trin.* 2.3.5 (CCSL 50: 86); 4.20.29 (CCSL 50: 199); 5.11.12 (CCSL 50: 219); *Tract. Ev. Jo.* 92.1–2 (CCSL 36: 556–7).

16:7,[46] John 16:13–14,[47] and Acts 2:1–4.[48] The eschatological handover of the kingdom is considered with reference to Dan 7:13–14[49] and 1 Cor 15:24–28,[50] the beatific vision with reference to Matt 5:8[51] and 1 Cor 13:12,[52] and the final judgment with reference to John 5:22[53] and John 5:27.[54] In addition to these, Phil 2:6–7 plays a crucial role in discerning whether texts refer to the Son in the *forma servi* or in the *forma dei* and in directing the ascent of faith.[55] Augustine does not offer extensive exegetical treatments of each text that he cites; some are

46. *Trin.* 1.8.18 (CCSL 50: 53); *Tract. Ev. Jo.* 94.4 (CCSL 36: 563); *Serm.* 143 (PL 38: 785–6); 270 (PL 38: 1239).

47. *Trin.* 1.8.18 (CCSL 50: 52–3); 2.3.5 (CCSL 50: 85–6); 2.13.23 (CCSL 50: 111); *Tract. Ev. Jo.* 46.4.2 (CCSL 36: 400); 96–101 (CCSL 36: 568–94); *Arian.* 22.18–23.20 (CCSL 87A: 229–32); 30.28 (CCSL 87A: 241–2).

48. *Trin.* 2.5.10 (CCSL 50: 93); *Tract. Ev. Jo.* 6.3 (CCSL 36: 54); 17.5 (CCSL 36: 172); 32.6 (CCSL 36: 303); 44.5 (CCSL 36: 383); 72.2 (CCSL 36: 508); 93.4 (CCSL 36: 561); 99.2 (CCSL 36: 583); 103.1 (CCSL 36: 598); 109.2 (CCSL 36: 619); 122.8 (CCSL 36: 674); *Coll. Max.* 14.19 (CCSL 87A: 419); *Maxim.* 1.19 (CCSL 87A: 532).

49. *Trin.* 2.18.33 (CCSL 50: 123–4); *Civ.* 18.34 (CCSL 49: 628).

50. *Trin.* 1.8.15–1.10.20 (CCSL 50: 46–57); 1.13.28 (CCSL 50: 70–1); 1.13.31 (CCSL 50: 193); *Tract. Ev. Jo.* 19.18 (CCSL 36: 201); 25.2 (CCSL 36: 248); 30.5 (CCSL 36: 291); 34.10 (CCSL 36: 317); 41.13 (CCSL 36: 365); 65.1 (CCSL 36: 491); 83.3 (CCSL 36: 536); *Arian.* 37 (CCSL 87A: 253–4); *Coll. Max.* 13 (CCSL 87A: 406); 14 (CCSL 87A: 419); 15 (CCSL 87A: 450); *Maxim.* 1.8 (CCSL 87A: 511); 1.19 (CCSL 87A: 528); 2.14 (CCSL 87A: 600); 2.18 (CCSL 87A: 615, 617).

51. *Trin.* 1.8.17 (CCSL 50: 51); 1.13.28 (CCSL 50: 70); 1.13.30 (CCSL 50: 74); 1.13.31 (CCSL 50: 78); 8.4.6 (CCSL 50: 275); *Tract. Ev. Jo.* 1.7 (CCSL 36: 4); 3.18 (CCSL 36: 28); 18.6 (CCSL 36: 183); 19.16 (CCSL 36: 199); 20.11 (CCSL 36: 209); 21.15 (CCSL 36: 221); 26.18 (CCSL 36: 268); 53.12 (CCSL 36: 458); 68.3 (CCSL 36: 499); 111.3 (CCSL 36: 630).

52. *Trin.* 1.8.16 (CCSL 50: 49–50); 1.13.28 (CCSL 50: 70); 1.13.31 (CCSL 50: 78); 2.17 (CCSL 50: 117); 8.4.6 (CCSL 50: 274); 9.1.1 (CCSL 50: 293); 12.14.22 (CCSL 50: 375); 14.2.4 (CCSL 50: 425); 14.17.23 (CCSL 50: 455); 14.19.25 (CCSL 50: 457); 15.8.14 (CCSL 50: 479); 15.11.21 (CCSL 50: 490); 15.13 (CCSL 50: 494); 15.21.40 (CCSL 50: 517); 15.23.44–15.24 (CCSL 50: 522); *Tract. Ev. Jo.* 34.9 (CCSL 36: 315); 43.7 (CCSL 36: 375); 86.1 (CCSL 36: 541); 96.4 (CCSL 36: 572); 101.5 (CCSL 36: 593); 102.3 (CCSL 36: 595); 124.5 (CCSL 36: 685); 124.7 (CCSL 36: 687); *Coll. Max.* 15.26 (CCSL 87A: 464).

53. *Trin.* 1.13.29–1.13.30 (CCSL 50: 72–3); 2.1.3 (CCSL 50: 82); *Tract. Ev. Jo.* 19.5 (CCSL 36: 190); 19.16 (CCSL 36: 199–200); 21.13 (CCSL 36: 219–20); 22.11 (CCSL 36: 229); 23.13 (CCSL 36: 242); 36.12 (CCSL 36: 331); 43.4 (CCSL 36: 374); 54.5–6 (CCSL 36: 461); 99.1 (CCSL 36: 582); *Coll. Max.* 15.18 (CCSL 87A: 451); *Maxim.* 2.18.6 (CCSL 87A: 615); *Arian.* 11.9 (CCSL 87A: 205).

54. *Trin.* 1.13.30 (CCSL 50: 73); 2.1.3 (CCSL 50: 82); *Tract. Ev. Jo.* 19.15–19.16 (CCSL 36: 198–9); 23.15 (CCSL 36: 243); 99.1 (CCSL 36: 582); *Arian.* (CCSL 87A: 206).

55. *Trin.* 1.6.12 (CCSL 50: 41–2); 1.7.14 (CCSL 50: 44–6); 1.8.18 (CCSL 50: 52–3); 1.10.20 (CCSL 50: 56–7); 1.10.21 (CCSL 50: 58); 1.11.22 (CCSL 50: 60–1); 1.13.29–1.13.30 (CCSL 50: 71–5); 2.1.3–2.3.5 (CCSL 50: 82–6).

simply passing citations. In many cases he is simply contesting the poorly executed exegesis of his interlocutors. Nevertheless, this extensive yet incomplete list shows that Augustine is very much committed to tying his doctrine of the Trinity to "the biblical statements about the economy of salvation." Rahner, despite his insistence on a "biblical" starting point, does not cite a single biblical text in *Der Dreifaltige Gott*. As noted earlier, though we are told at the beginning of part 3 that we have "*listened* very carefully and patiently" to what the Scriptures say about the Trinity,[56] the reader is given nothing but a few tangential footnotes to exegetical studies.[57] Meanwhile, as emphasized earlier, Augustine makes hundreds of appeals to the "biblical statements about the economy of salvation" in his Trinitarian writings.

The Biblical Backdrop of the Psychological Analogy

According to Rahner (as well as Schmaus, Harnack, and others), Augustine's psychological analogy is the main conceptual culprit for isolating the Trinity from the Scripture and the economy. However, even if the later tradition had focused on the analogy at the expense of the Bible and the economy, the same cannot be said of Augustine's version of the analogy. The first four books of *Trin.*—with all of their attention to Scripture and the events of the economy—are foundational to Augustine's penetration of the psychological analogy in books 8–15. Augustine intends for the fifteen books to be treated as a unit. When, in the prologue, he laments the premature publication of the first twelve books (the last few of which concern the psychological analogy), Augustine states that it had been his intention to publish the books together rather than individually "because the inquiry progresses in a tight-laced

---

2.5.9 (CCSL 50: 92); 2.11.20 (CCSL 50: 107); 2.17.31 (CCSL 50: 122); 3.proem.3 (CCSL 50: 129); 5.3.4–5.6.7 (CCSL 50: 208–12); 6.3.5–6.6.8 (CCSL 50: 233–6); 7.3.5 (CCSL 50: 253); *Tract. Ev. Jo.* 9.10 (CCSL 36: 96); 12.6 (CCSL 36: 124); 14.11 (CCSL 36: 149); 17.16 (CCSL 36: 179); 19.16 (CCSL 36: 199); 19.18 (CCSL 36: 201); 21.13–21.15 (CCSL 36: 221); 23.6 (CCSL 36: 236); 23.15 (CCSL 36: 244); 47.13 (CCSL 36: 13); 53.12 (CCSL 36: 457); 55.7 (CCSL 36: 466); 57.1 (CCSL 36: 495); 76.4 (CCSL 36: 519); 78.1-3 (CCSL 36: 523–5); 109.1 (CCSL 36: 582); *Coll. Max.* 14.17 (CCSL 87A: 418); 15.2 (CCSL 87A: 421); 15.15 (CCSL 87A: 444, 447); 15.26 (CCSL 87A: 465); *Maxim.* 1.5 (CCSL 87A: 501–4); 1.15 (CCSL 87A: 524); 1.17 (CCSL 87A: 526); 1.19 (CCSL 87A: 530–1); 2.9.2 (CCSL 87A: 550); 2.11 (CCSL 87A: 557); 2.14.7 (CCSL 87A: 581); 2.15.1 (CCSL 87A: 587); 2.26.13 (CCSL 87A: 688); *Arian.* 8.6 (CCSL 87A: 197–8).

56. Rahner, "Der Dreifaltige Gott," 596: "sehr ausführlich und geduldig *gehört* wurde, was Schrift, Dogmengeschichte und kirchenamtliche Lehre über die Trinität sagen."

57. On pages 513, 533, and 561 Rahner references Schulte, "Die Selbstschliessung des Dreifaltigen Gottes." On page 513, 557, and 583, he refers to Franz Josef Schierse, "Die Neutestamentliche Trinitätsoffenbarung," in *Mysterium Salutis*, ed. Johannes Feiner and Magnus Löhrer (Einsiedeln: Benziger, 1967), 82-131. On page 581, he refers to Rahner, "Theos im Neuen Testament."

development from first to last."[58] Ferri notes that "Augustine's fall-back not to greatly modify the books already published and his dissatisfaction with the overall result of the work explains—at least in part—the difficulties in interpreting the structure and development of the individual parts of the *De Trinitate*."[59] While this may be true, it

58. *Trin.* prologus (CCSL 50: 25): "Non enim singillatim sed omnes simul edere ea ratione decreueram, quoniam praecedentibus consequentes inquisitione proficiente nectuntur." Cf. *Ep.* 174 (CSEL 44: 650).

We know from the preface that production of the work faced interruptions. The bishop states that he laid the work aside upon learning that it had been stolen and published. At this stage, the prologues of the first four or five books, the back half of book 12, and books 13–15 were not complete. Augustine would later resume writing at the urgent request of many of his supporters, correcting the book as best he could, though less than he might have liked. Unfortunately, we cannot be certain of the extent to which Augustine corrected the books, nor of what precisely it means for him to have done so. While scholarship recognizes the delay in Augustine's writing, there is debate as to its precise timing. There are three main hypotheses for the starting point. Hendrikx argues that Augustine began writing in the summer of 399 (Ephraem Hendrikx, "La date de composition du *De Trinitate*," in *La Trinité I: Le Mystere*, Bibliothèque Augustinienne 15 (Paris: Desclée de Brouwer, 1955), 558). Hombert argues that he began between 400 and 405 (P. M. Hombert, *Nouvelles Recherches de Chronologie Augustinienne* (Paris: Institut d'Études Augustiniennes, 2000), 53–6), and, in her mature work, La Bonnardière suggests sometime after December 12, 404 (Anne-Marie la Bonnardière, "Recherche sur la structure du *De Trinitate* de saint Augustin," *Annuaires de l'École pratique des hautes études*, no. 82 (1973): 293–7). According to Hendrikx, Augustine wrote the first five books in 399–400 (Hendrikx, "La date de composition du *De Trinitate*," 558). La Bonnardière suggests that book 1 was written sometime after 404, and books 2–4 sometime between 411 and 414 (La Bonnardière, "Recherche sur la structure du *De Trinitate* de saint Augustin"). Hombert argues that book 1 was written from 400 to 403, books 2–3 from 411 to 413 and book 4 in the period 414–15 (Hombert, *Nouvelles Recherches de Chronologie Augustinienne*, 638).

As for the ending, Hendrikx argues that the work was completed in 419 (Hendrikx, "La date de composition du *De Trinitate*," 559), La Bonnardière suggests sometime between 420 and 426 (Anne-Marie la Bonnardière, *Recherches de chronologie Augustinienne* (Paris: Études Augustiniennes, 1965), 69, 166), and Kany between 420 and 427 (Kany, *Augustins Trinitätsdenken*, 44). Hombert only considers the dating of the first four books, and, more recently, Wilson has offered a convincing argument based on the references to the walls of Carthage for the work's completion between 425 and 427 (Andrew Wilson, "The Walls of Carthage and the Date of Augustine's *De Trinitate*," *Journal of Theological Studies*, vol. 70, no. 2 (2019): 680–705). For the purposes of this work, it will suffice to recognize that writing commenced sometime between 399 and 404 and was completed somewhere between 419 and 427, probably between 425 and 427. Thus, as well as being Augustine's principal work on the Trinity, it offers a mature account of Augustine's Trinitarian thought.

59. Riccardo Ferri, "Il *De Trinitate* di Agostino d'Ippona: Commento al Libro Primo," *Lateranum*, vol. 78, no. 3 (2012): 551: "In secondo luogo, il ripiego di Agostino di non modificare troppo i libri già pubblicati e la sua non totale soddisfazione per il risultato

also demonstrates that Augustine truly thought of the work as coherent and unified. This coherence and unity is reinforced in Augustine's summary of the first fourteen books in 15.3.5 as Augustine lays out the sequence of his argument.[60] Augustine expects his reader to appreciate the necessity of his scriptural foundation for his later reflection on the analogy. Hence, we cannot isolate Augustine's "speculative" and "psychological" theology in books 8–15 from his treatment of the economy in books 1–4. The bishop's attention to the economy forms the backdrop for his discussion of the psychological analogy.

A similar development can be discerned in his *Serm.* 52 (*c.* AD 410–412),[61] where the bishop employs the psychological analogy to make sense of what he reads in Scripture. In this sermon, Augustine begins with the baptism scene from Matt 3:14–17.[62] Upon encountering the difficulties of understanding how the three are one in this episode,[63] he eventually turns to the psychological analogy to make sense of the apparent problem.[64] Admittedly, we must avoid drawing too close a connection between the structure of the sermon and the structure of *Trin.* As Kany notes, the end of the sermon only really hints at what unfolds in *Trin.*[65] Nevertheless, the sermon still demonstrates that, in Augustine's thought, the psychological analogy is less distant from the economy than is often suggested. In both *Trin.* and the sermon, the bishop attempts to explore how the three revealed to be one in the economy are truly one.

Furthermore, as will be discussed in greater detail when we turn to the doctrine of creation, Augustine identifies biblical grounds for his analogy (e.g., John 1:3; Gen 1:26).[66] At the very least, a careful reader of Augustine must concede that, even when embarking upon his most "speculative" and "psychological" penetrations of the Trinitarian mystery, the bishop still affords greater attention to the Scriptures than Rahner does in *Der Dreifaltige Gott*, the very work that is supposed to begin from the "biblical starting point" and do justice to "the biblical statements about the economy of salvation." Thus, and somewhat ironically, even with respect to the psychological analogy, Augustine's *Trin.* satisfies Rahner's criteria for a biblically grounded Trinitarian theology more successfully than his own *Der Dreifaltige Gott*.

---

complessivo dell'opera spiega—almeno in parte—le difficoltà interpretative sulla struttura e sullo svolgimento delle singole parti del *De Trin*."

60. *Trin.* 15.3.5 (CCSL 50A: 463–7).

61. For the dating of this sermon, see Edmund Hill, comments on *Sermons on the New Testament (51–94)*, by Augustine of Hippo. vol. 3, The Works of Saint Augustine: A Translation for the 21st Century 3 (ed. John E. Rotelle; trans. Edmund Hill; Brooklyn: New City, 1991), 63.

62. *Serm.* 51.1 (CCSL 41Aa: 9–12).

63. *Serm.* 52.2–16 (CCSL 41Aa: 12–39).

64. *Serm.* 52.17–23 (CCSL 41Aa: 39–58).

65. Kany, *Augustins Trinitätsdenken*, 160.

66. Cf. pp. 48–9.

2. De Deo Uno *and* De Deo Trino

The Western Tradition and the Separation of the De Deo Uno *and* De Deo Trino

Rahner is concerned that the split of the treatises *De Deo uno* and *De Deo trino* in Neo-Scholastic theology ignores the biblical starting point he deems necessary. While recognizing that this split only took place formally from the time of Thomas, Rahner traces the split back to Augustine's conception of the Trinity. According to Rahner, Augustine's doctrine of the Trinity begins "with the One, the one essential God as a whole, and only then constitutes him as three persons."[67] In contrast, Rahner maintains: "Biblically and with the Greeks, we should start from the one absolutely unoriginate God, who is the *Father*, even when nothing is yet known about generation and spiration, because he is known as the one absolutely unoriginate hypostasis who is not *positively* thought of as 'absolute,' even if it is not already explicitly known as relative" (emphases in original).[68]

The narrative employed by Rahner is often associated with the paradigm outlined by the French Jesuit theologian Theodore de Régnon (1831–1893).[69] According to de Régnon,

> Latin philosophy first considers nature in itself and continues to the agent; Greek philosophy first considers the agent and then penetrates it to find the nature. The Latin considers personality as a mode of nature, while the Greek regards nature as the content of the person. … Also, the Latin says "three persons in God"; the Greek says: "one God in three persons."[70]

---

67. Rahner, "Der Dreifaltige Gott," 527: "Man ist zunächst einmal bei dem einen, einwesentlichen Gott im ganzen und konstituiert ihn erst danach als dreipersönlich."

68. Ibid., 527: "Biblisch und griechisch wäre auszugehen von dem einen, schlechthin ursprunglosen Gott, der auch dann der *Vater* ist, wo noch nicht gewußt wird, daß er der Zeugen—de und Hauchende ist, weil er als die eine schlechthin ursprunglose Hypostase gewußt wird, die nicht wieder *positiv* als "absolute" gedacht werden darf, auch wenn sie nicht schon ausdrücklich als relative gewußt wird."

69. For analysis of the development of this narrative in twentieth-century theology, see Barnes, "De Régnon Reconsidered"; Kristin Hennessy, "An Answer to de Régnon's Accusers: Why We Should Not Speak of 'His' Paradigm," *The Harvard Theological Review*, vol. 100, no. 2 (2007): 179–97; Ables, *Incarnational Realism*, 17–36.

70. Régnon, *Études de Théologie Positive sur la Sainte Trinité*, 1892, 433-4

> La philosophie latine envisage d'abord la nature en elle-même et poursuit jusqu'au suppôt; la philosophie grecque envisage d'abord le suppôt et y pénètre ensuite pour trouver la nature. Le Latin considère la personnalité comme un mode de la nature, le Grec considère la nature comme le contenu de la personne. … Aussi le Latin dit «trois personnes en Dieu»; le Grec dit: «un Dieu en trois personnes».

Strictly speaking, de Régnon does not present the Cappadocians as the peak of the "Greek" view, nor does he portray Augustine as the epitome of the Latin view. Thomas is the "most illustrious representative" of the Latin view.[71] In fact, de Régnon argues that Augustine's Trinitarian thought was heavily influenced by the school of Antioch, which he sees as "the link [*le lien*] between Eastern and Western dogmatics."[72] Nevertheless, de Régnon's typology suited the narrative of Augustine's later critics. For example, Schmaus argued that the psychological conception of the Trinity went hand in hand with the bishop's alleged overemphasis on divine unity: "The divine being, the one divine being, forms the starting point of the discussion about the Trinity. Augustine sharply developed this way of understanding the Trinity and made it decisive for the time that followed in the West."[73] Like Rahner after him, Schmaus believed that this inevitably gave rise to the later division of the *De Deo uno* and *De Deo trino*.[74] Elsewhere he would write that "the salvation-historical function ascribed to individual persons by Scripture seems to have no place in the Augustinian conception. The image of a Trinitarian 'God in himself' emerges."[75] Kärkkäinen rightly observes that in Augustinian scholarship of the late nineteenth and early mid-twentieth century, Augustine's Neoplatonic tendencies were said to result in a stress on the unity of the divine essence that had a hard time accounting for distinctions in the Godhead. He concludes that according to these scholars, this too "would of course mean that his approach would be diametrically opposed to the Eastern view."[76]

Augustine's Integration of the De Deo Uno *and* De Deo Trino

As Hill notes, one need not "quarrel with Rahner's description of the consequences of what he calls the Augustinian and western approach." One can, however, "deny that it is Augustinian."[77] Augustine does not start with the One independent of

---

71. Ibid., 305.

72. Régnon, *Études de Théologie Positive sur la Sainte Trinité*, 1898, 141–2.

73. Schmaus, *Die psychologische Trinitätslehre des heiligen Augustinus*, 102: "Wie für diese bildet für den afrikanischen Denker das göttliche Sein, das eine göttliche Wesen den Ausgangspunkt der Diskussion über die Trinität. Augustinus hat diese Art die Trinität aufzufassen aufs schärfste ausgebildet und sie für die Folgezeit im Abendland maßgebend gemacht."

74. Ibid., 102, n. 1.

75. Schmaus, "Die Spannung von Metaphysik und Heilsgeschicte in der Trinitätslehre Augustins," 511: "So scheint die von der Schrift den einzelnen Personen zugeschriebene heilsgeschichtliche Funktion in der augustinischen Konzeption keinen Platz zu haben. Es entsteht das Bild eines trinitarischen „Gottes an sich."

76. Veli-matti Kärkkäinen, "Is the Spirit Still the Dividing Line Between the Christian East and West? Revisiting an Ancient Problem of *Filioque* with a Hope for an Ecumenical Rapprochement," *Perichoresis*, vol. 9, no. 2 (2011): 127.

77. Hill, "Karl Rahner's 'Remarks on the Dogmatic Treatise *De Trinitate* and St. Augustine,'" 68.

the Three. His attention to "the biblical statements concerning the economy of Scripture" forces him to begin with both. As has already been seen, from the earliest chapters of *Trin.* the bishop seeks to account for the fact that "the *Trinity is the one*, only, and true God and how rightly that *the Father, the Son, and the Holy Spirit* are said to be of *one and the same substance or essence*."[78] It is the intention of the entire work to hold the two "treatises" together. This intention is reiterated again and again. In 1.4.7, he seeks "to teach in accordance with the Scriptures that *the Father, the Son, and the Holy Spirit* constitute a *divine unity* of one and the same substance in an indivisible equality."[79] When recapping his argument in book 15, he writes: "In the first book the *unity* and equality of that highest *Trinity* is shown according to the Holy Scriptures. The same is continued in the second, third, and fourth books."[80] Looking beyond *Trin.*, we even see that Augustine's exegetical method requires him to begin with the Three before the One. For example, his exegetical method in his first tractate on John's Gospel requires him to begin with "God," whom he identifies with the Father, and "the Word."[81] Similarly, in starting *Serm.* 52 with Matthew's depiction of the Jordan baptism, he must consider the Three as divine persons before he can penetrate their unity by means of the psychological analogy.

As Hill rightly asks, "Is this, in Rahner's commonplace categories, Greek and biblical, starting from the history of salvation, or is it Latin (Augustinian) and *a priori*, starting from a metaphysical idea of the unity of the divine substance?"[82] If anything, it is the former. Augustine certainly emphasizes the *unity* of the three persons. This is necessary to fend off any hint of Subordinationism. Nevertheless, it is the unity of the *three persons*. The *De Trinitate* must be differentiated from later Latin works where God's simplicity and oneness is discussed extensively before there is any hint of Triunity. We need not again revisit Augustine's copious attention to the salvation–historical events as outlined in 1.2.4 and expounded throughout the rest of *Trin.* and his other Trinitarian works. It will suffice to note than in all of these events—the Christ's virgin birth, baptism, transfiguration, crucifixion, burial, resurrection, ascension, and Pentecost—Augustine recognizes the distinction as well as the unity of the divine persons. The Scriptures lead him

---

78. Emphasis added. *Trin.* 1.2.4 (CCSL 50: 31): "Quapropter adiuuante domino deo nostro suscipiemus et eam ipsam quam flagitant, quantum possumus, reddere rationem, quod trinitas sit *unus et* solus et *uerus deus*, et quam recte pater et filius et spiritus sanctus *unius eiusdem* que *substantiae* uel *essentiae* dicatur."

79. Emphasis added. *Trin.* 1.4.7 (CCSL 50: 35): "hoc intentionerunt secundum scripturas docere, quod pater et filius et spiritus sanctus *unius substantiae* inseparabili aequalitate."

80. Emphasis added. *Trin.* 15.3.5 (CCSL 50A: 463): "In primo libro secundum scripturas sanctas unitas et aequalitas summae illius trinitatis ostenditur. In secundo et tertio et quarto eadem."

81. *Tract. Ev. Jo.* 1.1 (CCSL 36: 1).

82. Hill, "Karl Rahner's 'Remarks on the Dogmatic Treatise *De Trinitate* and St. Augustine,'" 71.

to consider the involvement of the Father and/or Son and/or Spirit as distinct but united persons in these events. In so doing, the bishop is able to refute the claims of his Homoian–Arian opponents and, in the process, pre-empts what Rahner desires.

The Inseparabilis Operatio

Of course, Augustine does not support Rahner's every nuance. There are times when Augustine stresses their unity of action beyond what is directly expressed in the Scriptures when applying the *inseparabilis operatio*. For example, in 1.8.16 Augustine speaks of the Son handing the kingdom to himself at the eschaton. Similarly, in 2.5.9 the bishop speaks of the Son sending himself. Though Augustine's Neoplatonic tendencies may well be lurking in the background, it must be understood that Augustine's application of the *inseparabilis operatio* is not simply the imposition of a philosophical paradigm onto the text of Scripture. Firstly, Augustine believes that he has exegetical warrant for a strong application of the *inseparabilis operatio* in John 10:30.[83] Secondly, even though Augustine does not have explicit exegetical warrant for saying that the Son sends—or hands the kingdom to—himself, it is not as if he is overlooking the Scriptures. The comments on the kingdom transfer emerge in a long discussion of 1 Cor 15:24–28. Even though this particular text only speaks of the Son handing over the kingdom to the Father, Augustine emphasizes again and again with reference to John 16:15 that everything the Father has is the Son's. There is at least a sense in which, after the transfer, the Son still "has" the kingdom. As for the Son sending himself, it should be noted that Augustine arrives at such a conclusion through reasoning from the Scriptures, citing John 10:36, 17:19; Rom 8:32; Gal 2:20; and Matt 1:18. Thirdly, in both cases, Augustine still differentiates the coactivity of the Father from the Son. In 1.8.16, he still recognizes the Son's peculiar role as the mediator who brings believers to a direct contemplation of God.[84] In 2.5.9, Augustine still recognizes a degree of appropriation in the indivisible work of the three. Just as the Father "delivered" the Son (citing Rom 8:32), so the Son "delivered himself" as "Saviour" (citing Gal 2:20), with the enabling of the Spirit (citing Matt 1:18). As questionable as Augustine's exegesis may be, he still attends to "the biblical statements about the economy of salvation"—as opposed to Rahner—and still manages to preserve *something* of the peculiarity of the three.

God the Father and the Trinity

We also know that Rahner struggles with the Augustinian use of the name "God." In his essay *Theos im Neuen Testamentum*, Rahner convincingly argues that ὁ θεος always signifies the Father in the New Testament unless the context specifically

---

83. *Trin.* 1.8.17–1.8.18 (CCSL 50: 50–3); 1.12.25 (CCSL 50: 64); 2.1.3 (CCSL 50: 82).
84. *Trin.* 1.8.16 (CCSL 50: 49–50).

suggests otherwise (e.g., "the Word was God"; John 1:1). From as early as *Trin.* 1.2.4, Augustine is content to use "God" (*Deus*) to denote the Trinity (*trinitas*), which Behr considers a "radically new" use of the former term.[85] The work likewise finishes with the infamous prayer to the "God" who is Father, Son, and Spirit in 15.28.51.[86] For Rahner, this is most inappropriate. Nevertheless, Augustine's attention to Scripture ultimately requires him to recognize a distinct sense in which the Father is "God." For example, when discussing John 1:1, he is forced to recognize that the "God" who is "with" the Word refers to the Father.[87] When exegeting 1 Cor 1:24, Augustine must recognize that the "God" to whom Wisdom belongs is the Father.[88] Similarly, when exegeting Gal 4:4–6 he is pressed to concede that the "God" who sends the Son and the Spirit is primarily the Father, even if there is a sense in which the Son and the Spirit are involved in the sending.[89] Gal 4:4 also forces the bishop to recognize the Father's primary identification as "God" in the closing prayer of 15.11.28.[90] From Rahner's perspective, this would not excuse Augustine of so readily applying the title "God" to the Trinity. Nevertheless, we see that Augustine's attention to the biblical particularities brings him much closer to what Rahner would prefer, thus partially exonerating the bishop.

A growing number of scholars now dismiss the "Latin" characterization of Augustine with respect to the One and Three as a "serious mistake,"[91] "unwarranted,"[92] and having "no evidence."[93] Williams writes that Augustine "never for a moment allows that you can separate divine life from the agents who live it."[94] While some of these conclusions may be slightly overstated, we can at the very least conclude that Augustine does not fit as neatly into the East–West paradigm as Rahner suggests.[95] This is due—in large part—to Augustine's "biblical" starting

---

85. John Behr, "Calling Upon God as Father: Augustine and the Legacy of Nicaea," in *Orthodox Readings of Augustine*, ed. George E. Demacopoulos and Aristotle Papanikolaou (New York: St Vladimir's Seminary Press, 2008), 161.

86. *Trin.* 15.28.51 (CCSL 50A: 533–4).

87. *Trin.* 1.6.9 (CCSL 50: 38); 2.5.9 (CCSL 50: 91); 4.1.3 (CCSL 50: 162); 6.2.3 (CCSL 50: 230); 7.1.1 (CCSL 50: 245); 7.3.4 (CCSL 50: 252); 15.10.19 (CCSL 50: 485).

88. *Trin.* 1.6.10 (CCSL 50: 39); 6.1.1 (CCSL 50: 228); 7.1.1 (CCSL 50: 244); 7.3.4 (CCSL 50: 251).

89. *Trin.* 2.5.8–2.5.9 (CCSL 50: 89–92); 2.7.12 (CCSL 50: 97); 4.19.26 (CCSL 50: 194–5); 15.26 (CCSL 50: 524–5); 15.28.51 (CCSL 50: 534).

90. *Trin.* 15.28.51 (CCSL 50A: 534).

91. Rowan Williams, *On Augustine* (London: Bloomsbury, 2016), 137.

92. Lewis Ayres, "The Fundamental Grammar of Augustine's Trinitarian Theology," in *Augustine and His Critics*, ed. Robert Dodaro and George Lawless (New York: Routledge, 2005), 67.

93. Mary A. Clark, "*De Trinitate*," in *The Cambridge Companion to Augustine*, ed. Norman Kretzmann and Eleonore Stump (Cambridge: CUP, 2001), 91.

94. Williams, *On Augustine*, 137.

95. It is also worth noting that the two main conceptual culprits for the East–West characterization—Augustine's doctrine of *inseparabilis operatio* and the psychological

point and attention to "the biblical statements about the economy of salvation." Rahner has overlooked these biblical statements in his own treatise on the Trinity, while failing to notice the extent to which the bishop's attention to these statements supports his agenda on the *De Deo uno* and *De Deo trino*.

3. Trinity and Christology

The Western Tradition and the Separation of Trinity and Christology

According to Rahner, whereas earlier theologians—certainly "the Greeks"—had assumed that only the Son could take on flesh, Augustine altered the course of the West. As we saw in the introduction, this claim is made again and again throughout Rahner's works.[96] If any of the three persons might assume flesh, the incarnation reveals nothing of the Logos himself. This would have implications for the connection between missions and processions, Christian sonship, and the way we read Scripture:

> There would then no longer be any real connection between "mission" and inner-Trinitarian life. Our sonship in grace would in truth have absolutely nothing to do with the sonship of the Son, since it could just as well be justified as absolutely the same by another incarnated person. In what God is for us, one could in no way experience what he is in himself, Triune.[97]

---

analogy—are not uniquely Latin, nor are they first discovered in Augustine. Augustine regards the *inseparabilis operatio* as his "faith inasmuch as it is the Catholic faith" (*Trin.* 1.5 (CCSL 50: 36)). The doctrine is found not only in Ambrose (*Spir.* 1.12.131 (CCSL 151: 71); 2.10.101 (CCSL 151: 125)) and Hilary (*Trin.* 7.17-18 (CCSL 62: 277-8)) but also in Basil's epistle to Eustathius (*Ep.* 189.6-8 (PG 32: 693-6)). Similarly, the psychological analogy was anticipated by Origen (*Princ.* 1.2.6 (PG 11: 134-5); 1.2.9 (PG 11: 137-8)), Athanasius (*C. Gent.* (PG 25: 89)), and Gregory of Nyssa (*Or. cat.* 1 (PG 45: 15)).

96. He attributes this problem to Augustine in *Der Dreifaltige Gott*, 543, as well as in Rahner, "Über den Begriff des Geheimnisses in der Katholischen Theologie," 97; Rahner, "Bemerkungen zum Dogmatischen Traktat 'De Trinitate,'" 119; Rahner, "Zur Theologie der Menschwerdung," 139; Rahner, "Dogmatische Fragen zur Osterfrömmigkeit," 162; Rahner, "Natur Und Gnade," 222-3; Rahner, "Zur Theologie des Symbols," 292-3.

97. Rahner, "Der Dreifaltige Gott," 545:

> Zwischen "Sendung" und dem innertrinitarischen Leben bestände dann überhaupt kein wirklicher Zusammenhang mehr. Unsere Sohnschaft in Gnade hätte in Wahrheit mit der Sohnschaft des Sohnes schlechthin nichts zu tun, da sie als absolut dieselbe ja ebensogut durch eine andere inkarnierte Person begründet werden könnte. An dem, was Gott für uns ist, wäre in keiner Weise zu erfahren, was er—dreifaltig—in sich selbst ist. Daß solche und viele ähnliche Folgerungen.

Conclusions that differ from this are said to "go against the whole inner flow of the Holy Scriptures."[98] In response, Rahner wishes to affirm in the strongest possible terms that the economic Logos is the immanent Logos and vice versa: "The Logos is as he appears in revelation, the one who reveals the Triune God (not as one of the possible revealers) on the basis of his only personal being, the Logos of the Father, which is peculiar to him."[99] The Logos is not wearing a "mask" (*Larve*) in the economy.[100] Rather, "What Jesus is and does as a man is the existence of the Logos as our salvation with us; this reveals the Logos himself. ... Here the Logos with God and the Logos with us, the immanent and the economic Logos, are strictly the same."[101] By "strictly the same," Rahner is not promoting an Hegelian Christology in which the economic Logos constitutes the immanent Logos. This is clear from the footnote, in which he states that this "sameness" is in keeping with Ephesus and Chalcedon.[102] Rahner is simply stating that the Logos who emanates from the Father immanently is the same Logos who is sent from the Father economically.

As noted earlier, Rahner never cites any texts from Augustine stating that the Father or the Spirit could become incarnate. Edmund Hill writes: "I myself am not aware of any text in *Trin.* in which Augustine so much as speculates on the possibility of the Father or the Holy Spirit becoming man."[103] These words are telling, coming from one of the leading Augustinian scholars of the twentieth century. According to LaCugna, Anselm of Canterbury was the first to argue this case.[104] Certainly *Trin.* stresses divine unity and equality. Benner writes that "Augustine is generally careful to maintain divine freedom and omnipotence, so at first glance it is possible to imagine Augustine's arguing for Anselm's later position."[105] Arnold also suggests that Rahner may have come to think Augustine held to this position due to his emphasis on the *inseparabilis operatio* or his exegesis of the Old Testament theophanies.[106] De Régnon and Scheffczyk suggested that the

---

98. Ibid.: "gegen den ganzen inneren Duktus der Heiligen Schrift sind."

99. Ibid., 547: "der Logos der ist, als der er in der Offenbarung erscheint, als der (nicht als einer der möglichen) Offenbarer des Dreifaltigen Gottes auf Grund seines nur ihm eigentümlichen persönlichen Seins, des Logos des Vaters."

100. Ibid., 549.

101. Ibid., 549–51: "Das, was Jesus als Mensch ist und tut, ist das den Logos selbst offenbarende Dasein des Logos als unseres Heiles bei uns. ... Hier ist der Logos bei Gott und der Logos bei uns, der immanente und der ökonomische Logos streng derselbe."

102. Ibid., 549, n. 28.

103. Hill, "Karl Rahner's 'Remarks on the Dogmatic Treatise *De Trinitate* and St. Augustine,'" 71.

104. Lacugna, *God for Us*, 98–9.

105. Benner, "Augustine and Karl Rahner on the Relationship between the Immanent Trinity and the Economic Trinity," 30.

106. Arnold, "Begriff und heilsökonomische Bedeutung der göttlichen Sendungen in Augustinus' *De Trinitate*," 66.

Old Testament theophanies undermine the Son's incarnational peculiarity,[107] while Schindler argued that "it cannot ultimately be made clear why the *Word* became *flesh* and why the Trinity or divinity did not become one human being" (emphases in original) because of the psychological analogy.[108] Nevertheless, Rahner seems unaware of their comments. The only source Rahner offers for his claim about Augustine is found in a footnote in *Zur Theologie des Symbols* where he cites Schmaus's influential work *Die psychologische Trinitätslehre des hl. Augustinus*.[109] Schmaus, however, never claims that Augustine allows for the Father or the Spirit to take on flesh in *Die psychologische Trinitätslehre*. He only notes that Augustine alters the tradition with respect to the Old Testament theophanies, a matter to be explored further in the next chapter.[110] Nevertheless, as we turn to Augustine's attention to the "inner flow of the Holy Scriptures," we will see that Rahner's charge does not stick. Augustine upholds not only the *fittingness* but also the *necessity* of the Son's incarnation. For Augustine, it must be precisely the Son who takes on flesh. Thus, he is able to affirm Rahner's Christological axiom while also linking the missions with the processions and human sonship with Divine Sonship.

Augustine's Strategies for Preserving Christological Peculiarity

The Form *Rule* First, Augustine's *form* rule—otherwise known as his *form-of-a-servant* rule or even his "Panzer"[111]—supports Rahner's claim that the economic Logos reveals the immanent Logos and demonstrates how this is so. After introducing the work and arguing that the Son must be "true God" and equal with the Father, Augustine cuts through "the sophistries and errors of the heretics"[112] and "identifies an architectonic problem with those who misread texts which suggest the Father's superiority to the Son."[113] The "heretics"—especially the Homoians—fail to recognize that there are some texts in the Scriptures that refer to the Son "in the form of a servant" (*in forma serui*) and others "in the form of God" (*in forma dei*), drawing on the language of Phil 2:6–7. Augustine distils this distinction into a *canonica regula* or rule, one he most probably inherited from Hilary and Ambrose.[114] This will function as "a hermeneutical rubric governing the dual ways

107. Régnon, *Études de Théologie Positive sur la Sainte Trinité*, 1892, 261–2; Scheffczyk, "Lehramtliche Formulierungen und Dogmengeschichte der Trinitätslehre," 146.
108. Alfred Schindler, *Wort und Analogie in Augustins Trinitätslehre* (Tübingen: Mohr, 1965), 145: "kann letzten Endes doch nicht klarwerden, warum das *Wort* Fleisch *ward*, und warum nicht entweder die Trinität bzw. Gottheit als ganze Mensch wurde."
109. Rahner, "Zur Theologie des Symbols," 293, n. 12.
110. Schmaus, *Die psychologische Trinitätslehre des heiligen Augustinus*, 20, 160–3.
111. Ayres, *Augustine and the Trinity*, 146.
112. *Trin.* 1.7.14, (CCSL 50: 44): "haereticorum tales calumnias uel errores."
113. Ayres, *Augustine and the Trinity*, 146.
114. For more on the genesis and chronology of this rule, as well as the second, see Marie-François Berrouard, "Introduction," in Augustine, *Homélies Sur l'Évangile de Saint Jean XVII–XXXIII*, by Augustine, vol. 72, Bibliothèque Augustinienne (Paris: Desclée de

Scripture speaks of Christ."[115] The rule enables Augustine to make sense of how the Son is sometimes referred to as less than the Father (John 14:28), emptying himself (Phil 2:7), made of a woman (Gal 4:4), or doing the will of the Father (John 6:38), while at other times he is spoken of as Creator (John 1:3), "one" with the Father (John 10:30), or possessing "life in himself" (John 5:26).[116] Ayres reminds us that the division "is not simply between the two 'natures' of Christ, but relies on an understanding of Christ as one subject who may be spoken of as he is eternally and as he is having assumed flesh."[117] Hence, the rule enables the believer to discern not only *that* the economic Logos is the immanent Logos, the former revealing the latter, but *how* this is so. It manages to preserve the Son's peculiar identity, both in the economy and immanently. At the same time, it protects against elevating or de-temporalizing economic-specific aspects of the Son's activity—particularly his subordination—into the immanent Trinity, a potential risk often associated with Rahner's *Grundaxiom*.[118] That this way of reading Scripture is derived from Phil 2:6–7 suggests that Augustine is attempting to move with "the inner flow of the Holy Scriptures." To quote Ayres, the *form* rule "follows in reverse the movement by which the Word is manifest in the Incarnation, one that understands how the immaterial and transcendent Word manifests the divine mystery in flesh and in words adapted to fallen human comprehension."[119] In this way, the economic Logos *is* or *reveals* the immanent Logos.

The From Rule Second, Augustine's other Christological *regula*—the *from* or *God-from-God* rule—complements the first *regula*. Whereas the *form* rule enables one to say with precision that economic Logos reveals the immanent Logos, the *from* rule lays down the conceptual roots as to why this is so. At the commencement of book 2, Augustine recognizes that some texts reveal that the Son is neither less than nor equal to the Father, but rather, intimate a genitive relationship; he is "of" or "from" the Father via eternal generation. Texts belonging to this category

---

Brouwer, 1977); Gioia, *The Theological Epistemology of Augustine's* De Trinitate, 27, n. 15; Ayres, *Augustine and the Trinity*, 156–7.

115. Ables, *Incarnational Realism*, 41.

116. *Trin*. 1.7.14 (CCSL 50: 44–6); 1.11.22 (CCSL 50: 60–1). Of course, the rule is more than just an exegetical sieve. As Ayres (*Augustine and the Trinity*, 146–7) writes:

> It is a rule which Augustine presents as implying and revealing a comprehensive conception of what it means to read Scripture at this point in the life of faith, at a point when we should seek to see what is said and done in *forma servi* as a drawing of our desires and intellects towards the *forma Dei* that will remain hidden until the *eschaton*.

117. Ayres, *Augustine and the Trinity*, 146.
118. Cf. pp. 106–8.
119. Ayres, *Augustine and the Trinity*, 187.

include John 5:19 and 5:26.¹²⁰ According to Augustine, we cannot apply the *form* rule to these verses. If read simply in *forma dei* these texts would intimate the Son's inferiority, but they cannot be read in *forma serui* for they refer to the Son's eternal generation. Hence, they must be understood to intimate the Son's being *from* the Father in *forma dei* without opening the door for a Subordinationist reading. This distinction lays the conceptual foundation for Augustine's horizontal doctrine of eternal generation.

Augustine will later link this understanding of eternal generation with his reading of the Son's mission. In book 4 of *Trin.*, Augustine states:

> Therefore, as the Father begot and the Son was begotten, so the Father sent and the Son was sent. ... For as being born means for the Son his being *from* the Father, so his being sent means his being known to be *from* him.¹²¹

According to Augustine, the Son's being *from* the Father in his mission reveals that he is eternally *from* the Father in his eternal generation precisely because his mission is grounded in his generation. While this reasoning alone may not preclude the possibility of the Spirit taking on flesh at the incarnation, it certainly precludes the possibility of the Father being sent, and by implication, taking on flesh. From this, we have at least some warrant to conclude with Ayres that the *from* rule, within the broader context of Augustine's Trinitarian theology, enables us to see that "the manifestation of the divine Word is a manifestation of the eternal relationship of Father and Son."¹²² In the following chapter we will explore the exegetical particularities of Augustine's account of the missions and processions in more detail. Here it will suffice to say that the *from* rule facilitates the close connection between the missions and processions in such a way that it would be inconceivable for Augustine that the Father should be sent and thus assume flesh.

Eternal Generation and Inseparabilis Operatio Third, in addition to the *form* and *from* rules, the relationship between Augustine's doctrine of eternal generation and *inseparabilis operatio* lends support to Rahner's Christological claims. Augustine

---

120. *Trin.* 2.1.3 (CCSL 50: 82–4). Curiously, Augustine has previously cited John 5:26 as belonging to the *forma dei* rule (1.11.22). One may speculate that this was added some time after its original composition, and that this rule is something of a mature reflection. The fact that the rule does not appear in Augustine's homilies on John 5:19–26 (*Tract. Ev. Jo.* 18–22, the latter three of which can be dated to 418–19) might support this speculation. Regardless, Augustine has previously been adamant that John 5:26 must refer to the Son's eternal generation. Cf. *Trin.* 1.12.26 (CCSL 50: 66).

121. Emphasis added. *Trin.* 4.20.29 (CCSL 50: 199): "Sicut ergo pater *genuit, filius genitus est*; ita *pater misit*, filius missus est. ... Sicut enim natum esse est filio *a patre esse*, ita mitti est filio cognosci quod ab illo sit."

122. Ayres, *Augustine and the Trinity*, 187.

discerns a strong parallel between the inseparable activity of the Father and the Son and their ontological unity. Soon after his discussion of the specific features of the economic activity of the Father, Son, and Spirit back in *Trin.* 1.4.7, Augustine writes: "The Father, the Son, and the Holy Spirit, as they are inseparable (*sicut inseparabiles sunt*), so they work inseparably (*ita inseparabiliter operentur*)."[123] In other words, the doctrine of inseparable operations parallels the doctrine of inseparable persons. In *Trin.* 2.1.3 we discern an asymmetry in this parallel: "The work of Father and Son is inseparable, and yet the Son's working is from the Father just as he himself is from the Father."[124] Just as the Son's person (inseparable from the Father) is *from* the Father, so his work (inseparable from the Father) is *from* the Father. The asymmetry in their immanent unity is reflected in the asymmetry of their economic unity. But, more than that, the asymmetrical unity of the former *is* the asymmetrical unity of the latter. This point is made clear in *Tract. Ev. Jo.* 20.8 where Augustine writes:

> Therefore, the works of Father and Son are inseparable. But to say, "The Son can do nothing on his own" [John 5:19], is the same thing as if he said, "The Son is not from himself." If he is the Son he was begotten; if he was begotten he is from the one of whom he was begotten.[125]

For Augustine, there is a sense in which the economic unity of the Father and the Son in the Son's works are so closely identified with the unity of their immanent life that they can be described as "the same thing." The Son's activity, given him *from* the Father, is inseparable from the Father's activity because the Son himself is *from* the Father. The asymmetry in the immanent relation not only reveals but also grounds the asymmetry of the economic activity. The inseparable operations of the divine persons *ad extra* reveal and are grounded in the divine relations *ad intra*. Thus, Augustine's doctrine of inseparable operations supports Rahner's Christological rule. The economic Son whose external works (inseparable from the works of the Father) are given him *from the Father* is the immanent Son who, through eternal generation, is *from the Father* and immanently inseparable from the Father. Importantly, Augustine arrives at these conclusions through recourse to John 5:19[126] and John 10:30.[127]

---

123. *Trin.* 1.4.7 (CCSL 50: 36): "pater et filius et spiritus sanctus sicut inseparabiles sunt, ita inseparabiliter operentur."

124. *Trin.* 2.1.3 (CCSL 50: 83): "et inseparabilis est operatio patris et filii, sed tamen ita operari filio de illo est de quo ipse est, id est *de patre*."

125. *Tract. Ev. Jo.* 20.8 (CCSL 36: 207): "Inseparabilia sunt ergo opera Patris et Filii. Sed hoc est: *Non potest Filius a se quidquam facere*, quod esset si diceret: non est Filius a se. Etenim si Filius est, natus est; se natus est, ab illo est de quo natus est."

126. *Trin.* 2.1.3 (CCSL 50: 83); *Tract. Ev. Jo.* 20.1–20.8 (CCSL 36: 202–8).

127. *Trin.* 2.1.3 (CCSL 50: 82); *Tract. Ev. Jo.* 20.3 (CCSL 36: 204).

The Son as Wisdom and Word Fourth, Augustine highlights the peculiarity of the Son as God's Wisdom and Word in book 7. Why does 1 Cor 1:24 appropriate the term "Wisdom" to the Son even though it could be attributed to any of the three persons?

> Is it perhaps to commend to us for our imitation the wisdom by whose imitation we are formed, that Wisdom in those books never speaks or has anything said about her but what presents her as born of God or made by him, although the Father too is wisdom itself? For the Father utters her to be his Word ...; and she by enlightening us utters to us whatever needs to be uttered to men about herself and about the Father. Thus, the reason it says, "No one knows the Son but the Father, and no one knows the Father but the Son and whoever the Son chooses to reveal him to" [Matt 11:27], is that it is through the Son that the Father makes his revelation, that is through his Word.[128]

As Hill concludes from this text, "Here Augustine touches on an important idea, first given currency by Irenaeus, that it is the special province of the Son as Logos to reveal the Father."[129] This "special province" does not belong to the Father or Spirit in the same way. It is peculiar to the Son as "Word."

The Soteriological Importance of the Son's Peculiarity Fifth, in discerning a parallel between divine and human sonship, Augustine also supports Rahner's claim regarding the soteriological importance of the Son's peculiarity. In book 13, Augustine writes that

> if the Son of God by nature became a son of man by mercy for the sake of the sons of men ..., how much more credible is it to believe that the sons of men by nature can become sons of God by grace and dwell in God, in whom alone and thanks to him alone they can be blessed become partakers of his immortality; and that we might be convinced of this, the Son of God was made a partaker of our mortality?[130]

128. *Trin.* 7.3.4 (CCSL 50: 251):

> An propterea non loquitur in illis libris sapientia uel de illa dicitur aliquid nisi quod eam de deo *natam* ostendat aut *factam*, quamuis sit et pater ipsa sapientia, quia illa nobis sapientia commendanda erat et imitanda cuius imitatione formamur? Pater enim eam dicit ut uerbum eius sit ... et inluminando dicit nobis et de se et de patre quod dicendum est hominibus. Ideoque ait: *Nemo nouit filium nisi pater, et nemo nouit patrem nisi filius et cui uoluerit filius reuelare* quia per filium reuelat pater, id est per uerbum suum.

129. Hill, "Karl Rahner's 'Remarks on the Dogmatic Treatise *De Trinitate* and St. Augustine,'" 74.

130. *Trin.* 13.9.12 (CCSL 50A: 399): "Si enim natura *dei filius* propter filios hominum misericordia factus est *hominis filius* ..., quanto est credibilius natura filios hominis gratia

While this does not assert the *necessity* of the Son taking on flesh, Augustine demonstrates a firm belief in the *fittingness* and sensibility of it being precisely the divine *Son* who should be born as a son of man and offer sonship to "the sons of men." Augustine, like Rahner, does not think that our "sonship in grace" has "absolutely nothing to do with the sonship of the Son." Moreover, Augustine makes his point in the context of a discussion of the "inner flow of the Scriptures," as he exegetes John's prologue. He is led to speak of human sonship from John 1:12–13 and divine Sonship from John 1:14.

Christological Peculiarity and the Psychological Analogy Finally, even Augustine's discussion on the psychological analogy supports Christological peculiarity. When discussing the title "Word" in book 15, Augustine writes:

> In the likeness of our word, there is also this likeness of the Word of God, that our word can exist and yet no work may follow it, but we cannot have a work which is not preceded by a word, just as the Word of God could be, even without any creation coming into existence, but there could not be any creation except through that Word through which all things were made. And the reason why it was not God the Father, not the Holy Spirit, not the Trinity itself, but only the Son who is the Word of God that became flesh although by the grace of the Trinity, is that we might live rightly by our word following and imitating his example; that is by our having no falsehood either in the contemplation or in the operation of our word.[131]

According to Augustine, only the Word can assume flesh, so that humankind may imitate his example in their word. This clearly demonstrates Augustine's conviction that it had to be precisely the Word who assumed flesh at the incarnation, not the Father or the Spirit. From this it is evident that Augustine pre-empts Rahner's Christological rule. The economic Logos is revealed and grounded in the immanent Logos. The fact that these remarks arise in the context of a discussion of the psychological analogy demonstrates that the analogy is by

---

dei *fieri dei filios* et habitare in deo in quo solo et de quo solo esse possint beati participes immortalitatis eius effecti, propter quod persuadendum *dei filius* particeps nostrae mortalitatis effectus est?"

131. *Trin.* 15.11.20 (CCSL 50A):

> Est et haec in ista similitudine uerbi nostri similitudo uerbi dei quia potest esse uerbum nostrum quod non sequatur opus; opus autem esse non potest nisi praecedat uerbum sicut uerbum dei potuit esse nulla exsistente creatura; creatura uero nulla esse posset nisi per ipsum per quod facta sunt omnia. Ideoque non deus pater, non spiritus sanctus, non ipsa trinitas, sed solus filius quod est *uerbum* dei *caro factum* est quamuis trinitate faciente, ut sequente atque imitante uerbo nostro eius exemplum recte uiueremus, hoc est nullum habentes in uerbi nostri uel contemplatione uel operatione mendacium.

no means incompatible with—or conceptually opposed to—the incarnational peculiarity of the Word. Importantly, he comes to this conclusion as he considers the "inner flow of Scriptures," once again drawing upon the language of John's prologue. Thus, despite Rahner's inclination to distance himself from Augustine, the bishop's attention to the "biblical statements about the economy of salvation" once again come to the aid of the Jesuit's programme.

4. Trinity and Creation

The Western Tradition and the Separation of Trinity and Creation

As mentioned in the introduction, Rahner also laments the isolation of the doctrine of creation from the doctrine of the Trinity in contemporary theology. As we saw in the introduction, Rahner laments the fact that the doctrine of the "image of the Trinity" and "the vestiges" are thought to be nothing but pious speculation, telling us nothing about the Trinity or created reality which we did not know from other sources.[132] Bonaventure is lauded as the classical exception to this more recent trend. Though he does not explicitly lay the blame on Augustine, Rahner certainly holds the doctrine of *inseparabilis operatio* responsible for this disconnect and Augustine was the early champion of this doctrine.[133] Moreover, Rahner holds the West's "speculative" and inward-looking doctrine of the Trinity responsible for this disconnect, which implicitly lays the blame on Augustine.[134] Thus, it would not be rash to suggest that Rahner ultimately holds Augustine responsible for the isolation of the doctrine of the Trinity from the doctrine of creation. Nevertheless, Rahner offers no worked corrective to the problem he diagnoses. In contrast, Augustine's integration of the doctrine of creation with the doctrine of the Trinity pays greater attention to Scripture than what we see in both Rahner and Bonaventure. In what follows, we consider how John 1:3, Gen 1:26, Rom 1:20, and the Genesis creation narratives inform Augustine's doctrine of the Trinity, especially with respect to the *inseparabilis operatio*, psychological analogy, and *vestigia*.

John 1:3 and the Inseparabilis Operatio

Augustine's frequent use of John 1:3 is key to this integration. In *Trin.* 1.6.9, it forms the exegetical basis of Augustine's insistence on the inseparable or—to use Rahner's idiom—"common" operations of the divine persons in creation. If "all things were made through him" (John 1:3), Augustine reasons that the Word was not made by the one through whom all things were made. "And if he was not made, then he is not a creature; but if he is not a creature, then he is of the same

---

132. Cf. pp. 6–7.
133. Rahner, "Der Dreifaltige Gott," 521–3.
134. Ibid., 523–5.

substance [*substantiae*] with the Father. For every substance [*substantia*] which is not God is a creature, and that which is not a creature is God."[135] Shortly after, Augustine then reasons:

> If, however, all things were made through the Father, and all things were made through the Son, then the same things were made through the Father that were made through the Son. Therefore, the Son is equal to the Father and the Father and the Son work inseparably [*inseparabilis operatio*].[136]

Thus, Augustine's Trinitarian account of creation upholds the distinction of the divine persons—the Father creates *through* the Son—and yet, in the same move, establishes a biblical grounding for the *inseparabilis operatio*, the very thing Rahner holds responsible for the divorce of the doctrines of creation and the Trinity.[137] Thus, Augustine has managed to integrate the doctrines of creation and Trinity via Scripture while establishing an exegetical basis for the doctrine said to separate the two.

John 1:3 and the Psychological Analogy

In 15.11.20,[138] Augustine's integration of the doctrines of Trinity and creation via John 1:3 even forms the backdrop for his comments on the psychological analogy and the Word's incarnational peculiarity. He writes that "just as it is said of that Word, 'All things were made through him' [John 1:3], where God is said to have made all things through his Only Begotten Word, so too there are no works of man which are not first said in the heart."[139] Augustine is making the point that just as the Father begets the divine Word, so do our hearts beget words. Similarly, just as no creature can exist except through the Word whom God made all things, similarly, a word can exist in our minds and yet no work follows it. No work can

---

135. *Trin.* 1.6.9 (CCSL 50: 38): "Vnde liquido apparet ipsum factum non esse *per quem facta sunt omnia*. Et si factus non est, creatura non est; si autem creatura non est, *eiusdem cum patre substantiae* est. Omnis enim substantia quae deus non est creatura est, et quae creatura non est deus est."

136. *Trin.* 1.6.12 (CCSL 50: 42): "Si autem omnia per patrem et omnia per filium, eadem per patre quae per filium. *Aequalis* ergo est *patri* filius, et inseparabilis operatio est patris et filii."

137. For other examples of Augustine integrating the doctrines of the Trinity and creation with the *inseparabilis operatio* via John 1:3, see *Trin.* 1.6.12 (CCSL 50:42); *Tract. Ev. Jo.* 20.3 (CCSL 36: 204); 20.7 (CCSL 36: 207); 21.1-2 (CCSL 36: 211-13).

138. Cf. p. 47.

139. *Trin.* 15.11.20 (CCSL 50A: 488): "Animaduertenda est in hoc aenigmate etiam ista uerbi dei similitudo quod sicut de illo uerbo dictum est: *Omnia per ipsum facta sunt*, ubi deus per unigenitum uerbum suum praedicatur uniuersa fecisse, ita hominis opera nulla sunt quae non prius dicantur in corde."

exist unless the word precedes it. This forms the basis for what Augustine then says about the Word's incarnational peculiarity, all the while making the Trinity and the psychological analogy relevant to Christian piety.[140]

Gen 1:26 and the Psychological Analogy

Augustine also connects the Trinity with the doctrine of creation in his exposition of Gen 1:26. In a passing comment in book 1, he writes that "if the Father had made man alone without the Son, it would not have been written: 'Let us make man in our image and likeness.'"[141] Similarly, in book 7 he writes:

> "Let us make" and "our" are in the plural and should not be understood except as relational terms. For he did not mean that gods might make in the "image" and "likeness" of gods, but that the Father and the Son and the Holy Spirit might make in the image of Father and Son and Holy Spirit, so that man might subsist as the image of God; and God is Trinity.[142]

Here and elsewhere, Augustine clearly reads the first-person plural verb as an intra-Trinitarian reference, thus, once again connecting the doctrines of Trinity and creation.[143]

More importantly, this understanding of Gen 1:26 will prove foundational to his discussion of the psychological analogy, the very analogy Rahner blames for disconnecting the Trinity from Scripture. Augustine insists that Gen 1:26 directs us to the belief that the Father, Son, and Spirit created man to subsist as the image of the God who is Trinity. Like Rahner, Augustine believes that the "image of the Trinity" is found in the world, especially in humanity. Humanity is created not only in the image of the Son but of the whole Trinity:

> Man is said to be "the image" on account of an imperfect likeness, and, therefore, "our image," in order that man might be the image of the Trinity, not equal to the Trinity as the Son and Father, but approaching it, as has been said by a certain likeness, as one can speak of a certain distance between things, but of a sort of imitation. For to this it says: "Be transformed by the renewing of your mind"

---

140. Cf. pp. 59–60.

141. *Trin.* 1.7.14 (CCSL 50: 46): "Nam si pater tantum sine filio fecisset hominem, non scriptum esset: *Faciamus hominem ad imaginem et similitudinem nostram*."

142. *Trin.* 7.6.12 (CCSL 50: 266): "Et *faciamus* et *nostram* pluraliter dictum est et nisi ex relatiuis accipi non oportet, non enim ut facerent dii aut *ad imaginem* et similitudinem deorum, sed ut facerent pater et filius et spiritus sanctus ad imaginem ergo patris et filii et spiritus sancti ut subsisteret homo *imago dei*; deus autem trinitas."

143. For further examples of this interpretation of Gen 1:26, see *Trin.* 12.6.6–7 (CCSL 50: 360–2); 14.19.25 (CCSL 50: 456); *Arian.* 16.9 (CCSL 87A: 216–17): *Coll. Max.* 15.26 (CCSL 87A: 463); *Maxim.* 2.26.2–3 (CCSL 87A: 662–4).

[Rom 12:2]; and it also says: "So be imitators of God as dear children" [Eph 5:1.] For it is said to the new man: "Who is being renewed in the knowledge of God, after the image of him who created him" [Col 3:10].[144]

According to Augustine, since we are made in the image of the God who is a Trinity, we can therefore expect some kind of "likeness" to God—perhaps even his Triunity—in ourselves. The Scriptures teach that our minds are being transformed and renewed in our knowledge as the image of God. By attending to the text of Scripture, Augustine brings creation, the *imago dei*, and the Trinity together, just as Rahner desires. This then sets the stage for Augustine's turn to the psychological analogy in books 8–15, where he likens the human mind to a "trinity" of *mens, notitia sui*, and *amor sui* (book 10) and then (*mens, notitia sui*, and *voluntas*) in book 11. Augustine speaks of a trace or "vestigium" of the Trinity in both the inner and outer man because both the inner and outer man are made in the *imago Dei*.[145] While the particular intricacies and details of Augustine's analogy may not arise directly from Scripture, Augustine's psychological penetration is certainly not without a scriptural basis. In fact, as much as one might wish to raise issues with his exegetical manoeuvres, a strong argument can be made that Augustine's psychological analogy is more closely tied to the text of Scripture than Rahner's transcendental scheme in section 3 of *Der Dreifaltige Gott* and his four triads: (1) Origin–Future, (2) History–Transcendence, (3) Invitation (offer)–Acceptance, (4) Knowledge–Love.[146] As Ormerod comments, "It is hard to see how these are

---

144. *Trin.* 7.6.12 (CCSL 50: 267):

> Sed propter imparem ut diximus similitudinem dictus est homo *ad imaginem*, et ideo *nostram* ut *imago* trinitatis esset homo, non trinitati *aequalis* sicut filius *patri*, sed accedens ut dictum est quadam similitudine sicut in distantibus significatur quaedam uicinitas non loci sed cuiusdam imitationis. Ad hoc enim et dicitur: *Reformamini in nouitate mentis uestrae*; quibus item dicit: *Estote itaque imitatores dei sicut filii dilectissimi*. Nouo enim homini dicitur: *Qui renouatur in agnitionem dei secundum imaginem eius qui creauit eum*.

145. *Trin.* 11.1.1 (CCSL 50: 333).

146. Cf. Rahner, "Der Dreifaltige Gott," 65–8. Marmion and van Neuwenhove provide a clear summary of Rahner's dense argument:

> The first aspect of each of these four pairs refers to God's self-communication in the Son, the second to the Holy Spirit. As addressee of God's self-communication, the human person has an origin and a future; we are embedded in history but our history is situated in a wider horizon which always transcends us. Constituted as beings who are history in transcendence, and a duality of origin and future, we are essentially free being, free to accept the invitation of Gods self-communication. Finally, we are knowing and loving beings.

any less hypothetical than the psychological analogy, and indeed the final pair of aspects clearly relates to it."[147] At least Augustine's analogy is grounded in "biblical statements concerning the economy of salvation." Augustine would certainly agree with Rahner that the doctrine of the image cannot be dismissed as pious speculation.

Rom 1:20 and the Vestigia

Like Rahner, Augustine also insists upon a more general *vestigia* in the created order revealing the Trinity. For example, there are those things in creation that reveal God's unity, form, and order. He writes:

> So then, as we direct our gaze at the creator by "understanding the things that are made" [Rom 1:20], we should understand him as Trinity, whose vestige [*vestigium*] appears in creation in a way that is fitting. In that supreme Trinity is the source of all things, and the most perfect beauty, and wholly blissful delight.[148]

Augustine believes that the *vestigia* in creation teach us about the Trinity because the Scriptures direct him to this conclusion. Augustine turns to Romans 1:20, the classic prooftext for natural revelation. Of course, he does not think that one can come to an understanding of the Trinity through natural reason alone. Moments later he adds, with reference to 1 Cor 13:12, that the one who sees the Trinity through the *vestigia* "sees this, either in part, through a mirror, or in an obscure manner."[149] Nevertheless, one can hardly deny that Augustine stands alongside Bonaventure in connecting the doctrines of creation and the Trinity through the *vestigia*. As with the image, Augustine would certainly agree with Rahner that the *vestigia* cannot be dismissed as pious speculation.

> A self-communication of God to us must present itself as a self-communication of absolute truth and absolute love.

Declan Marmion and Rik van Nieuwenhove, *An Introduction to the Trinity* (Cambridge: CUP, 2011), 169. Rahner demonstrates the unity of the four former aspects in each pair, the unity of the four latter aspects, and the connectedness of the opposing and thus distinct constituents in each pair.

147. Neil Ormerod, *The Trinity: Retrieving the Western Tradition* (Milwaukee: Marquette University Press, 2005), 138.

148. *Trin.* 6.10.12 (CCSL 50: 242): "Oportet igitur ut creatorem *per ea quae facta sunt intellecta conspicientes* trinitatem intellegamus cuius in creatura quomodo dignum est apparet *vestigium*. In illa enim trinitate summa origo est rerum omnium et perfectissima pulchritudo et beatissima delectatio."

149. *Trin.* 6.10.12 (CCSL 50: 243): "Qui uidet hoc uel *ex parte* uel *per speculum in aenigmate.*"

A Trinitarian Reading of Gen 1–3

Augustine's Trinitarian reading of creation also permeates his biblical commentaries on Gen 1–3.[150] For example, in *De Genesi ad litteram libri duodecim* he writes:

> It is the Trinity that is presented as creating. For, when Scripture says, "In the beginning God created heaven and earth," by the name "God" we understand the Father, and by the name "Beginning," the Son, who is the beginning, not of the Father, but, first, for the spiritual creation and then also for all creatures. When Scripture says, "And the Spirit of God moved above the water," we observe a complete enumeration of the Trinity. So in the conversion and in the perfecting of creatures by which their species are separated in due order, the same Trinity is presented: the Word and the Father of the Word, as indicated in the statement, "God said"; and then the holy goodness, by which God finds pleasure in all the measured perfections of his creatures, which please him, as indicated by the words, "God saw that it was good."[151]

Aspects of his exegesis will draw scepticism from modern readers, especially the link between the Son and the Beginning. Nevertheless, this goes to show, once again, just how enmeshed the doctrine of the Trinity is with Augustine's doctrine of creation.[152]

Evidently, through his attention to "the biblical statements about the economy of salvation," Augustine regularly and intentionally connects his doctrines of creation and the Trinity. Meanwhile, it is difficult to find a text in which Rahner manages to integrate the three. Rahner connects his doctrine of the Trinity to creation in texts such as *Der Dreifaltige Gott*,[153] *Fragen der Kontroverstheologie*

---

150. For example, *Gen. litt.*, 1.6.12 (CSEL 28,1: 10); 2.6 (CSEL 28,1: 40); 3.19 (CSEL 28,1: 84); 9.15 (CSEL 28,1: 286); *Gen. litt. inp.* 1 (CSEL 28,1: 459); 16 (CSEL 28,1: 497, 500–2). For further exploration of these commentaries, see Dunham, *The Trinity and Creation in Augustine*.

151. *Gen. litt.*, 1.6.12 (CSEL 28,1: 10):

> trinitas insinuatur creatoris—nam dicente scriptura: in principio fecit deus caelum et terram intellegimus patrem in dei nomine et filium in principii nomine, qui non patri, sed per se ipsum creatae primitus ac potissimum spiritali creaturae et consequenter etiam uniuersae creaturae principium est, dicente autem scriptura: et spiritus dei superferebatur super aquam conpletam commemorationem trinitatis agnoscimus —, ita et in conuersione atque perfectione creaturae, ut rerum species digerantur, eadem trinitas insinuetur, uerbum dei scilicet et uerbi generator, cum dicitur: dixit deus, et sancta bonitas, in qua deo placet quidquid ei pro suae naturae modulo perfectum placet, cum dicitur: uidit deus quia bonum est.

152. For other examples of Augustine's Trinitarian reading of creation, one could appeal to *Tract. Ev. Jo.* 1–3 (CCSL 36: 1–31); *Conf.* 11–13 (CCSL 27: 194–273), and *Civ.* 11 (CCSL 48: 321–55); 13 (CCSL 48: 385–414).

153. Rahner, "Der Dreifaltige Gott," 531–3.

über die Rechtfertigung,[154] *Überlegungen zur Methode der Theologie*,[155] and *Über die Verborgenheit Gottes*,[156] but avoids discussion of the biblical text. In his reflections on creation in *Theologisches zum Monogenismus*, he considers some of the biblical foundations of the doctrine, but never so much as mentions the Trinity.[157] The nearest we come to a theological integration of the doctrines of Trinity and creation that pays heed to the testimony of Scripture is found in *Theos im Neuen Testament*, but even here the discussion of creation is peripheral at best.[158] For Augustine, the doctrine of creation will prove to be central when he comes to the latter part of *Trin.*, and the doctrine of the Trinity is central in his works on creation such as *Gen. litt. inp.* and *Gen. litt.* Moreover, the bishop clearly pays closer attention to "the biblical statements about the economy of salvation" than Rahner does.

Augustine and Bonaventure: A Comparison

Bonaventure, whom Rahner lauds as the model for integrating the doctrines of Trinity and creation, fares a little better. Part 1 of the *Breviloquium*, Bonaventure's most influential work, closes with the doxology of Rom 11:33–36 but offers no reflection on its Trinitarian significance.[159] Bonaventure discusses the Trinity in Part 2 on creation.[160] However, for the most part, he offers an abridged summary of what Augustine has already said. In his only comments specifically on Gen 1:1–2 he echoes Augustine's interpretation in *De Genesi ad litteram*: "Here the eternal Trinity is also hinted at: the Father is named God Creating; the Son is named Beginning; and the Holy Spirit named the Spirit of God."[161] Notably, like Augustine, he treats the term Beginning as a reference to the Son. Likewise, when referring to the "image," Bonaventure embraces Augustine's psychological understanding though in far less detail.[162] His discussion of the *vestigia* also sounds eerily similar to Augustine's.[163] Though Bonaventure pays closer attention to the biblical testimony

---

154. Karl Rahner, "Fragen der Kontroverstheologie über die Rechtfertigung," in *Schriften zur Theologie*, vol. 4, 16 vols (Einsiedeln: Benziger, 1960), 261–71. Here, Rahner is more concerned with Christology than Trinity.

155. Karl Rahner, "Überlegungen zur Methode der Theologie," in *Schriften zur Theologie*, vol. 9, 16 vols (Zürich: Benziger, 1970), 119–20.

156. Karl Rahner, "Über die Verborgenheit Gottes," in *Schriften zur Theologie*, ed. Karl H. Neufeld, vol. 12 (Zürich: Benziger, 1975), 285–305.

157. Karl Rahner, "Theologisches zum Monogenismus," *Zeitschrift für Katholische Theologie*, vol. 76, no. 2 (1954): 187–223.

158. Rahner, "Theos im Neuen Testament."

159. Bonaventure, *Brev.* 1.9.7 (BTTS 9: 56).

160. Bonaventure, *Brev.* 2.4.1–2.12.5 (BTTS 9: 69–98).

161. Bonaventure, *Brev.* 1.2.5 (BTTS 9: 32).

162. Bonaventure, *Brev.* 2.6.3 (BTTS 9: 77–8); 2.9.1 (BTTS 9: 84–5); 2.9.3 (BTTS 9: 85–6).

163. Bonaventure, *Brev.* 2.1.2 (BTTS 9: 60–1); 2.12.1–2.12.4 (BTTS 9: 96–8); 7.1.2 (BTTS 9: 266–8).

concerning creation than Rahner does, he pays very little direct attention to the textual particularities of those verses key to Augustine's integration of creation and Trinity. For example, Bonaventure never cites John 1:3 and offers little more than vague allusions to texts such as Gen 1:26 and Rom 1:20.[164] A strong case can be made that Augustine offers an account of creation and Trinity that is more tightly intertwined and pays greater attention to the Scriptures than Bonaventure's, thus providing greater exegetical support for Rahner's cause.

5. Trinity and Faith

The Western Tradition and the Separation of Trinity and Faith

Finally, we turn to what is arguably Rahner's strongest lament, that the doctrine of the Trinity has been annexed from the Christian's act of faith. As was noted in the introduction, Rahner famously bemoans the fact that contemporary Christians "are almost merely 'monotheists' in the religious conduct of their lives."[165] They have nothing to do with the mystery of the Trinity except to know something "about it" through revelation.[166] With his axiom he seeks to do justice to "the biblical statements about the economy of salvation" and to help Christians see "that the Trinity also occurs and must occur in the practice of the Christian faith as a belief in salvation and in Christian life."[167] In the introduction we also saw Augustine and his emphasis on God's inner life portrayed as the villain.[168]

Rahner was not alone in this lament. Adolf von Harnack asserted that "Augustine's great work, *De Trinitate*, hardly promoted piety anywhere nor at any time."[169] According to Michael Schmaus, Augustine's Trinitarian theology represented "a heavy burden for the exercise of faith itself."[170] There was still a sense

---

164. For Gen 1:26, see note 250. For Rom 1:20, see Bonaventure, *Brev*, 7.7.2 (BTTS 9: 292).

165. Rahner, "Der Dreifaltige Gott," 517: "Christen ... religiösen Daseinsvollzug beinahe nur "Monotheisten" sind."

166. Ibid., 523.

167. Ibid., 535: "dieses Axioms ... verstehen läßt, daß die Trinität auch im Vollzug des christlichen Glaubens als Heilsglaubens und im christlichen Leben vorkommt und vorkommen muß."

168. Rahner, *Grundkurs des Glaubens*, 140: "sich seit Augustinus die christliche Theologie das innere Leben Gottes in Selbstbewußtsein und in Liebe so vorzustellen sucht, daß ein gewisses ahnendes Verständnis der Dreipersönlichkeit Gottes daraus resultiert, ein Verständnis, das ganz unbezüglich zu uns und unserer christlichen Existenz sich gleichsam ein inneres Leben Gottes ausmalt, im letzten Grunde doch nicht sehr hilfreich sind."

169. Harnack, *Lehrbuch der dogmengeschichte*, 2:295: "Das grosse Werk Augustin's *de trinitate* hat schwerlich irgendwo und zu irgend einer Zeit die Frömmigkeit befördert."

170. Schmaus, "Die Spannung von Metaphysik und Heilsgeschicte in der Trinitätslehre Augustins," 514: "Die augustinische Trintitätslehre stellt ... eine Hypothek für den Glaubensvollzug selbst dar."

in which the conceptual progress brought about by the psychological analogy "must be paid for with a loss of salvation-historical and religious dynamism."[171] Du Roy would similarly write that "the Augustinian scheme of the Trinity gradually produced a depiction of the Trinity that weakened Trinitarian piety in the West."[172] However, in what follows we see that Augustine's doctrine of the Trinity is much more integrated with Christian piety than he is often given credit for. The bishop articulates a doctrine of the Trinity that starts with faith, comes to be understood through prayer and meditation, and reaches its climax in eschatological contemplation. More to the point, unlike Rahner, Augustine achieves this through copious attention to "the biblical statements about the economy of salvation."

The Starting Point of Faith

From the opening sentence of book 1 when Augustine warns against those who mock "the starting point of faith" (the *initium fidei*),[173] the centrality of faith for Augustine's doctrine of the Trinity is established. For Augustine, theological knowledge "cannot rely on reason alone, but requires that we start from faith, a faith that welcomes what God has revealed of himself, and, on this premise, performs an intellectual investigation of what has been revealed."[174] An incorrect use of reason, prescinding from the starting point of faith, is exactly what has led astray those whom Augustine seeks to refute. The starting point of faith requires a turn to Holy Scripture, so that "the human mind may be purified from errors of this kind."[175] The content of this faith—the *catholica fidei*—is outlined at length in 1.4.7.[176] For Augustine, it is the *catholica fidei* because it is taught in Scripture. It is his faith (*haec et mea fides est*) because it is the *catholica fidei*, but his continual return to the Scriptures confirms this faith.

It is difficult to comprehend these things without a *purgatio mentis* (intellectual purification). For Augustine, this *purgatio* is bound up in the work of Christ, but in the individual, it finds its starting point in faith: "We are strengthened by faith

---

171. Ibid., 17: "Die hohe Begrifflichkeit, die hier waltet, der Fortschritt, der in der Dimension der begrifflichen Durchdringung erreicht wurde, muß mit einem Verlust an heilsgeschichtlicher und religiöser Dynamik bezahlt werden."

172. Du Roy, *L'Intelligence de la Foi en la Trinité selon Saint Augustin*, 462: "le schéme augus tinien de la Trinité a progressivement accrédité une représentation de la Trinité qui a affaibli la piété trinitaire en Occident."

173. *Trin.* 1.1.1 (CCSL 50: 27).

174. Ferri, "Il *De Trinitate* di Agostino d'Ippona: Commento al Libro Primo," 552: "La conoscenza teologica, la conoscenza di Dio-Trinità non può dunque appoggiarsi soltanto sulla ragione, ma richiede che si parta dalla fede (una fede che accoglie la rivelazione che Dio ha fatto di se stesso) e, su tale presupposto, compie poi un'indagine intellettuale di quanto rivelato."

175. *Trin.* 1.1.2 (CCSL 50: 28): "ab huiusmodi falsitatibus humanus animus purgaretur."

176. Cf. p. 28.

and are led along more accessible roads, in order that we may gain the proficiency and skill to grasp that reality."[177] Thus, for Augustine, any explanation—and understanding—of God's Triunity requires "the help of the Lord our God."[178] The "weak eye of the human mind cannot be fixed on a light so excellent, unless it has been invigorated by the nourishment of the righteousness of faith."[179] We should not be surprised that Augustine would begin like this in *Trin*. As Hill writes, "If there is one absolutely established Augustinian principle, it is that you must first believe if you would understand."[180]

In what ensures, we see that faith is likewise crucial for the spiritual journey towards contemplation of the Trinity. The spiritual attitude of the reader is of vital importance:

> Thus, let us enter together on the path of charity in search of him of whom it is said: "Seek his face evermore" [Ps 104:4]. This is the sacred and safe compact into which I, in the presence of the Lord our God (*coram* Domine *deo*), shall enter with those who read what I am writing, in all my writings.[181]

Since the project takes place in the presence of God (*coram deo*) and with his help, Augustine therefore recognizes the need for his own meditation on Scripture and prayer, following the example of the psalmist:

> As for me, "I meditate on the law of the Lord," if not "day and night," at least during the few moments of time that I can, and lest my meditations escape from me through forgetfulness I hold on to them by my pen. … I pray and place this trust and my own desires in his hands, who is wholly capable of guarding what he has given and of fulfilling what he has promised.[182]

---

177. *Trin*. 1.1.3 (CCSL 50: 30): "qua nondum praediti fide nutrimur, et per quaedam tolerabiliora ut ad illud capiendum apti et habiles efficiamur itinera ducimur."

178. *Trin*. 1.2.4 (CCSL 50: 32): "adiuuante domino deo."

179. *Trin*. 1.2.4 (CCSL 50: 31): "mentis humanae acies inualida in tam excellenti luce non figitur nisi *per iustitiam fidei* nutrita uegetetu."

180. Hill, "Karl Rahner's 'Remarks on the Dogmatic Treatise *De Trinitate* and St. Augustine,'" 69.

181. *Trin*. 1.3.5 (CCSL 50: 32): "Ita ingrediamur simul caritatis uiam tendentes ad eum de quo dictum est: *Quaerite faciem eius semper*. Et hoc *placitum* pium atque tutum *coram domino deo* nostro cum omnibus inierim qui ea quae scribo legunt et in omnibus scriptis."

182. *Trin*. 1.3.5 (CCSL 50: 33-4)

> Ego tamen *in lege domini meditabor*, si non *die ac nocte*, saltem quibus temporum particulis possum, et meditationes meas ne obliuione fugiant stilo alligo sperans de misericordia dei quod in omnibus ueris quae certa mihi sunt perseuerantem me faciet; … Hoc oro et hoc depositum desideriumque meum penes ipsum habeo, qui mihi satis idoneus est et custodire quae dedit et reddere quae promisit.

Augustine likewise promotes prayer and meditation on Scripture for his readers. Soon after saying this, he (rightly) expresses a concern that others—those "who are slower of comprehension"—will misunderstand him.[183] When addressing this group again in 15.27.49, he advises them to strive to understand more deeply what they believe through prayer, meditation on Scripture, by asking questions, and in holy living.[184] Evidently, there is still a strong sense in which Augustine's Trinitarian theology was intended to promote piety.

Praying to the Father and the Trinity

Furthermore, *Trin.* concludes with a soliloquy (15.27.50) and prayer (15.28.51). The prayer—to the "Lord our God" who is the "Father and Son and Holy Spirit"—is the kind that troubles Rahner. In *Der Dreifaltige Gott* he denounces modern prayers for applying "Our Father" to the three divine persons without differentiation.[185] Michael Schmaus was similarly critical of Augustine for doing the same with the concluding prayer of *Trin.*: "The personality of God itself is presented as the personality of the Father, the Son and the Holy Spirit, not as a personality specific to the one God himself." Hence in Augustinian thought, "Prayer to the Lord God as such only seems possible if one imagines the Being itself in a vague way, so that one can address it."[186] While Augustine's prayer would be problematic for Rahner, it is worth emphasizing two points. First, it is noteworthy that the bishop attempts to integrate Trinity and piety through prayer. Though Rahner would not approve the prayer, it certainly cannot be written off as lacking "religious dynamism," placing "a heavy burden for the exercise of faith," or failing to "promote piety." Augustine's Trinitarian theology is a spiritual affair, fuelled by and directed towards meditation on Scripture and prayer. Secondly, Augustine's attention to Scripture somewhat mitigates his proclivity to direct prayers to the undifferentiated Trinity. Amidst his discussion of the psychological analogy in book 15, Augustine recognizes that Christians pray specifically to the Father.[187] On several occasions in *Tract. Ev. Jo.*, Augustine explicitly identifies "God" with the "Father" to whom we pray.[188] By observing Augustine's citations of Matt 6:9 across his corpus, it is unambiguously clear that he encourages and expects Christians to pray specifically to the Father.[189]

---

183. *Trin.* 1.3.6 (CCSL 50: 34).
184. *Trin.* 15.27.49 (CCSL 50A: 530–1).
185. Rahner, "Der Dreifaltige Gott," 519.
186. Schmaus, "Die Spannung von Metaphysik und Heilsgeschicte in der Trinitätslehre Augustins," 512–13.
187. *Trin.* 15.13 (CCSL 50: 494–5).
188. *Tract. Ev. Jo.* 17.16 (CCSL 36: 178); 53.8 (CCSL 36: 456); 67.3 (CCSL 36: 496).
189. See *Ep.* 187.16 (CSEL 57: 94); 217.6 (CSEL 57: 407); *Spec.* 25 (CSEL 12: 158); *Serm. Dom.* 2.4.15 (CCSL 35: 104–5); 2.5.18 (CCSL 35: 108); *Tract. Ev. Jo.* 21.3 (CCSL 36: 213); 81.4 (CCSL 36: 531); *Enarrat. Ps.* 54.14 (CCSL 39: 667); 65.21 (CCSL 39: 854); *Serm.* 1.1 (CCSL 41Aa: 221); 9A (Weidmann 5, Jensen 1); 56.4.5 (CCSL 41Aa: 156); 57.2.2 (CCSL 41Aa: 178); 59 auctus (= Poque 1) 61A.7 (CCSL 41Aa: 287); 71.15.25 (CCSL 41Ab: 48);

Similarly, Gal 4:6 and Rom 8:15 force Augustine to recognize time and again that Christian prayers are directed specifically to "Abba, Father."[190] For example, in *Arian.*, he notes that the apostle, "in saying, 'Abba, Father,' does not plead with the Son, but with the Father."[191] While the prayer to the three in *Trin.* is located in a prominent location in his major work on the Trinity and thus warrants attention, Augustine is certainly aware of the biblical impulse to pray specifically to the Father. The Scriptures force him to recognize that Christians can and should pray to the Father, just as Rahner insists.

Faith as the End

Faith is also intricately connected with the end goal of Augustine's work. As previously mentioned, Augustine intends for those "invigorated by the nourishment of the righteousness of faith" to go beyond merely thinking of God and to *experience* and *see* (or contemplate) the God in whom they believe. This experience reaches its climax in the beatific "face to face" vision.[192] According to Augustine, those who will see the beatific vision are "the just who live by faith" (*iustos ex fide*; cf. Hab 2:4),[193] "the faithful" (*credentes*).[194] Drawing on 1 John 3:2, he argues that contemplation is promised to the believer as the end for their labours and the fullness of their joy.[195] Similarly, drawing on Acts 15:9 he states: "Contemplation is indeed the reward of faith, and our hearts are purified by faith for this reward, as it is written: 'Purifying their hearts by faith.'"[196] With reference to Matt 5:8, he then adds: "It is proved, however, that our hearts will be

---

114 (RBén 73: 26); 136C (= Lambot 11; ReAug 24: 91); 139.1 (EAA 195: 422); 156 (CCSL 41Ba: 158); 181 (CCSL 41Bb: 695); 211 (SC 116: 160); 229L (= Guelferbytanus 10; MiAg 1: 473); 252A (= Wilmart 13; MiAg 1: 715); 315 (PL 38: 1431); 357 (PL 39: 1585).

190. See *Ep.* 140.52 (CSEL 44: 198); 194.17 (CSEL 57: 189); 194.17 (CSEL 57:189); *Quaest. Hept.* 2.55 (CCSL 33: 95); *Cons.* 3.4.13 (CSEL 43: 284); 3.4.14 (CSEL 43: 285); *Serm. Dom.* 3.14 (CCSL 35: 105–6); 11.38 (CCSL 35: 129–30); *Exp. Gal.* 31 (CSEL 84: 96–8); *Serm.* 71.17.28 (CCSL 41Ab: 55); 156 (CCSL 41Ba: 158–60).

191. *Arian.* 25.21 (CCSL 87A: 234): "Vt autem secundum ipsorum sensum sic accipiamus clamantem, tamquam non clamare nos faciat, sed ipse clamet, ecce dicendo: *Abba, Pater,* non interpellat Filium, sed Patrem." For a similar interpretation of these verses, see *Maxim.* 2.13 (CCSL 87A: 401).

192. Augustine's discussion of this vision arises when opposing the Homoian–Arian challenge to the Son's equality with the Father. The Homoians point to the Son's visibility as proof of his inequality with the Father.

193. *Trin.* 1.8.16–1.8.17 (CCSL 50: 49–50).

194. *Trin.* 1.8.16 (CCSL 50: 49); 1.9 (CCSL 50: 55); 1.10.20 (CCSL 50: 56); 1.10.21 (CCSL 50: 57).

195. *Trin.* 1.8.17 (CCSL 50: 50).

196. *Trin.* 1.8.17 (CCSL 50: 151): "Contemplatio quippe merces est fidei, cui mercedi per fidem corda mundantur, sicut scriptum est: *Mundans fide corda eorum.*"

purified for that contemplation by this sentence: 'Blessed are the pure of heart for they shall see God.'"[197]

The "sight" of the eschatological vision is more epistemological than optical. As Barnes writes, "for Augustine 'to see' means 'to know.'"[198] Indeed, Augustine also sees the essence of eternal life as "knowing God," drawing on John 17:3.[199] As will be discussed in the following chapter, the Son is not visible in the Old Testament. He is visible only as an object of faith in the incarnation. The purification that comes through faith is thus necessary to truly "see" (or "know") the Triune God at the eschaton, for it is the man Jesus Christ in the *forma servi* who will lead the believers to the contemplation of God and the Father in the *forma dei*. However, Augustine adds the qualification that this contemplation of the Father is bound up in "seeing" the Son, due to his unity with the Father. In 1.8.16 Augustine turns to Jesus' discourse with Philip in John 14 to argue that the vision of the Son *is* the vision of the Father, for, as Jesus says, "I am in the Father and the Father is in me" (John 14:10). Augustine's argument enables him to refute his Homoian opponents. On the one hand, since Christ is only optically visible in the incarnation in the *forma servi*, he cannot be said to be ontologically inferior to the Father. On the other hand, it enables Augustine to do justice to the beatific promise in Matt 5:8 that the pure of heart *will* see God.

Of course, Rahner is sceptical of appeals to the beatific vision as a means of integrating the Christian with the inner life of the Triune God. He wonders how such a vision can take place if there is no real ontological relationship between each of the persons and the believer beyond "mere Appropriation" (*bloße Appropriation*).[200] We have already begun to see how, according to Augustine, the economic Logos is the immanent Logos and vice versa, thus somewhat curtailing this concern. Our discussion of Augustine's doctrine of the missions and processions in the following chapter will further tease out the "real ontological relationships" between the divine persons and the believer. Pertinent to the present discussion, Augustine's appeal to the beatific vision demonstrates an attempt to integrate faith with the doctrine of the Trinity via the testimony of Scripture.

Faith and the Psychological Analogy

Finally, it is important to note that Augustine's psychological analogy does not place a wedge between the doctrine of the Trinity and Christian piety as Rahner and others suppose. Several comments can be made in this regard. First, as Bourassa remarks, "Augustine *does not* use this analogy in his dogmatic approach, that is to say for *the justification of faith* (books 1 to 7), but only in his search for the *intellect*"

---

197. *Trin.* 1.8.17 (CCSL 50: 51): "Probatur autem quod illi contemplationi corda mundentur illa maxime sententia: *Beati mundicordes quoniam ipsi deum uidebunt.*"
198. Barnes, "The Visible Christ and the Invisible Trinity," 331.
199. *Trin.* 1.8.17 (CCSL 50: 51).
200. Rahner, "Der Dreifaltige Gott," 523–5.

(emphases in original).[201] Second, Augustine's real concern with the psychological analogy is "the way those moments of our mental operation participate in and are elevated in the missions of Son and Spirit."[202] Thus, third, as Hill writes, "Augustine's doctrine of the Trinitarian image in man is largely designed to make the mystery of the Trinity relevant to the practice of the Christian life."[203] Fourth, Augustine uses the psychological analogy as a pedagogical tool in the life of the church to enable his hearers to comprehend various aspects of the Triune life. This is particularly evident in his *Serm.* 52 where he transitions from the Jordan baptism to the psychological analogy. Finally, his analogies have had a significant impact on the devotional lives of many, from medieval times through to the present. Wilken points to the impact of Augustine's psychological analogy on the piety of Richard of St. Victor and Bonaventure.[204] Wilken is joined by Pecknold in identifying the pastoral dimension to Augustine's psychological analogy and in encouraging its contemporary application to the life of piety.[205] Thus, even if Rahner *can* attribute the isolation of Trinity and faith to the psychological analogy in later Western theology, he cannot directly blame Augustine.

6. Summary

In summary, we have seen from these five themes emerging in book 1 of *Trin.* that several of the charges levelled against Augustine by Rahner fail to stick. In fact, we have begun to see that Augustine's *Trin.* supports Rahner's Trinitarian agenda on multiple fronts. Augustine's account is rooted in the text of Scripture; it thoroughly integrates the *De Deo Uno* with the *De Deo trino*; it preserves the peculiarity of the Son with respect to the incarnation; it integrates the doctrines of the Trinity and creation; and it is closely tethered to faith and piety. Moreover, it does so with great attention to the biblical statements about the economy of salvation, as opposed to Rahner's account in *Der Dreifaltige Gott* which seems to be as disconnected from the Scriptures as the Neo-Scholastic textbooks he denounces. A portrait of Rahner begins to emerge in which the Jesuit priest appears totally unaware

---

201. Bourassa, "Théologie Trinitaire chez Saint Augustin," 683: "Augustin n'utilise *aucunement* cette analogìe en sa démarche dogmatique, c'est-à-dire pour la *justification de la foi* (LL. 1 à 7), mais seulement dans sa recherche d'*intellectus*."

202. Ables, *Incarnational Realism*, 39.

203. Hill, "Karl Rahner's 'Remarks on the Dogmatic Treatise *De Trinitate* and St. Augustine,'" 79.

204. Robert Louis Wilken, "The Resurrection of Jesus and the Doctrine of the Trinity," *Word & World*, vol. 2, no. 1 (1982): 27–8.

205. C. C. Pecknold, "How Augustine Used the Trinity: Functionalism and the Development of Doctrine," *Anglican Theological Review*, vol. 85, no. 1 (2003): 127–41; cf. Benner, "Augustine and Karl Rahner on the Relationship between the Immanent Trinity and the Economic Trinity," 26.

of the resources at his disposal in the theologian he holds most responsible for the theological superficiality of his day. On the one hand, we are left puzzled by Rahner's complete lack of attention to his required "biblical starting point" and to "the biblical statements about the economy of salvation." On the other hand, we are beginning to see that much of what Rahner requires in a treatise on the Trinity is already there in Augustine's writings, especially given the bishop's exhaustive consideration of the Scriptures. In the next chapter, we see how this picture continues to develop as we turn to the bishop's treatment of the Old Testament, the doctrine of salvation, and the divine missions and processions.

Chapter 3

AUGUSTINE AND THE ECONOMY: THE OLD TESTAMENT, SOTERIOLOGY, AND THE MISSIONS AND PROCESSIONS

1. Introduction

In the previous chapter we began to see that there are considerable resources in Augustine's theology not only to meet Rahner's complaints but also to enhance his aspirations for Trinitarian theology. We saw that several motifs first arising in (though not restricted to) book 1 of Augustine's *Trin.* address the weaknesses Rahner discerns in the "Augustinian-Western" tradition and pre-empt the solutions Rahner proposes. These included Augustine's integration of the Trinity with Scripture more generally, his integration of the *De Deo uno* and *De Deo trino*, and his connection of the doctrine of the Trinity with Christology, creation, and faith or piety. In particular, it was demonstrated that Augustine's attention to "the biblical statements about the economy of salvation, its Triune structure and the explicit biblical sentences with regard to the Father, Son and Spirit"[1] supports and enhances Rahner's thesis. On each of these fronts, Augustine affords greater attention to these details than the Jesuit priest does.

In this chapter, we consider how three further motifs arising in (though not restricted to) books 2–4 further corroborate the findings of the previous chapter. To overcome the weaknesses of the "Augustinian-Western tradition," Rahner desires a doctrine of the Trinity that pays attention to the Old Testament, the doctrine of salvation, and to the connection between the missions and processions. This is precisely what Augustine provides in *Trin.* books 2–4. In these books, Augustine seeks to answer three related questions, laid out in *Trin.* 2.7.13: first, which divine person(s) appeared in the Old Testament theophanies? Augustine wants to know whether it was "the Father, or the Son, or the Holy Spirit, or sometimes the Father, sometimes the Son, sometimes the Holy Spirit; or the one and only without any

---

1. Rahner, "Der Dreifaltige Gott," 535: "die biblischen Aussagen über die Heilsökonomie, deren dreifaltige Struktur und über die expliziten biblischen Sätze im Blick auf den Vater, Sohn und Geist."

distinction of persons, that is, the Trinity appeared to the Fathers through those created forms."[2] Second, how did God manage these appearances? He must decide

> whether a creature was formed just for this purpose, in which God would be revealed to human sight in such a way as he judged right; or whether angels who already existed were so sent as to speak in the person of God; in such a case they could either have taken a material form from a material creature for the purpose of carrying out their service.[3]

Third, what *are* "missions"? He investigates

> whether the Son and the Holy Spirit were also sent before, and if so sent, the difference between that sending and the one we read of in the Gospel; or whether neither of them was sent except when either the Son was made from the Virgin Mary, or when the Holy Spirit appeared to be visible in the form of dove or in the form of fiery tongues.[4]

As will be seen, in answering the first two questions, Augustine pays significant attention to the Old Testament, and by answering the third question he devotes considerable space to the doctrine of grace and the missions–processions dynamic. Thus, yet again, the bishop meets Rahner's complaints and enhances his aspirations for Trinitarian theology. Moreover, Augustine does so with significantly greater attention to "the biblical statements about the economy of salvation" than what Rahner offers.

2. Trinity and the Old Testament Theophanies

Rahner on the Trinity and the Old Testament

Rahner seeks an account of the Trinity that pays heed to the Old Testament preparations for the doctrine. He argues that the isolation of the doctrine of the Trinity from the broader scheme of theology has resulted in "the fearfulness

---

2. *Trin.* 2.7.13 (CCSL 50: 97): "utrum pater an filius an spiritus sanctus; an aliquando pater, aliquando filius, aliquando spiritus sanctus; an sine ulla distinctione personarum sicut dicitur *deus unus et solus*, id est ipsa trinitas, per illas creaturae formas patribus apparuerit."

3. *Trin.* 2.7.13 (CCSL 50: 97–8): "utrum ad hoc opus tantummodo creatura formata sit in qua deus sicut tunc oportuisse iudicauit humanis ostenderetur aspectibus, an angeli qui iam erant ita mittebantur ut ex persona dei loquerentur assumentes corporalem speciem de creatura corporea in usum ministrii sui sicut cuique opus esset."

4. *Trin.* 2.7.13 (CCSL 50: 98): "utrum filius an spiritus sanctus et antea mittebantur, et si mittebantur, quid inter illam missionem et eam quam in euangelio legimus distet; an missus non sit aliquis eorum nisi cum uel filius factus esset *ex Maria uirgine* uel cum spiritus sanctus uisibili specie siue in columba siue in igneis linguis apparuit."

with which one fends off attempts, analogies, premonitions, preparations for this doctrine outside of Christianity or in the Old Testament."[5] He goes on to write that

> the patriarchs of the Old Testament already knew something about it [the Trinity] in their faith, and Augustine granted the great philosophers a knowledge of this with a generosity that would cause offense today. Newer Catholic apologetics consistently and harshly rejects such attempts to discover an anticipation of this mystery outside of the New Testament. And this with indisputable consequence: if the Trinity does not appear as a reality for this theology in the world and salvation history, then it is at least unlikely that there will be even the slightest knowledge of it. And so it is tacitly assumed, more or less, even before the a posteriori question of fact, whether such traces are actually to be found or not (to which, of course, the answer is not a priori yes), that this *cannot* be at all. In any case, however, there will be little tendency to assess echoes and analogies in the history of religion or in the Old Testament positively. Almost everywhere one *only* emphasizes the incommensurability of these doctrines inside and outside Christianity. (emphases in original)[6]

Rahner believes that God *himself* converses with the Old Testament patriarchs through his actions in history.

Rahner also insists that this "revelatory self-presentation is primarily mediated in the Old Testament (next to the angel of Yahweh and the like) through the 'Word,' which on the one hand allows God himself to be powerfully present and yet represents him, and in the 'Spirit,' who helps people to understand and proclaim

---

5. Rahner, "Der Dreifaltige Gott," 531–3: "die Ängstlichkeit, mit der man Versuche abwehrt, Analogien, Ahnungen, Vorbereitungen dieser Lehre außerhalb des Christentums oder im Alten Testament nachzuweisen."

6. Ibid., 533:

> Die Patriarchen des Alten Testaments wußten in ihrem Glauben schon etwas davon, und Augustinus gestand den großen Philosophen eine diesbezügliche Kenntnis in einer Großzügigkeit zu, die heute Ärgernis erregen würde. Die neuere katholische Apologetik lehnt durchgängig schroff solche Versuche ab, eine Ahnung dieses Geheimnisses außerhalb des Neuen Testamentes zu entdecken. Und dies mit unbestreitbarer Konsequenz: Wenn für diese Theologie in der Welt und Heilsgeschichte die Trinität als Wirklichkeit nicht vorkommt, dann ist es mindestens nicht wahrscheinlich, daß sich da auch nur die leiseste Kenntnis von ihr findet. Und so wird doch stillschweigend mehr oder minder schon vor der aposteriorischen Tatsachenfrage, ob sich solche Spuren tatsächlich finden oder nicht (worauf natürlich auch nicht apriorisch mit ja zu antworten ist), vorausgesetzt, daß dies gar nicht sein *könne*. Jedenfalls aber wird die Neigung gering sein, Anklänge und Analogien in der Religionsgeschichte oder im Alten Testament positiv zu werten. Man hebt so gut wie überall *nur* die Inkommensurabilität dieser Lehren innerhalb und außerhalb des Christentums hervor.

the Word."[7] As mentioned in the previous chapter, this point concerning the "primary mediation" of the Word is probably the root of Rahner's being convinced that Augustine rejects the Son's incarnational peculiarity. Though Rahner regularly asserts that Augustine rejects this,[8] only once does he cite direct evidence for his claim. As mentioned in the introduction, when arguing that Augustine's purported view on incarnational peculiarity has "no clear roots in the earlier tradition and still less in Scripture," Rahner cites Schmaus's *Die psychologische Trinitätslehre des hl. Augustin* as evidence.[9] However, at the location cited, Schmaus argues that Augustine deviated from the traditional interpretation of the theophanies.[10] Moreover, in the introduction to *Der Dreifaltige Gott*, Rahner states that he "assumes the statements made so far" by the authors of the previous chapters, including the chapter by Scheffczyk. Scheffczyk had argued that Augustine's interpretation of the Old Testament theophanies results in a lack of differentiation in the economic Trinity.[11] So it is highly likely that Rahner considers Augustine's account of the theophanies to be a factor contributing to the problems he seeks to address with his *Grundaxiom*.

Augustine's Approach to the Theophanies

Augustine indubitably satisfies Rahner's requirement that an account of the Trinity should not "fend off" the witness of the Hebrew Scriptures. This has already been demonstrated with respect to his exegesis of the opening chapter of Genesis.[12] It is also commonly overlooked that nearly 10 per cent of *Trin.* focuses on the Old Testament theophanies. He likewise devotes space to the theophanies in *Maxim.* and *Serm.* 6 and 7.[13] His understanding of the theophanies differs from

---

7. Ibid., 561: "Diese enthüllende Selbstdarbietung ist aber im Alten Testament vor allem (neben dem Engel Jahwes u. ä.) vermittelt durch das "Wort," das Gott selbst einerseits machtvoll anwesend sein läßt und ihn doch vertritt, und im "Geist," der das Wort verstehen und verkündigen läßt."

8. Rahner, "Über den Begriff des Geheimnisses in der Katholischen Theologie," 97; Rahner "Bemerkungen zum Dogmatischen Traktat 'De Trinitate,'" 119; Rahner, "Zur Theologie der Menschwerdung," 139; Rahner, "Dogmatische Fragen zur Osterfrömmigkeit," 162; Rahner, "Natur Und Gnade," 222–3; Rahner, "Zur Theologie des Symbols," 292–3; Rahner, "Der Dreifaltige Gott," 519.

9. Rahner, "Zur Theologie des Symbols," 293: "die sicher keinen klaren Anhaltspunkt in der Augustin vorausgehenden Tradition (und noch weniger in der Schrift)."

10. Schmaus, *Die psychologische Trinitätslehre des heiligen Augustinus*, 20: "Trotzdem glauben sie vor Augustinus fast ausnahmslos, in den Theophanien des Alten Testaments sei der Sohn Gottes erschienen."

11. Scheffczyk, "Lehramtliche Formulierungen und Dogmengeschichte der Trinitätslehre," 146.

12. Cf. pp. 49–53.

13. Cf. *Maxim.* 2.26.1–12 (CCSL 87A: 661–87); *Serm.* 6 (CCSL 41: 62–7); 7 (CCSL 41: 70–6).

Rahner's. In answer to the first question laid out in *Trin.* 2.7.13—who appeared in the theophanies?—Augustine argues in the latter half of book 2 "that the Father was not the only one who appeared, nor only the Son, nor only the Holy Spirit, but the one who did appear was either the Lord God, by which we understand the Trinity without any distinction of persons, or else it was some person of the Trinity, which the text of the narrative expresses."[14] Unlike Rahner, the mature Augustine is not convinced that the divine presence in the Old Testament is mediated primarily through the Word. Nevertheless, Augustine's account of the Trinity certainly "attempts to discover an anticipation of this mystery outside of the New Testament," as Rahner insists upon.

Augustine and the Tradition

In setting forth his mature view, Augustine deviates from the majority of his theological forebears. Theologians as diverse as Justin,[15] Theophilus,[16] Irenaeus,[17] Clement of Alexandria,[18] Origen,[19] Novatian,[20] Tertullian,[21] Athanasius,[22] Cyril of Jerusalem,[23] and Basil of Caesarea[24] each espouse a Christological interpretation of the Old Testament theophanies. According to Justin,

> He who has but the smallest mind (κἂν μικρὸν νοῦν ἔχων) will not dare to suggest that the Maker and Father of all things, having left all heavenly matters, was visible on a little portion of the earth.[25]

The Christological interpretation was likewise maintained by Hilary of Poitiers[26] and Ambrose of Milan,[27] Augustine's immediate Latin forebears.

---

14. *Trin.* 3.proem.3 (CCSL 50: 130): "Iam enim quaesitum atque tractatum est in illis antiquis corporalibus formis et uisis non tantummodo patre nec tantummodo filium nec tantummodo spiritum sanctum apparuisse, sed aut indifferenter dominum deum qui trinitas ipsa intellegitur aut quamlibet ex trinitate personam quam lectionis textus indiciis circumstantibus significaret."
15. Justin, *Dial.* 60 (PG 6: 612).
16. Theophilus, *ad Autol.* 1.2 (PG 6: 1026–8).
17. Irenaeus, *Haer.* 4.11–42 (PG 7: 1002–8).
18. Clement, *Paed.* 1.7 (PG 8: 312–14).
19. Origen, *Hom. Gen.* 4.5. (PG 12: 186–8).
20. Novatian, *Trin.* 18–19 (PL 3: 918–25).
21. Tertullian, *Prax.* 14 (PL 2: 170–2); 16 (PL 2: 174–6).
22. Athanasius, *C. Ar.* 3.13–14 (PG 26: 348–51).
23. Cyril of Jerusalem, *Catech.* 12.16 (PG 33: 744).
24. Basil, *Eun.* 2.18 (PG 29: 609–12).
25. Justin, *Dial.* 60 (PG 6: 612).
26. Hilary, *Syn.* 50 (PL 10: 517); cf. 38.14 (PL 10: 511); *Trin.* 4.15 (CCSL 62: 116–17), 4.23–24 (CCSL 62: 125–7), 5.11 (CCSL 62: 161).
27. Ambrose, *Fid.* 1.13.79–84 (PL 16: 547–50).

However, this does not mean that Augustine is out of keeping with the "tradition" preceding him as Rahner suggests in *Zur Theologie des Symbols*. Firstly, in the bishop's anti-Manichean treatise *Contra Adimantum* (*c.* AD 393), Augustine employs a Christological line of exegesis. The bishop writes to oppose the view that the theophanies contradict Jesus' testimony about God and thus cannot be accepted as revealing the God of Jesus Christ. Augustine responds to this by saying:

> The Son himself, the Word of God, made the Father known to those he wished not only in latter times, when he deigned to appear in the flesh, but also before, from the founding of the world, whether by speaking or by appearing, whether by means of angelic power or by means of some creature.[28]

Augustine argues that it is the Word who is seen in Jacob's struggle and at the burning bush, and yet he is seen as an angel. Kloos notes that in Augustine's reasoning, "there is a unity of the Old and New Testaments because in *both* the Son is the proper agent of revelation to creation. Thus, any stories in which God appears visibly must be manifestations of the Son."[29] Though Augustine's interpretation of the theophanies at this stage emphasizes mediation more than his predecessors, it is certainly rooted in the earlier tradition of Justin et al.

Secondly, Augustine's mature interpretation of the theophanies in *Trin.* was by no means the first time a major theologian challenged the Christological interpretation. In *Refutatio confessionis Eunomii*, Gregory of Nyssa compares the reference to the "Lord" (Heb.: יהוה) in Isa 6 with the citation of the same text in John 12:41 and Acts 28:25–26, where the title "Lord" is ascribed to the Son and Spirit, respectively. For Gregory, this means that "every specially divine vision, every theophany, every word uttered in the person of God, is to be understood to refer to the Father, the Son, and the Holy Spirit."[30] As de Régnon notes, "Certainly, here is a very Augustinian explanation of the theophanies."[31] In his *De Trinitate*, Didymus the Blind of Alexandria reproduces Gregory's argument and arrives at the same conclusion.[32] According to the *de Fide* of Epiphanius of Salamis, "This Father, Son and Holy Spirit has always graciously appeared in visions to his saints,

---

28. *Adim.* 9 (CSEL 25: 131): "Ipse Filius, quod est Verbum Dei, non solum novissimis temporibus, cum in carne apparere dignatus est, sed etiam prius a constitutione mundi, cui voluit de Patre annuntiavit, sive loquendo sive apparendo, vel per angelicam aliquam potestatem, vel per quamlibet creaturam."

29. Kari Kloos, "Seeing the Invisible God: Augustine's Reconfiguration of Theophany Narrative Exegesis," *Augustinian Studies*, vol. 36, no. 2 (2005): 409.

30. Gregory of Nyssa, *Ref. Eun.* 193–194 (GNO 2: 394): ὅτι πᾶσα ὀπτασία θειοτέρα, καὶ πᾶσα θεοφάνεια, καὶ πᾶς λόγος ἐκ προσώπου Θεοῦ λεγόμενος, ἐπὶ τοῦ Πατρὸς νοεῖται, καὶ ἐπὶ τοῦ Υἱοῦ, καὶ ἐπὶ τοῦ Πνεύματος τοῦ ἁγίου.

31. Régnon, *Études de Théologie Positive sur la Sainte Trinité*, 1898, 137: "Certes, voici une explication bien augustinienne des théophanies."

32. Didymus, *Trin.* 1.19 (PG 39: 366).

as each was able to receive the vision in accordance with the gift which had been given him by the Godhead."[33] The Father appeared to Daniel as the Ancient of Days, while the Spirit appeared to Ezekiel. De Régnon notes that we are very close to Augustine here as well.[34]

Schmaus claims that Augustine's predecessors accept the Christological interpretation of the theophanies "almost without exception" (*fast ausnahmslos*). However, two pages later Schmaus admits that Didymus, Epiphanius, Gregory of Nyssa, and even Gregory of Nazianzus diverge from the Christological interpretation, but this is glossed over.[35] While no one could dispute that the Christological interpretation was the majority position of the early church, one would have to admit that these exceptions are fairly significant exceptions. It is notable that all four of these writers were from the East, and that two are Cappadocians, whom Rahner lauds as the peak of early Greek theology.[36] It would not be entirely fair to say that Augustine's interpretation is "clearly rooted" in these earlier Eastern theologians. Augustine gives no evidence of dependence on these earlier works. Nevertheless, there is certainly precedent for this alternate viewpoint. Thus, it would be inaccurate to say that his approach to the theophanies has *no* roots in the tradition.

Thirdly, Augustine's mature interpretation of the theophanies is designed to defend "the tradition" against Homoian–Arianism. This is particularly evident in his debate and subsequent response to the Homoian–Arian bishop Maximinus (*Coll. Max.* and *Maxim.*). According to Maximinus, the Son's difference from and inferiority to the Father was evident in both the incarnation and the Old Testament theophanies. In *Coll. Max.*, Maximinus declares that

> Christ did not come to teach us that the Father is greater than the form of the servant. But the Truth has come to us to teach and instruct us that the Father is greater than the Son and greater than this Son who is the great God. … You say that the divinity showed itself to the patriarchs, and just before that you said that the divinity was invisible. The Father, who is invisible, surely did not show himself. Otherwise, if we say that the Father was seen, we render the apostle a liar, who says, "No human being has seen him or can see him" [1 Tim 6:16]. Moreover, we find ourselves not only resisting the New Testament, but we also find ourselves contrary to the Old. After all, Moses says thus: "No one can see God and live" [Exod 33:20].[37]

---

33. Epiphanius, *Exp. Fid.* 14 (PG 42: 809): καὶ τοῦτον τὸν Πατέρα καὶ Υἱὸν καὶ ἅγιον Πνεῦμα τοῖς αὐτοῦ ἁγίοις καὶ ἀπ' αἰῶνος καταξιώσαντα ἐν ὀπτασίαις φανῆναι, καθάπερ ἠδύνατο ἕκαστις χωρεῖν κατὰ τὸ χάρισμα αὐτοῦ διὰ τῆς Θεότητος.

34. Régnon, *Études de Théologie Positive sur la Sainte Trinité*, 1898, 139.

35. Schmaus does not cite any works by Gregory of Nazianzus where this view is affirmed.

36. Rahner, "Der Dreifaltige Gott," 529, note (n.) 14.

37. *Coll. Max.* 2.25–26 (CCSL 87A: 462):

Thus, as Kloos summarizes, the Homoian–Arian view is that the Son's "visibility and materiality, in contrast to the Father's invisibility and impassibility, show his inferiority to the Father not merely in his office but in himself."[38] According to the Homoian-Arians, the Son's unique manifestation in the Old Testament theophanies was evidence of his ontological subordination. Though Augustine's debate with Maximinus took place two decades after he initially penned books 2 and 3 of *Trin.*, the similar manner in which Augustine interprets the theophanies in both indicates that *Trin.* refutes an argument similar to that refuted in his debates with Maximinus.[39] While it is true that Augustine deviates from the majority viewpoint on the theophanies, it is important to recognize that he does so to preserve the pro-Nicene tradition against a Subordinationist threat. As Boulnois writes, Augustine's argument in books 2 and 3 "is inseparable from the polemical desire to undermine one of the syllogisms most frequently used by the Arians: the Father is invisible; the Son made himself seen by the patriarchs; therefore he is visible and inferior to the Father."[40] Such arguments can be found in Augustine's debates with Maximinus.[41] Even Schmaus recognizes Augustine's preservation and continuation of the tradition in this respect:

> Augustine deprived this argument of all strength by breaking with the almost unanimously traditional teaching and, as a logical consequence of his standpoint regarding the unity of the Trinity, he explained the Old Testament revelations in such a way that his teaching on this was a continuation and further development of that which appears in Gregory of Nyssa, Didymus and Epiphanius.[42]

> Nec enim ob hoc uenit Christus, ut nos instrueret quod ad formam serui maior est Pater. Sed ideo ueritas ad nos uenit, ut utique doceret nos atque instrueret quod enim Pater Filio maior est, et huic Filio qui magnus Deus est. ... Dicis quod se diuinitas patribus ostendit, et paulo ante prosecutus es quod utique diuinitas sit inuisibilis. Ostendit se sane, non Pater qui est inuisibilis; ne si dicamus Patrem uisum fuisse, apostolum reddamus mendacem, qui ait: *Quem uidit hominum nemo, neque uidere potest.* Et non solum inuenimur nouo resistere testamento, uerum etiam et ueteri pari modo contrarii inuenimur. Denique sic ait Moyses: *Non potest quisque Deum uidere et uiuere.*

38. Kloos, *Christ, Creation, and the Vision of God: Augustine's Transformation of Early Christian Theophany Interpretation*, 135.

39. Cf. Michel R. Barnes, "The Arians of Book V, and the Genre of 'De Trinitate,'" *Journal of Theological Studies*, vol. 44, no. 1 (1993): 193, n. 42.

40. Boulnois, "Le *De Trinitate* de Saint Augustin: Exégèse, logique et noétique," 37: "cette recherche est inséparable de la volonté polémique de saper l'un des syllogismes les plus fréquemment utilisés par les ariens: le Père est invisible, or le Fils s'est fait voir des patriarches, il est donc visible et inférieur au Père."

41. See, for example, *Coll. Max.* 2.26 (CCSL 87A: 462–6).

42. Schmaus, *Die psychologische Trinitätslehre des heiligen Augustinus*, 160: "Augustinus nahm diesem Argument jede Kraft, indem er mit der fast einhellig tradierten Lehre brach und in logischer Auswirkung seines Standpunktes bezüglich der Einheit Dreiheit die

The bishop deviates from the Christological interpretation for the sake of being pro-Nicene. In this sense, it is difficult to maintain Rahner's implied criticism that Augustine's account of the theophanies has "no clear roots" in the tradition.

Augustine's Exegesis

More importantly, it is by attending to "the biblical statements about the economy of salvation" that Augustine manages to preserve the tradition. In *Zur Theologie des Symbols*, Rahner implies that Augustine's mature interpretation of the theophanies has "no clear roots" in the *Scriptures*. The bishop's extensive treatment of the theophanies in books 2 and 3 makes this argument difficult to maintain. Moreover, he raises significant exegetical dilemmas that Rahner has not accounted for when insisting that God's self-presentation is "primarily mediated" through the Word in the Old Testament.

The Eden Theophany Augustine's challenge to the Christological reading of the Eden theophany (cf. Gen 2) offers a first case in point. He reasons that one usually attributes the words "Let there be light" of Gen 1 to the Father, for "he made all things through his Word, because we know by the right rule of faith that his Word is his only Son."[43] Since "the narrative of Scripture nowhere passes obviously from one person to another, the one who speaks to the first man appears to be the same as the one who had said 'Let there be light.'"[44] It could be that Scripture passes imperceptibly from the Father in Gen 1 to the Son in Gen 2 and 3, but this is not made explicit.[45] Thus, "why should we not take it to be the Father who appeared to Abraham and Moses, and indeed to anyone he liked in any way he liked?"[46] Moreover, even if Adam "saw" the Father in some sense other than with his physical eyes, "there is nothing in this text to prevent us from taking those

---

alttestamentlichen Offenbarungen in der Weise erklärt, daß seine Lehre hierüber als eine Fortsetzung und Weiterbildung derjenigen eines Gregor von Nyssa, eines Didymus und eines Epiphanius erscheint."

43. *Trin.* 2.10.17 (CCSL 50: 102): "Omnia enim per uerbum suum fecit, uod *uerbum* eius *unicum filium eius* secundum rectam fidei regulam nouimus."

44. *Trin.* 2.10.17 (CCSL 50: 102): "Contextio quidem ipsa scripturae nusquam transire sentitur a persona ad personam; sed ille uidetur loqui ad primum hominem qui dicebat: *Fiat lux.*"

45. He makes a similar argument in *Maxim.* 2.26.2 (CCSL 87A: 664):

> On what basis do you decide that the Father said, "Let there be light" [Gen 1:3] and the rest, and that the Father said, "Let us make man" [Gen 1:26], but that the Son said, "Let us make a helper for him" [Gen 2:18], when in all these cases Scripture tells you only, 'God said'? What is the rashness? What is this presumptuousness?

46. *Trin.* 2.10.17 (CCSL 50: 102): "cur non iam ipse intellegatur apparuisse Abrahae et Moysi et quibus uoluit quemadmodum uoluit …?"

voices which Adam heard as not only being produced by the Trinity, but also as manifesting the person of the same Trinity."[47] Here, there are "clear biblical roots" for Augustine's hesitancy to affirm the Word as the one who "primarily mediated" God's Old Testament presence.

The Abraham Theophanies Augustine's treatment of the Abrahamic theophanies exposes similar difficulties for the Christological interpretation. When the "Lord" appears to Abraham in Gen 12:7, Augustine admits that it could be the Son who is called "Lord" in 1 Cor 8:5. However, by the same reasoning, he suggests that it could be the Father or Spirit who appears; the Father is called "Lord" in Ps 2:7[48] and 110:1,[49] as is the Spirit in 2 Cor 3:17.[50] To this Augustine could have followed Gregory and Didymus in observing the attribution of the title "Lord" to the Spirit in Acts 28:25–26. Thus we cannot automatically assume that "Lord" refers to the second person in the Trinity: "it is not evident here, whether any person of the Trinity, or whether God himself the Trinity appeared to Abraham, of which one God it is said, 'The Lord your God shall you fear; him alone shall you serve [Gen 12:7]."[51] To be fair to someone disputing Augustine's view, the New Testament disproportionately refers to Christ as "Lord." Even so, given the references to the Father and Spirit as "Lord," Augustine's conservatism should not be dismissed lightly without ironclad New Testament proof that this (or any) instance necessarily refers to the second person.

Turning to the Mamre episode, Augustine suggests that there is not enough evidence to dismiss the possibility that the three angels do not represent the three divine persons.[52] The fact that the three are sometimes addressed in the singular (such as in Gen 18:1, 18:3–5; cf. Gen 19:18) points to their unity. Since the three are referred to and speak as a collective, Augustine argues that we cannot exclude the possibility that the Father or the Spirit may have appeared in this theophany. What about the two men who separate from the third man in Gen 18:22, only to re-emerge as two "angels" in Gen 19:1? Augustine notes that in Gen 19:18, Lot speaks to the two angels (i.e., "to them") in the singular: "Please, *Lord*." He writes:

> Why does he say "Please, *Lord*," and not "Please, *Lords*"? Or if he wanted to address one of them, why does Scripture say, "And Lot said to them, 'Please,

---

47. *Trin.* 2.10.18 (CCSL 50: 104): "Nec nos aliquid prohibet illas uoces factas *ad Adam* non solum a trinitate factas intellegere sed etiam personam demonstrantes eiusdem trinitatis accipere."

48. Also quoted in Acts 13:33; Heb 1:5, 5:5.

49. Also quoted in Matt 22:44.

50. In Acts 28:25–27, Paul identifies the Spirit with the Yahweh of Isa 6.

51. *Trin.* 2.10.19 (CCSL 50: 106): "Neque hic ergo euidenter apparet utrum aliqua ex trinitate persona an deus ipse trinitas, de quo uno deo dictum est: *Dominum deum tuum adorabis et illi soli seruies, uisus* fuerit *Abrahae*."

52. *Trin.* 2.10.19–2.12.22 (CCSL 50: 106–9).

Lord, since your servant has found favour before you?'" Or do we here also understand two persons indicated by the plural number? And when the two are addressed as one, is it the one Lord God of the same substance?"[53]

From here, Augustine asks why these two angels cannot be divine persons like the third. The bishop is content to leave the matter open-ended. Whatever the case, to maintain a Christological interpretation of the Old Testament theophanies, attention must be afforded to the exegetical dilemmas posed by Augustine in this episode.[54] Rahner makes no such attempt.

The Exodus Theophanies In Exodus, Augustine discerns a certain fittingness to holding that it was the Son who appeared at the burning bush. In Exod 3, the Angel of the Lord is referred to as "God" and in Rom 9:5 the Christ who appeared to the Jewish forefathers is referred to as "God." Therefore, Augustine reasons that there is a case for arguing that this refers to the Son.[55] Nevertheless, if it was, in fact, one of the angels who appeared,

> How can anyone easily tell whether the task imposed on him was to represent the person of the Son, or of the Holy Spirit, or of God the Father, or simply of the Trinity itself who is the one and only God, in saying, "I am the God of Abraham and the God of Isaac and the God of Jacob" [Exod 3:6]? We cannot possibly say that the God of Abraham and the God of Isaac and the God of Jacob is the Son of God but is not the Father.[56]

How can we say that it was not the Father who appeared in the Exodus theophanies? As Augustine mentions, Rom 1:20 says that "the invisible things of God [*invisibilia dei*] may be intelligibly perceived from the world's creation

---

53. Emphasis added. *Trin.* 2.12.22 (CCSL 50: 109): "Cur dicitur, *Rogo, domine*, et non, '*Rogo*, domini'? Aut si unum ex eis uoluit appellare, cur ait scriptura: *Dixit autem Loth ad eos: Rogo, domine quoniam inuenit puer tuus ante te misericordiam*? An et hic intellegimus in plurali numero personas duas, cum autem idem duo tamquam unus conpellantur, *unius substantiae unum dominum deum*?"

54. Augustine rehearses the same exegetical argument in *Maxim.* 2.26.5-8 (CCSL 87A: 668–72); *Serm.* 7.6 (CCSL 41: 74–5).

55. *Trin.* 2.13.23 (CCSL 50: 110).

56. *Trin.* 2.13.23 (CCSL 50: 110–11):

> Si enim unus ex angelis erat, quis facileaffirmare possit utrum ei filii persona nuntianda imposita fuerit an spiritus sancti an dei patris an ipsius omnino trinitatis qui est unus et solus deus, ut diceret: *Ego sum deus Abraham et deus Isaac et deus Iacob*? Neque enim possumus dicere deum Abraham et deum Isaac et deum Iacob filium dei esse et patrem non esse.

through the things that are made, as also his eternal might and divinity."[57] Clearly the Father reveals himself through created means. Thus, Augustine reasons that "it was by creatures made submissive that all these visible and intangible exhibitions were displayed, in order to represent the invisible and intelligible God—not only the Father, but also the Son too and the Holy Spirit."[58] We cannot rule out the possibility that the Father manifested himself through creaturely means. He pursues this argument further in book 3.[59]

Augustine also proposes that there is a certain fittingness to suggesting that the Holy Spirit appeared at Sinai. He observes that the stone tablets were inscribed upon by the "finger of God" (*digito dei*; cf. Exod 31:18) and notes that the Spirit is indicated by the name "finger of God" in the Gospels (cf. Luke 11:20; Matt 12:28).[60] He also observes similarities between Sinai and Pentecost, the (supposed) parallel in the fifty-day gap between Passover and Sinai and the Resurrection and Pentecost,[61] and the parallel between the manifestation of fire at Sinai (Exod 19:18) and at Pentecost (Acts 2:1). Even still, as far as he can tell, here "we do not discern any one person of the Trinity by some proper sign, as far I can discern from my senses."[62] From the various Exodus manifestations, Augustine concludes that "though neither Father, Son, nor Holy Spirit was either named or unmistakably indicated in them, they still contained enough likely hints and probabilities to make it impossible without rashness to say that God the Father never appeared to the patriarchs or prophets under visible forms."[63] Even if one remains unconvinced by certain points in his argument, it is difficult to challenge his conclusion that there is not enough evidence to dismiss the possibility that it might have been the Father, the Spirit, or the Trinity appearing through some created and/or angelic medium in these episodes.

---

57. *Trin.* 2.15.25 (CCSL 50: 114).

58. *Trin.* 2.15.25 (CCSL 50: 114): "Sed per subiectam, ut saepe diximus, creaturam exhibentur haec omnia uisibilia et sensibilia ad significandum *invisibilem* atque intellegibilem *deum*, non solum patrem sed et filium et spiritum sanctum."

59. Augustine rehearses a similar argument in *Maxim.* 2.26.11 (CCSL 87A: 684–5); *Serm.* 7.4 (CCSL 41: 72–3).

60. *Trin.* 2.15.26 (CCSL 50: 114). See also *Trin.* 3.7.12 (CCSL 50: 139); 3.9.18 (CCSL 50: 145); *Maxim.* 2.21.2 (CCSL 87A: 628); *Serm.* 8.18 (CCSL 41: 99); 155.3 (CCSL 41Ba: 110); 155.5 (CCSL 41Ba: 112).

61. There is no biblical evidence for this first fifty-day gap.

62. *Trin.* 2.15.26 (CCSL 50: 115): "Sed aliquam ex trinitate personam signo quodam proprio, quantum ad mei sensus capacitatem pertinet, non uidemus."

63. *Trin.* 2.17.32 (CCSL 50: 123): "Multa enim talia uisa facta sunt illis temporibus non euidenter nominato et designato in eis uel patre uel filio uel spiritu sancto, sed tamen per quasdam ualde probabiles significationes nonnullis indiciis exsistentibus ut nimis temerarium sit dicere deum patrem numquam patribus aut prophetis per aliquas uisibiles formas apparuisse."

The Daniel Theophany While his argument against the traditional reading mainly revolves around ambiguity and inconclusiveness, at the end of book 2 Augustine discerns in Dan 7 conclusive evidence against an exclusively Christological interpretation of theophanies. If the "Son of Man" receiving the kingdom is the Son, surely the Ancient of Days visibly giving him the kingdom is the Father. Here they are both visibly present before the prophet. This being the case, "how can they say that the Father never appeared to the prophets, and so alone can be regarded as the invisible one 'whom no man has seen, nor can see' [1 Tim 6:16]?"[64] From Dan 7, Augustine concludes that there are biblical grounds for asserting that the Father can appear: "So it is not unbecoming to believe that God the Father was also accustomed to appear in that sort of way to mortals."[65] The transcendent creator can do whatever he wants.

Created Mediation Importantly, Augustine does not say that the divine persons are revealed in the theophanies according to their substance (*substantia*). The main aim of book 3 is to establish that this does not happen, as the bishop sets himself to address the second question laid out in 2.7.13. According to Augustine,

> It is clear that all of those things shown to the fathers, whenever God showed himself to them, unfolding his plan of salvation according to the times, were manifested through created objects. Even if we do not know how he did these things with angels to assist him, that they were done through angels is not something we made up from our own discernment.[66]

From where does this idea come? "There is the authority of the divine Scriptures, from which our minds should not deviate, leaving the solid ground of the divine book, being thrown down into the abyss of our own thoughts, where neither our senses can guide us nor the clear reason of truth shine forth."[67] For Augustine, the

---

64. *Trin.* 2.18.33 (CCSL 50: 123–4): "quomodo isti dicunt *patrem* numquam uisum esse prophetis et ideo solum debere intellegi *inuisibilem, quem nemo hominum uidit nec uidere potest*?"

65. *Trin.* 2.18.33 (CCSL 50: 124): "Non ergo inconuenienter creditur etiam deus pater eo modo solere apparere mortalibus."

66. *Trin.* 3.11.22 (CCSL 50: 150–1): "Proinde illa omnia quae patribus uisa sunt cum deus illis secundum suam dispensationem temporibus congruam praesentaretur per creaturam facta esse manifestum est. Et si nos latet quomodo ea ministris angelis fecerit, per angelos tamen esse facta non ex nostro."

67. *Trin.* 3.11.22 (CCSL 50: 151): "Exstat enim auctoritas diuinarum scripturarum unde mens nostra deuiare non debet, nec relicto solidamento diuini eloquii per suspicionum suarum abrupta praecipitari ubi nec sensus corporis regit nec perspicua ratio ueritatis elucet."

Scriptures—especially Heb 1:3, Acts 7:30, and Gal 3:19—are his "solid ground," or, to use Rahner's idiom, his "clear roots."[68]

Conclusion Modern readers may well remain unconvinced by certain aspects of Augustine's exegesis. However, no one can claim that Augustine's theophanic non-peculiarity lacks "clear roots" in Scripture. This is simply not the case. Augustine does not deny that there are some biblical indications that it was the Son who appears in the theophanies. Nevertheless, the substantial weight of many, if not most, of his exegetical objections to this interpretation force one to seriously consider the possibility that Rahner's Christological reading is at greater risk than Augustine's of lacking "clear roots" in Scripture or the tradition. In any case, Augustine certainly provides greater attention to the narrative particularities of the Old Testament preparations for the Trinity than Rahner does.

3. Trinity and Salvation

Rahner on the Trinity and Salvation

Next, Rahner is also concerned that in isolating the doctrine of the Trinity from the economy and from the rest of theology, the Augustinian-Western tradition has disconnected the doctrine of the Trinity from soteriology. As such, like the incarnation, the doctrine of grace tells us nothing of the Trinity:

> The doctrine of satisfaction, and thus the doctrine of redemption with its theory that is customary today of a double moral subject in Christ, conceives an act of redemption, which from the outset is directed equally to all three divine persons, so that this doctrine in no way expressly reflects on the fact that the satisfaction is precisely from the *verbum* incarnatum (and not simply from the Deus–homo). One could just as easily imagine that another divine person could have given the Triune God a satisfactio condigna as a human, and that such a condition would just as well be conceivable for us, without the Trinity being assumed as a condition of its possibility at all.[69]

---

68. *Trin.* 3.11.22–3.11.27 (CCSL 50: 150–8); cf. *Serm.* 6.2 (CCSL 41: 63); 7.6 (CCSL 41: 75).

69. Rahner, "Der Dreifaltige Gott," 519–21:

> daß die heute übliche Satisfaktions- und somit die Erlösungslehre mit ihrer Theorie eines doppelten moralischen Subjekts in Christuss eine Erlösungstat konzipiert, die sich von vornherein an alle drei göttlichen Personen in gleicher Weise richtet, daß also diese Lehre in keiner Weise darauf ausdrücklich reflektiert, daß die Genugtuung gerade vom *Verbum* incarnatum (und nicht einfach vom Deus-homou) geleistet wurde, und daß man sich darum ebensogut denken könnte, daß eine andere göttliche Person als Mensch dem dreifaltigen Gott eine satisfactio condigna v hätte

As seen in the introduction, Rahner believes that this is a flow-on effect from the non-peculiarity of the divine persons in the Western tradition and the psychological analogy, which can be traced to Augustine.

Rahner wishes to correct this tradition:

> It will now have to be said that this isolation of the treatise on the Trinity proves to be wrong simply because of this fact: it *cannot* be like that. The Trinity is a mystery of *salvation*. Otherwise, it would not be revealed. But then it must also become clear why it is such a thing. But then it must also become clear in all treatises of dogmatics that the realities of salvation dealt with therein cannot themselves be understood without recourse to this mystery of the origins of Christianity. (emphases in original)[70]

Rahner insists that the doctrine of the Trinity is integral to the doctrine of salvation and that the latter cannot be separated from or understood apart from the former. He argues that a reintegration of these two doctrines is made possible through attention to the economy. In what follows, we see that this is precisely what Augustine offers. In so doing, Augustine interacts with the philosophy of his day, but as will be seen, he does not do so "with a generosity that would cause offense today" as Rahner suggests.[71] Augustine certainly recognizes a degree of consonance between the Christian doctrine of God and elements of ancient philosophy. As such, Augustine like Rahner appreciates certain anticipations of the Christian God outside of the New Testament Scriptures, in this case, among

---

> leisten können, ja auch eine solche ebensogut für uns denkbar wäre, ohne daß die Trinität als Bedingung ihrer Möglichkeit überhaupt vorausgesetzt würde.

70. Rahner, "Der Dreifaltige Gott," 533:

> Man wird nun sagen müssen, daß diese Isoliertheit des Trinitätstraktats sich schon einfach durch ihre Tatsache als falsch erweist: So *kann* es nicht sein. Die Trinität ist ein *Heils*mysterium. Sonst wäre sie nicht geoffenbart. Dann aber muß auch deutlich werden, warum sie ein solches ist. Dann aber muß auch in allen Traktaten der Dogmatik deutlich werden, daß die darin behandelten Heilswirklichkeiten selbst nicht verständlich werden können ohne Rückgriff auf dieses Ursprungsmysterium des Christentums.

This quotation has sometimes been misunderstood, in part due to Donceel's translation. Donceel adds an interpretive gloss between the first and second sentences, writing, "There *must* be a connection between Trinity and man." (Karl Rahner, *The Trinity*, trans. Joseph Donceel (New York: Herder, 1970), 21). This gloss is misleading—particularly the italicised *must*—and has caused some to view Rahner as collapsing the Trinity into the doctrine of salvation. However, Rahner is making the point that the doctrine of the Trinity is integral to the doctrine of salvation and that the latter cannot be separated from or understood apart from the former.

71. Cf. Rahner, "Der Dreifaltige Gott," 533. Cf. p. 64.

the philosophers. However, his attention to the biblical statements about the economy of salvation will force him to reject philosophy as a saving mediator or means to purification.

The Place of Trin. *4 in Augustine's Argument*

In the first eighteen sections of book 4 (*Trin.* 4.1.2–4.18.24) Augustine turns to the outworking of the Son's mission. Some have struggled to see how this section fits into the development of Augustine's argument. Augustine has proceeded to answer the first two questions raised in *Trin.* 2.7.13 in books 2 and 3, respectively, but will only begin explicitly answering the third question—what *are* the missions?—from 4.19.25. Thus, according to Hombert, "One has the impression of a break in the original program, and it is as if the part dedicated to Christ the Redeemer and Mediator were an added piece."[72] However, as Hill notes, throughout the preceding material of book 4 Augustine is "engaged all along in describing in concrete, actual terms what it means for the Word to be sent."[73] His mission requires him to take on flesh and to offer an acceptable sacrifice as mediator for our purification. He has not been "sent" to do so until he begins to accomplish this mission, and, hence, his mission only begins in the New Testament. Thus, Augustine is actually answering his third question in the earlier parts of book 4.

The Exegetical Backdrop

Importantly, as Augustine answers this question, his teaching on the soteriological ends of the Son's mission is rooted in the text of Scripture as Rahner demands. Book 1 has already provided the exegetical foundation for his core soteriological categories. There (as in many of his other works), Augustine relies heavily upon 1 Tim 2:5 for the theme of mediation,[74] Matt 5:8 for purification and contemplation,[75]

---

72. Hombert, *Nouvelles Recherches de Chronologie Augustinienne*, 68: "On a l'impression d'une rupture dans le programme primitif, et tout se passe comme si la partie consacrée au Christ Rédempteur et Médiateur était une pièce rapportée."

73. Edmund Hill, notes on *The Trinity: Introduction, Translation and Notes*, by Augustine. vol. 5, The Works of Saint Augustine: A Translation for the 21st Century 1 (ed. John E. Rotelle; trans. Edmund Hill; Brooklyn: New City, 1991), 173.

74. *Trin.* 1.7.14 (CCSL 50: 44); 1.8.16 (CCSL 50: 48); 1.8.17 (CCSL 50: 50); 1.10.20 (CCSL 50: 57). Cf. *Trin.* 3.11.26 (CCSL 50: 157); 13.10.13 (CCSL 50A: 399); 13.18.23 (CCSL 50A: 413); 15.25 (CCSL 50: 523); *Ep.* 137.12 (CCSL 31B: 265); 140.8.21 (CSEL 42: 172); 149.2.17 (CSEL 44: 364); 166.5 (CSEL 44: 553); 187.2.3 (CSEL 57: 83); *Tract. Ev. Jo.* 16.7 (CCSL 36: 169); 17.7 (CCSL 36: 174); *Serm.* 51.31 (CCSL 41Aa: 45); *Arian.* 9.7 (CCSL 87A: 202).

75. *Trin.* 1.8.17 (CCSL 50: 51); 1.13.28 (CCSL 50: 70); 1.13.30 (CCSL 50: 74); 1.13.31 (CCSL 50: 76, 78). Cf. *Trin.* 8.4.6 (CCSL 50: 275); *Ep.* 92.4 (CCSL 31A: 162); 119.5 (PL 33: 451); 130.2.5 (CCSL 31B: 215); 147 (CSEL 44: 274–331); 148.2.9 (CSEL 44: 339); 148.3.11 (CSEL 44: 341); 148.3.12 (CSEL 44: 342); 169.1.3 (CSEL 44: 613); 171A.2 (CSEL

and Acts 15:9 for the connection between purification (or cleansing) and faith.[76] While these verses are no longer cited in book 4, the themes are central to Augustine's discourse.

The book begins with the statement that God "has absolutely nothing changeable, neither in eternity, nor in truth, nor in will, because there is eternal truth, eternal love; there the love is true, eternity true; and there eternity is loved, truth loved."[77] Humanity, however, has been exiled from this unchanging joy and made subject to darkness and foolish minds, blinded by depraved desires and unbelief.[78] Drawing upon Rom 5:8–9 and 8:31, Augustine argues that God chose to persuade sinful humanity of his love for us, so that the power of his love for us would be brought to perfection in faith and humility, lest we grow proud.[79] Then, turning to John's prologue, Augustine argues that humanity is restored to truth through the Word who, full of life, provides enlightenment (*inluminatio*) to all of humankind.[80] Enlightenment is to participate (*participatio*) in the Word, but "the only thing to cleanse the unjust and the proud is the blood of the just and the humility of God."[81] Only then can mankind contemplate God. Echoing 2 Pet 1:4 and (presumably unintentionally) Athanasius before him, he writes:

> God [*Deus*], therefore, became a just man and interceded with God [*Deo*] for sinful man. The sinner did not accord with [*congruit*] the just, but man did accord with man. So he, applying to us the likeness of his humanity, removed the dissimilarity of our iniquity, and, becoming a partaker of our mortality, made us partakers of his divinity.[82]

44: 635); *Tract. Ev. Jo.* 1.7 (CCSL 36: 4); 3.18 (CCSL 36: 28); 18.6 (CCSL 36: 183); 19.16 (CCSL 36: 199); 20.11 (CCSL 36: 209); 21.15 (CCSL 36: 221); 26.18 (CCSL 36: 268); 53.12 (CCSL 36: 458); 68.3 (CCSL 36: 499); 111.3 (CCSL 36: 630); *Serm.* 53.6 (CCSL 41Aa: 91–2); 53.7–9 (CCSL 41Aa: 94–5); *Civ.* 20.21 (CCSL 48: 373); *Coll Max* 14.15 (CCSL 87A: 417); *Maxim.* 2.12.2 (CCSL 87A: 563); *Arian.* 9.7 (CCSL 87A: 202).

76. 15:9 *Trin.* 1.8.17 (CCSL 50: 51). Cf. *Serm.* 53.10–11 (CCSL 41Aa: 97); *Tract. Ev. Jo.* 68.3 (CCSL 36: 499).

77. *Trin.* 4.proem.1 (CCSL 50: 160): "Omnino enim dei essentia qua est nihil habet mutabile nec in aeternitate nec in ueritate nec in uoluntate quia aeterna ibi est ueritas, aeterna caritas; et uera ibi est caritas, uera aeternitas."

78. *Trin.* 4.1.2–4.2.4 (CCSL 50: 161–3).

79. *Trin.* 4.1.2 (CCSL 50: 161–2).

80. *Trin.* 4.2.4 (CCSL 50: 163).

81. Ibid.: 163–4: "Porro iniquorum et superborum una mundatio est *sanguis iusti* et humilitas dei."

82. Ibid.: 164: "Deus itaque factus homo iustus intercessit deo pro homine peccatore. Non enim congruit peccator iusto, sed congruit homini homo. Adiungens ergo nobis similitudinem humanitatis suae abstulit dissimilitudinem iniquitatis nostrae, et factus particeps mortalitatis nostrae fecit participes diuinitatis suae."

One can imagine Rahner objecting to the seemingly indiscriminate ("a-Trinitarian?") use of *Deus* in this citation, were it to be read in abstraction. However, we must remember that in the previous breath Augustine has been discussing the Word with specific reference to John's prologue. Rather than blurring the distinctions between the divine persons, Augustine is speaking of the Word as *Deus* as distinct from the Father as *Deus* following the model of John 1:1.

Mediation, the One, and the Many

From *Trin.* 4.2.4–4.12, Augustine works out the Son's mediation numerologically against the backdrop of the Plotinian problematic of the one and the many. For Augustine, the incarnation provides the solution: "The single of our Lord and Saviour Jesus Christ matches our double."[83] From Rom 8:10 Augustine argues that "we died both soul and body, soul on account of sin, body on account of the punishment of sin, and thus also of body on account of sin."[84] However, "the one death of our Saviour saved us from our two deaths, and one resurrection afforded us two resurrections, since his body was in both things—that is, both in death and in resurrection—was served to us as a kind of medical remedy, suitable for both the mystery of the inner man and the type of the outer man."[85] The numerology will strike many modern readers as somewhat fanciful, especially in 4.4.7–4.6.10. However, it cannot be denied that Augustine's account pays extensive attention to the economy of salvation and the testimony of Scripture. This is evidenced by the dozens of biblical citations and allusions,[86] as well as the allusion to 1 Tim 2:5 where Augustine brings the "many" into relationship with Christ, the "one" and the "mediator":

> We the many members had been preceded by the one head, in whom we have been purified by faith and will then be made completely whole by sight, and that

---

83. *Trin.* 4.3.5 (CCSL 50: 165): "simplum domini et saluatoris nostri Iesu Christi duplo nostro congruat."

84. Ibid.: 165: "anima et corpore mortui sumus, anima propter peccatum, corpore propter poenam peccati ac per hoc et corpore *propter peccatum*."

85. Ibid.: 169: "Vna ergo mors nostri saluatoris duabus mortibus nostris saluti fuit, et una eius resurrectio duas nobis resurrectiones praestitit cum corpus eius in utraque re, id est et in morte et in resurrectione, et in sacramento interioris hominis nostri et exemplo exterioris medicinali quadam conuernientia ministratum est."

86. In *Trin.* 4.4.7, he cites or alludes to Gen 1:5; 1:26–27; 2:1–2; 9:6; Exod 20:11; 31:17; Ps 56:7; Eccl 17:1; Dan 7:13; Sap 2:23; Matt 1:17; Luke 13:11–13, 13:16; John 1:14; Rom 5:13; 6:14; 2 Cor 3:18; 4:16; Eph. 4:23; Phil. 2:7; Tit 3:5–7; 1 John 3:8 (CCSL 50: 169–71). In 4.4.8, he cites or alludes to Isa 7:14; Matt 1:21; 12:40; 26:61; 27:40; 27:60; Mark 14:58; 15:46; Luke 1:31, 23:52; John 2:19–21; 19:41; and Eph 4:12 (CCSL 50: 172–3). In 4.6.10, he cites or alludes to Gen 1:4–5; Matt 26:61; 27:40; 27:45–46; Mark 14:58; 15:25; 15:33–37; John 2:19–20; 19:14; 27:46, 27:50; 2 Cor 4:6; and Eph 5:8 (CCSL 50: 173–5).

thus, fully reconciled to God by him, the mediator, we may be able to cling to the one, enjoy the one, and remain for ever one.[87]

It is obvious that Augustine is sympathetic with Plotinian metaphysics. However, this is far from granting the great philosophers such a knowledge of the Trinity that it would "cause offense" today as Rahner supposes.[88] In fact, this interaction with the Neoplatonic problematic begins to set the stage for the strong critique of Neoplatonism that follows in 4.15.20–4.18.24. But before turning to this critique, we must consider his exposition of Christ's mediation in 4.10.13–4.14.

Mediation, Christ, and the Devil

Having presented Christ's mediation as restoring harmony to a sin-plagued world (4.2.4–4.9), Augustine then contrasts Christ's mediation with the Devil's false mediation (4.10.13–4.14). Augustine presents the Devil as the "mediator of death" (*mediatorem mortis*),[89] who in his pride brought proud man down to death. He grew high to seemingly become "a great man, a leader among the legions of demons through whom he rules the kingdom of lies" and "inflates man with false philosophy or engulfs him in sacrilegious or sacred things, in which he also holds him captive by magical trickery, while he hurls the minds of the more curious and the more proud into deceit and delusion."[90] Referencing 2 Cor 11:14 and 2 Thess 2:9, Augustine argues that the Devil promises a kind of purification by transforming himself into an angel of life, using all sorts of deceptive signs and portents.[91] However, these are of no use at all for purifying the soul and reconciling it to God, for "the way to death was through sin in Adam" and the Devil "was the mediator of this way, persuading us to sin and hurling us into death; he used his own single death to bring about our double death."[92] Another kind of mediation is required.

---

87. *Trin.* 4.7.11 (CCSL 50: 176): "multa *membra* intueremur praecessisse nos *caput unum* in quo *nunc per fidem* mundati et *tunc per speciem* redintegrati et per mediatorem deo reconciliati haereamus uni, fruamur uno, permaneamus unum."

88. Cf. Rahner, "Der Dreifaltige Gott," 533.

89. *Trin.* 4.10.13 (CCSL 50: 178).

90. Ibid.: 178: "magnus homini uidebatur princeps in legionibus daemonum per quos fallaciarum regnum exercet. Sic hominem per elationis typhum potentiae quam iustitiae cupidiorem aut per falsam philosophiam magis inflans aut per sacra sacrilega inretiens, in quibus etiam magicae fallaciae curiosiores superbioresque animas deceptas inlusasque praecipitans, subditum tenet."

91. Ibid.: 178–9.

92. *Trin.* 4.12.15 (CCSL 50: 180): "Via nobis fuit ad mortem *per peccatum in Adam*: ... Huius uiae mediator diabolus fuit, persuasor peccati et praecipitator in mortem; nam et ipse ad operandam duplam mortem nostram simplam attulit suam." Cf. *Ep.* 53.7 (CCSL 31: 225); *Conf.* 10.42.67 (PL 32: 807–8); *Civ.* 2.26 (CCSL 47: 61–2); 9.10 (CCSL 47: 258–9).

Christ's mediation overcomes the Devil's false mediation. He is the "mediator of life" (*mediatorem uitae*) and in his humility raises the obedient, humble, and lowly to life. Drawing upon 1 Cor 15:21, Augustine discerns a penal-substitutionary dimension to the atonement:

> The mediator of life, showing that death, which cannot now be avoided by human condition, is not to be feared. Rather, godlessness, which can be avoided by faith, is to be feared. It meets us at the end in which we have come, but not on the road by which we have come. For we come to death through sin, he through justice; and therefore, since our death is the punishment for sin, his death has become the propitiation [*hostia*] for sin.[93]

Augustine presents Christ's mediation as a moral example. He allowed himself to be tempted by the Devil in the desert so that, in overcoming temptation, "he might be a mediator not only through help but also by example."[94] From Col 2:15, Augustine also seems to advocate a kind of "Devil's rights" model of the atonement: "For by his death—by his one and most true sacrifice for us—he purged, abolished, and destroyed whatever there was of guilt, on account of which the principalities and the powers rightfully held us captive in order to make us atone for our guilt."[95] Importantly, each of the three aspects to Christ's mediation mentioned here—as well as the language of "mediation" itself—is grounded in biblical statements about the economy of salvation.

The Inadequacy of Philosophy

The inadequacy of philosophy comes into sharper focus in *Trin.* 4.15.20–4.18.24. Here, the emphasis shifts from a Neoplatonist philosophy—perhaps infused with pagan elements, such as what we might find in Apuleius (and even Porphyry)—to a more intellectual philosophy characteristic of someone like Plotinus. This kind of philosopher thinks "that they can purify themselves for contemplating

---

93. *Trin.* 4.12.15 (CCSL 50: 181): "uitae mediator ostendens quam non sit mors timenda quae per humanam conditionem iam euadi non potest sed potius impietas quae per fidem caueri potest, occurrit nobis ad finem quo uenimus sed non qua uenimus. Nos enim ad mortem *per peccatum* uenimus, ille *per iustitiam*; et ideo cum sit mors nostra poena peccati, mors illius facta est hostia pro peccato."

Augustine also explains the atonement in penal-substitutionary categories using 1 Cor 15:21 in *Civ.* 13.23 (CCSL 48: 405–8) and *Ep.* 166.7.21 (CSEL 44: 575–7).

94. *Trin.* 4.13.17 (CCSL 50: 183): "mediator esset non solum per adiutorium uerum etiam per exemplum."

95. *Trin.* 4.13.17 (CCSL 50: 183): "Morte sua quippe uno uerissimo sacrificio pro nobis oblato quidquid culparum erat unde nos principatus et potestates ad luenda supplicia iure detinebant purgauit, aboleuit, exstinxit." Cf. *Trin.* 13.18.23 (CCSL 50A: 413–14); *Conf.* 7.21.27 (PL 32: 747–8); 9.13.36 (PL 32: 778–9).

God and cleaving to him by their own virtue, such that they are most defiled by pride."⁹⁶ On the basis of Rom 1:20, Augustine recognizes that these philosophers have the ability to understand "the sublime and unchanging substance through the things that were made."⁹⁷ Like Rahner after him, Augustine is willing to entertain the possibility that there are preparations for the doctrine of the Christian God outside of Christianity.⁹⁸

Nevertheless, at the same time, "we ought not to consult the philosophers concerning the succession of the ages or the resurrection of the dead, not even those who have understood, within their capacity, the eternity of the creator in whom we live and move and have our being."⁹⁹ Returning to Rom 1:20, he adds that these philosophers have not glorified God as he is, or given thanks. Rather, by calling themselves wise they have become fools. Since humankind is "unable to attain eternal things, weighed down by the filth of our sins, which we had contracted by our love of temporal things, and which had become almost a natural growth on our mortality, we needed purifying."¹⁰⁰ Only the Son of God who was sent can provide this purification and the faith purification requires. In the mission of the Son, "the eternal allied himself to us in our originated condition, and so provided us with a bridge to his eternity."¹⁰¹ As Levering aptly surmises,

---

96. *Trin.* 4.15.20 (CCSL 50: 187): "Sunt autem quidam qui se putant ad contemplandum deum et inhaerendum deo uirtute propria posse purgari, quos ipsa superbia maxime maculat."

97. *Trin.* 4.16.21 (CCSL 50: 188): "praecelsam incommutabilemque substantiam *per illa quae facta sunt* intellegere potuerunt." Cf. *Trin.* 13.19.24 (CCSL 50A: 415–17); *Conf.* 7.20.26 (PL 32: 746–7); *Civ.* 8.6 (CCSL 47: 224); 8.10 (CCSL 47: 226); 8.12 (CCSL 47: 229).

98. Cf. Rahner, "Der Dreifaltige Gott," 531–3. Gioia outlines the positive reception Augustine affords to Plato's physics, logic, and ethics in book 8 of *De ciuitate Dei* as follows:

> (i) In his account of *physics*, Augustine argues that "Platonists" have found the incorporeality, the immutability, and the simplicity of God and have seen God as the origin of everything which has being [Cf. *Civ.* 8.6 (CCSL 47: 223)]. (ii) Concerning *logic*—which corresponds to epistemology—he credits "Platonists" with the view that "the creator of all things is the light of the mind which makes possible every acquisition of knowledge" [Cf. *Civ.* 8.7 (CCSL 47: 224)]. (iii) Finally, with regard to *ethics*, he identifies Plato's highest good (*summum bonum*) with God [Cf. *Civ.* 8.8 (CCSL 47: 224)].

Gioia, *The Theological Epistemology of Augustine's* De Trinitate, 61.

99. *Trin.* 4.17.23 (CCSL 50: 190): "Ergo de successionibus saeculorum et de resurrectione mortuorum philosophos nec illos consulere debemus qui creatoris aeternitatem *in quo uiuimus, mouemur et sumus* quantum potuerunt intellexerunt."

100. *Trin.* 4.18.24 (CCSL 50: 191): "Quia igitur ad aeterna capessenda idonei non eramus sordesque peccatorum nos praegrauabant temporalium rerum amore contractae et de propagine mortalitatis tamquam naturaliter inolitae, purgandi eramus."

101. Ibid.: 192: "aeterno per ortum nostrum nobis sociato ad aeternitatem ipsius traiceremur." We here adopt the translation of Hill in Augustine, *The Trinity: Introduction,*

without this mission "we could not purify ourselves for worship, and so we could not participate in God the Trinity as we were created to do."[102] This being the case, all that philosophy can really tell us is that there is a simple and immutable God. According to Augustine, traces or hints of the Trinity may be discerned in the created order, but these will be insufficient to purify one's soul for contemplation of the Triune God.[103] By implication, paganism or pagan-infused philosophy will also prove inadequate to mediate between God and man. Importantly, Augustine's conclusion on the philosophers is grounded in biblical statements concerning the economy of salvation. Again, his conclusion on philosophy does not exude "a generosity that would cause offense today" as Rahner suggests.[104]

Conclusion

Rahner requires a doctrine of the Trinity that is thoroughly integrated with Scripture and the economy—and doctrine of—salvation. We have already noted the almost complete absence of attention to the biblical statements concerning the economy of salvation in Rahner's *Der Dreifaltige Gott*. What is perhaps even more surprising is Rahner's neglect of the doctrine of the atonement. As Benner highlights, one would thus expect "a close relationship between his Trinitarian theology and the doctrine of the atonement. However, his belief that God's desire for incarnation motivates God's activity of creation removes the soteriological impetus for the incarnation. His treatment of the economic Trinity is left without any connection either to the atonement or to humanity's need for reconciliation

---

Translation and Notes, ed. John E. Rotelle, trans. Edmund Hill, vol. 5, The Works of Saint Augustine: A Translation for the 21st Century 1 (Brooklyn: New City, 1991), 202.

102. Matthew Levering, *The Theology of Augustine: An Introductory Guide to His Most Important Works* (Grand Rapids: Baker, 2013), 121.

103. Gioia also notes that throughout his exploration of the threefold classification of philosophy ascribed to Plato in *Civ.* 8

> Augustine does not mention the Trinity at all. He rather focuses on the "cause of existence" (*causa subsistendi*), the "principle of reason" (*ratio intellegendi*) and the "rule of life" (*ordo uiuendi*) of everything according to the philosophy he ascribes to "Platonists" and he finds that their answer corresponds to that which Christians know even without the study of Plato's three branches of philosophy. (p. 61)

Gioia identifies a number of other passages that one might consider to defend Rahner's assertion about the philosophers discovering the Trinity (pp. 47–67), but reads these in the light of "the most unambiguous disavowal of the attribution of knowledge of the Trinity to philosophers" in book 11 of *Civ.* (p. 63). Gioia, *The Theological Epistemology of Augustine's De Trinitate*. Cf. *Civ.* 8.8 (CCSL 47: 224–5); 11.25 (CCSL 48: 344).

104. Rahner, "Der Dreifaltige Gott," 533.

with God."[105] This is exacerbated by Rahner's lack of concern for soteriology in the systematic outline in the third section of *Der Dreifaltige Gott*.

Rahner's doctrine of salvation is particularly difficult to crystallize, even in works explicitly dealing with the doctrine. Mansini doubts whether Rahner's Jesus causes salvation at all.[106] Peterson argues that "Rahner's soteriology is a person-centred, representative one, with Christ as the True Human in whom all the blessed freely and eternally participate."[107] Vass notes that Rahner shuns words such as "expiation," "ransom," "sacrifice," and "propitiation," and even discerns similarities between Rahner's soteriology and Hegel's.[108]

Difficult as it may be to pin down, Rahner's soteriology clearly differs from Augustine's and pays significantly less attention to "the biblical statements concerning the economy of salvation." With a few exceptions—such as his doctoral thesis, unpublished until 1999[109]—one struggles to find more than a few biblical references in his most significant soteriological works.[110] Moreover, one finds very little on the doctrine of the Trinity in these works. Conversely, one finds the Scriptures integrated with the doctrines of salvation and the Trinity throughout Augustine's writings.[111] Once again and despite their significant differences,

---

105. Benner, "Augustine and Karl Rahner on the Relationship between the Immanent Trinity and the Economic Trinity," 36.

106. Guy Mansini, *The Word Has Dwelt among Us: Explorations in Theology* (Ave Maria, FL: Sapientia, 2008), 98–9.

107. Brandon R. Peterson, *Being Salvation: Atonement and Soteriology in the Theology of Karl Rahner* (Minneapolis: Fortress Press, 2017), 264.

108. George Vass, *Understanding Karl Rahner: The Atonement and Mankind's Salvation*, vol. 4. A Pattern of Doctrines (London: Bloomsbury, 1998), 17–18.

109. Karl Rahner, "E latere Christi: Der Ursprung der Kirche als zweiter Eva aus der Seite Christi des zweiten Adam; Eine Untersuchung über den typologischen Sinn von Joh 19,34.51," in *Sämtliche Werke*, vol. 3, 32 vols (Zürich, Düsseldorf: Benziger, 1999), 3–84.

110. His most significant soteriological works include Karl Rahner, "Kirchliche Christologie zwischen Exegese und Dogmatik," in *Schriften zur Theologie*, vol. 9 (Einsiedeln: Benziger, 1970), 197–226; Rahner, *Grundkurs des Glaubens*; Karl Rahner, "Kleine Anmerkungen zur Systematischen Christologie Heute," in *Schriften zur Theologie*, vol. 15, 16 vols (Zürich: Benziger, 1983), 225–35; Karl Rahner, "Probleme der Christologie von Heute," in *Sämtliche Werke*, vol. 12, 32 vols (Freiburg im Brisgau: Herder, 2005), 261–301.

111. In addition to *Trin.* book 4, see *Trin.* 13 (CCSL 50A: 381–420); *Tract. Ev. Jo.* 3.18–3.20 (CCSL 36: 28–30); 9.8–10 (CCSL 36: 94–7); 19.10 (CCSL 36: 193–4); 19.18 (CCSL 36: 200–1); 21.10–12 (CCSL 36: 217–19); 22.2–3 (CCSL 36: 223–4); 22.6 (CCSL 36: 226); 22.12 (CCSL 36: 230); 23.14–15 (CCSL 36: 242–3); 27.5 (CCSL 36: 271–2); 34.4 (CCSL 36: 312–13); 76.4 (CCSL 36: 519); 77.1 (CCSL 36: 520); 94.5 (CCSL 36: 564); 97.1 (CCSL 36: 572–3); 121.4 (CCSL 36: 667); *Serm.* 52.4.12–52.4.13 (CCSL 41Aa: 67–8); 53.6.6 (CCSL 41Aa: 91); 53.9.9–53.10.10 (CCSL 41Aa: 95–7); 53.15.16 (CCSL 41Aa: 103–4); 71.15.25 (CCSL 41Aa: 48–50); 71.17.28 (CCSL 41Aa: 54–6); *Ep.* 120 (CCSL 31B: 143–59).

Augustine appears to satisfy Rahner's criteria for a treatise on the Trinity more substantially than Rahner himself does. Augustine's doctrine of the Trinity is more comprehensively integrated with the doctrine of salvation, the economy of salvation, and the text of Scripture. Close attention to Augustine's account also demonstrates that the bishop's penchant for extra-biblical philosophy is drastically less "offensive" than Rahner suggests.

4. Trinity, Missions, and Processions

Rahner on the Missions and Processions

Finally, central to Rahner's axiom is the interconnectedness of the missions and processions. Rahner implicitly traces their detachment to Augustine's (alleged) emphasis on the non-peculiarity of the divine persons and his psychological analogy. As mentioned in the introduction, Rahner argues that if Jesus is not simply God in general but the Son, there must then be at least one mission that is peculiar to him. If this were not true, there would "no longer be any real connection between 'mission' and inner-Trinitarian life."[112] For Rahner, the missions cannot be an afterthought to one's doctrine of the Trinity:

> In order to imagine the content of the doctrine of the Trinity, one can always refer back to the experience of salvation and grace (Jesus and the Spirit of God at work in us), because in it one really already has the Trinity itself as such, then there shouldn't be a Trinitarian treatise in which the doctrine of the "missions" is appended at the end of this treatise at most as a relatively secondary and subsequent comment. Any such treatise should be animated by this doctrine from the start, even if it were only dealt with, didactically, as an explicit topic in itself at the end of the Trinitarian treatise or even only in other sections of dogmatics. One could almost say: the less a doctrine of the Trinity is afraid of being economically beneficial, the more it has prospects of the immanent Trinity to say the real thing and really bring this real thing close to a theoretical and existential understanding of faith.[113]

---

112. Rahner, "Der Dreifaltige Gott," 545: "Zwischen "Sendung" und dem innertrinitarischen Leben bestände dann überhaupt kein wirklicher Zusammenhang mehr."
113. Ibid., 559–61:

> um sich den Inhalt der Trinitätslehre zu vergegenwärtigen, immer auf die heils- und gnadengeschichtliche Erfahrung (Jesu und des in uns wirkenden Geistes Gottes) zurückgreifen kann, weil man darin die Trinität selbst schon als solche wirklich hat, dann dürfte es keinen Trinitätstraktat geben, in dem die Lehre von den "Sendungen" höchstens noch als ein relativ nebensächliches und nachträgliches Scholion dieses Traktates am Schluß angehängt wird. Jeder solche Traktat müßte von vornherein aus dieser Lehre leben, selbst wenn sie didaktisch als explizites Thema für sich erst

The missions must be central, even the "starting point" (*Ansatzpunkt*).[114] This does not mean that he is collapsing the immanent Trinity into the economy. This *Ansatzpunkt* is epistemological rather than ontological. "Basically, this cannot be disputed by any theology, because in the history of revelation it is simply the case that we know about the Trinity because the Word of the Father entered our history and communicated his Spirit to us."[115] Rahner simply begins from the economy because that is where the doctrine is first revealed.

Rahner's insistence on the interconnectedness of the missions and processions is made pointedly clear in his *Trinität* entry in *Sacramentum Mundi*:

> The economic Trinity is already immanent because one could not speak of a self-communication from God if the two missions and the "persons" given for us—in whom we have God—did not belong to God 'in himself' but only to God in the creaturely realm. The "missions" are real (assuming the divine freedom of choice for self-communication) "processions" (*processiones*) in God himself.[116]

Speaking of missions as "processions" or *processiones* in God himself could be misread as making the immanent Trinity dependent on the economy. Later he is even happy to speak of the economic and immanent Trinity as being "identical" (*identisch*). However, it is worth observing his qualifications. First, he assumes divine freedom for the missions. Later he describes the internal "missions" (*Sendungen*) as "possibilities" (*Möglichkeiten*) which "are not to be thought of as potentialities [*Potentialitäten*] that must be actualized [*aktualisiert*] in God."[117] This may sound strange at first glance, but, as shall be seen, it is not all that different from Augustine. Second, when speaking of the economic and immanent Trinity as *identisch*, he qualifies this with references to divine freedom:

> am Ende des Trinitätstraktats oder gar erst in anderen Abschnitten der Dogmatik behandelt würde. Man könnte geradezu sagen: Je weniger eine Trinitätslehre sich scheut, heilsökonomisch zu sein, um so mehr hat sie Aussicht, von der immanenten Trinität das Eigentliche zu sagen und dieses Eigentliche einem theoretischen und existentiellen Glaubensverständnis auch wirklich nahezubringen.

114. Ibid., 573.
115. Ibid.: "Grundsätzlich kann das von keiner Theologie bestritten werden, weil es offenbarungsgeschichtlich einfach so ist, daß wir von der Trinität wissen, weil das Wort des Vaters in unsere Geschichte eingetreten ist und uns seinen Geist mitgeteilt hat."
116. Rahner, "Trinität," 1016: "Die ökonomische T. ist schon die immanente, weil von einer Selbstmitteilung Gottes nicht geredet werden könnte, wenn die beiden Sendungen und die damit für uns gegebenen 'Personen,' in denen wir Gott haben, nicht Gott 'an sich' zukämen, sondern bloß dem geschöpflichen Bereich angehörten. Die 'Sendungen' sind real (der göttliche Freiheitsentschluß zur Selbstmitteilung vorausgesetzt) 'Hervorgänge' (processiones) in Gott selbst."
117. Ibid., 1017.

Of course, this identity does not deny that there is an economic Trinity, as identical [*identisch*] with the immanent one, only because of God's free decision for his (supernatural) self-communication. But borne by this freedom, the gift in which God communicates himself to the world is precisely God as the Triune himself (not something efficiently produced by him that represents him), and in such a way that—because he is threefold [*dreifaltige*]—this "Trinity" [*Dreifaltigkeit*] also determines the giving of the gift and makes it threefold [*dreifaltig*].[118]

The Trinity freely (*Dreifaltigkeit*) chooses to reveal himself as he is, as "threefold" (*dreifaltig*). Third, Rahner also articulates the identity between the processions and missions in terms of *correspondence*: "The two immanent 'processions' in God correspond [*entsprechen*] with the two "missions" (in identity)."[119] Rahner is seeking to preserve the peculiarity of each divine person by emphasizing the correspondence of the missions and processions, but he wishes to avoid undermining God's freedom in the economy.

Augustine's Definition of "Missions"

The interconnectedness Rahner discerns between the missions and processions is not all that different to what Augustine writes at the end of book 4 of *Trin*. Here, Augustine finally comes to terms with the third question raised in 2.7.13: what are the missions? In 4.19.25 he begins to answer this question by turning to the purpose of the missions:

> Look, the purpose for which the Son of God was sent, and, indeed, the Son of God has been sent. Everything that has been done in time to produce the faith, by which we are cleansed for the contemplation of the truth, in things that had a beginning, has been brought forth from eternity and is referred back to eternity, and was either testimony of this mission or the very mission of the Son of God.[120]

---

118. Ibid., 1011:

> Diese Identität bestreitet natürlich nicht, daß es eine heilsökonomische T., als mit der immanenten identisch, nur gibt aufgrund des freien Entschlusses Gottes zu seiner (übernatürlichen) Selbstmitteilung. Aber getragen von dieser Freiheit, ist die Gabe, in der sich Gott der Welt mitteilt, eben Gott als der dreifaltige selbst (nicht ein von ihm effizient Hervorgebrachtes, das ihn vertritt), und zwar so, daß—weil er der dreifaltige ist—diese "Dreifaltigkeit" auch das Gegebensein der Gabe mitbestimmt und diese dreifaltig macht.

119. Ibid., 1012: "daß den zwei immanenten 'Hervorgängen' in Gott zwei 'Sendungen' (in Identität) entsprechen."

120. *Trin*. 4.19.25 (CCSL 50: 193): "Ecce ad quod missus est *filius dei*; immo uero ecce quod est missum esse filium dei. Quaecumque propter faciendam fidem qua mundaremur

Augustine's definition of "mission" is bound up with the salvific work of the incarnate Son, depicted earlier in book 4. The Old Testament theophanies preempt the coming of the Son's mission but are not to be confused with the mission itself. As Ayres surmises, "The visible human nature assumed by the Word is offered so that we might have a faith that may be consummated in the contemplation of eternity when we truly see that which the visible Christ represents."[121] This purpose paves the way for Augustine's transition from the missions to the processions.

The Correspondence of the Son's Mission and Procession

In 4.19.26–4.20.28, Augustine begins to tease out the correspondence of the Son's mission with his generation. If, as the Homoian–Arians claim, being "sent" makes the Son less than the Father, he is only less insofar as he was man.[122] In 4.20.27, Augustine states his own position:

> But if the Son is said to have been sent by the Father in this sense, because one is the Father, the other the Son, this in no way prevents us from believing that the Son is equal, consubstantial, and co-eternal with the Father, and yet that the Son has been sent by the Father. Not because the former is greater and the other lesser, but because one is the Father, the other is the Son; the one is the begetter, the other the begotten; the one is he, from whom the one who is sent has his being, the other is he, who has his being from the one who sends. For the Son is from the Father, not the Father from the Son. Accordingly, it can now be understood that the Son has not only been sent, therefore, because the Word was made flesh, but that he was sent, therefore, in order that the Word might be made flesh, and might fulfill through his bodily presence those things which were written; that he was sent to become a man, because he was not sent according to his unequal power, or substance, or anything which in him is not equal to the Father, but in respect to this: that the Son is from the Father, not the Father from the Son.[123]

---

ad contemplandam ueritatem in rebus ortis ab aeternitate prolatis et ad aeternitatem relatis temporaliter gesta sunt aut testimonia missionis huius fuerunt aut ipsa missio filii dei."
 121. Ayres, *Augustine and the Trinity*, 184.
 122. *Trin.* 4.19.26 (CCSL 50: 194–5).
 123. *Trin.* 4.20.27 (CCSL 50: 195–6):

> Si autem secundum hoc missus *a patre* filius dicitur quia ille pater est, ille filius, nullo modo impedit ut credamus *aequalem patri* esse filium et *consubstantialem* et coaeternum et tamen a patre missum filium. Non quia ille *maior* est et ille *minor*; sed quia ille pater est, ille filius; ille genitor, ille genitus; ille a quo est qui mittitur, ille qui est ab eo qui mittit. Filius enim *a patre* est, non pater a filio. Secundum hoc iam potest intellegi non tantum ideo dici missus filius quia *uerbum caro factum est*, sed ideo missus ut uerbum caro fieret et per praesentiam corporalem illa quae scripta sunt operaretur, id est ut non tantum homo missus

The importance of this excerpt cannot be underestimated. First, this passage is foundational to Augustine's insistence on the peculiarity of the Son. The Son is not sent on his salvific mission as one of three who might have been sent; he is sent because he is "from the Father" *ad intra*. While we cannot establish from this excerpt alone that it would be inappropriate for the Spirit to take on flesh, we can safely conclude that, for Augustine, it would be most inappropriate for the Father to be sent to take on flesh. He is not "from" the Son.

Second, in connecting the mission and procession in this way, Augustine avoids compromising the Son's equality and unity with the Father. He is equal, consubstantial, and co-eternal with the Father precisely because he is the Son, begotten of the Father. This prevents the economic subordination of the Son being read into the divine life, the critique often levelled at Rahner's rule.[124]

Third, like Rahner, Augustine does not restrict the mission to the created temporal realm. Since the Son is sent *in order that* he might be made flesh, his mission is not entirely restricted to his physical incarnation in creaturely time. Or, as Ferri writes, the Son's mission "is not simply identified with the incarnation but is rather the presupposition of the incarnation."[125] The way Augustine teases this out has been the subject of debate. For Schmaus, "Augustine understands the mission to be the eternal procession of one person from the other *combined with* an external manifestation of the emerging person."[126] According to this view, Augustine sees the procession as constitutive of the mission, and thus not entirely distinct from it. According to Schindler, the notion of "procession" does not constitute the "mission" because the "mission" means to be known externally.[127] Schindler also believes that one could not speak of an external mission if this were not preceded by an intra-Trinitarian procession, but does not go so far as to affirm, with Schmaus, that the procession is a constitutive part of the concept of "mission."[128] There is no overlap between the procession and the mission. Ferri argues that

> intellegatur quod uerbum factum est, sed et uerbum missum ut homo fieret quia non secundum imparem potestatem uel substantiam uel aliquid quod in eo patri non sit aequale missus est, sed secundum id quod filius *a patre* est, non pater a filio.

124. Cf. p. 106.

125. Riccardo Ferri, "Le Missioni Divine nel *De Trinitate* di Agostino d'Ippona: Commento ai libri II–IV," *Lateranum*, vol. 82, no. 1 (2016): 70: "La missione del Figlio, allora, non si identifica semplicemente con l'incarnazione, ma è piuttosto il presupposto dell'incarnazione."

126. Emphasis added. Schmaus, *Die psychologische Trinitätslehre des heiligen Augustinus*, 164: "Unter Sendung versteht Augustinus vielmehr den ewigen Heryorgang einer Person von der anderen, verbunden mit einer äußeren Manifestation der hervorgehen den Person."

127. Schindler, *Wort und Analogie in Augustins Trinitätslehre*, 144.

128. Ibid., 164.

Augustine emphasizes that the Word of God is described as "sent" not because he was generated by the Father, but because he manifested himself to humankind. With this we want to establish not an identification, but rather a distinction between generation and mission. Sending is put in parallel with generating (as well as being sent with being generated), but the specific thing about sending consists in "making it knowable."[129]

This best interprets what Augustine describes here in book 4, while doing justice to the bishop's definition of "missions." The mission is distinct from the procession but still reveals and is grounded in the procession. However, Schmaus's interpretation is not entirely without basis. Elsewhere, Augustine writes:

> But to say, "the Son can do nothing on his own" [John 5:19] is the same thing as if he said, "the Son is not from himself." Obviously, if he is the Son he was generated. If he was generated he is from the one by whom he was generated.[130]
> The Father shows the Son what he is doing, and by showing he begets the Son.[131]

For Augustine, what the Son "does" is outward. This is obvious from the surrounding appeals to John 1:3.[132] But this "doing" is the same thing as to say that the Son is not from himself, which is to say that the Son was eternally generated.[133] The

---

129. Ferri, "Le Missioni Divine Nel *De Trinitate*," 71–2:

> Agostino infatti sottolinea che il Verbo di Dio è detto mandato non perché generato dal Padre, ma perché si è manifestato agli uomini. Con ciò si vuol stabilire non un'identificazione, ma semmai una distinzione tra generazione e missione. Il mandare è messo in parallelo col generare (così come l'essere mandato con l'essere generato), ma lo specifico del mandare consiste nel "rendere conoscibile."

Cf. Arnold, "Begriff und heilsökonomische Bedeutung der göttlichen Sendungen in Augustinus' *De Trinitate*," 27–8.

130. *Tract. Ev. Jo.* 20.8 (CCSL 36: 207): "Sed hoc est: *Non potest Filius a se quidquam facere*, quod esset si diceret: Non est Filius a se. Etenim si Filius est, natus est: si natus est, ab illo est de quo natus est."

131. *Tract. Ev. Jo.* 23.9 (CCSL 36: 238): "Pater ostendit Filio quod facit, et ostendendo Filium gignit."

132. *Tract. Ev. Jo.* 20.7 (CCSL 36: 207); 23.7 (CCSL 36: 236); 23.13 (CCSL 36: 242).

133. At this juncture, it may seem that Augustine comes awfully close to collapsing the creator–creature divide. Augustine would likely defend himself against this charge by pointing to his exegesis of John 5:26 and his comments on divine simplicity. Because Augustine understands John 5:26 as referring to the Son's eternal generation, he therefore understands the Son to have "life in himself"; he is "a se." Cf. *Tract. Ev. Jo.* 19.11–15 (CCSL 36: 194–9); 22.9–10 (CCSL 36: 228–30). Augustine argues that the Father's eternal generation of the Son in this way constitutes divine simplicity in *Tract. Ev. Jo.* 23.9 (CCSL 36: 238–9).

precise language of *processio* and *missio* is not used in this context. Nevertheless, this shows a kind of identification between the Son's generation and his economic activity which is close to Schmaus's understanding of Augustine, one that is very close to Rahner's understanding.

Exegetical Support for the Correspondence of the Son's Mission and Procession

More importantly, Augustine also provides exegetical support for the kind of relationship between the missions and processions envisioned by Rahner. In 4.19.26, Augustine returns to Gal 4:4—a favourite text when discussing the Son's mission—as exegetical support for the Son's mission commencing at the virgin birth.[134] This verse explains why the language of "missions" does not apply to the Old Testament theophanies: "How, then, before this 'fullness of time' [Gal 4:4], in which it was fitting for him to be 'sent,' could he be seen by the Fathers before he was sent, when certain angelic visions were shown to them, if he could not be seen as he is, equal to the Father, even after he had already been sent?"[135] It is not appropriate to understand the Son as having been sent in the Old Testament, prior to the virgin birth, because it was not yet the "fullness of time."

In 4.20.27, the bishop's argument for the Son's mission paralleling his procession is explained in the language of John's prologue and with reference to Wisdom 7. The Word is the one "through whom all things were made" (John 1:3) and the "Word *became* flesh" (John 1:14). "Word" is not a title only fitting in the economy, but proper to who he is. Therefore, he must have been sent "in order for the Word to become flesh, and by his bodily presence to do all that was written."[136] Thus, his sending precedes his taking flesh. Augustine then uses Wisdom 7 to defend the propriety of the Son's being sent while still being consubstantial, co-eternal, and co-equal with the Father, as well as the way the Son appeared in the Old Testament. Because the Son is "the pure outflow of the glory of God almighty" (Wis 7:25), it makes sense that "what flows out and what it flows out from are of one and the same substance."[137] The Father and Son are consubstantial. Because the Son (or "Wisdom") "is the brightness of eternal light" (Wis 7:26), it follows that the Son is

---

134. Cf. *Trin.* 1.11.22 (CCSL 50: 60–1); 2.5.8 (CCSL 50: 89); 2.5.9 (CCSL 50: 90); 2.7.12 (CCSL 50: 97); 3.proem.3 (CCSL 50: 128); 4.7.11 (CCSL 50: 175); 4.20.28 (CCSL 50: 198); 4.20.30 (CCSL 50: 201); 15.28.51 (CCSL 50A: 534); *Tract. Ev. Jo.* 3.2 (CCSL 36: 20); 8.9 (CCSL 36: 88); 28.5 (CCSL 36: 279); 31.5 (CCSL 36: 296); 104.2 (CCSL 36: 602); 124.5 (CCSL 36: 684); *Serm.* 52.4.9 (CCSL 41Aa: 65); 52.4.11 (CCSL 41Aa: 66); 69.3.4 (CCSL 41Aa: 464) *Ep.* 140.6 (CSEL 44: 158); *Arian.* 6.6 (CCSL 87A: 192).

135. *Trin.* 4.19.26 (CCSL 50: 194): "Quomodo ergo ante istam plenitudinem temporis qua eum mitti oportebat priusquam missus esset uideri a patribus potuit cum eis angelica quaedam uisa demonstrarentur, quando nec iam missus sicut *aequalis* est *patri* uidebatur?"

136. *Trin.* 4.20.27 (CCSL 50: 196): "ut uerbum caro fieret et per praesentiam corporalem illa quae scripta sunt operaretur."

137. Ibid.: "quod manat et de quo manat *unius eiusdemque* substantiae est."

co-eternal and co-equal with the Father. As this light flows from the Father's light, it cannot be greater or less than the Father's light: "therefore, it is equal [*aequalis est ergo*]." Since Wisdom "inserts herself into holy souls and makes them friends of God and prophets" (Wis 7:27), the Son was able to fill angels and operate through them whatever belongs to the functions they perform. Augustine contrasts this with what happened at the incarnation:

> When the fullness of time came he was not sent to fill the angels nor even to be an angel—except in the sense that he declared the Father's counsel which was also his—nor that he should be with men or among men, since he had already been like this among the patriarchs and prophets; no, it was in order that the Word might become flesh, that is, to become man.[138]

Though confessional biases will cause some to question the legitimacy of Augustine's appeal to the book of Wisdom, as a Jesuit priest, Rahner himself could mount no such objection to the use of a deuterocanonical writing.[139]

In Augustine's *Tract. Ev. Jo.* we find further exegetical support for the interconnectedness of the missions and processions. In his exegesis of John 7:29 we find the sending of the Son grounded in the Son's eternal generation. In *Tract. Ev. Jo.* 31.4, Augustine writes:

> Finally, when he had said, "But the one who sent me, whom you do not know, is true," [John 7:28] to show them from where they could learn what they did not know he added, "I know him myself." [John 7:29] Ask me, therefore, if you want to know him. But how do I know him? Because "I am from him, and he sent me" [John 7:29]. He demonstrated both on a grand scale. "I am from him," he says, because the Son is from the Father, and whatever the Son is, it is from the one whose Son he is. That is why we say that the Lord Jesus is "God from God." We do not call the Father "God from God," but just "God." And we call the Lord Jesus "Light from Light." We do not call the Father "Light from Light," but only "Light."[140]

---

138. Ibid.: 197: "*Cum* autem *uenit plenitudo temporis*, missa est non ut impleret angelos, nec ut esset angelus nisi in quantum consilium patris annuntiabat quod et ipsius erat, nec ut esset cum hominibus aut in hominibus, hoc enim et antea in patribus et prophetis; sed ut ipsum uerbum caro fieret, id est homo fieret."

139. For similar treatment of Wisdom 7, see *Tract. Ev. Jo.* 20.13 (CCSL 36: 211); 21.2 (CCSL 36: 213); 22.10 (CCSL 36: 229); *c. adu. Leg.* 1.11.15 (PL 42: 611); *Ep.* 170.4 (CSEL 44: 625); 238.24 (CSEL 57: 552); *Serm.* 117.8.11 (RBén 124: 241); 118.2.2 (PL 38: 672).

140. *Tract. Ev. Jo.* 31.4 (CCSL 36: 295):

> Denique cum dixisset: *Sed est uerus qui misit me, quem uos nescitis*, ut ostenderet eis unde possent scire quod nesciebant, subiecit: *Ego scio eum.* Ergo a me quaerite, ut sciatis eum. Quare autem scio eum? *Quia ab ipso sum, et ipse me misit.* Magnificate utrumque monstrauit. *Ab ipso*, inquit, *sum*; quia Filius de

According to Augustine, the literary correspondence found in John 7:29—between "I am from him" and "he sent me"—underscores the correspondence between the procession and mission.[141]

We find a similar correspondence in his exegesis of John 8:42:

> "I did not come of myself; he sent [*misit*] me. I proceeded [*processi*] from God and came" [John 8:42]. Remember what we frequently say: he came from him, and he came with him from whom he came. The sending [*missio*] of Christ, then, is the incarnation. Indeed, that the Word proceeded [*processit*] from God is an eternal procession [*procession*]; he does not have a time, through whom time was made.[142]

Again, Augustine detects a parallel between the literary correspondence and the actual correspondence of the mission and procession. Of particular significance, the Latin text of this verse brings together the actual vocabulary of *missio* and *processio*. The *missio* corresponds to the *processio*. Exegetes may well question whether John 7:29 and 8:42 actually refer to the Son's eternal procession. Nevertheless, one can hardly argue that Augustine overlooks the "biblical statements about the economy of salvation" when seeking to connect the Son's mission and procession. He certainly affords more attention than Rahner does.

The Correspondence of the Spirit's Mission and Procession

In *Trin*. 4.20.29–4.21.31 Augustine considers the correspondence of the Spirit's procession and mission. The transition from Son to Spirit begins with a definition of "mission" or "being sent" common to Son and Spirit:

> For just as being born means for the Son to be from the Father, so his being sent means his being known to be from him. And just as for the Holy Spirit his being the Gift of God means his proceeding from the Father, so his being sent means his being known to proceed from him. Nor can we say that the Holy Spirit does not proceed from the Son; for it is not in vain that the Spirit of the Father and the Spirit of the Son are said to be the same.[143]

> Patre, et quidquid est Filius, de illo est cuius est Filius. Ideo Dominum Iesum Dicimus Deum de Deo; Patrem non dicimus Deum de Deo, sed tantum Deum; et dicimus Dominum Iesum Lumen de Lumine; Patrem non dicimus Lumen de Lumine, sed tantum Lumen.

141. This is the only citation of John 7:29 in Augustine's entire corpus.

142. *Tract. Ev. Jo.* 42.8 (CCSL 36: 368): "*Non a meipso ueni, ille me misit, a deo processi et ueni*. Mementote quid soleamus dicere: ab illo uenit; et a quo uenit, cum illo uenit. christi ergo missio, est incarnatio. quod uero de deo processit uerbum, aeterna processio est; non habet tempus, per quem factum est tempus."

143. *Trin*. 4.20.29 (CCSL 50: 199): "Sicut enim natum esse est filio *a patre* esse, ita mitti est filio cognosci quod ab illo sit. Et sicut spiritui sancto *donum* dei esse est *a patre* procedere,

These sentences are three of the most important in *Trin.* thus far. As Hill notes, the first two sentences are "the culmination of the whole discussion of the divine missions from book 2 onward. They justify the space devoted to the topic, for they state that it is the missions which reveal the inner core of the Trinitarian mystery."[144] In Rahner's coinage, they announce that the economic Trinitarian relations reveal the immanent Trinitarian relations. Ayres suggests that Augustine's treatment of the Spirit offers no indication of how the Spirit's mission "*uniquely* reveals the Spirit's relationship to the Father" (emphasis in original).[145] However, in view of the third sentence, we can at least say that the peculiarity of the Son and Spirit in Augustine's thought is bolstered. If the Spirit's "being sent" by Father and Son is grounded in his procession from both the Father and the Son, it is difficult to see how—in Augustine's thought—the Spirit could be sent prior to the Son for the purpose of taking on flesh. Augustine is saying that the two missions reveal and are ultimately grounded in the two processions.

The tight correlation Augustine envisions between the Spirit's procession and mission is perhaps most acute in his ninety-ninth tractate on John's Gospel:

> So then, we ought to accept what has been said of the Holy Spirit. "For he will not speak of himself; but whatever he will hear, he will speak" [John 16:13], so that we may understand that he is not of himself. For the Father alone is not of another. The Son was born of the Father, and the Holy Spirit proceeds from the Father, but the Father is neither born of another, nor will he proceed. Nor is there any disparity in that supreme Trinity that should occur to human thought. For the Son is equal to the one from whom he was born, and the Holy Spirit is equal to the one from whom he proceeds. ... Therefore "he will not speak of himself" because he is not of himself. "But whatever he will hear, he will speak"; he will hear from him from whom he proceeds. To hear him is to know, but to know is to be, as was discussed earlier. Since, therefore, he is not of himself but of him from whom he proceeds, and his knowledge is of him of whom his essence is, therefore from him is his hearing, which is nothing other than his knowledge.[146]

---

ita mitti est cognosci quod ab illo procedat. Nec possumus dicere quod spiritus sanctus et a filio non procedat; neque enim frustra idem spiritus et *patris et filii spiritus* dicitur."

144. Hill, comments in *The Trinity: Introduction, Translation and Notes*, by Augustine, 218, n. 96.

145. Ayres, *Augustine and the Trinity*, 186.

146. *Tract. Ev. Jo.* 99.4 (CCSL 36: 584–5):

> Sic itaque debemus accipere quod de spiritu sancto dictum est: *Non enim loquetur a semetipso, sed quaecumque audiet, loquetur,* ut intellegamus non eum esse a semetipso. Pater quippe solus de alio non est. Nam et filius de patre natus est, et spiritus sanctus de patre procedit; pater autem nec natus est de alio, nec procedet. Nec ideo sane aliqua disparilitas in summa illa trinitate cogitationi occurrat humanae; nam et filius ei de quo natus est, et spiritus sanctus ei de quo procedit, aequalis est. ... *Non ergo loquetur a semetipso,* quia non est a semetipso. Sed

The economic speech of the Spirit is not "of himself" because the Spirit himself is not "of himself" immanently. The Spirit's speech is transferred to him via "hearing." Hearing is the same as knowing and knowing is the same as being. Hence, the Spirit's economic speech is about as close to his ontological being as one can imagine. But far from compromising the equality or simplicity of the Trinity, for Augustine, this tight correspondence between procession and economic activity preserves and is the grounds for both.

Exegetical Support for the Correspondence of the Spirit's Mission and Procession

As with the Son, Augustine grounds the interconnectedness of the Spirit's mission and procession in Scripture. When transitioning from the mission and procession of the Son to that of the Spirit in 4.20.29, Augustine reasons that since the Father and the Son are one (John 10:30), so the sender and sent are one. Since the Spirit is also sent, the Spirit must be one with the Father and the Son. This conclusion is supported by the Johannine comma: "These three are one" (1 John 5:7). The bishop then infers from John 20:22 that the Son's breathing on the disciples was a "symbolic demonstration that the Holy Spirit proceeds from the Son as well as from the Father."[147] Why the Spirit is twice given (here and at Pentecost) is delayed until book 15. Nevertheless, this certainly indicates in no uncertain terms that Augustine detects a strong correlation between the economic and immanent Son–Spirit relationship.

In 4.20.29, Augustine likewise infers from John 14:26 (together with 15:26) that the Son's sending of the Spirit is indicative of the Spirit's eternal procession from the Son:

> What the Lord then says—"Whom I will send you from the Father" [John 15:26]—shows that the Spirit is of Father and of the Son. For even when he said, "Whom the Father will send," he added, "in my name" [John 14:26] … showing that the Father is the origin [*principium*] of the whole Godhead [*diuinitatis*], or if you prefer, the deity [*deitatis*].[148]

> *quaecumque audiet, loquetur*; ab illo audiet a quo procedit. Audire illi scire est; scire uero esse, sicut superius disputatum est. Quia ergo non est a semetipso, sed ab illo a quo procedit, a quo illi est essentia, ab illo scientia; ab illo igitur audientia, quod nihil est aliud quam scientia.

147. *Trin.* 4.20.29 (CCSL 50: 200): "demonstratio per congruam significationem non tantum *a patre* sed *et a filio* procedere spiritum sanctum." Augustine makes the same argument from John 20:22 in *Tract. Ev. Jo.* 99.7 (CCSL 36: 586) and *Maxim.* 2.14.1 (CCSL 87A: 568).

148. *Trin.* 4.20.29 (CCSL 50: 200): "Quod ergo ait dominus: *Quem ego mittam uobis a patre*, ostendit *spiritum* et *patris* et *filii*. Quia etiam cum dixisset: *Quem mittet pater*, addidit *in nomine meo* … uidelicet ostendens quod totius diuinitatis uel si melius dicitur deitatis principium pater est."

When later commenting on John 15:26 in book 5, the Son is described as the *principium* of the Spirit: "It must be admitted that the Father and Son are the origin [*principium*] of the Holy Spirit; not two origins, but just as Father and Son are one God, and with reference to creation one creator and one Lord, so relative to the Holy Spirit they are one origin [*principium*]."[149] This lays the theological foundation for the controversial addition of the *Filioque* to the Niceno-Constantinopolitan Creed in subsequent centuries.[150]

In his exegesis of John 5:26 in book 15, Augustine grounds the Spirit's procession from the Son in eternal generation, thus establishing the Father as the person from whom the Spirit principally (*principaliter*) proceeds. He writes:

> And anyone who can understand that when the Son says, "As the Father has life in himself, so he has given the Son to have life in himself" [John 5:26], he means but that the Father had begotten him without time, that the life which the Father gave to the Son when begetting should be co-eternal with the life of the Father who gave; let him understand that just as the Father has in himself that the Holy Spirit proceeds from him, so he has given to the Son that the same Holy Spirit proceeds from him in eternity. And so it is said that the Holy Spirit proceeds from the Father, that it may be understood that what proceeds from the Son is something which the Son has from the Father. For if the Son has whatever he has from the Father, he has from the Father that the Holy Spirit also proceeds from him. … But the Son is born of the Father and the Holy Spirit is from the Father principally [*principaliter*], and since the Father gives without any interval of time, he proceeds from both [*utroque*] in a general way.[151]

---

149. *Trin.* 5.14.15 (CCSL 50: 223): "fatendum est patrem et filium principium esse spiritus sancti, non duo principia, sed sicut pater et filius *unus deus* et ad creaturam relatiue *unus creator* et *unus dominus*, sic relatiue ad spiritum sanctum unum principium sicut *unus creator* et *unus deominus*."

150. In Augustine's time, the Niceno–Constantinopolitan Creed was still recited without the *Filioque*.

151. *Trin.* 15.26.47 (CCSL 50A: 529):

> Et qui potest intellegere in eo quod ait filius: *Sicut habet pater uitam in semetipso* sic dedit filio uitam patrem dedisse sed ita eum sine tempore genuisse ut uita quam pater filio gignendo dedit coaeterna sit uitae patris qui dedit, intellegat sicut habet pater in semetipso ut et de illo procedat spiritus sanctus sic dedisse filio ut de illo procedat idem spiritus sanctus et utrumque sine tempore, atque ita dictum spiritum sanctum de patre procedere ut intellegatur quod etiam procedit de filio, de patre esse filio. Si enim quidquid habet de patre habet filius, de patre habet utique ut et de illo procedat spiritus sanctus. … Filius autem de patre natus est, et spiritus sanctus de patre principaliter, et ipso sine ullo interuallo temporis dante, communiter de utroque procedit.

According to Augustine, the Spirit proceeds from both Father and Spirit as one *principium*, but this is only the case for the Son because he has it from the Father, from whom the Spirit proceeds principally (*principaliter*).[152] Coffey helpfully notes that this distinction "shows that though Orthodox and Catholics may differ on the question of the Filioque, they are at one on the more basic question of the Father as the sole 'cause' (αιτια) of the Son and the Holy Spirit."[153] Zizioulas questions whether the expression *principaliter* necessarily precludes "making the Son a kind of secondary cause in the ontological emergence of the Spirit."[154] He argues that the *Filioque* still seems to suggest two sources of the Spirit's personal existence, the Father as primary cause, the Son as secondary cause. Nevertheless, at the very least, we must conclude that the *principaliter* qualification brings the Western model significantly closer to the Eastern model. This comes through extensive reflection on the economy of salvation.

Moments later, Augustine quotes at length from his ninety-ninth tractate on John's Gospel, a sermon on John 16:13–15. In that tractate, Augustine appeals to a host of verses to argue that the one Spirit who is both the Spirit of the Father and of the Son (or of Christ) proceeds from both Father and Son.[155] How can it be that the Spirit also proceeds from the Son? Augustine answers:

> But from the one from whom the Son has it that he is God (for he is God from God), from him he certainly has it that the Holy Spirit proceeds from him as well, and by the same token the Holy Spirit has it from the Father himself that he would also proceed from the Son, just as he proceeds from the Father.[156]

According to Augustine, this cannot mean that the Spirit proceeds "from the Father to the Son." Rather, "he proceeds jointly [*quoque*] from both, although the

---

152. Augustine also uses the term *principaliter* to distinguish the Spirit's unique procession from the Father from his joint procession from the Father and the Son in *Trin.* 15.17.29 (CCSL 50A: 503–4) and *Serm.* 71.16.26 (CCSL 41Ab: 51). Congar notes that Tertullian uses the term in *Prax* 3 (PL 2: 158). Cf. Yves Congar, *Je Crois en l'Esprit Saint: Le Fleuve de Vie Coule en Orient et en Occident*, vol. 3 (Paris: Cerf, 1980), 125, n. 26.

153. David Coffey, "The Roman 'Clarification' of the Doctrine of the Filioque," *International Journal of Systematic Theology*, vol. 5, no. 1 (2003): 6.

154. John D. Zizioulas, "One Single Source: An Orthodox Response to the Clarification on the Filioque," Orthodox Research Institute, 2017, http://www.orthodoxresearchinstitute.org/articles/dogmatics/john_zizioulas_single_source.html (accessed February 10, 2021).

155. Augustine appeals to Matt 10:20; Luke 1:34–35, 6:19, 8:46, 24:49; John 7:16, 15:26, 20:22; Acts 1:8; Gal 4:6; Eph 4:4–6; Rom 8:9–11; Gal 4:6; Eph 4:4–6. *Tract. Ev. Jo.* 99.6–8 (CCSL 36: 585–7).

156. *Tract. Ev. Jo.* 99.8 (CCSL 36: 587): "A quo autem habet Filius ut sit Deus, (est enim de Deo Deus), ab illo habet utique ut etiam de illo procedat Spiritus sanctus; ac per hoc Spiritus sanctus ut etiam de Filio procedat, sicut procedit de Patre, ab ipso habet Patre." Cf. 15.27.48 (CCSL 50A: 529–30).

Father gives it to the Son that he [the Spirit] proceeds from him [the Son] just as he [the Son] proceeds from him [the Father]."[157] The Father gives to the Son that the Spirit should also proceed from him jointly.[158] Regardless of whether or not this avoids the traditional Eastern criticism of the West, we must recognize that, in contrast to Rahner, Augustine is at least trying to reckon with Scripture.

Conclusion

Modern scholars will likely object to certain aspects of Augustine's exegesis, especially concerning the processions. One expects that he will be criticized for inferring from the economic "sendings" to the immanent processions of the Son and the Spirit. Many today suggest that the reference to the Spirit's *processio* in John 15:26 (Gk.: ἐκπορεύεται) should be read as an economic procession, paralleling the Son's "sending" of the Spirit in the same verse.[159] Godet raises the point that ἐκπορεύεται is in the present-tense form, while πέμψω is in the future-tense form.[160] Perhaps this criticism is not as strong as modern biblical scholars contend. But even if one or both criticisms are valid and these verses do not provide a convincing exegetical basis for a tight association between the missions and processions, Augustine is at least *attempting* to use Scripture to connect the missions and processions. His attempt goes well beyond what Rahner offers.

5. Summary

In summary, we have seen that the themes emerging in books 2–4 satisfy three further requirements of Rahner's Trinitarian agenda. First, Augustine pays detailed attention to the Old Testament theophanies prefiguring the manifestation of the Trinity in the New Testament. While it certainly differs from Rahner's account, Augustine's interpretation of the Old Testament theophanies has clear roots in the text of Scripture and—in some ways—the tradition as well. His

---

157. *Tract. Ev. Jo.* 99.9 (CCSL 36: 587): "Spiritus autem sanctus non de Patre procedit in Filium, et de Filio procedit ad sanctificandam creaturam, sed simul de utroque procedit; quamuis hoc Filio Pater dederit, ut quemadmodum de se, ita de illo quoque procedat." Cf. 15.27.48 (CCSL 50A: 530).

158. Augustine employs a similar argument in *Maxim.* 2.14.1. He writes: "The Father begot a Son and, by begetting him, gave it to him that the Holy Spirit proceeds from him as well."

159. This general line of thought is criticized by C. K. Barrett, *The Gospel According to St. John* (Philadelphia: Westminster, 1978), 482; D. A. Carson, *The Gospel According to John* (Grand Rapids: Eerdmans, 1990), 529; George R. Beasley-Murray, *John*, vol. 36, Word Biblical Commentary (Nashville: Thomas Nelson, 1999), 276.

160. Frédéric Louis Godet, *Commentary on the Gospel of John: With an Historical and Critical Introduction*, vol. 2 (New York: Funk & Wagnalls, 1886), 304–5.

attention to the narrative particularities of the theophanies raises significant exegetical objections to the traditional interpretation, objections Rahner does not account for. Second, through attention to the Scriptures, Augustine integrates the doctrines of the Trinity and grace. Moreover, though Augustine is sympathetic to Neoplatonic metaphysics, he does not grant ancient philosophers a knowledge of the Trinity that would cause the kind of offense today that Rahner warns of. In *Trin.* 4 (as elsewhere) the bishop demonstrates the insufficiency of philosophy to grant knowledge of the Trinity. Finally, Augustine's account of the missions and processions exhibits almost precisely what Rahner desires in an account of the Trinity. As Cipriani writes, "Using the language of Rahner, we could say that for Saint Augustine the immanent Trinity corresponds to the economic Trinity, as we only know the Triune God through the saving history of Christ."[161] The parallels articulated by the bishop fundamentally support Rahner's Rule. Moreover, just as we have seen with the seven other themes observed in this and the previous chapter, Augustine's account of the missions and processions pays considerable attention to "the biblical statements concerning the economy of salvation," far more than what is found in Rahner's work. Hence, from these two chapters we can discern eight ways in which Augustine's attention to the Scriptures address the alleged weaknesses in the Augustinian-Western tradition, thus pre-empting many of Rahner's positive proposals. Ironically, Augustine provides the attention to the biblical particularities that Rahner promised but failed to deliver. In the next two chapters, we pivot to consider how Augustine's exegetical reading strategy avoids most (if not all) of the exegetical objections raised against Rahner's Rule. In particular, we will begin to see how the bishop's vision of a tight association between the missions and processions guides this strategy.

---

161. Nello Cipriani, *La teologia di sant'Agostino: introduzione generale e riflessione trinitaria*, Kindle ed. (Rome: Institutum Patristicum Augustinianum, 2015), loc. 679: "Usando il linguaggio di K. Rahner, potremmo dire che anche per sant'Agostino alla Trinità economica corrisponde la Trinità immanente, nel senso che conosciamo la Trinità di Dio solo attraverso la storia salvifica di Cristo."

Chapter 4

THE FATHER-SON RELATIONSHIP: RAHNER'S RULE, CONTEMPORARY OBJECTIONS, AND AUGUSTINE'S EXEGESIS

1. Introduction

In the previous two chapters we have seen that Augustine's exegesis—especially in *De Trinitate* books 1–4—supports Rahner's Trinitarian programme at critical junctures. Several of Rahner's objections to Augustine were called into question and the bishop was seen to have achieved many of the things to which the Jesuit theologian aspired. The bishop's attention to the "biblical statements about the economy of salvation" certainly exceeded that of the Jesuit priest. Chapter 2 included an exploration of Augustine's Christological rules while Chapter 3 finished with a close examination of the tight association Augustine envisions between the missions and processions. In this and the next chapter, we pivot to the exegetical objections contemporary theologians have levelled against Rahner's Rule. Again, it will be seen that the bishop's attention to Scripture comes to Rahner's aid. These chapters argue that through commitment to both his Christological rules and the tight correspondence of the missions and processions, Augustine offers an alternative reading strategy that largely avoids the exegetical difficulties said to challenge Rahner's Rule.

Rahner and Scripture

One familiar with Rahner's doctrine of Scripture and revelation may wonder whether Rahner would find this line of inquiry acceptable. For example, Rahner distances himself from propositional revelation[1] and a miraculous conception of inspiration.[2] At times he disagrees with the literal sense of Scripture.[3] Jowers also suggests that

---

1. For example, Karl Rahner, "Geschichtlichkeit der Theologie," in *Schriften zur Theologie*, vol. 8, 16 vols (Zürich: Benziger, 1967), 67–8.
2. For example, Karl Rahner, "Buch Gottes-Buch der Menschen," in *Schriften zur Theologie*, vol. 16, 16 vols (Einsiedeln: Benziger, 1984), 284.
3. For example, Karl Rahner, "Jungfräulichkeit Marias," in *Schriften zur Theologie*, vol. 13, 16 vols (Zürich: Benziger, 1978), 369–70.

one could argue that a person who marshals biblical texts in support of or in opposition to Rahner's *Grundaxiom* commits a category mistake. For such a person might seem to confuse the *Grundaxiom*, a principle that concerns how one ought to interpret Scripture, with a first-order assertion concerning a state of affairs with which assertions of Scripture may agree or conflict. Scriptural arguments of this nature would manifest only the confusion of their author, not any merits or inadequacies of Rahner's *Grundaxiom*.[4]

However, Rahner regularly characterizes Scriptures as the "*norma non normata*" for theology and the church.[5] Moreover, as has been emphasized throughout this book, Rahner insists that his Rule must do justice to the "biblical statements about the economy of salvation."[6] Thus, Rahner would have to admit that his Rule must be able to withstand significant exegetical objections. Though Rahner's doctrine of Scripture and revelation certainly differs from Augustine's, these differences do not prove decisive. What matters is whether Augustine's scriptural reading strategy, one that has already addressed so many of Rahner's theological concerns, can match exegetical concerns of others with Rahner's theological project.

Defining Rahner's Rule

Before proceeding, it is pertinent that we clarify what Rahner means by his Rule. Jowers lists four of the most common misunderstandings of the *Grundaxiom*. First, Jowers notes that Rahner does not mean to insinuate a "trivially obvious identity."[7] Jowers cites Cary who notes that "Rahner must be claiming more than just the identity of the Father, Son, and Holy Spirit of salvation-history with the three persons of the immanent Trinity; for that is an identity already written into the Creed, which no Trinitarian theology could possibly want to contest."[8] Second, Jowers notes that Rahner does not affirm an "absolute identity" that renders "the distinction between the immanent and the economic Trinity superfluous."[9] Rahner himself states that "the 'immanent' Trinity is the necessary condition of the possibility of God's free self-communication," meaning that the two must

---

4. Jowers, "Test of Rahner's Axiom," 428.

5. For example, Karl Rahner, "Was Ist Eine Dogmatische Aussage?," in *Schriften zur Theologie*, vol. 5, 16 vols (Zürich: Benziger, 1962), 67, 77–9; Karl Rahner, "Exegese und Dogmatik," 85.

6. Rahner, "Der Dreifaltige Gott," 533.

7. Dennis W. Jowers, "An Exposition and Critique of Karl Rahner's Axiom: 'The Economic Trinity *is* the Immanent Trinity and Vice Versa,'" *Mid-America Journal of Theology*, vol. 15 (2004): 166.

8. Phillip Cary, "On Behalf of Classical Trinitarianism: A Critique of Rahner on the Trinity," *The Thomist: A Speculative Quarterly Review*, vol. 56, no. 3 (1992): 367. Cf. Jowers, "Exposition and Critique of Rahner's Axiom," 166–7.

9. Jowers, "Exposition and Critique of Rahner's Axiom," 167.

therefore still be distinguished.[10] Thus, for Rahner—and in contrast with the likes of Schoonenberg, Moltmann, and LaCugna—the two cannot be collapsed into one another.[11] Third, Jowers asserts that Rahner does not view the economic Trinity as "a mere manifestation of the immanent Trinity through the divine acts of salvation history."[12] Rahner states in no unclear terms that the way God behaves toward humanity is "not only an image or an analogy to the inner Trinity," even if it is communicated as free and gracious.[13] Fourth, Jowers states that Rahner does not consider the "correspondence between the eternal Trinity and the Trinity which communicates itself to humanity as merely *de facto* and unnecessary in itself."[14] If "there is a real *self*-communication with a real distinction in that which is communicated as such, that is, 'for us,' then God must 'in himself' ... carry this distinction" (emphasis in original).[15] While there is a mimetic correspondence between the economic and immanent divine relations, this correspondence is not accidental or unintentional.

According to Rahner, the Rule—including the vice versa—implies that

> exactly [*denn*] what is communicated is precisely [*gerade*] the Triune personal God, and likewise the communication (which is given to the creature in free grace), *if* it happens freely, can only be in the inner-divine way of the two communications of the divine being from the Father to the Son and Spirit. Any other communication could not communicate what is being communicated here, since the divine persons are nothing different from their own way of communicating themselves. (emphasis in original)[16]

---

10. Rahner, "Der Dreifaltige Gott," 611: "die "immanente" Trinität die notwendige Bedingung der Möglichkeit der freien Selbstmitteilung Gottes."

11. Piet Schoonenberg, "Trinität—Der Vollendete Bund: Thesen zur Lehre vom Dreipersonlichen Gott," *Orientierung*, vol. 37 (1973): 115–17; Moltmann, *Trinität und Reich Gottes*, 177; Lacugna, *God for Us*, 211.

12. Jowers, "Exposition and Critique of Rahner's Axiom," 167.

13. Rahner, "Der Dreifaltige Gott," 553: "Gott verhält sich zu uns dreifaltig, und ebendies dreifaltige (freie und ungeschuldete) Verhalten zu uns *ist* nicht nur ein Abbild oder eine Analogie zur inneren Trinität, sondern ist diese selbst, wenn auch als frei und gnadenhaft mitgeteilte." Cf. Rahner, "Über den Begriff des Geheimnisses in der Katholischen Theologie," 95; Rahner, "Über die Verborgenheit Gottes," 301.

14. Jowers, "Exposition and Critique of Rahner's Axiom," 168.

15. Rahner, "Der Dreifaltige Gott," 555, note (n.) 35: "Handelt es sich aber wirklich um eine *Selbst*mitteilung, in der im Mitgeteilten als solchem, also 'für uns,' ein wirklicher Unterschied gegeben ist, dann muß Gott 'an sich selbst,' unbeschadet seiner Einheit ... unterschiedlich sein."

16. Ibid., 553:

> Denn eben das Mitgeteilte ist gerade der dreifaltige persönliche Gott, und ebenso kann die (an die Kreatur in freier Gnade geschehende) Mitteilung, *wenn* sie frei geschieht, nur in der innergöttlichen Weise der zwei Mitteilungen des göttlichen

As Jowers surmises, for Rahner, "The immanent constitution of the Trinity forms a kind of *a priori* law for the divine self-communication *ad extra* such that the structure of the latter cannot but correspond to the structure of the former."[17] Hence, the relations between the divine persons in the economy should correspond to their relations in the immanent Trinity. The Father–Son, Son–Spirit, and Father–Spirit relations in the economy always reflect their *ad intra* relations because the former are grounded in the latter. For Rahner, there exists a true, consistent, yet distinguishable correspondence between the economic and immanent divine relations. It is "true" in the sense that the correspondence is both intentional and more than a copy or image. The correspondence is certainly mimetic, but this is not a *de facto* correspondence. It is "consistent" in the sense that Rahner expects the Rule to apply consistently across the "biblical statements about the economy of salvation." By "distinguishable," we mean that, for Rahner, a distinction can still be made between the economic Trinity and the immanent Trinity, though, as the Rule affirms, the former is still the latter and vice versa. References to the Rule over the next two chapters assume this interpretation.

Alleged Difficulties for Rahner's Rule

Though Rahner strongly commends the Eastern approach to Trinitarian theology, he still commits himself to the particularities of the Catholic magisterium. As well as considering "the biblical statements about the economy of salvation," Rahner insists that his Rule must do justice to the "really binding data of the doctrine of the Trinity according to the church's official statements."[18] As such, any application of Rahner's Rule to "biblical statements" must produce results consistent with official Catholic pronouncements, such as those concerning Subordinationism, eternal generation, and the *Filioque*.[19] Rahner's critics cite various exegetical objections to the kind of correspondence he envisions with his Rule. The portrayal of the economic Father–Son and Son–Spirit relationships in various biblical texts is said to be incongruous with the traditional Western conception of the immanent relations. The next two chapters consider how Augustine's reading of these problem texts largely avoids the objections raised. While Chapter 5 explores Augustine's reading of the biblical texts said to challenge Rahner's Rule regarding the Son–Spirit relationship, this chapter focuses on the exegetical issues raised by scholars pertaining to the Father–Son relationship.

Wesens vom Vater an den Sohn und Geist geschehen, weil eine andere Mitteilung gar nicht das mitteilen könnte, was hier mitgeteilt wird, die göttlichen Personen, da diese gar nichts von ihrer eigenen Mitteilungsweise Verschiedenes sind.

17. Jowers, "Exposition and Critique of Rahner's Axiom," 168.
18. Rahner, "Der Dreifaltige Gott," 535: "Gelingt es dort nämlich, mit Hilfe dieses Axioms eine Trinitätslehre systematisch zu entwickeln, die *erstens* den wirklich verbindlichen Daten der kirchenamtlichen Trinitätslehre gerecht wird."
19. Cf. Rahner, "Der Dreifaltige Gott," 574–95.

The main issues for the Father–Son relationship revolve around Subordinationism, reversibility or "reversed subordination," triadic patterns, and the ascension. First, it is alleged that Rahner's Rule requires the Son's economic subordination and obedience to be read into the immanent Trinity, thus producing a kind of Subordinationism inconsistent with the Catholic magisterium. Second, it is suggested that texts speaking of the Father's transfer of authority and power to the Son indicate reversibility or interchangeability in the economic Father–Son relationship. From this, it is suggested that Rahner's Rule invariably results in reversibility, interchangeability, or reversed subordination in the immanent Father–Son relationship. Such a conclusion would be inconsistent with magisterial pronouncements which assume the irreversibility of the Father's eternal generation of the Son (e.g., DS 15, 19, 39, 40, 86).[20] Similarly, third, it is suggested that texts which speak of the Father and the Son's mutual glorification, mutual knowledge and revelation, mutual love and mutual indwelling inevitably result in a reversal in the Father–Son relationship that is incompatible with the immanent Father–Son relationship. Fourth, some argue that the various patterns in which the divine persons are named in certain biblical texts (Son–Spirit–Father, Son–Father–Spirit, Spirit–Son–Father, etc.) constitute alternative economic τάξεις to the Father–Son–Spirit τάξις. As such, an application of Rahner's Rule to those texts naming the Son prior to the Father would result in a reversal of the immanent Father–Son relationship. Fifth, it is suggested that no "eternal analogue" can be found for the Son's ascension to the Father. Thus, many argue that applying Rahner's Rule to certain economic occurrences produce results inconsistent with Western (and even Nicene) orthodoxy.

Preview

It became apparent in the previous chapter that Augustine discerns a tight association between the missions and processions, one that fundamentally supports Rahner's Rule.[21] This chapter considers the extent to which Augustine's conception of this association can account for the kinds of exegetical difficulties mentioned earlier. It argues that Augustine offers a reading strategy that largely avoids these difficulties perceived to result from an application of Rahner's Rule to the Father–Son relationship. In what follows, we consider how Augustine handles various exegetical difficulties, branching out from *Trin.* to consider his treatment of relevant passages across his entire corpus. Given the relative lack of interest in Augustine's exegesis, engagement with Augustinian scholars will be less than might be desired. Though in some cases his treatment of certain texts will be irrelevant to the task at hand, a consistent picture will emerge from the analysis of his exegesis of the considerable number of relevant biblical citations or allusions.

20. Cf. p. 13.
21. Cf. pp. 88–99.

The economic references to the Father–Son relationship reflect the τάξις of this relationship *ad intra*. Thus, Augustine's attention to Scripture supports Rahner's programme yet again.

2. Subordinationism

The Problem of Subordinationism

Perhaps the most serious criticism of Rahner's Trinitarianism is its alleged predisposition towards Subordinationism. According to Giles, there is no support for "the claim that Rahner believed in a hierarchically ordered Trinity where the Son is set under the Father."[22] At one point Rahner asks whether the term "Son" simply refers to eternal generation or "whether from the synoptic Jesus' concept of the Son we must eliminate his relationship of obedience, his adoration, and his subjection from the incomprehensible will of the Father?"[23] For Rahner, these concepts are to be understood as properties (*Eigenschaften*) of the Son, though not constitutive moments (*konstitutive Momente*) of his Sonship. Pages earlier Rahner describe Subordinationism as an error (*Mißverständnis*) akin to Tritheism or Modalism,[24] so whatever he means later, it is unlikely that he means a kind of ontological subordination of the Son to the Father. Nevertheless, this is what Benner deduces from the citation earlier.[25] Moreover, Benner argues that Rahner is unable "to avoid Subordinationism as a consequence of his basic axiom."[26] Similarly, according to Sanders, "a consistent exegetical application of Rahner's Rule suggests that Christ's relation of devotion and obedience to the first person of the Trinity is not merely a condition of the incarnation, but belongs to his personal character as the Son of God."[27] This, argues Sanders, produces the kind of ontological Subordinationism Nicaea rejected.[28] Though it does not necessarily follow for Rahner that an application of his Rule inevitably leads to Subordinationism, he does not account for why this might be the case. On this front, the bishop offers a way forward.

---

22. Kevin Giles, *Jesus and the Father: Modern Evangelicals Reinvent the Doctrine of the Trinity* (Grand Rapids: Zondervan, 2009), 266.

23. Rahner, "Der Dreifaltige Gott," 583: "Kann man in der Tat ohne weiteres sagen, daß im Sohnbegriff des synoptischen Jesus sein Verhältnis des Gehorsams, seiner Anbetung, des Untertanseins unter den unbegreiflichen Willen des Vaters auszuscheiden sei?"

24. Cf. Rahner, "Der Dreifaltige Gott," 578.

25. Benner, "Augustine and Karl Rahner on the Relationship between the Immanent Trinity and the Economic Trinity," 35.

26. Ibid., 36.

27. Sanders, *The Image of the Immanent Trinity*, 8.

28. Ibid.

Augustine's Strategy for Preventing Subordinationism

With his *form* rule, Augustine offers a strategy for determining how the economic Father–Son relationship corresponds with the immanent relationship without compromising the Son's equality. His line or argument is summarized most pointedly in 1.11.22:

> Therefore, knowing this rule for understanding the Scriptures about the Son of God, in order to distinguish what resonates in them, according to the form of God [*formam dei*] in which he is, and is equal to the Father, and according to the form of a servant [*forma serui*] which he received and in which he is less than the Father, we will not be confused by the seemingly contrary and incompatible statements in the holy books. For in the form of God the Son is equal to the Father, and so is the Holy Spirit, because neither of them is a creature, as we have already shown; but according to the form of a servant, he is less than the Father, because he himself said, "The Father is greater than I" [John 14:28]; he is also less than himself, because it is said of him that "he emptied himself" [Phil 2:7].[29]

In this section, Augustine goes on to write that the Son is only less than the Father in the *forma serui*, the form in which he was made of a woman (Gal 4:4), does the Father's will rather than his own (John 6:38), and is sorrowful to the point of death (Matt 26:38; Phil 2:8). Read with the following sections of book 1, it becomes apparent that Augustine finds it entirely inappropriate to read any kind of subordination into the Godhead from the Son's economic subordination.

Recent scholarship has challenged this conclusion. Several evangelical scholars have boldly attempted to argue from his discussion of the processions at the end of book 4 that Augustine advocated a kind of "eternal functional subordination," distinct from Subordinationism but encompassing authority and submission within the immanent Trinity.[30] At one point, Ayres (seemingly

---

29. *Trin.* 1.11.22 (CCSL 50: 60):

> Quapropter cognita ista regula intellegendarum scripturarum de filio dei ut distinguamus quid in eis sonet secundum *formam dei* in qua est et *aequalis* est *patri*, et quid secundum *formam serui* quam accepit et *minor* est *patre*, non conturbabimur tamquam contrariis ac repugnantibus inter se sanctorum librorum sententiis. Nam secundum *formam dei aequalis* est *patri* et filius et spiritus sanctus quia neuter eorum creatura est sicut iam ostendimus; secundum *formam* autem *serui minor* est *patre* quia ipse dixit: *Pater maior me est*; minor est se ipso quia de illo dictum est: *Semetipsum exinaniuit*.

30. Bruce Ware, "Equal in Essence, Distinct in Roles: Eternal Functional Authority and Submission among the Essentially Equal Divine Persons of the Godhead," *JBMW*, vol. 13, no. 2 (2008): 52; Wayne Grudem, *Evangelical Feminism and Biblical Truth: An Analysis of More Than 100 Disputed Questions* (Wheaton: Crossway, 2012), 418; John Starke, "Augustine and His Interpreters," in *One God in Three Persons: Unity of Essence, Distinction*

inadvertently) couches Augustine's doctrine of eternal generation in terms of the Son's "dependence" on the Father. When discussing the *from* rule at the start of *Trin.* book 2, Ayres writes that "Augustine's fundamental concern here is to point not simply to the Son's equality to the Father, but to the Son's dependence on the Father, his birth from the Father as one who is equal to the Father."[31] As will be seen in the rest of this chapter, Augustine certainly maintains the irreversibility of the Father–Son relationship. This is the whole point of the *from* rule.[32] However, he deploys the *form* rule to ensure precision in the language he uses to describe this relationship *ad intra*. As Plantinga argues with respect to Augustine's *forma dei* and *forma serui* distinction, "Any subordination relations of Jesus to the Father— surely any statement to the effect that the Father is greater than he—belong to the latter category," the *forma serui*.[33] Augustine is careful to avoid explaining the immanent relationship with language that offers even a hint of Subordinationism, such as "dependence," "authority," "obedience," and "submission," or a qualified kind of "subordination." He must be highly selective in his language to avoid giving ammunition to the Homoian–Arian theologians he seeks to refute.[34]

Though Augustine's ruled reading of Scripture may limit the properties of Sonship that Rahner wishes to preserve immanently (properties which are not constitutive of Sonship), it succeeds in staving off criticisms of Subordinationism. It is unfair to assume that Rahner's Rule automatically and necessarily leads to the heresy of Subordinationism, even if we concede that his brief and peripheral comments on obedience veer slightly in that direction.[35] Rahner ultimately wishes to emphasize the connectedness of the missions and processions, showing that the missions reveal and are grounded in the processions, much like Augustine in *Trin.* books 2–4. What Rahner lacks is a clear strategy for discerning *how* the Scriptures depicting divine economic co-activity reveal immanent coexistence. Augustine's ruled reading of Scripture provides a weighty example of how this can be done. It maintains the interconnectedness of the missions and processions but clearly evades the error of Subordinationism. In this way, Augustine's ruled reading offers a helpful supplement for applying Rahner's Rule without landing in Subordinationist territory.

---

of Persons, Implications for Life, ed. Bruce A. Ware and John Starke (Wheaton: Crossway, 2015), 155–73.

31. Ayres, *Augustine and the Trinity*, 179.

32. See Chapter 2.

33. Cornelius Plantinga, "The Fourth Gospel as Trinitarian Source Then and Now," in *Biblical Hermeneutics in Historical Perspective: Studies in Honor of Karlfried Froelich on His Sixtieth Birthday*, ed. Mark S. Burrows and Oaul Rorem (Grand Rapids: Eerdmans, 1991), 318.

34. For more on the Homoian–Arians, cf. p. 70.

35. Rahner himself would adamantly refuse to equate this with the heresy of Subordinationism. He maintains the Son's equality of nature, substance, and essence and never degrades the Son in status or rank.

3. Reversibility and the Transfer of Authority

The Problem of Reversibility and the Transfer of Authority

A second challenge to Rahner's Rule concerns the problem of interchangeability, reversibility, or "reversed subordination." It is sometimes argued that certain biblical texts depict an economic reversal of the Father–Son relationship as the Father transfers authority and power to the Son. According to Tinkham, a "functional subordination of the Father and Son is most apparent in the complex Pauline passage, 1 Cor 15:24–28."[36] Whereas the content of verses 24 and 28 asserts the Son's "delegation" or "subordination" to the Father, Tinkham argues that the Father's putting "all things under Christ's feet" (1 Cor 15:27) constitutes a "delegation" or "subordination" of the Father to the Son.[37] Pannenberg and Sanders adopt a similar reading of this passage, though with less attention to the textual particularities.[38] Tinkham likewise cites John 3:35, 13:3, and 16:15 as evidence that the Father has "surrendered everything pertaining to the plan of redemption to the Son's authority," thus constituting a "subordination" of the Father to the Son.[39] Gruenler argues from John 5:19–30 that the Father "defers to the Son in giving him all authority to judge. The Father submits to the good judgment of the Son and trusts his judgment completely."[40] Canale cites Matt 28:18 and Phil 2:9 as evidence that the Father's subordination to the Son continues after the ascension, along with references to the Son being seated at the Father's right hand (Heb 10:12–13; 1 Pet 3:22).[41] In addition to these verses, one might also cite Dan 7:13–14, Luke 1:32, Eph 1:10, 20–22, and Rev 2:27 (cf. Ps 2:9) as examples of the Father granting authority to the Son and thus potentially submitting to him. Pannenberg, Sanders, and Harrower suggest that if verses such as these constitute a reversal of the Father–Son relationship in the economy, an application of Rahner's Rule inevitably leads to a reversal in their immanent relationship.[42] Such a reversal would be inconsistent with the traditional doctrine of eternal generation.

In what follows, we consider Augustine's approach to the various texts listed earlier, those directly cited by scholars as well as those parallel passages conveying a similar idea. It is argued that the bishop provides a framework that supports Rahner's Rule without introducing reversibility into the economic or immanent Father–Son relationship. At times, Augustine's exegesis of certain "problem

---

36. Tinkham, "Neo-Subordinationism," 269.

37. Ibid., 270. Cf. Fernando L. Canale, "Doctrine of God," in *Handbook of Seventh-Day Adventist Theology*, ed. Raoul Dederen, Seventh-Day Adventist Bible Commentary Reference Series 12 (Hagerstown, MD: Review & Herald, 2001), 149.

38. Pannenberg 1:328–30; Sanders, *The Image of the Immanent Trinity*, 168.

39. Tinkham, "Neo-Subordinationism," 269.

40. Gruenler, *The Trinity in the Gospel of John*, 37.

41. Canale, "Doctrine of God," 149, 209–11.

42. Pannenberg, 1:328–30; Harrower, *Trinitarian Self and Salvation*, 104–9; Sanders, *The Image of the Immanent Trinity*, 168.

texts" will be irrelevant to our discussion. This is to be expected. Augustine does not always set out with the explicit purpose of demonstrating how these texts correspond with the Son's eternal generation. However, it will become apparent that Augustine never interprets these texts in a way that introduces reversibility or interchangeability into the Father–Son relationship. Conversely, his treatment of these texts regularly assumes and sometimes provides an exegetical basis for the doctrine of eternal generation.

1 Cor 15:24–28

To begin with, Augustine's treatment of 1 Cor 15:24–28 never entertains the prospect that the Father submits to the Son in giving him authority and rule,[43] not even in his extended treatment of the passage in *Trin.* 1.8.15–1.13.31.[44] As Gioia notes, this text was among the apparent Subordinationist texts of the New Testament used to deny the Son's full divinity.[45] Studer adds that this view was championed by Palladius, the Homoian–Arian bishop of Dalmatia. When citing 1 Cor 15:27 in *De diuersis quaestionibus octoginta tribus liber unus*, likely Augustine's response to Palladius,[46] he writes:

> But when it says that "all things are subject to him" [1 Cor 15:27a], as the prophet said in the Psalms [cf. 8:6], "it is clear that it makes an exception of him who has placed all things under him" [1 Cor 15:27b]. The intent is that the Father be understood as having placed all things under the Son (as the same Lord in many places in the Gospel teaches and proclaims), not only by reason of his form as a slave, but also by reason of the principle from which he is and by which he is equal to him from whom he is. For he is wont to refer everything to one principle whose image, as it were, he is, but in him dwells all the fulness of the Godhead.[47]

43. For example, *Tract. Ev. Jo.* 25.2 (CCSL 36: 248); 68.2 (CCSL 36: 498); *Div. quaest. LXXXIII* 69.1–10 (CCSL 44A: 184–96); *C. Jul. op. imp.* (CSEL 85,2: 442); *Coll Max* 14.19 (CCSL 87A: 419); *Maxim.* 1.19 (CCSL 87A: 527); *Civ.* 18.49 (CCSL 48: 647); 19.15 (CCSL 48: 683); 20.22 (CCSL 48: 741); 22.29 (CCSL 48: 859); 22.30 (CCSL 48: 862).
44. *Trin.* 1.8.15–1.13.31 (CCSL 50: 46–79).
45. Gioia, *The Theological Epistemology of Augustine's* De Trinitate, 31.
46. So suggests Studer, *Augustins* De Trinitate, 168–70.
47. *Div. quaest. LXXXIII* 69.6 (CCSL 44A: 190–1):

> *Cum autem dixerit quia omnia subiecta sunt*—dixit hoc utique propheta in psalmis—*manifestum quia praeter eum qui subiecit illi omnia*, patrem uult intellegi omnia filio subiecisse, sicut multis locis idem dominus in euangelio commendat et praedicat, non solum propter formam serui, sed etiam propter principium de quo est et de quo aequalis est ei de quo est. Amat enim ad unum principium referre omnia tamquam imago eius, sed in quo inhabitat omnis plenitudo diuinitatis.

Bardy and Mosher suggest that questions 66–75 of *Div. quaest. LXXXIII* were probably written at a time when Augustine was involved in a systematic study of the Pauline letters.

According to Augustine, verse 27 does not speak of a reversed subordination. As the verse clearly states, the Father's placement of everything under the Son "does not include God himself." Rather than viewing verse 27 as an example of reversed subordination, Augustine reads this verse as an economic expression of the Son being "from" the Father in eternity. Hence, contra Tinkham, Pannenberg, and Sanders, Augustine offers a strategy for reading this verse that does not introduce an economic reversed subordination as authority is transferred from the Father to the Son. Rather, he reads the verse as indicative of an irreversible economic Father–Son relationship that parallels their immanent relationship. At the same time, it does not result in the Son's economic subordination being read into his immanent relationship with the Father. To this extent, the bishop's reading of the verse thus supports Rahner's Rule.[48]

John 5:22, 5:26, 5:27; Phil 2:9

Next, Augustine's treatment of John 5:22—considered together with John 5:26 and 5:27 and Phil 2:9 in *Trin.*—does not result in an economic reversal either. Towards the end of *Trin.* book 1, the Son's authority and power to judge is tied to his eternal generation. In 1.12.26–27, Augustine discerns a parallel between the Son's eternal generation and earthly authority. The Son of Man judges not on human authority but on the authority of the Word, the Son of God. The Son of God possesses this authority as the one whom the Father has "given" to have life in himself (John 5:26). The Son of God possesses this authority as the one whom the Father has begotten. There is not a hint of reverse subordination.

A few chapters later Augustine considers the parallel use of the verb "to give" (Lat.: *dedit*) in John 5:22; 5:26, 5:27, and Phil 2:9. In 1.13.29–30, Augustine draws a sharp distinction between the "giving" per eternal generation and the "giving" of temporal authority and judgment to the Son. The Father's giving the Son "to have life in himself" (John 5:26) is not the same as his giving him the authority to judge (John 5:22) and "the name above every name" (Phil 2:9). The former kind of "giving" is immanent, referring to the Son of God in the *forma dei*; the latter is economic, referring to the Son of Man in the *forma serui*. However, though they may be differentiated, Augustine still discerns a strong parallel between these two

---

Around AD 394–95 Augustine composed treatises on Romans (*Expositio quarandum propositionum ex Epistla ad Romanos; Epistulae ad Romanos incoata expositio*) and Galatians (*Expositio Epistulae ad Galatas*). Hence, they conclude that these questions were probably written at a similar time. Gustave Bardy, J.-A. Beackaert, and J. Boutet, eds., *Œervres de Saint Augustin*, Bibliothèque Augustinienne 10 (Paris: Desclée de Brouwer, 1952), 30–6; David L. Mosher in *Eighty-Three Different Questions*, trans. David L. Mosher, vol. 70, The Fathers of the Church: A New Translation (Washington, DC: CUA Press, 1982), 18–20.

48. Admittedly, the transfer of power depicted in verse 24 raises the difficulty of the ascension for Rahner's Rule. How does the Son's return to the Father complement the doctrine of eternal generation? This will be addressed later in the chapter.

kinds of "giving." The Son judges with the Father because the Father has "given" him to have life in himself. The Son judges without the Father because he has "given" judgment to the Son exclusively in the form of man.[49] As the Father gives the Son life, so he gives him judgment. The latter follows and is grounded in the former. The Son of Man's authority and power to judge is not an economic reversal of the eternal Father–Son relationship but an economic expression of it. In fact, as Ferri highlights, the Father gives judgment to the Son in *forma serui* precisely because he is "less than" the Father.[50]

Augustine's exegesis of these verses highlights a difficulty in assuming that the "giving" of judgment and authority constitutes a reverse subordination. If "giving" results in a reverse subordination in John 5:22 and 5:27 and Phil 2:9, why not also in John 5:26? If this were the case, the giving of life in John 5:26 would also constitute a reverse subordination in the doctrine of eternal generation itself. Nobody would assume that the Father's giving the Son "to have life in himself" constitutes a reversal in the Father–Son relationship. As such, why would these parallel "givings" indicate a reversal? It follows much more naturally that the giving of "judgment" and "authority" parallels the giving of "life in himself." Augustine thus provides a framework for interpreting these texts that resists the kind of economic reversal in the Father–Son relationship suggested by Gruenler and Tinkham. Given that the Son in *forma serui* judges precisely because he is less than the Father, Augustine would find it unthinkable that this text could even hint at a reversal in the Father–Son relationship. In fact, by demonstrating how the economic expression of the Father–Son relationship parallels the immanent Father–Son relationship, Augustine provides exegetical support for Rahner's Rule.

John 16:15

Similarly, contra Tinkham's interpretation of John 16:15, Augustine does not see the Son's possession of what belongs to the Father as evidence of the Father handing authority to the Son such that their relationship is reversed. In a passing comment in *Trin.* 2.3.5, the Son's declaration that "everything that the Father has is mine" (John 16:15a) is understood to refer to eternal generation while 15b refers to the Spirit's joint procession from both.[51] As Gioia comments regarding 15a, the Son is able to reveal the Father "precisely because he is equal to the Father and yet from the Father, he is God and yet 'God from God.'"[52] This association comes into sharper focus in *Tract. Ev. Jo.* 100.4.1:

> "Everything," he said, "that the Father has is mine. Therefore, I said that he will receive from me and he will show it to you" [John 16:15]. What more do you

---

49. Cf. *Tract. Ev. Jo.* 19.15 (CCSL 36: 198).
50. Ferri, "Il *De Trinitate* di Agostino d'Ippona: Commento al Libro Primo," 569.
51. *Trin.* 2.3.5 (CCSL 50: 85–6).
52. Gioia, *The Theological Epistemology of Augustine's* De Trinitate, 122.

4. The Father-Son Relationship 113

want? Therefore, the Holy Spirit receives from the Father from whom the Son receives, because in this Trinity the Son is born from the Father, the Holy Spirit proceeds from the Father. But he who is born of no one proceeds of no one, [for he] is the Father alone.[53]

The reception of "all things" is cast in terms of the internal life of the Godhead.[54] The Son receives "all things" through his eternal generation. This strategy is also used to make sense of John 17:10, which speaks of the Son having all that the Father has and vice versa. The Son has what the Father has because he was begotten by the Father; the Father has what the Son has because he begot the Son.[55] John 16:15 need not be interpreted as a reversed subordination. Thus, it is not incompatible with Rahner's Rule, and so Augustine's exegesis comes to Rahner's aid yet again.

Several modern commentators challenge this interpretation of John 16:15, observing that the verse is primarily about the capacity to know and thus reveal the Father in the economy; it is not about the internal processions.[56] Nevertheless, both interpretations highlight that the text can be interpreted in a way that does not imply a "reversed subordination." If Augustine's interpretation is correct and the Son's reception of "all things" refers to his generation, the verse obviously cannot indicate a reverse subordination. Alternatively, if this other modern interpretation is correct, the Son's reception of that which belongs to the Father in 16:15a—specifically, this capacity to know and reveal—can be understood in a manner like Augustine's interpretation of John 5:22 and 5:27 and Phil 2:9 earlier. That is, just as the Father eternally gives the Son "to have life in himself," so the Father has given the Son to have that capacity to know and reveal the Father on earth. It is an earthly reflection of an eternal reality. This need not imply that the Father is somehow subordinate to the Son.

---

53. *Tract. Ev. Jo.* 100.4 (CCSL 41: 590): "*Omnia*, inquit, *quaecumque habet pater, mea sunt; propterea dixi quia de meo accipiet, et annuntiabit uobis*. Quid uultis amplius? Ergo de Patre accipit Spiritus sanctus, unde accipit Filius, quia in hac trinitate de patre natus est Filius, de patre procedit Spiritus sanctus. qui autem de nullo natus sit, de nullo procedat, pater solus est."

54. Augustine offers a similar interpretation of John 16:15 in *Tract. Ev. Jo.* 107.2 (CCSL 41: 613); *Serm.* 135.2.3 (PL 38: 746-7); *Maxim.* 2.9.2 (CCSL 87A: 551); 2.11-12 (CCSL 87A: 558); 2.14.7 (CCSL 87A: 579-81); *Arian.* 23.19-20 (CCSL 87A: 231-2). When citing John 16:15a in *Tract. Ev. Jo.* 49.8 (CCSL 36: 423-4); 99.9 (CCSL 36: 587); *Serm.* 16A (CCSL 41: 228); and *Serm.* 76.3 (CCSL 41Ab: 183), Augustine does not read the verse as a reference to eternal generation, but he does not see it as evidence for a reversed subordination either.

55. *Tract. Ev. Jo.* 104.1 (CCSL 36: 601); 107.2 (CCSL 36: 613-14); cf. *Serm.* 135.2.3 (PL 38: 746-7).

56. For example, Carson, *The Gospel According to John*, 541; Herman Ridderbos, *The Gospel of John: A Theological Commentary*, trans. John Vriend (Grand Rapids: Eerdmans, 1997), 536; Beasley-Murray, *John*, 283.

Dan 7:13–14

Augustine likewise associates the Father's economic "giving" of the kingdom to the Son with eternal generation when citing Dan 7:13–14. In *Trin.* 2.18.33, Augustine attempts to show his Homoian-Arian opponents that the Father also appears in the Old Testament, thus undermining their argument that the Son's visibility insinuates his ontological subordination. He argues that the Ancient of Days, from whom the Son of Man receives the kingdom in Dan 7, is "the one who says to him in the Psalms, 'You are my Son; I have begotten you today; ask of me and I will give you the nations as your inheritance' [Ps 2:7] and he who has 'put all things under his feet' [1 Cor 15:27]."[57] We have already seen that Augustine interprets the handing of the kingdom to the Son in 1 Cor 15:24–28 as an economic expression of his eternal generation. Elsewhere in his corpus, Augustine employs Ps 2:7 as a proof-text for the Son's eternal generation.[58] Thus, in appealing to these two texts to interpret the Son's reception of the kingdom in Dan 7:13–14, it is difficult to imagine Augustine discerning a reversal in the Father–Son relationship.[59] Consequently, Augustine's exegesis seems to be entirely consistent with Rahner's Rule yet again.

Matt 28:18

The bishop's exegesis of Matt 28:18 is likewise consistent with Rahner's Rule. In his debate with Maximinus, Augustine discusses the giving of power to the Son in Matt 28:18. According to Teske, "Maximinus probably takes the fact that the power was given to Jesus by the Father as indicating that it is less than the power of the Father."[60] This is, of course, the complete opposite to the interpretation of those like Canale who discern in the giving of authority a reversed subordination. Nevertheless, Augustine's response is relevant for both assertions. Perplexed by the point Maximinus is trying to make, Augustine states:

> He did not say, "Power has been given to me by my God," did he? If he had said this, it should be clear that it was because of the human form. But because he did not say this, I do not understand what you meant with this. Yes, I understand that you did this so that you might speak more. For if this power was given to him as if by God, the Father gave it to him at his birth, not to one lacking, for

---

57. *Trin.* 2.18.33 (CCSL 50: 123): "ab illo scilicet qui ei dicit in psalmis: *Filius meus es tu; ego hodie genui te; postula a me, et dabo tibi gentes haereditatem tuam*, et qui *omnia subiecit sub pedibus eius.*"

58. *Conf.* 11.13.15 (CCSL 27: 202); *Enchir.* 14.49 (CCSL 46: 75–6).

59. When citing Dan 7:13–14 elsewhere, Augustine is not concerned with the Father–Son relationship. Cf. *Civ.* 18.34 (CCSL 48: 628).

60. Roland J. Teske in *Arianism and Other Heresies*, ed. John E. Rotelle, trans. Roland J. Teske, vol. 1, The Works of Saint Augustine: A Translation for the 21st Century (Hyde Park, NY: New City, 1995), 307, n. 99. Cf. *Coll. Max.* 15.16 (CCSL 87A: 447).

he gave it by begetting him, not by adding something to him. But if this power was given to him as man, what is the matter? Did you perhaps want to call our attention to the fact that the Lord commanded that the nations "be baptized in the name of the Father and of the Son and of the Holy Spirit" [Matt. 28:19]? There you hear one name, but you do not wish to understand one deity.[61]

If Matt 28:18 is specifically about the Father giving power to the Son, it does not make the Son less than the Father. If the power is given to the Son in the *forma dei*, it is through eternal generation. If given in the *forma serui*, it still cannot result in the Son's ontological subordination due to their sharing the divine name in Matt 28:19. For Augustine (and even his Homoian–Arian opponent), it is unthinkable that the Father's giving of power might result in a reversed subordination.[62] If we adopt Augustine's interpretation, Matt 28:18 cannot be used to undermine Rahner's Rule. Hence, the bishop comes to the aid of the Jesuit once again.

Summary

In summary, we have seen that Augustine provides a framework for reading texts purported to result in an economic reversal of the Father–Son relationship. The granting of authority, judgment, and power to the Son can be read as an economic expression of the Father granting the Son to have life in himself. In other words, the transfer of authority to the Son can be read through the lens of eternal generation. Admittedly, Augustine does not attend to every possible verse that could be used to imply a reversal in the Father–Son relationship. For example, when citing texts such as Luke 1:32;[63] John 13:3;[64] Eph

---

61. *Maxim.* 2.16.2 (CCSL 87A: 600):

> Numquid enim ait, data est mihi a Deo meo potestas? Quod si dixisset, propter ipsam humanam formam dictum fuisse ambigi non deberet. Quia uero non dixit, quid isto testimonio uolueris agere, non intellego. Immo intellego te id egisse, ut abundantius loquereris. Si enim tamquam Deo data est haec potestas, nascenti eam Pater dedit, non indigenti, quia gignendo dedit, non augendo. Si uero tamquam homini data est haec potestas, quid habet quaestionis? An forte nos admonere uoluisti, quod baptizari Dominus iusserit gentes in nomine Patris et Filii et Spiritus sancti? Ubi audis unum nomen, et unam non uis intellegere deitatem.

62. In the only other place where Augustine cites Matt 28:18, *Cons.* 3.25.79 (CSEL 43: 384), the bishop does not specifically discuss the transfer of power.

63. *Cons.* 2.5.14 (CSEL 43: 95); 2.5.17 (CSEL 43: 102); *Priscill.* 7.8 (PL 42: 673); *Serm.* 51.11.18 (CCSL 41Aa: 29).

64. Augustine only ever addresses John 13:3, which speaks of the Father "handing all things over" to the Son, in *Tract. Ev. Jo.* 55.3 (CCSL 36: 465) and 55.5–6 (CCSL 36: 465–6). We saw above that Tinkham cites this verse as an example of "reverse subordination." Though Augustine is not concerned with the Trinitarian dimension of the verse in *Tract. Ev.*

1:10,⁶⁵ 1:20–22;⁶⁶ Heb 10:12–13;⁶⁷ 1 Pet 3:22;⁶⁸ and Rev 2:27 (cf. Ps 2:9),⁶⁹ his comments offer little insight one way or the other. However, the strategy considered earlier offers a clear picture as to how he would likely have interpreted these texts if pressed. Augustine's exegesis follows through on his commitment to the tight association of the missions and processions and thus, once again, comes to the aid of Rahner's Trinitarian agenda.

4. Reversibility and Mutuality

The Problem of Reversibility and Mutuality

A third alleged problem for Rahner's Rule concerns those verses that speak of the Father and the Son's mutual glory (13:31–32, 17:1–5), knowledge (Matt 11:27; Luke 10:22; John 10:15), love (John 3:35, 5:20, 10:17, 14:31), and indwelling (John 10:38, 14:10, 17:23). As with those texts considered in the previous section, some suggest that if we read these mutual aspects of the economic Father–Son relationship into the immanent Trinity, we introduce reversibility in the immanent Trinity, and even mutual submission and mutual hierarchy. Dukeman argues that a "hierarchy of the Son over the Father may be seen in the fact that the Father is *dependent* upon the Son."⁷⁰ He cites the mutual glorification in John 17:1–5 as evidence that "the Father is dependent upon the Son's glorious work in order that the Father may be glorified in the world."⁷¹ Harrower, who concurs with this interpretation of John 17,⁷² also argues that the mutual revelation and "knowing" in Luke 10:22 (par. Matt 11:27) produces reversibility in the economic Father–Son relationship.⁷³ Since Jesus is the sole person who reveals the Father, the Father is dependent on the will of the Son. He warns that applying Rahner's Rule to this verse—as well as several of the verses mentioned above—produces a subordination of the Father to the Son that is inconsistent with Trinitarian orthodoxy. For Erickson, the divine persons "are bound to one another in love, *agapē* love, which therefore

---

Jo. 55, one imagines that, if pressed, he would interpret this in much the same way he does the similar phrase from John 3:35 in *Tract. Ev. Jo.* 14.11 (CCSL 36: 148–9).

65. *Praed.* 18.35–36 (PL 44: 986–7); *perseu.* 7.15 (PL 45: 1002); *Serm.* 1.3 (CCSL 41: 4).

66. *Conf.* 9.4.9 (CCSL 27: 138); *C. Jul. op. imp.* 6.37 (CSEL 85,2: 442); *Civ.* 22.18 (CCSL 48: 837); cf. *Div. quaest. LXXXIII* 69.10 (CCSL 44A: 195–6).

67. *Enarrat. Ps.* 109.9 (CCSL 40: 1609); 109.10 (CCSL 40: 1610).

68. *Ep.* 164.10 (CSEL 44: 530).

69. *exp. prop. Rm.* 54 (CSEL 84: 39); *Enarrat. Ps.* 44.18 (CCSL 38: 506); 47.5 (CCSL 38: 542); 47.15 (CCSL 38: 550); 58.1.1 (CCSL 39: 730); *C. litt. Petil.* 2.92.202 (CSEL 52: 254); *cath. fr.* 8.20 (CSEL 52: 254).

70. Dukeman, *Mutual Hierarchy*, 74.

71. Ibid.

72. Harrower, *Trinitarian Self and Salvation*, 54.

73. Ibid., 111.

unites them in the closest and most intimate relationships. This unselfish *agapē* love makes each more concerned for the other than for himself. There is therefore mutual submission of each to the other and a mutual glorifying of one another."[74] It is not difficult to imagine how a similar strategy could be applied to those texts that speak of the mutual indwelling of the Father and the Son (John 10:38, 14:10, 17:23). As we turn to Augustine, it quickly becomes apparent that none of these verses concerning economic Father–Son mutuality need be read as indicative of a reversal in their relationship, such that a parallel cannot be drawn with the nature of their immanent relationship. According to Augustine, a parallel can be discerned between the immanent Father–Son relationship and their economic mutuality. Yet again, Augustine's exegesis supports Rahner's Rule.

Mutual Glorification

To begin with, Augustine discerns an asymmetry in the Father and the Son's mutual glorification that supports Rahner's Rule. Immediately after an important discussion of the processions in 2.3.5, Augustine broaches the topic of reciprocal glorification in 2.4.6. Ayres has demonstrated that Homoian–Arians read the Son's high priestly prayer—"Father, glorify me" (John 17:1, 5)—as proof of the Father being greater than the Son.[75] Following this logic, Augustine determines that the Spirit must be greater than the Son because he also glorifies the Son (John 16:14). "Of course, let them be careful, lest the Holy Spirit should be thought of as greater than both, since he glorifies the Son, who glorifies the Father, yet it is not said that he is glorified by either the Father or the Son."[76] Then, turning to John 17:4, Augustine highlights the folly of suggesting that intra-Trinitarian glorification entails submission or subordination. If one person glorifying another implies subordination, the Father is subordinate to the Son *and* Spirit because the Son glorifies the Father (John 17:4) and the Spirit glorifies the Son (John 16:14).[77] As Ayres surmises, "This mutual glorification ... is founded in the Father's gift of what he is to Son and Spirit."[78] Thus it cannot imply subordination. Augustine likewise states in no unclear terms in *Tract. Ev. Jo.* 43.14 that glorification is not indicative of subordination: "If the Father glorifies the Son and the Son glorifies the Father, set aside your obstinacy, acknowledge their equality, correct your perversity."[79] Mutual glorification points to equality, not subordination.

74. Erickson, *God in Three Persons*, 331.
75. Ayres, *Augustine and the Trinity*, 100–3. Augustine identifies this line of thinking with the Arians specifically in *Tract. Ev. Jo.* 43.14 (CCSL 36: 379).
76. *Trin.* 2.4.6 (CCSL 50: 87): "Sane caueant ne putetur spiritus sanctus maior ambobus quia glorificat filium quem glorificat pater, ipsum autem nec a patre nec a filio glorificari scriptum est."
77. Ibid.
78. Ayres, *Augustine and the Trinity*, 180.
79. *Tract. Ev. Jo.* 43.14 (CCSL 36: 379): "Si et ille Filium glorificat, et Filius Patrem glorificat; pone peruicaciam, agnosce aequalitatem, corrige peruersitatem."

In *Tract. Ev. Jo.* 105,[80] it becomes apparent that this mutuality, though indicative of equality, is not symmetrical. Augustine writes: "The Son was glorified by the Father in the form of a servant, which the Father raised from the dead and set at his right hand, and no Christian doubts that."[81] The real question concerns how the Son can glorify the Father without diminishing nor increasing his divine perfection. Augustine reasons:

> But if the Son had only died and had not arisen, doubtless he would neither have been glorified by the Father nor would he have glorified the Father. But now, glorified by the Father in the resurrection, he glorifies the Father in the preaching of his resurrection. For this is the order of words he himself opens with: "Glorify," he says, "your Son, that your Son may glorify you" [John 17:1], as though he were to say, "Raise me up that you may be made known to the whole world through me."[82]

This mutual glorification is asymmetrical. The Father glorifies the Son by raising him from the dead; the Son glorifies the Father by making him known. The Son prays for the former so that the latter may take place. Drawing on 17:3, Augustine states that this "making known" was the purpose for which the Son was sent.[83] It should now be apparent that, for Augustine, "sending" is grounded in eternal generation. From this, we can assume that the Son's glorification of the Father corresponds with his eternal generation.

As for the Father's glorification of the Son, Augustine later turns to 17:4, where the Son prays, "Glorify me, Father, with yourself, with the glory which I had before the world was, with you." Drawing on Eph 1:4, Augustine reasons: "For if the Apostle said of us, 'As he chose us in him before the creation of the world,' why is it [that is, John 17:4] thought to be averse to the truth, if the Father then glorified our Head when he chose us in him to be his members?"[84] The Father's glorifying the Son is akin to his choosing the elect in the Son prior to creation.

---

80. This tractate was likely written sometime shortly after 419. Cf. Bonnardière, *Recherches de chronologie Augustinienne*, 75.

81. *Tract. Ev. Jo.* 105.1 (CCSL 36: 603): "Glorificatum a Patre Filium secundum formam serui, quam Pater suscitauit a mortuis, et ad suam dexteram collocauit, res ipsa indicat, et nullus ambigit christianus."

82. Ibid.: 604: "Si autem tantummodo mortuus fuisset Filius, nec resurrexisset, procul dubio nec a Patre clarificatus esset, nec Patrem clarificasset; nunc autem resurrectione clarificatus a Patre, resurrectionis suae praedicatione clarificat Patrem. Hoc quippe aperit ordo ipse uerborum: *Clarifica*, inquit, *Filium tuum, ut Filius tuus clarificet te*, tamquam diceret: resuscita me, ut innotescas toti orbi per me."

83. *Tract. Ev. Jo.* 105.3 (CCSL 36: 602–3).

84. *Tract. Ev. Jo.* 105.7 (CCSL 36: 607): "Si enim de nobis dixit apostolus: Sicut *elegit nos in ipso ante mundi constitutionem*, cur abhorrere putatur a uero, si tunc Pater caput nostrum glorificauit, quando nos in ipso, ut membra eius essemus, elegit?"

While Augustine does not explicitly ground the Father's glorification of the Son in eternal generation, he does connect it with the Father–Son relationship in eternity.

In *Tract. Ev. Jo.* 106,[85] the parallel between the Son's glorification of the Father and the doctrine of eternal generation becomes clearer. Augustine reaffirms that the Son glorifies the Father by making him known.[86] Then he turns to John 17:6–8 and reasons that the Son's revelation (by which he glorifies the Father) is given to him from the Father:

> For the Father gave all things at the same time as when he begot the one who will have all things. "Because the words," he says, "which you gave me I have given to them; and they have received them" [John 17:8]; that is, they have understood and kept them. For a word is received when it is perceived by the mind.[87]

According to Augustine, the Son glorifies the Father by revealing him. The Son reveals the Father by speaking words that were given to him from the Father. This "giving" takes place at the same "time" as the Son's eternal generation. Therefore, if we follow Augustine's logic, the Son's glorification of the Father must correspond with his eternal generation. The Father's "giving" to the Son is grounded in generation. Augustine's thought is now distilled into something of an axiom with which he interprets most purported "reverse subordination" texts: "whatever God the Father gave to God the Son, he gave by begetting."[88] In contrast to Erickson, Dukeman, and Harrower, Augustine demonstrates that passages referring to the mutual glorification of the Father and the Son need not imply a kind of mutuality that is inconsistent with the immanent Father–Son relationship. A strong parallel can be discerned between the economic mutual glorification of the Father and the Son and their immanent relationship. Thus, Augustine's perspective on mutual glory is congruent with Rahner's Rule.

Mutual Knowledge and Revelation

Augustine's interpretation of Luke 10:22 (par. Matt 11:27) likewise supports Rahner's Rule. In *Trin.* 7.3.4, the bishop discerns no reverse subordination in the

---

85. This tractate was also written sometime shortly after 419. Cf. Bonnardière, *Recherches de chronologie Augustinienne*, 65–87.

86. *Tract. Ev. Jo.* 106.3 (CCSL 36: 609–10).

87. *Tract. Ev. Jo.* 106.6 (CCSL 36: 612): "Simul enim Pater dedit omnia, cum genuit qui haberet omnia. *Quia uerba*, inquit, *quae dedisti mihi, dedi eis, et ipsi acceperunt*; id est, intellexerunt atque tenuerunt. Tunc enim uerbum accipitur, quando mente percipitur."

88. *Tract. Ev. Jo.* 106.7 (CCSL 36: 613): "quidquid deus pater deo filio dedit, gignendo dedit." In *Tract. Ev. Jo.* 63.3 (CCSL 36: 484), Augustine briefly attends to the mutual glory between Father and Son in John 13:31–32, the other "mutual glory" text. Though his comments on the reciprocity are brief, it is evident that he discerns an asymmetry to this reciprocity.

mutual "knowing" of Father and Son, nor in the Son's delegated "revealing" of the Father. After considering the Son's designation as "Word" prior to space and time, he writes: "'No one knows the Son but the Father, and no one knows the Father except the Son, and to whom the Son wishes to reveal' [Luke 10:22], because the Father reveals by the Son, that is, by his own Word."[89] The Son's revelation of the Father is tied to his identity as the Word. As Word, he is spoken from the Father in eternity. Then he switches to the language of Wisdom:

> Therefore, "Christ is the Power and Wisdom of God" [1 Cor 1:24], because he is Power and Wisdom from the Father who is Power and Wisdom, just as he is Light from the Father who is Light, and the Fountain of Life with God the Father who is of course the Fountain of Life. "Because with you," he says, "is the Fountain of Life, and in your light, we shall see light" [Ps 36:10], because "just as the Father has life in himself, so he has given the Son to have life in himself" [John 5:26].[90]

Here, Christ's revelation of the Father is grounded in his being the Wisdom and Power of the Father, as well as his being the Father's Word. Or, as Ayres surmises, "The distinct Word and Wisdom reveals the Father truly only because the Father has shared all that he is with his consequently consubstantial Son and Image."[91] This identity is grounded in eternal generation. There is no hint of a reversed subordination.

In *Serm.* 68,[92] Augustine discusses the reciprocity of the "revealing" in this text more specifically. The mutuality is once again tied to eternal generation. He argues that the Father and the Son only reveal one another—and can only be acknowledged—precisely because the Father has a Son and vice versa:

> Therefore, if he is only Father because he has a Son, the Father reveals the Son. By the very fact that paternity is recognised in him, the offspring is required; if he is the Father, you ask whom he has begotten; the answer is God the Christ.

---

89. *Trin.* 7.3.4 (CCSL 50: 251): "*Nemo nouit filium nisi pater, et nemo nouit patrem nisi filius et cui uoluerit filius reuelare* quia per filium reuelat pater, id est per uerbum suum."

90. *Trin.* 7.3.4 (CCSL 50: 251–2): "Et ideo *Christus uirtus et sapientia dei* quia de patre uirtute et sapientia etiam ipse *uirtus* et *sapientia* est sicut *lumen de* patre *lumine* et *fons uitae* apud deum patrem utique fontem uitae. *Quoniam apud te*, inquit, *fons uitae, in lumine tuo uidebimus lumen, quia sicut pater habet uitam in semetipso, sic dedit filio uitam habere in semetipso*."

91. Ayres, *Augustine and the Trinity*, 228.

92. Composed *c.* 425–30. Edmund Hill, notes on *Sermons on the New Testament (51–94)*, by Augustine. vol. 3, The Works of Saint Augustine: A Translation for the 21st Century 3 (ed. John E. Rotelle; trans. Edmund Hill; Brooklyn: New City, 1991), 483.

> If Christ is the Son, you ask by whom he was begotten; the answer is God the Father.[93]

Far from constituting a reversal in the Father–Son relationship, Augustine sees the Son's revelation as a function of his eternal generation.
Elsewhere, Augustine specifically addresses the mutual "knowing" in the text. Immediately after citing John 1:18 and Luke 10:22 in *Tract. Ev. Jo.* 31.4,[94] Augustine returns to his sermon text from John 7, stating:

> Finally, when he had said, "But he is true who has sent me, whom you do not know" [John 7:27], in order to show them from whom they could know what they did not know, he added, "I know him" [7:29]. Seek, therefore, of me that you may know him. But how do I know him? "Because I am from him, and he has sent me" [7:29]. He showed them both magnificently. "I am from him," he said, because the Son is from the Father and whatever the Son is, it is from him of whom he is the Son.[95]

According to Augustine, this is why we are able to say that Jesus is "God from God" and "Light from Light." Evidently, Augustine ties the Son's "knowing" the Father to eternal generation. The Son knows the Father because he is "from him," God from God, Light from Light. In *Tract. Ev. Jo.* 47.3,[96] Augustine treats the other mutual "knowing" text, John 10:15, alongside Luke 10:22 and John 1:18.[97] Though brief, he at the very least hints that the Son's knowledge of and capacity to reveal the Father is contingent upon his being "the Only Begotten Son."[98] While Augustine does not comment on *how* the Father knows the Son in either tractate, it is not difficult to imagine what he might say. The Father knows the Son because he begot him in eternity. Augustine demonstrates that "mutual knowledge" and "mutual revelation"

---

93. *Serm.* 68.9 (CCSL 41Aa: 447): "Ergo, si non est Pater, nisi quia Filium habet, reuelat Pater Filium. Hoc ipso, quod in eo paternitas agnoscitur, proles inquiritur; si Pater est, quaeris quem genuit: ipse est Deus Christus. Christus si Filius est, quaeris a quo genitus sit: ipse est Deus Pater."

94. Composed *c.* 419-21. For the dating of *Tract. Ev. Jo.* 24–54, see Bonnardière, *Recherches de chronologie Augustinienne*, 87–117.

95. *Tract. Ev. Jo.* 31.4 (CCSL 36: 295): "Denique cum dixisset: *Sed est uerus qui misit me, quem uos nescitis*, ut ostenderet eis unde possent scire quod nesciebant, subiecit: *Ego scio eum*. Ergo a me quaerite, ut sciatis eum. Quare autem scio eum? *Quia ab ipso sum, et ipse me misit*. Magnifice utrumque monstrauit. *Ab ipso*, inquit, *sum*; quia Filius de Patre, et quidquid est Filius, de illo est cuius est Filius."

96. Composed *c.* 419-21. For the dating of *Tract. Ev. Jo.* 24–54, see Bonnardière, *Recherches de chronologie Augustinienne*, 87–117.

97. This is the only time in his entire corpus that Augustine treats the reciprocal "knowing" of the Father and the Son.

98. *Tract. Ev. Jo.* 47.3 (CCSL 36: 405–6).

texts need not be read as indicative of reversed subordination. In fact, he would have found the idea that the Son's revelation of the Father implies the inferiority of the latter illogical. As Barnes notes, the Homoian–Arians of Augustine's day argued that "the Son's role as revealer of the Father means that the Son cannot be God as the Father is God."[99] As has been seen, Augustine counters by asserting that texts referring to the Son's revelation of the Father should be read as depicting an asymmetry that closely parallels the immanent Father–Son relationship. In this way, Augustine yet again corroborates Rahner's Rule.

Mutual Love

Augustine's treatment of those texts depicting the mutual love between the Father and the Son likewise supports Rahner's Rule. Fundamental to Augustine's discussion of intra-Trinitarian love is the assertion that "God is Love" or "Charity" (1 John 4:8, 16).[100] He famously reaches the conclusion that, "if the charity by which the Father loves the Son and the Son loves the Father ineffably demonstrates the communion of them both, what is more fitting than that he who is the common Spirit of them both should properly be called Charity?"[101] Augustine clearly discerns a reciprocal love in the Father–Son relationship. Coffey observes that Augustine fails to provide "reasonable biblical foundation for identifying the Holy Spirit with the love of God."[102] Curiously, he likewise offers very little consideration of biblical texts that refer more directly to the mutual love of Father and Son in *Trin.* (e.g., John 3:35, 5:20, 10:17, 14:31, 17:24; 1 John 4:7).[103] For this we turn more directly to *Tract. Ev. Jo.*

As Augustine exegetes John 3:35 in *Tract. Ev. Jo.* 14,[104] he considers both the Father's expression of love for the Son and the basis for which he loves the Son. He writes:

---

99. Barnes, "The Visible Christ and the Invisible Trinity," 330.

100. For example, *Trin.* 6.5.7 (CCSL 50: 236); 7.3.6 (CCSL 50: 254); 8.7.11 (CCSL 50: 286); 8.8.12 (CCSL 50: 287); 9.1.1 (CCSL 50: 294); 15.6.10 (CCSL 50A: 472); 15.17.27 (CCSL 50A: 502); 15.17.31 (CCSL 50A: 505); 15.19.37 (CCSL 50A: 513).

101. *Trin.* 15.19.37 (CCSL 50A: 513): "Et si caritas qua pater diligit filium et patrem diligit filius ineffabiliter communionem demonstrat amborum, quid conuenientius quam ut ille proprie dicatur caritas qui spiritus est communis ambobus?"

102. David Coffey, "The Holy Spirit as the Mutual Love of the Father and the Son," *Theological Studies*, vol. 51, no. 2 (1990): 201.

103. Augustine largely ignores the reference to the Father's love for the Son in each of the citations of John 10:17 in *Trin.* 4.13.16 (CCSL 50: 182); *Tract. Ev. Jo.* 47.7 (CCSL 36: 407); *Enarrat. Ps.* 3.5 (CCSL 38: 9); 42.7 (CCSL 38: 479); 86.5 (CCSL 39: 1202); 88.2.10 (CCSL 39: 1242).

104. Composed *c.* 407–8. Bonnardière, *Recherches de chronologie Augustinienne*, 61–2. This verse could also be used as an example of the Father handing over authority to—and thus submitting to—the Son.

> "The Father loves the Son and has placed all things in his hand" [John 3:35]. He added, "He has placed all things in his hand," to let you know here too in what distinct way he said, "The Father loves the Son." What is the reason? … The Father loves the Son, but in the same way as a father loves a son, not as a master loves a slave. He loves him as his only Son, not as an adopted son. And so, "He placed all things in his hand." What does "all things" mean? That the Son should be as great as the Father. For he begot as his equal the one for whom it would not be robbery for him to be, in the form of God, equal to God.[105]

The Father expresses his love for the Son by placing "all things" in his hands. He expresses this love for the Son as a human father loves his son. The expression of this love does not result in an economic or immanent subordination of the Father to the Son. Rather, the Father's expression of this love in placing all things in the Son's hand is equated with the begetting of an equal. The expression of the Father's love for the Son is thus grounded in, and a reflection of, his eternal generation of the Son.[106]

In his exegesis of John 10:17 in *Tract. Ev. Jo.* 47, Augustine recognizes that the Father's love for the Son is tied to his redemptive work:

> "The Father loves me for this," he says, "that I lay down my life to take it up again" [John 10:17]. What does he say? The Father loves me because I die to rise again.[107]

---

105. *Tract. Ev. Jo.* 14.11 (CCSL 36: 149):

> *Pater diligit Filium, et omnia dedit in manu eius.* Adiecit: omnia dedit in manu eius, ut nosses et hic qua distinctione dictum sit: Pater diligit Filium. Quare enim? … *Pater diligit Filium*, sed quomodo pater filium, non quomodo dominus seruum; quomodo unicum, non quomodo adoptatum. Itaque *omnia dedit in manu eius*. Quid est, *omnia*? Ut tantus sit Filius, quantus est Pater. Ad aequalitatem enim sibi genuit eum, cui rapina non esset in forma Dei esse aequalem Deo.

106. Curiously, Augustine ignores the reference to the Father's love for the Son in John 5:20. While the verse is cited in *Tract. Ev. Jo.* 18.9 (CCSL 50: 185); 19.3–4 (CCSL 50: 189); 21.2 (CCSL 50: 212–13); 23.7 (CCSL 50: 236–7); and 23.12 (CCSL 50: 241), this is always to comment on the manner in which the Father "shows" the Son all he does. Augustine equates this "showing" with eternal generation. Like 3:35, this verse contains (1) a statement of the Father loving the Son, (2) a copula, and (3) a description of movement toward the Father that Augustine equates with eternal generation. Thus, if pressed, it seems likely that he would interpret the Father's love here in much the same way as in *Tract. Ev. Jo.* 14.11 (CCSL 36: 148–9).

107. *Tract. Ev. Jo.* 47.7 (CCSL 36: 407): "*Propterea me Pater diligit*, inquit, *quia ego pono animam meam, ut iterum sumam eam*. Quid ait? *Propterea me Pater diligit*: quia morior ut resurgam."

At the end of the tractate, Augustine acknowledges that the Son lays down his life in conformity with the Father's commandment, a commandment that exists within himself by means of his eternal generation:

> "This commandment," he said, "I received from my Father" [John 10:18]. The Word did not receive the commandment by a word, but in the Only Begotten Word of the Father every commandment exists. But when the Son is said to receive what he has in a substantial way, as it was said, "As the Father has life in himself, so he has given to the Son to have life in himself" [John 5:26], since the Son himself is life, his power is not diminished, but his generation is shown. For the Father did not add something to that Son who was born imperfect; but in his begetting, he gave all things to him whom he begot as a perfect being. Thus, he gave him his equality, whom he did not beget unequal.[108]

Through his eternal generation, the Son receives all that he has from the Father, including "this commandment." The Father loves the Son because the Son does what the Father commands. The Son receives the Father's command through generation but this does not result in his subordination. In this round-about way, the Father's love of the Son is once again connected with eternal generation. There is certainly no hint of a reversal in the Father–Son relationship.

Augustine only cites the reference to the Son's love for the Father in John 14:31 (the only verse explicitly stating the Son's love for the Father) in *Tract. Ev. Jo.* 79.2, *Quaest. Hept.* 5.55,[109] and *Coll. Max.* 15.24,[110] the latter two citations bearing no relevance to this investigation. In *Tract. Ev. Jo.* 79, Augustine demonstrates an awareness that the Son expresses his love for the Father in obeying the Father's commandment to lay down his life. Admittedly, Augustine does not dwell on the point for long. However, it is probably fair to deduce that, for Augustine, if (1) obeying the Father's commandment is the Son's economic expression of his love for the Father, and (2) this commandment was received through his generation, then 3) the economic expression of the Son's love for the Father reflects something of his eternal generation. Obviously, for Augustine the love must be mutual and reciprocal. However, there is no sense in which the mutuality of the love indicates

---

108. *Tract. Ev. Jo.* 47.14 (CCSL 36: 412):

> *Hoc*, inquit, *mandatum accepi a Patre meo*. Verbum non uerbo accepit mandatum, sed in uerbo Unigenito Patris est omne mandatum. Cum autem dicitur Filius a Patre accipere quod substantialiter habet, quomodo dictum est: *Sicut habet Pater uitam in semetipso, sic dedit Filio habere uitam in semetipso*, cum Filius ipse sit uita; non potestas minuitur, sed generatio eius ostenditur. Quoniam Pater non quasi ei Filio qui imperfectus est natus, aliquid addidit; sed ei quem perfectum genuit, omnia gignendo dedit. Ita illi dedit suam aequalitatem, quem non genuit inaequalem.

109. *Quaest. Hept.* 5.55 (CCSL 33: 308).
110. *Coll. Max.* 15.24 (CCSL 87A: 461).

a kind of symmetry that implies reversal or mutual subordination as Erickson suggests. The Father loves the Son as *Father*; the Son loves the Father as *Son*. Or, as Ayres writes, "It makes sense only to read him as saying that the Father from eternity establishes the Son as one who is all that the Father is, and as one who loves the Father in and with the love that is God from God and also all that the Father is."[111] Thus, it seems prudent to conclude that, for Augustine, the mutual love of the Father and the Son in the economy reveals and is grounded in the immanent relationship. Hence, the bishop's interpretation of these texts provides exegetical support for Rahner's Rule.

Mutual Indwelling

Finally, Augustine's treatment of texts referring to the mutual indwelling (i.e., *circumincession* or περιχώρησις) of the Father and the Son likewise support Rahner's Rule. Gioia notes that Augustine identifies "love" with "mutual indwelling" when discussing the relationship between God and humanity.[112] Thus one might expect that the mutual indwelling of the Father and the Son might reflect the assymetrical nature of their mutual love. This turns out to be the case, especially in the bishop's exegesis of John 14:10.

According to Schmaus, John 14:10 was often used by the Sabellians and Homoian–Arians of Augustine's era to justify their respective positions.[113] Augustine sought to build upon the work of his Latin forebears to destabilize these readings. Ayres notes that for Hilary, perichoretic language "qualifies continuing pro-Nicene use of the traditional Trinitarian order or *taxis* by insisting that the Father's speaking of the Word and breathing of the Spirit eternally gives rise to three who exist incomprehensibly 'in' one another."[114] Likewise, Ayres writes that for Ambrose, "The notion of existence 'in' one another is used both to argue that Son and Spirit are dependent on the Father, and to show that the Father's acts of generation and spiration without division result in a true sharing of existence."[115]

In his tractate on John 14:7–10 (*Tract. Ev. Jo.* 70),[116] Augustine similarly interprets the mutual indwelling of the Father and the Son through the lens of eternal generation, thus ensuring the distinction and equality of the two. He writes:

> "For as the Father has life in himself," and of course the life that he has is nothing other than what he who has it is, "so has he given to the Son to have life in himself" [John 5:26], since he himself is the same life that he has in himself. But

---

111. Ayres, *Augustine and the Trinity*, 579.
112. Gioia, *The Theological Epistemology of Augustine's* De Trinitate, 136.
113. Schmaus, *Die psychologische Trinitätslehre des heiligen Augustinus*, 114.
114. Ayres, *Augustine and the Trinity*, 50. Cf. Hilary, *Trin*. 8.52 (CCSL 62A: 364–5).
115. Ayres, 51. Cf. Ambrose, *Fid*. 3.11.89 (CSEL 78: 140).
116. Composed sometime shortly after 419. Cf. Bonnardière, *Recherches de chronologie Augustinienne*, 65–87.

will we be the same "life" that he is, when we begin to be in that life, that is, in him? No, of course, because by existing, he, the Life, has life, and he is what he has, and what life is in him, he is in himself; but we are partakers of life, not life itself, and although we shall be there, yet we cannot be in ourselves what he is, but we ourselves, though not the life, may have him as life who has himself as life because he is life. In short, he is both unchangeably in himself and inseparably in the Father.[117]

Through generation the Son receives the "life in himself" that belongs to the Father. Through this transmission of "life in oneself" from the Father to the Son, the Father indwells the Son who thus likewise indwells the Father. Hence, the mutual indwelling of the Father and the Son is a consequence of eternal generation. The Father indwells the Son through begetting, while the Son indwells the Father in his being begotten. The mutual indwelling of the Father and the Son—whether viewed economically or immanently—does not result in a reversal of the Father-Son relationship. Rather, it is entirely consistent with and parallel to the doctrine of eternal generation. Admittedly, as Ayres has pointed out, Augustine does not make extensive use of this perichoretic language.[118] Nevertheless, when he does, it certainly seems to provide further support for Rahner's Rule.[119]

Summary

In summary, we have seen that Augustine provides a framework for reading the "mutual" texts purported to result in an economic reversal of the Father-Son relationship. According to Augustine, the mutual glory, knowledge, love, and indwelling of the Father and the Son does not result in a kind of reversed

---

117. *Tract. Ev. Jo.* 70.1 (CCSL 36: 502–3):

> *Sicut enim habet Pater uitam in semetipso*, et utique non aliud est uita quam habet, nisi quod est ipse qui hanc habet, *sic dedit Filio habere uitam in semetipso*, cum ipse sit eadem uita quam habet in semetipso. Numquid autem nos uita quod est ipse, hoc erimus, cum in illa uita, hoc est in ipso esse coeperimus? Non utique, quia ipse exsistendo uita habet uitam, et ipse est quod habet, et quod uita est in ipso, ipse est in seipso; nos autem non ipsa uita, sed ipsius uitae participes sumus, atque ita ibi erimus, ut in nobis ipsis non quod ipse est esse possimus, sed nos ipsi non uita, ipsum habeamus uitam, qui seipsum habet uitam, eo quod ipse sit uita. Denique ipse et in seipso est inmutabiliter, et in Patre inseparabiliter.

118. Ayres, *Augustine and the Trinity*, 221.
119. Augustine only ever directly cites John 10:38 in *Tract. Ev. Jo.* 48.10 (CCSL 36: 418), and only in passing. Likewise, he only cites John 17:23 ("Tu in me et ego in te") in *Tract. Ev. Jo.* 110.4 (CCSL 36: 624) and *Ep.* 238.28 (CSEL 57: 554), and then, only in passing. The bishop does not read these verses as indicative of reversed subordination. However, one assumes he would likely interpret these two verses as he interprets John 14:10.

subordination that is inconsistent with the immanent Father–Son relationship. Rather, these aspects of the Father–Son relationship reflect and are grounded in the doctrine of eternal generation. Thus, far from undermining Rahner's Rule, by following through on his commitment to the tight association between the missions and processions, Augustine's attention to the biblical witness comes to the aid of Rahner's Rule.

5. Reversibility and Triadic Patterns

The Problem of Reversibility and Triadic Patterns

Next, some discern a reversal in the Father–Son relationship from biblical texts that mention each of the three divine persons, but with the Son mentioned prior to the Father. The ταξις discerned within these texts is said to be incompatible with Latin Trinitarianism, which conceives of the Trinity in the Father–Son–Spirit pattern, the Father begetting the Son and spirating the Spirit together with the Son. Bobrinskoy argues that a "study of the New Testament allows us to discern in it several 'movements' of Trinitarian revelation that complement one another, and all seem to have their inevitability."[120] While the "messianic schema" of Father–Spirit–Son is said to be the primary schema, Bobrinskoy highlights 2 Cor 13:14 as an example of a New Testament schema that places the Son before the Father.[121] For Harrower, the divergent patterns in which the divine persons are mentioned in 2 Cor 13:14, 1 Cor 12:4–6, and Eph 4:4–6 demonstrates "the lack of a consistent order of relations" between the divine persons.[122] Each of these verses mention the Son prior to the Father, thus introducing a reversal into the Father–Son relationship. Consequently, according to Harrower, applying Rahner's Rule to these verses would introduce a reversal into the immanent Father–Son relationship.

In Rodrick Durst's encyclopaedic study of the seventy-five New Testament instances of the three divine persons mentioned within close proximity,[123] three of the six possible triadic patterns place the Son prior to the Father. These include

---

120. Bobrinskoy, *The Mystery of the Trinity*, 65.
121. Ibid., 68.
122. Harrower, *Trinitarian Self and Salvation*, 158.
123. Durst offers three classifications for these seventy-five triadic patterns. The forty-four "Grade A" texts are usually contained within one verse, with no or very few intervening words (e.g., Matt 28:19; 2 Cor 13:14). For the eighteen "Grade B" texts, the triadic usage is usually found with intervening words over two or three verses (e.g., Acts 2:32–33; Eph 4:4–6). The twelve "Grade C" texts contain a triadic pattern over two to five verses with intervening words (e.g., Acts 11:15–17; Rom 8:1–3). Rodrick Durst, *Reordering the Trinity: Six Movements of God in the New Testament* (Grand Rapids: Kregel Academic & Professional, 2015), 74–5.

passages that refer to the divine persons in the order Son–Father–Spirit,[124] Son–Spirit–Father,[125] and Spirit–Son–Father.[126] These passages account for thirty-seven occurrences, or just under 50 per cent of the triadic patterns in the New Testament, compared with the eighteen occurrences of the traditional Western Father–Son–Spirit τάξις, which accounts for 24 per cent of all triadic patterns.[127] If the order in which the divine persons are mentioned is indicative of the immanent τάξις, this poses a significant challenge for Rahner's Rule.[128] As well as doing justice to the Scriptures, Rahner insists that his rule must "do justice to the really binding data of the church's official doctrine of the Trinity."[129] If (1) Trinitarian τάξις can be discerned from word order, (2) there are multiple τάξεις in the New Testament, and (3) economic τάξις reflects and is grounded in immanent τάξις; it should then follow that (4) there are multiple τάξεις in the immanent Trinity, and thus, (5) application of Rahner's Rule to the economic Father–Son relationship produces results inconsistent with Rahner's Latin understanding of the immanent Father–Son relationship. We now consider Augustine's treatment of the various triadic texts outlined by Durst following the Son–Father–Spirit, Son–Spirit–Father, and Spirit–Son–Father patterns. As will be seen, Augustine provides an overarching strategy for interpreting (most of) these thirty-seven texts—one that reflects his commitment to the tight association of the missions and processions—that

---

124. Luke 11:13, 24:49–50; John 3:34, 14:16, 14:25–26; Acts 1:4–5, 2:32–33; Rom 7:4–6, 15:12–13; 2 Cor 13:14; Eph 2:21–22; Heb 2:3–4, 3:1–7, 10:12–15. Cf. Durst, *Reordering the Trinity*, 199–220.

125. Matt 3:16–17; Mark 1:10–11; Luke 3:32, 10:21; John 1:33–34; Acts 2:38; Rom 8:1–3, 15:30; 1 Cor 6:11; 2 Cor 3:3; Eph 2:17–19; Heb 9:14, 10:29; 1 John 5:6–9; Rev 22:17–18. Cf. Durst, *Reordering the Trinity*, 183–98.

126. John 15:26, 16:7–9, 16:14–15; Acts 4:8; 1 Cor 12:4–6; Eph 4:4–6, 5:18–20; 1 John 4:2. Cf. Durst, *Reordering the Trinity*, 265–5.

127. Durst, *Reordering the Trinity*. For other discussions on the triadic patterns in the New Testament, see Tinkham, "Neo-Subordinationism," 266–8; Gordon D. Fee, *God's Empowering Presence: The Holy Spirit in the Letters of Paul* (Peabody, MA: Hendrickson, 1994), 839–942; Robert Letham, *The Holy Trinity: In Scripture, History, Theology, and Worship* (Phillipsburg: P&R, 2004), 63–9; Arthur William Wainwright, *The Trinity in the New Testament* (London: SPCK, 1962), 237–47. It is worth recognizing that the precise number of passages in each category can be disputed. As Giles notes, in "several cases members of the Godhead are mentioned more than once in the one context, and so where one begins and ends, the selected passage determines the answer." Giles, *Jesus and the Father*, 109, n. 71.

128. When briefly discussing Rahner's Rule, Durst recognizes that the Father–Son–Spirit τάξις underlies the other triadic patterns. However, Durst does not conclude that each triadic pattern should be read into the immanent Trinity. Durst, *Reordering the Trinity*, 302–3.

129. Rahner, "Der Dreifaltige Gott," 535: "den wirklich verbindlichen Daten der kirchenamtlichen Trinitätslehre gerecht wird."

is congruent with Rahner's Western conception of the immanent Father–Son relationship.

Son–Father–Spirit Texts

Luke 24:49–50 We begin by considering Augustine's treatment of triadic texts in the Son–Father–Spirit pattern, starting with Luke 24:49–50.[130] Augustine is often more interested in the Son's sending of the Spirit in this text.[131] Nevertheless, we can still discern two points about his conception of the Father–Son relationship. First, Augustine quotes Luke 24:49–50 in *Tract. Ev. Jo.* 99,[132] a foundational text for his understanding of Trinitarian τάξις. As Ayres notes, this tractate "emphasizes the importance of viewing the Father as the cause and source of the Trinitarian communion."[133] Indeed, Augustine repeatedly speaks of the Son's eternal generation.[134] Barnes notes concerning the section of *Tract. Ev. Jo.* 99 where the verses are quoted that the "subject of Augustine's theologizing is again that the Holy Spirit proceeds from both the Father *and the Son*."[135] In other words, the bishop cites these verses in a context in which he is defending his traditional Western understanding of τάξις with respect to the Spirit. When citing Luke 24:49–50, he does not consider the order in which the divine persons are named a serious threat to his conception of the Father–Son relationship, nor the Father–Son–Spirit τάξις.[136] Second, Augustine recognizes that the text speaks of the Son sending the promised Spirit *from his Father*.[137] John 15:26 likewise speaks of the Son sending the Spirit from the Father. This text is foundational to his understanding of economic and immanent τάξις. It indicates (with John 14:26) "that the Father is the source [*principium*] of the Godhead, or if it is better said, of all Deity,"[138] and hence the *principium* of the Son. Given that Luke 24:49–50 mirrors John 15:26 so closely, it is difficult to imagine Augustine discerning a reversed Father–Son τάξις in the Lucan text based purely on word order. At the very least, we can conclude that the Son's being mentioned prior to the Father and Spirit in this verse does not appear

---

130. This text refers to the Spirit only as the Father's promise. Durst includes it as a triadic text.

131. For example, *Tract. Ev. Jo.* 99.7 (CCSL 36: 586–7); *Tract. Ep. Jo.* 2.3 (PL 35: 1389–90); *Serm.* 175.3 (CCSL 41Bb: 528–9); 265D.6 (MiAg 1: 662); 378.1 (PL 39: 1673–4); *Conf.* 9.4.9 (CCSL 27: 138).

132. *Tract. Ev. Jo.* 99.7 (CCSL 36: 586–7).

133. Ayres, *Augustine and the Trinity*, 264.

134. *Tract. Ev. Jo.* 99.2 (CCSL 36: 583); 99.4 (CCSL 36: 584–5); 99.9 (CCSL 36: 587).

135. Barnes, "Augustine's Last Pneumatology," 225.

136. *Tract. Ev. Jo.* 99.7 (CCSL 36: 586).

137. *Serm.* 229.2–3 (MiAg 1: 30–2).

138. *Trin.* 4.20.29 (CCSL 50: 200): "quod totius diuinitatis uel si melius dicitur deitatis principium pater est."

to introduce a reversal into the Father–Son relationship. As such, this triadic text need not be seen to challenge Rahner's Rule.

John 3:34 Likewise, Augustine remains unperturbed by the fact that the Son is mentioned prior to the Father and Spirit in John 3:34. In *Tract. Ev. Jo.* 14,[139] he states: "'For the one sent by God speaks the words of God' [John 3:34]. He is the true God, and God sent him. God has sent God."[140] As we saw in the previous chapter, for Augustine, the Son's being "sent" is an economic extension of his eternal generation. Ayres reminds us that this distinction is crucial to Augustine's "refutation of the Homoian objection that the one who sends must be greater than the one who is sent."[141] It is unlikely that Augustine will reverse his conception of the Father–Son relationship because the Son is mentioned first in this text. He is even more unlikely to do so when the Son is referred to as the one "sent." When Augustine cites John 3:34 in *Tract. Ev. Jo.* 74.3,[142] he does so to discuss the Son–Spirit relationship. However, moments later he refers to the Son as begotten of the Father. Unsurprisingly, the word order in 3:34 does not introduce a reversal into the Father–Son relationship, one that does not parallel Augustine's conception of paternity and filiation. This triadic text poses no challenge for Rahner's Rule. Moreover, the fact that the text speaks of the Son being "sent" is more likely to support Rahner's Rule, given the correspondence the bishop discerns between missions and processions.

John 14:16 Augustine typically comments on John 14:16 when discussing the Spirit's mission rather than the Father–Son relationship.[143] Though he never explicitly discusses the Father–Son relationship directly from the verse, he often discusses their relationship within proximity to citations of the verse. We just saw in *Tract. Ev. Jo.* 74 (his tractate on John 14:15–17) that Augustine never so much as flinches simply because the Son is mentioned prior to the Father. Soon after commenting on John 14:16 in *Trin.* 1.9.19, he concludes: "Yet they are not to be understood as separated from each other because of the unity of Trinity and the one substance and Godhead of the Father and the Son and the Holy Spirit."[144] That is, he rearranges the order in which the persons are mentioned to match the

---

139. Composed *c.* 407–8. Bonnardière, *Recherches de chronologie Augustinienne*, 61–2.

140. *Tract. Ev. Jo.* 14.9 (CCSL 36: 147–8): "Quem enim misit deus, uerba dei loquitur. Ipse est deus uerax, et misit illum Deus; Deus misit Deum." Cf. *Tract. Ev. Jo.* 74.3 (CCSL 36: 514).

141. Ayres, *Augustine and the Trinity*, 181.

142. Composed sometime shortly after 419. Bonnardière, *Recherches de chronologie Augustinienne*, 65–87.

143. For example, *Trin.* 1.9.19 (CCSL 50: 55); *Tract. Ev. Jo.* 74 (CCSL 36: 515–17); *Maxim.* 2.26.14 (CCSL 87A: 691); *Conf.* 9.4.9 (CCSL 36: 138); *Fund.* 6 (CSEL 25,1: 199).

144. *Trin.* 1.9.19 (CCSL 50: 56): "non tamen aliis separatis intelleguntur propter eiusdem trinitatis unitatem unamque substantiam atque deitatem patris et filii et spiritus sancti."

Father–Son–Spirit sequence. For Augustine, the order in which the persons are mentioned is inconsequential. He sees no reason not to revert to the Father–Son–Spirit order when summarizing the fruit of his exegesis. What a text actually says about the relationship of the three is more important than the order in which they are mentioned. Hence, this triadic text need not challenge Rahner's Rule.

John 14:25–26 John 14:25–26 also supports Augustine's conception of τάξις, despite the divergent word order.[145] In his discussion of the *inseparabilis operatio* in *Trin.* 1.12.25, he notes that the Son sends the Spirit (John 16:7) and the Father sends the Spirit in the Son's name (14:25–26). These verses feed into Augustine's argument that both the Son and the Spirit have been sent into the world in which they were previously present. Augustine asserts that the Son sends the Spirit because the Father has enabled him to do so by giving him all that the Father has, citing John 16:15. In other words, the Son is able to send the Spirit because the Father begot him. Thus, it is hardly surprising that Augustine concludes from John 14:25–26 (alongside John 15:26) "that the Father is the source of the Godhead, or if it is better said, of all Deity."[146] As Schmaus indicates, John 14:26 thus feeds into Augustine's account of the Spirit's eternal joint procession from the Father and the Son.[147] Ayres goes so far as to assert that John 14:26, with 15:26, signifies "that Father and Son together send the Spirit who is the Spirit of Father and Son: their sending of the Spirit in the economy of salvation manifests the Spirit's eternal status."[148] Far from introducing a reversal by mentioning the Son prior to the Father, this text proves foundational to his paradigm of Trinitarian τάξις and hence the Father–Son relationship.[149] Augustine interprets this text through the

---

145. The reasoning by which Durst classifies John 14:25–26 as a Son–Father–Spirit text is somewhat suspect. One could easily argue that it better fits the Son–Father–Spirit model. Durst recognizes that "the triadic order is Son–Son–Spirit–Father–Spirit–Son–Son." He goes on to argue that the

> logical reconstruction of the advent of the Counselor is that (1) the Father sent Him, and (2) that sending was upon the request of the Son or in the Son's name. So the initiation is the Son's, the permission or commission is the Father's, and the results are the Spirit's. Jesus intends His disciples to understand the movement of the sending of the Spirit to be Son–Father–Spirit. (Durst, *Reordering the Trinity*, 204)

The fact that Durst must be so selective to reach his proposed ordering highlights a key weakness of searching for Trinitarian order through word order.

146. *Trin.* 4.20.29 (CCSL 50: 200): "quod totius diuinitatis uel si melius dicitur deitatis principium pater est."

147. Schmaus, *Die psychologische Trinitätslehre des heiligen Augustinus*, 165.

148. Ayres, "Spiritus Amborum," 215.

149. Augustine treats the text similarly in *Tract. Ev. Jo.* 77.1 (CCSL 36: 520); 104.1 (CCSL 36: 601); *Arian.* 4 (CCSL 87: 189); *Serm.* 71.20.33 (CCSL 41Ab: 62); *Serm.* 265A.1 (MiAg 1: 392).

lens of eternal generation and thus discerns a parallel between the economic activity in view and the immanent Father–Son relationship.

Son–Spirit–Father Texts

Matt 3:16–17; Mark 1:10–11; Luke 3:22; John 1:33–34 Next, we consider Augustine's treatment of those verses presenting the persons in the Son–Spirit–Father pattern, beginning with the Jordan baptism scene (Matt 3:16–17; Mark 1:10–11, Luke 3:22; John 1:33–34). Ayres notes that Augustine's Latin predecessors, Ambrose and Hilary, treat the baptism scene as evidence for the Son being the Father's "proper Son."[150] His economic sonship in this episode is indicative of his eternal generation. Though Augustine is not usually as explicit as this,[151] his interpretation is at least consistent with his forebears.

In many of his references to the baptism scene, Augustine shows little concern whatsoever for divine order.[152] Though, at other times, Augustine *is* concerned with divine order when addressing this scene, he doesn't allow the order in which the persons are introduced to dictate his conception of divine τάξις. In fact, when referring to the baptism scene in *Tract. Ev. Jo.* 6,[153] Augustine rearranges the order, to match Matt 28:19. He states:

> The Trinity appeared in the most obvious way: the *Father* in the voice, the *Son* in the man, the *Spirit* in the dove. Let us see what we see about where the apostles were sent in the name of this Trinity and what is surprising is what those people do not see. For they do not really see, but close their eyes to what strikes their face. Where were the disciples sent, "in the name of the Father and of the Son and of the Holy Spirit" [Matt 28:19], by the one of whom it was said, "This is the one who baptizes" [John 1:33]? For that was said to his ministers by the one who held this authority for himself.[154]

---

150. Ayres, *Augustine and the Trinity*, 87. Cf. Hilary, *Trin.* 6.37 (CCSL 62: 241–2); Ambrose, *Fid.* 2. *pro.* 2 (CSEL 78: 58).
151. Possible exceptions including *Trin.* 2.10.18 (CCSL 50: 103–5); *Arian.* 4.4 (CCSL 87A: 190).
152. For example, *Trin.* 2.1.2–2.4.6 (CCSL 50: 81–7); *Tract. Ev. Jo.* 4.16 (CCSL 36: 39–40); 10.6 (CCSL 36: 103–4); 99.2 (CCSL 36: 583); *Tract. Ep. Jo.* 7.11 (PL 35: 1442–3); *Serm.* 71.27 (CCSL 41Ab: 52); 210.2.3 (PL 38: 1048); 308A.5 (MiAg 1: 46–7).
153. Composed *c.* 405–7. Bonnardière, *Recherches de chronologie Augustinienne*, 46–51.
154. Emphasis added. *Tract. Ev. Jo.* 6.5 (CCSL 36: 56):

> Apparet manifestissima trinitas, Pater in uoce, Filius in homine, Spiritus in columba. In ista Trinitate quo missi sunt apostoli, uideamus quod uidemus, et quod mirum est quia illi non uident; non enim uere non uident, sed ad id quod facies eorum ferit, oculos claudunt. Quo missi sunt discipuli, in nomine Patris et Filii et Spiritus sancti, ab illo de quo dictum est: *Hic est qui baptizat*. Dictum est enim ministris ab eo qui sibi tenuit hanc potestatem.

4. The Father–Son Relationship

As we shall continue to see, Augustine often rearranges triadic texts to follow the Matt 28:19 pattern. Curiously, he never rearranges these texts to follow other notable triadic texts such as 2 Cor 13:14. In fact, as Kany observes, 2 Cor 13:14 is never cited in *Trin.*[155] and is most likely never cited in his entire corpus. With the exception of Matt 28:19, the order in which divine persons are mentioned is simply of no consequence to Augustine when determining the τάξις of the immanent Trinity.

Augustine certainly recognizes that the order in which the persons are mentioned differs between the Jordan baptism and Matt 28:19. In a sermon preached in Carthage in 397,[156] he states:

> For he was baptized, he came up from the baptism, the dove came down, and the voice resounded from heaven: "This is my beloved Son, in whom I am well pleased" [Matt 3:17]. The Son in the man, the Spirit in the dove, the Father in the voice.[157]

However, this does not cause him to break with the Matt 28:19 order. Moments earlier he has just stated:

> What do we believe? That the Father, the Son and the Spirit do not precede one another by any interval of time. Since, therefore, the Father, the Son and the Spirit do not precede each other by any interval of time, still I was unable to name Father and Son and Spirit without these names taking up time and being contained by their times.[158]

In this excerpt, Augustine mentions the divine persons in the Father–Son–Spirit pattern three times. The divergent order in which the persons are named in the Jordan baptism episode does not cause Augustine to rethink his conception of the Father–Son relationship. Why? Because the order in which the divine persons are mentioned in this text is of little consequence for Augustine's conception of

---

Augustine interprets the baptism scene along similar lines in *Serm.* 52.1 (CCSL 41Aa: 58–9); and 71.27 (CCSL 41Ab: 52–3).

155. Kany, *Augustins Trinitätsdenken*, 481.

156. Cf. Edmund Hill, notes on *Sermons on the New Testament (306–340A)* by Augustine, vol. 9, The Works of Saint Augustine: A Translation for the 21st Century 3 (ed. John E. Rotelle; trans. Edmund Hill; Brooklyn: New City, 1994), 55.

157. *Serm.* 308A.5 (MiAg 1: 47): "Baptizatus est enim, ascendit a baptismo, descendit columba, et sonuit uox de caelo: hic est Filius meus dilectus, in quo bene complacui. Filius in homine, Spiritus in columba, Pater in uoce."

158. *Serm.* 308A.5 (MiAg: 46): "Quid credimus? patrem et filium et spiritum sanctum nullo tempore se praecedere. Cum ergo pater et filius et spiritus sanctus nullo tempore se praecedant, non tamen potui nominare patrem et filium et spiritum sanctum, nisi ista nomina tempora tenerent, et temporibus suis tenerentur."

Trinitarian τάξις.[159] It certainly does not reverse the Son's relationship with the Father in *forma serui* such that it no longer corresponds to his relationship with the Father in *forma dei*.

Acts 2:38 Similarly, Augustine derives no significance from the order in which the divine persons are mentioned in Acts 2:38. Most citations are disconnected from comments on the Father–Son relationship.[160] However, in *Maxim.* Augustine interprets the text through the lens of Matt 28:19. Why does Peter command the Christians to "be baptized in the name of the Lord Jesus" (Acts 2:38) and not the in the name of the Father and the Spirit?

> But they were ordered to be baptized in the name of Jesus Christ without any mention of the Father and the Holy Spirit, and they are, nonetheless, understood to have been baptized "in the name of the Father and of the Son and of the Holy Spirit" [Matt 28:19].[161]

Augustine again uses the baptismal formula of Matt 28:19 to interpret a triadic text, as he explains that baptism in the name of the Son means baptism in the name of the Father, Son, and Spirit. In fact, elsewhere Augustine interprets Acts 2:38 through the lens of John 14:26.[162] As has been seen, John 14:26 also supports Rahner's Rule. Again, Augustine does not draw conclusions about divine τάξις from word order. Augustine sees no reversal in the economic Father–Son relationship emerging from this text, such that it no longer corresponds to the immanent relationship.

Rom 8:1–3 When citing Rom 8:1–3, Augustine is usually most concerned with the phrase concerning Christ being made "in the likeness of sin." His use of this text (and that phrase in particular) rarely has any bearing on his understanding of the Father–Son relationship.[163] However, Augustine sometimes cites the verse in

---

159. The baptism episode is more consequential to the Son–Spirit relation. It will be treated in greater detail in the following chapter.

160. For example, *Serm.* 16A.8 (CCSL 41: 225); 77.4 (41 Ab: 201); 175.4 (CCSL 41Bb: 530–1); 229E.2 (MiAg 1: 467–8); 316.3 (PL 38: 1433); 352.1.2 (RBén 129: 36–9); 94A.4 (MiAg 1: 254); 360B.18 (EAA 147: 260).

161. *Maxim.* 2.17.1 (CCSL 87A: 603): "non nominatis Patre et Spiritu sancto, in nomine Iesu Christi iussi sunt baptizari, et tamen intelleguntur non baptizati nisi in nomine Patris et Filii et Spiritus sancti."

162. *Serm.* 71.33 (CCSL 41Ab: 61–2).

163. For example, *Tract. Ev. Jo.* 41.1 (CCSL 36: 357); 42.1 (CCSL 36: 366); 95.3 (CCSL 36: 567); *Serm.* 19.3 (CCSL 41: 254); 110A.7 (EAA 147: 146–7); 184.2 (SPM 1: 75); 185.1 (PL 38: 997); 228B.2 (MiAg 1: 19); 233.4 (PL 38: 1114); 317.3 (PL 38: 1436); *Faust.* 18.6 (CSEL 25,1: 495).

proximity to comments on eternal generation.¹⁶⁴ He also sometimes highlights the Father's "sending" of the Son in 8:3.¹⁶⁵ As seen in the previous chapter, Augustine grounds the Son's mission in his procession. Thus, once again, the order in which the divine persons are mentioned in this chapter has no impact on his conception of the economic Father–Son relationship, nor on the question of economic and immanent τάξις more generally. If anything, given the reference to the sending of the Son and Augustine's tendency to read texts concerning the Father and the Son through the lens of "generation" and "sending," Augustine's interpretation of this verse most probably supports the parallel conception of the economic and immanent Father–Son relationship, and, thus, Rahner's Rule.

1 John 5:6–9 In *Trin.* 4.20.29, Augustine cites the Johannine comma when discussing the divine τάξις:

> Therefore, as the Father begot and the Son was begotten, so the Father sent and the Son was sent. But just as the begetter and the begotten are one, so are the sender and the sent, because the Father and the Son are one; so too the Holy Spirit is one with them, for "these three are one" [1 John 5:8].¹⁶⁶

This famous phrase follows and completes the late fourth-century interpolation in the Johannine text: "There are three that bear record in heaven, the Father, the Word, and the Holy Spirit." It is hardly surprising, then, that Augustine should cite the Johannine comma in a passage so decisive for his conception of divine τάξις and unity. The three divine persons are mentioned in the Father–Son–Spirit pattern. The wider unit of 1 John 5:6–9 is cited by Durst as an example of the Son–Spirit–Father pattern. In the UBS edition of 1 John, the three persons are still mentioned in close proximity, though without the interpolation. In Augustine's Bible, probably some variant of the *Vetus Latina*, the references to the Son and Spirit almost certainly would have closely preceded the interpolation. And still, the order in which the persons were named in these earlier verses did not cause him to reconsider his conception of divine τάξις. Is Augustine giving arbitrary preference to the Father–Son–Spirit order in the comma over and against the order in the wider unit? With respect to the Father–Son relationship in the citation earlier, it appears that he refers to the Father prior to the Son because

---

164. For example, *Tract. Ev. Jo.* 108.3–4 (CCSL 36: 617); *Serm.* 229H.1 (MiAg 1: 479); 246.5 (SC 116: 306).

165. For example, *Tract. Ev. Jo.* 108.4 (CCSL 36: 617); *Maxim.* 1.2 (CCSL 87A: 495); *Serm.* 136.4–6 (PL 38: 752–4); 152.8 (CCSL 41Ba: 42); 294.12 (PL 38: 1342–3).

166. *Trin.* 4.20.29 (CCSL 50: 199): "Sicut ergo pater *genuit, filius genitus* est; ita *pater misit*, filius missus est. Sed quemadmodum *qui genuit* et qui *genitus* est, ita est qui *misit* et qui missus est *unum* sunt quia pater et filius *unum* sunt; ita etiam spiritus sanctus unum cum eis est quia *haec tria unum sunt*." Cf. *Maxim.* 2.9 (CCSL 87A: 551).

he has begotten the Son. It has nothing to do with mere word order. It would be difficult to argue that Augustine's interpretation of this passage poses a threat to Rahner's Rule.

Spirit-Son-Father Texts

John 15:26 The same trend continues in Augustine's treatment of Spirit-Son-Father texts. We have already seen that John 15:26 is foundational for Augustine's conception of τάξις in *Trin.* 4.20.29.[167] In fact, as Wisse notes, Augustine cites this verse the only time he chooses to speak of the Father specifically as the *principium diviniatatis* or *deitatis*.[168] Or, as Lee observes, "Augustine explicitly interpreted John 15:26 as monopatrism."[169] Augustine argues that the Son sends the Spirit and is able to do so because the Father has given him the Spirit, just as the Spirit proceeds from the Son because the Father has given him the Spirit.[170] Ayres notes that in *Trin.* 5.11.12, Augustine cites John 15:26 alongside Rom 8:9 as evidence that the Spirit is Gift of both the Father and the Son.[171] In no way does the order in which the divine persons are mentioned in John 15:26 disrupt Augustine's conception of τάξις. This interpretation is consistent throughout *Trin.*[172] and the rest of his corpus.[173] After commenting on the verse in *Maxim.* he cites Matt 28:19 to explain that the three persons—mentioned in the Father-Son-Spirit pattern—are one God.[174] Augustine's treatment of John 15:26 further demonstrates the futility in looking to word order for divergent τάξεις. If the Spirit whom the Son sends is sent ultimately from the Father, surely this is scriptural proof of the congruity of the relations within the missions and Augustine's conception of the relations in the processions. This is the "rule of thumb" by which all texts are otherwise understood. Word order does not challenge Augustine's understanding of the Father-Son relationship. Yet again, the parallel Augustine discerns between the missions and processions supports the parallel conception of the economic and immanent Father-Son relationship, and, thus, Rahner's Rule.

---

167. Cf. p. 131.

168. Wisse, *Trinitarian Theology beyond Participation*, 159.

169. Chungman Lee, *Gregory of Nyssa, Augustine of Hippo, and the Filioque*, 169 (Leiden: Brill, 2021), 234.

170. Cf. pp. 157–80.

171. Ayres, *Augustine and the Trinity*, 251.

172. *Trin.* 2.3.5 (CCSL 50: 85); 5.11.12 (CCSL 50: 219); 5.14.15 (CCSL 50: 222); 12.5.5 (CCSL 50: 359); 15.26 (CCSL 50: 525); 15.26.47 (CCSL 50: 529); 15.27.48 (CCSL 50: 529); 15.28.51 (CCSL 50: 534).

173. For example, *Tract. Ev. Jo.* 92 (CCSL 36: 555–7); 99.8 (CCSL 36: 587); *Maxim.* 2.14.1 (CCSL 87A: 568); 2.22.3 (CCSL 87A: 638); *Serm.* 60A.2 (CCSL 41Aa: 254); 71.18.29 (CCSL 41Ab: 56); 214.10 (RBén 72: 20).

174. *Maxim.* 2.22.3 (CCSL 87A: 639).

John 16:7–9 We have already seen when discussing his treatment of John 14:25–26 in *Trin.* 1.12.21 that Augustine cites John 16:7 in defence of his conception of Trinitarian τάξις. Augustine likewise cites these texts together in *Arian*. He then comments:

> The Father alone is said not to have been sent, since he alone has no Originator from whom he is begotten or from whom he proceeds. And, therefore, the Father alone is not said to have been sent, not on account of a difference of nature, which is not found in the Trinity, but on account of his being the origin.[175]

Again, word order does not reverse the Father–Son relationship. Rather, this text is used to uphold Augustine's view of τάξις more generally. This should come as no surprise. As Gioia notes, Augustine's use of the *from* or *God from God* rule—the rule that undergirds Augustine's conception of τάξις—is particularly prominent in this work.[176] This rule is what guides his exegesis of John 16:7–9, not superficial attention to word order. Read in this way, Augustine's exegesis of John 16:7–9 thus supports the congruence of the economic and immanent Father–Son relationship, and, hence, Rahner's Rule. His use of this verse is consistent elsewhere.[177]

John 16:13–15 As previously mentioned, John 16:13–15 is crucial to Augustine's conception of τάξις, and, hence, the Father–Son relationship. In *Trin.* 1.12.25, Augustine cites John 16:15 to explain that the Son, like the Father, can send the Spirit since "all that the Father has" belongs to Jesus.[178] Gioia notes that Augustine's citation of John 16:13–15 in *Trin.* 2.3.5 supports the bishop's contention that

> the way the Holy Spirit is involved in the revelatory work of the Son depends on his inner-Trinitarian relation to the Father and the Son. If Jesus says that the Holy Spirit will speak—i.e. reveal—from what is his, this means that the Holy Spirit comes from the Father and the Son, even though the Son himself receives this "ability" to give the Holy Spirit from the Father.[179]

In fact, *Tract. Ev. Jo.* 99—the famous tractate cited at length at the heart of *Trin.* book 15, where Augustine lays down perhaps his most definitive statement on

---

175. *Arian.* 4.4 (CCSL 87A: 190): "Solus Pater non legitur missus, quoniam solus non habet auctorem a quo genitus sit, uel a quo procedat. Et ideo non propter naturae diuersitatem, quae in Trinitate nulla est, sed propter ipsam auctoritatem solus Pater non dicitur missus."

176. Gioia, *The Theological Epistemology of Augustine's* De Trinitate, 27, n. 14.

177. *Tract. Ev. Jo.* 94 (CCSL 36: 561–4); 95 (CCSL 36: 564–8); *Serm.* 71.24 (CCSL 41Ab: 48); 143.1 (PL 38: 735); 144.4 (PL 38: 788); 192.3 (PL 38: 1013); 267.1 (PL 38: 1230); 270.2 (PL 38: 1238).

178. *Trin.* 1.12.25 (CCSL 50: 64).

179. Gioia, *The Theological Epistemology of Augustine's* De Trinitate, 122.

Trinitarian τάξις—is a sermon on John 16:13. Both in this tractate and in *Trin.* book 15, the Spirit proceeds from the Son as well as the Father because the Father has begotten the Son. Moreover, in *Tract. Ev. Jo.* 99 and *Tract. Ev. Jo.* 100 (the tractate on John 16:13–15), Augustine constantly refers to the Son's eternal generation.[180] The fact that the persons are mentioned in the Spirit–Son–Father order is of no consequence to Augustine. The word order certainly does not result in a reversal of the Father–Son relationship.[181] Once again, Augustine's interpretation of this verse supports his view on the congruence of the Son's mission and procession, and, thus, Rahner's Rule.

1 Cor 12:4–6 While at times Augustine's use of 1 Cor 12:4–6 is irrelevant to his discussion of τάξις or the Father–Son relationship,[182] at other times it appears at critical junctures. Though the verse is only cited with respect to the Spirit in *Trin.* 4.20.29 and 5.13.14 and *Tract. Ev. Jo.* 74.3.2, each citation emerges near important comments by Augustine concerning the Father–Son τάξις. The citation of 1 Cor 12:6 in *Trin.* 4.20.29 comes shortly after Augustine climactically links the Father's begetting the Son with his sending the Son.[183] The citation in *Trin.* 5.13.14 follows shortly after stating:

> Therefore, the Father is called Father relationally, and he is also called the origin [*principium*] relationally, and by any name similar to these. But he is called Father with reference to the Son, and origin [*principium*] with reference to all things that are from him. Again, the Son is a relational term; he is also called Word and image relationally, and with all these names he is referred to the Father, while the Father himself is called none of these things.[184]

The citation of 1 Cor 12:4 in *Tract. Ev. Jo.* 74.3 likewise comes soon after commenting on the Son's eternal generation.[185] Once again, word order has no impact upon how Augustine conceives of Trinitarian τάξις nor does it reverse the Father–Son relationship. Augustine's interpretation of this verse supports the correspondence of the economic and immanent Father–Son relationship, and, thus, Rahner's Rule.

---

180. *Tract. Ev. Jo.* 99.2 (CCSL 36: 583); 99.4 (CCSL 36: 584–5); 99.9 (CCSL 36: 587); 100.3 (CCSL 36: 598–90); 100.4 (CCSL 36: 590).
181. Augustine's interpretation of the verse is similar in *Maxim.* 2.9.2 (CCSL 87A: 551); *Serm.* 135.2.3 (PL 38: 746–7).
182. For example, *Serm.* 272B.4 (REAug 44: 199); *Ep.* 48.3 (CCSL 31: 210).
183. *Trin.* 4.20.29 (CCSL 50: 200).
184. *Trin.* 5.13.14 (CCSL 50: 220–1): "Dicitur ergo relatiue pater idemque relatiue dicitur principium et si quid forte aliud; sed pater ad filium dicitur, principium uero ad omnia quae ab ipso sunt. Item dicitur relatiue filius; relatiue dicitur et uerbum et imago, et in omnibus his uocabulis ad patrem refertur; nihil autem horum pater dicitur."
185. *Tract. Ev. Jo.* 74.3 (CCSL 36: 514).

Eph 4:4-6 Gioia notes that the early verses of Eph 4 function as key "scriptural bases of Augustine's pneumatology."[186] These verses are crucial in *Trin.* for the bishop's conception of the Spirit as the Father and Son's joint Gift, as well as their Love and Unity.[187] As Gioia writes, "Through the Holy Spirit the Father and the Son are united to each other; through the Holy Spirit the Father (*gignens*) loves the Son (*genitus*) and the Son loves the Father, thus fulfilling their unity 'in virtue of their own being.'"[188] Thus, it comes as no surprise that the Spirit–Son–Father word order poses no threat to Augustine's conception of Trinitarian τάξις. The bishop can cite Eph 4:4-6 in *Tract. Ev. Jo.* 99 when addressing the Spirit's procession. Immediately after citing the text, he rearranges the order in which he speaks of the persons: "Since, therefore as there is one Father and one Lord, that is, Son, so there is also one Spirit, surely he is of both."[189] Just as the order in which the persons are mentioned in Eph 4:4-6 is of no consequence to Augustine's conception of Trinitarian τάξις, likewise the Son's being mentioned before the Father is not seen to alter the nature of their relationship. Moreover, immediately after citing Eph 4:4 in *Maxim.*, Augustine affirms that "the Son is not from matter nor from nothing but from whom he is begotten."[190] Augustine discerns no reversal in the economic or immanent Father–Son relationship pattern due to the order in which they are mentioned in this verse. Augustine's interpretation of this verse supports the congruence of the Son's mission and generation, and, thus, Rahner's Rule.

1 John 4:2 Similarly, Augustine discerns no tension between the order in which the divine persons are mentioned in 1 John 4:2 and the doctrine of eternal generation. This is most evident in *Serm.* 183,[191] a sermon dedicated entirely to this text. Here, Augustine considers the various heretical groups that acknowledge Christ's coming in the flesh. At one point, he affirms the eternal generation of the Son, alongside the Donatists.[192] Augustine's problem is that the Donatists deny Christ by their deeds, even though they affirm orthodox doctrines. The mention of eternal generation is just a passing comment. However, it demonstrates that Augustine does not waver on his conception of the Father–Son relationship when confronted with a text that mentions the persons in the Spirit–Son–Father pattern. It would be difficult to argue that, for Augustine, this verse upends the congruence

---

186. Gioia, *The Theological Epistemology of Augustine's* De Trinitate, 129.

187. Cf. *Trin.* 6.5.7 (CCSL 50: 235); 15.19.34 (CCSL 50: 509).

188. Gioia, *The Theological Epistemology of Augustine's* De Trinitate, 130.

189. *Tract. Ev. Jo.* 99.6.1 (CCSL 36: 586): "Cum ergo sicut unus Pater, et unus Dominus, id est Filius, ita sit et unus Spiritus, profecto amborum est."

190. *Maxim.* 2.14.2 (CCSL 87A: 570): "non de aliqua materia uel de nihilo est Filius, sed de quo est genitus."

191. Composed *c.* 417. Cf. Edmund Hill, comments on *Sermons on the New Testament (148-183)* by Augustine, vol. 5, The Works of Saint Augustine: A Translation for the 21st Century 3 (ed. John E. Rotelle; trans. Edmund Hill; Brooklyn: New City, 1992), 337.

192. *Serm.* 183.6.10 (CCSL 41Bb: 726).

of the missions and processions or the economic and immanent Father–Son relationship, and, thus, Rahner's Rule.

Summary

Thus, for Augustine, the order in which the divine persons are named in the texts earlier *never* results in a reversal of the Father–Son relationship, neither in the economy nor immanently. Augustine is unfazed by the fact that certain verses mention the Son prior to the Father. These verses (1) are cited in close proximity to comments on the Father–Son relationship, (2) are reordered to follow the Father–Son–Spirit pattern, (3) speak of the Father sending the Son, (4) are used to support the doctrine of eternal generation, and (5) mirror texts used to support eternal generation. If anything, Augustine's steadfast commitment to the tight association of the missions and processions—a commitment with exegetical warrant—means that he supports the Rule.

The remaining New Testament triadic texts mentioning the Son prior to the Father do not shift Augustine's conception of the Father–Son relationship. They are either left untreated in Augustine's major works (Acts 2:32-33; Acts 4:8-10; 2 Cor 13:14; Heb 9:14; 10:29-31; and Rev 22:17-18), or their treatment is irrelevant to and disconnected from his treatment of the Father–Son relationship (see, for example, Luke 10:21;[193] Acts 1:4-5;[194] Rom 7:4-6,[195] 15:12-13;[196] 1 Cor 6:11;[197] 2 Cor 3:3;[198] Eph 2:17-18,[199] 2:21-22,[200] 5:18-

---

193. *Serm.* 24.4 (CCSL 41: 329); 67.1.1 (CCSL 41Aa: 420); 69.1 (CCSL 41Aa: 460); 29B.2 (EAA 147: 24); 68.5.7 (CCSL 41Aa: 445); 184.1 (SPM 1: 74); *Enarrat. Ps.* 39.14 (CCSL 38: 436); 94.4 (CCSL 39: 1333); 117.1 (CCSL 40: 1658); *C. Jul. op. imp.* 3.106 (CSEL 85,1: 425); *Cons.* 2.33.80 (CSEL 43, 1: 183).

194. *Tract. Ev. Jo.* 101.6 (CCSL 36: 593); 122.8 (CCSL 36: 674); *Serm.* 71.19 (CCSL 41Ab: 40); 378.1 (PL 39: 1673-4); *Fund.* 9 (CSEL 25,1: 203-4); *C. litt. Petil.* 2.32.76 (CSEL 52: 65).

195. *Serm.* 153.2-3 (CCSL 41Ba: 50-3); 155.3 (CCSL 41Ba: 110); *Faust.* 11.8 (CSEL 25,1: 327); *Spir. et litt.* 25.14 (CSEL 60: 179); *C. du. ep. Pelag.* 1.8.13 (CSEL 60: 434); 3.4.12 (CSEL 60: 498).

196. *Serm.* 360A.2 (EAA 147: 233).

197. *Serm.* 20A (CCSL 41: 274); 213 (MiAg: 446); 294 (PL 38: 1338); 335I.4 (PLS 2: 834); 351.8 (PL 39: 1545); *Ep.* 29.5 (CCSL 31: 100); 149.8 (CSEL 44: 355); *Man.* (CSEL 90: 83); *Div. quaest. LXXXIII* 76.2 (CCSL 44A: 220); *Praed.* 8.33 (PL 44: 986-7).

198. *Serm.* 155.6 (CCSL 41Ba: 114); 272B.5 (REAug 44: 199); *Ep.* 29.4 (CCSL 31: 99); *Doctr. chr.* 3.34.48 (CCSL 32: 108); *Spir. et litt.* 14.24 (CSEL 60: 177); 17.30 (CSEL 46: 183).

199. *Enarrat. Ps.* 71.1 (CCSL 39: 971); 84.11 (CCSL 39: 1171); *Serm.* 112A (MiAg: 263); 202.1 (PL 38: 1033); 204.2 (BTT 3: 77-8); 204B:5 (CSEL 101: 71); *c. Fort.* 16 (CSEL 25,1: 93); *Faust.* 22.89 (CSEL 25,1: 696); *c. adu. leg.* 2:2.5 (PL 42: 641); *Pecc. merit.* 1.27.46 (CSEL 60: 45).

200. *Serm.* 156.15 (CCSL 41Ba: 159); 200.3.4 (PL 38: 1030-1); 306E.4 (EAA 147: 213).

20;[201] Heb 2:3–4,[202] 3:1–7,[203] 10:12–15).[204] Those like Bobrinskoy, Harrower, and Durst who place great stock in the order in which the divine persons are mentioned would likely criticize Augustine for under-emphasizing the significance of the various New Testament triadic patterns. However, if afforded the chance, Augustine would likely respond that these authors drastically overemphasize the significance of the order. Put simply, Augustine places no stock in the fact that texts or passages referring to the three divine persons sometimes mention the Son prior to the Father. His strategy for interpreting these triadic texts supports Rahner's contention that what is communicated of the Father–Son relationship in the economy corresponds with, reflects, and is grounded in the eternal Father–Son relationship. Hence, yet again, the bishop's exegesis supports the Jesuit's axiom.

6. The Ascension

Finally, some have suggested that the ascension presents a serious challenge to Rahner's Rule. Harrower argues that it would be "a grave mistake to employ the return of Jesus to his Father in heaven as a basis for speaking about the nature of the immanent relations within God" as it lacks an "eternal analogue."[205] If Rahner's Rule

> is to be applied evenly across the biblical text whenever there are references to relationships between persons of the Trinity, the ascension of Jesus would be included in this group. Yet, applying such a reading of Rahner's norm would prove to be problematic for the doctrine of God. It would entail a theology whereby in the immanent Trinity there is a return of Jesus to God the Father.[206]

This observation leads Sanders to ask: "If the economic sending of the Son from the Father has as its immanent analogue the eternal begetting of the Son from the Father (so the classic tradition of Trinitarian interpretation), then what is the immanent analogue of the economic return of the Son to the Father?"[207] If we apply the rule, "the ascension of Christ must also be reckoned with as some kind of revelation of an eternal receiving of the eternally returning Son by the eternal Father."[208] However, as shall now be seen, Augustine—with his commitment to the

---

201. *Tract. Ev. Jo.* 49.14 (CCSL 36: 427); *Serm.* 225.4 (CSEL 101: 118); 369.1 (RBén 79: 124); *Ep.* 48.3 (CCSL 31: 210).
202. *Trin.* 3.11.22 (CCSL 50: 151–2); 15.19.34 (CCSL 50A: 510); *Serm.* 57.5 (CCSL 41Aa: 181); *Civ.* 18.50 (CCSL 48: 648).
203. *Faust.* 22.69 (CSEL 25,1: 665).
204. *Enarrat. Ps.* 109.9 (CCSL 40: 1609); 109.10 (CCSL 40: 1610).
205. Harrower, *Trinitarian Self and Salvation*, 115.
206. Ibid. Cf. Harrower, "Bruce Ware's Trinitarian Methodology," 320–1.
207. Sanders, "Foreword," xiii.
208. Sanders, *The Triune God*, 112.

tight association of the missions and processions—yet again comes to Rahner's aid, offering two possible points of comparison that address this objection.

The Parallel Starting Point

Firstly, in his exegesis of John 16:28 in *Tract. Ev. Jo.* 102,[209] Augustine offers a potential starting point for discerning a parallel between the starting point of the Son's procession, mission, and ascension. He writes:

> "And you have believed," he says, "that I came forth from God. I came from the Father, and I came into the world; again I leave the world, and I go to the Father" [John 16:28]. Plainly we have believed. For it ought not seem incredible for this reason, because, coming to the world, he came from the Father in such a way that *he did not depart from the Father*; and he goes to the Father, the world left behind, in such a way that *he does not depart from the world*. For he came *from* the Father because he is *of* [*de*] the Father; he came into the world because he showed to the world his body, which he took of the virgin. He left behind the world by corporeal seceding; he made his way to the Father by the ascension of the man, and yet he did not depart from the world by the governing of his presence.[210]

In his mission the Son comes *from* the Father, *and yet remains*. In his ascension the Son departs *from* the world corporeally, *and yet remains*. As Ratzinger comments, for Augustine, "Christ, the one who ascended, also remains the one who descended."[211] In *Tract. Ev. Jo.* 103, Augustine discusses Jesus' saying that "the Father is with me" (John 16:32) immediately prior to his ascension. He posits that the Son in his ascension "goes to him who *is with him*."[212] Piecing these

---

209. This tractate was composed sometime after 419. Cf. Bonnardière, *Recherches de chronologie Augustinienne*, 65–87.

210. Emphasis added. *Tract. Ev. Jo.* 102.6 (CCSL 36: 597):

> *Et credidistis, inquit, quia a Deo exiui. Exiui a Patre et ueni in mundum; iterum relinquo mundum, et uado ad Patrem.* Plane credidimus. Neque enim propterea debet incredibile uideri, quia sic ad mundum ueniens exiit a patre, ut non desereret patrem, et sic uadit ad patrem relicto mundo, ut non deserat mundum. Exiit enim a Patre, quia de Patre est; in mundum uenit, quia mundo suum corpus ostendit quod de uirgine assumsit. Reliquit mundum corporali discessione, perrexit ad Patrem hominis adscensione, nec mundum deseruit praesentiae gubernatione.

211. Joseph Ratzinger, "The Holy Spirit as Communio: Concerning the Relationship of Pneumatology and Spirituality in Augustine," *Communio: International Catholic Review*, vol. 25 (1998): 335.

212. Emphasis added. *Tract. Ev. Jo.* 103.2 (CCSL 36: 599): "Quis uadit ad eum qui cum illo est."

together, perhaps we can say that in the ascension there is also a sense in which the Son comes forth *from* the Father—who prior to the ascension *is with him*—as he departs. Perhaps the *going to* assumes a *going from*. This would create an even stronger parallel between the starting points of the mission and ascension. Augustine does not draw this out himself. Nevertheless, one could argue that it is consistent with what Augustine has just said.

Augustine likewise discerns a correspondence between the starting point of the mission and the procession. His coming *from* the Father refers to his mission. He came *from* the Father in his mission because he is "of" or "from" (*de*) the Father as the eternally begotten Son. The latter is the ontological grounding of his mission. If (1) the Son's physical departure *from* the Father on earth below at his ascension parallels his coming *from* the Father above in his mission and 2) his coming *from* the Father in his mission is grounded in his being eternally *from* the Father; it therefore seems to follow that (3) the Son's physical departure *from* the Father on earth at his ascension parallels his eternal coming forth *from* the Father who begets him.

The Parallel End Point

Second, Augustine offers a parallel end point to the ascension. The bishop regularly emphasizes that the Son ascends physically to be with the Father, seated at his right hand.[213] He goes to be with him who is currently with him. The destination of the ascension is key to Augustine's defence against the Subordinationist interpretation of John 14:28 ("the Father is greater than I"). He understands Jesus as saying, "I must go to my Father, because while you see me like this you assume from what you see that I am less than the Father, and thus with all your attention on the creature and on the adopted condition, you do not understand the equality I have with my Father."[214] Christ's ascension to be *with* the Father signifies his equality with the Father.[215] As Barnes adds, the removal of the resurrected Jesus from sight via the ascension ensured "that faith would be both necessary and possible."[216]

For Augustine, the Son's ascending to be *with* the Father parallels his being begotten such that he is *with* the Father. In *Tract. Ev. Jo.* 78, Augustine's tractate on John 14:27–28, he comments:

Because the Son was therefore not equal to the Father, he was going *to the Father*, from whom he will come to judge the living and the dead. But insofar as the

---

213. For example, *Trin.* 1.8.18 (CCSL 50: 52–3); *Serm.* 17 (CCSL 41: 239); 53A.6 (CCSL 41Aa: 117); 215 (RBén 68: 24); 227 (SC 116: 238); 263 (MiAg 1: 509); 330 (PL 38: 1456).
214. *Trin.* 1.9 (CCSL 50: 54): "me oportet ire *ad patrem* quia dum me ita uidetis, et ex hoc quod uidetis aestimatis *minor* sum *patre*, atque ita circa creaturam susceptumque habitum occupati aequalitatem quam cum Patre habeo non intelligitis."
215. *Trin.* 1.9 (CCSL 50: 54).
216. Barnes, "The Visible Christ and the Invisible Trinity," 353, n. 58.

Only Begotten is equal to the Begetter, he never departs from the Father, but is *with him everywhere*, entirely, with the same divinity, which no place contains. (emphases added)[217]

Note the parallel between the ascension and the Son's generation. The Son ascends *to the Father*, that is, to be *with* the Father. Similarly, as the Only Begotten, he never departs from the Father but is *with him everywhere*. He is *with* the Father as his equal because he is begotten by the Father as his equal. Hence, the end point of the ascension has an "eternal analogue" with the Son's eternal generation, just as the starting point has an analogue.

Admittedly, Augustine never speaks of the Son being immanently *from* the Father *to* the Father. We can only see a parallel between the start point (*from*) and the end point (*with*) of the Son's ascension and generation. One assumes he would likely be content to speak of the Son being *from* the Father as the Son who is thus *with* and *in* the Father. The analogue to the Son's *return* might simply be his *being from* and thus *with* the Father as the eternally begotten Son. In the end, we can only speculate what Augustine might have said if pressed on this issue. However, given the tight relationship the bishop envisions between the missions and processions, it seems likely that the bishop would detect a strong connection between the Son's ascension *to* the Father and his eternal generation. At the very least, the fact that he discerns a parallel between the start and end point of the two suggests that an eternal analogue to the ascension is less puzzling than Harrower and Sanders would have us think. Thus, we can say that Augustine offers adherents to Rahner's Rule a starting point to overcome this particular objection.

7. Conclusion

In conclusion, we have seen that Augustine comes to Rahner's aid in fending off criticisms made against Rahner's Rule. First, Augustine's ruled reading offers Rahner a clear strategy for avoiding ontological Subordinationism when moving from the economic Trinity to the immanent Trinity. Second, Augustine demonstrates that it is possible to read texts that speak of the Son's exercising of power and judgment without reversing the Father–Son relationship. These texts can be read in parallel to the Father's eternal generation of the Son. Third, Augustine provides a similar strategy for reading texts that speak of the Father and Son's mutual glorification, mutual knowledge and revelation, mutual love, and mutual indwelling. Fourth, the bishop demonstrates that it is possible to read biblical texts mentioning all three divine persons—in this case, those citing the Son prior to the

---

217. *Tract. Ev. Jo.* 78.1 (CCSL 36: 524): "Per quod ergo Filius non est aequalis Patri, per hoc iturus erat ad Patrem, a quo uenturus est uiuos iudicaturus et mortuos; per illud autem in quo aequalis est gignenti unigenitus, numquam recedit a Patre, sed cum illo est ubique totus pari diuinitate, quam nullus continet locus."

Father—without compromising the τάξις of the immanent Trinity or reversing the Father–Son relationship. As Lee has observed, "Augustine did not allow for a reversal of the *taxis* (order) Father–Son–Spirit expressed in the baptismal formula. Otherwise, the Son would be a father of the Father, which in his eyes was ridiculous."[218] Fifth, Augustine offers a strategy—or at the very least, the starting point of a strategy—for discerning a parallel between the ascension and eternal generation. Just as the Son is *from* the Father in eternity and comes forth *from* the Father in his mission *and yet remains*, he ascends corporeally *from* earth (and *from* the Father) in time *and yet remains*. Just as the Son who is from the Father is eternally *with* the Father, he ascends to be *with* the Father, seated at his right hand. In the previous two chapters we saw how Augustine provided exegetical support for Rahner's Trinitarian agenda, an agenda aimed at addressing the weaknesses emerging from Augustine's legacy. By exploring how the bishop follows through on the tight association he envisions between the missions and processions, we begin to see that Augustine helps Rahner by overcoming the exegetical objections levelled at his solution. In the next chapter, we consider how Augustine continues to aid Rahner, this time with respect to the Son–Spirit relationship.

---

218. Chungman Lee, *Gregory of Nyssa, Augustine of Hippo, and the Filioque* (Leiden: Brill, 2021), 220.

Chapter 5

THE SON-SPIRIT RELATIONSHIP: RAHNER'S RULE, CONTEMPORARY OBJECTIONS, AND AUGUSTINE'S EXEGESIS

1. Introduction

In the previous chapter, we saw that Rahner discerns in his Rule a true, consistent, yet distinguishable correspondence between the economic and immanent divine relations. According to this understanding of the Rule, the Father–Son, Son–Spirit, and Father–Spirit relations in the economy should always reflect their *ad intra* relations. The previous chapter outlined several contemporary challenges to the Rule with respect to the Father–Son relationship. Theologians allege that applying the Rule to the particularities of the economy sometimes results in Subordinationism or relational reversibility, while at other times there simply is no "eternal analogue" to the economic activity. Then it was shown that Augustine—with his tight association of the missions and processions—offers an interpretive reading strategy that largely avoids these potential objections. In that way, Augustine's strategy supports Rahner's Rule.

In this chapter, we explore how Augustine's reading strategy likewise supports Rahner's Rule with respect to the Son–Spirit relationship and (to a lesser degree) the Father–Spirit relationship. Rahner insists that his *Grundaxiom* must do "justice to the really binding data of the church's official doctrine of the Trinity" and "the biblical statements about the economy of salvation."[1] This means that the particularities of the Son–Spirit relationship (and the Father–Spirit relationship) in the economy must reflect and be grounded in a Western conception of τάξις. Rahner is relatively quiet on the *Filioque*, preferring to speak of the Spirit's procession as "from the Father through [*durch*] the Son."[2] According to Rahner, this is not a capitulation to the Eastern model of the Spirit's procession. Rahner has magisterial warrant for this statement in the pronouncements of Florence (DS

---

1. Rahner, "Der Dreifaltige Gott," 535: "Gelingt es dort nämlich, mit Hilfe dieses Axioms eine Trinitätslehre systematisch zu entwickeln, die erstens den wirklich verbindlichen Daten der kirchenamtlichen Trinitätslehre gerecht wird, zweitens die biblischen Aussagen über die Heilsökonomie."

2. Ibid., 586. Cf. p. 12.

1300) and Gregory XIII (DS 1986). Beyond this, Rahner says little on the Spirit's place in the Trinitarian τάξις. Nevertheless, his commitment to the magisterium forces him to adhere to the *Filioque*. Therefore, if his Rule is to do justice to the statements of the magisterium and those of Scripture, the economic Son–Spirit relationship must correspond to a Filioquist articulation of the immanent Son–Spirit relationship. To use the idiom of Rahner's English translator, this means that the Spirit "cannot come before the Son" *ad extra* or *ad intra*.[3]

In what follows, we see that Rahner's commitment to the *Filioque* leads to several alleged difficulties for his Rule. Many biblical texts can be cited in demonstration of an alleged "inversion" or "reversal" in the economic Son–Spirit relationship. These texts can be grouped according to the virgin conception, Jordan baptism, messianic ministry, crucifixion, resurrection, and Pentecost and in the various triadic texts (i.e., texts referring to three divine persons). Applying Rahner's Rule to these kinds of texts is said to introduce inversions or reversals into the immanent Son–Spirit relationship, compromising the *Filioque* and necessitating a complementary *Spirituque*. It is suggested that this ultimately threatens the stability of the Trinitarian relations and undermines the doctrine of eternal generation. Moreover, as with the Father–Son relationship, it is suggested that no "eternal analogue" can be found for certain aspects of the Son–Spirit relationship. Even though, as will be seen, numerous solutions have been proposed to overcome these difficulties, further difficulties have been identified with these solutions.

Nevertheless, by turning to Augustine's exegesis, it becomes apparent that the above-mentioned difficulties—including difficulties said to arise from *some* of the proposed solutions—are not insurmountable. After outlining—at some length—these various difficulties and solutions, this chapter eventually turns to Augustine's treatment of the Son–Spirit relationship in texts concerning the virgin conception, Jordan baptism, messianic ministry, resurrection, and Pentecost and in triadic texts citing the Spirit prior to the Son (and, in some cases, the Father).[4] As will be seen, Augustine offers an alternative reading strategy to these economic particularities in which the economic Son–Spirit closely parallels the immanent Son–Spirit relationship. Barnes's assessment proves true: "Augustine reads virtually all statements about the relations of Son and Spirit as also signifying aspects of their eternal relationship."[5]

3. Rahner, *The Trinity*, 83, unnumbered footnote.
4. Heb 9:14 is the only verse cited earlier for the Spirit's involvement in the Son's crucifixion. Augustine never directly cites or alludes to this verse in his corpus. Given the consistent strategy that will emerge in the rest of this chapter, is highly unlikely that his interpretation of the Son–Spirit dynamic at the crucifixion would challenge Rahner's Rule. One could also turn to Luke 23:46 when, at the cross, the Son speaks of committing the Spirit (or *spirit*) into the Father's hands. Augustine's citation of this verse reveals nothing that challenges the τάξις of the Son–Spirit relationship. Cf. *Cons.* 3.18.55 (CSEL 43: 342–3); *Enarrat. Ps.* 30.1.6 (CCSL 38: 187); 30.2.1.11 (CCSL 38: 199); *Serm.* 316.3 (PL 38: 1433); 319.4 (PL 38: 1441); *Arian.* 9.7 (CCSL (CCSL 87A: 199–200).
5. Barnes, "Augustine's Last Pneumatology," 230. Cf. Ayres, "Spiritus Amborum," 207–21.

2. Alleged Difficulties for Rahner's Rule

As just mentioned, several difficulties have been levelled against Rahner's Rule regarding the economic Son–Spirit relationship. First, many biblical texts have been cited in demonstration of an alleged "inversion" or "reversal" in the economic Son–Spirit relationship. Von Balthasar cites texts concerning the Spirit's role in Jesus' virgin birth (Luke 1:35), childhood (Luke 1:80, 2:40), baptism (Matt 3:16; Luke 3:22; John 1:32–33), desert temptation (Luke 4:1), and anointing and ministry (Isa 61:1; Matt 12:28; Luke 4:14; 4:18; Acts 10:38) to speak of a "Trinitarian inversion" in the Son–Spirit relationship.[6] Harrower likewise discerns various economic "reversals" in the Son–Spirit relationship, drawing on the Son's "comprehensive subordination" to the Spirit in Luke 3:21–22, 4:1, 4:14, 4:18 and the Spirit's "comprehensive subordination" to the Son in Acts.[7] To these, Jowers adds Matt 1:20 concerning the virgin birth, Mark 1:12 concerning the Spirit and the desert leading, Heb 9:14 concerning the Spirit's involvement in the Son's death, and Rom 1:14 and 1 Pet 3:18 concerning the Spirit's involvement in the resurrection.[8] As we saw in the previous chapter, theologians like Bobrinskoy and Harrower suggest that these reversals may also be detected in those texts referring to the three divine persons in patterns that diverge from the Father–Son–Spirit formula.[9] Pertinent to this discussion are those texts placing the Spirit prior to the Son and/or the Father.

Second, it is then alleged—from multiple theological directions—that if the economic Son–Spirit relationship is indicative of the immanent Son–Spirit relationship, this relationship must be inconsistent with the kind of Filioquism that Rahner adheres to. For Orthodox theologian Paul Evdokimov, "The formula *per Filium* means and explains that the *Filioque* can be Orthodox only by being balanced by the corresponding formula of the *Spirituque*. … The Son in his generation receives the Holy Spirit from the Father and therefore in his being he is eternally inseparable from the Holy Spirit; he was born *ex Patre Spirituque*."[10] Though committed to the *Filioque* as expounded at Lyon and Florence,[11] Catholic

---

6. Hans Urs von Balthasar, *Dramatis Personae: Persons in Christ*, trans. Graham Harrison, vol. 3, Theo-Drama: Theological Dramatic Theory (San Francisco: Ignatius, 1992), 183–4, 520–4.

7. Harrower, *Trinitarian Self and Salvation*, 136–49.

8. Jowers, "A Test of Karl Rahner's Axiom," 434.

9. Bobrinskoy, *The Mystery of the Trinity*, 65–8; Harrower, *Trinitarian Self and Salvation*, 158.

10. Paul Evdokimov, *L'Esprit Saint dans la tradition orthodoxe* (Paris: Les Éditions du Cerf, 1969), 71–2: "C'est ici que la formule *per Filium* signifie et explique que le *Filioque* peut être orthodoxe qu'en étant équilibré par la formule correspondante du *Spirituque*. … Ainsi le Fils dans sa génération reçoit du Père l'Esprit Saint et donc dans son être il est éternellement inséparable de l'Esprit Saint; il est né *ex Patre Spirituque*."

11. Boff, *A Santíssima Trindade é a Melhor Comunidade*, 121–5.

theologian Leonardo Boff is content to adopt the same language as Bobrinskoy: "The Spirit belongs to the Father through the Son (*Patre Filioque*) as the Son recognizes himself in the Father through the love of the Spirit (*Patre Spirituque*)."[12] Boff even goes so far as to endorse a *Patreque* clause.[13] While for Boff, this is supposed to balance out the *Filioque* and *Spirituque*, thus ensuring there is no first cause within the Trinity, Weinandy is willing to entertain a *Patreque* if by this we mean "that the Spirit conforms the Father to be the Father as the Father breathes forth the Spirit."[14] Sanders and Harrower argue that an application of Rahner's Rule in this way introduces a kind of reversal into the Son–Spirit relationship *ad intra* which requires a *Spirituque* or "reverse successive subordinations."[15]

In the only monograph devoted to a biblical assessment of Rahner's Rule, Harrower alleges further difficulties. According to Harrower, if these "reversed economic relations" are read into the immanent τάξις, "a theology arises whereby God is a being who may morph at the ontological level."[16] As such, "little could be said about God's eternal being due to these changes, unless one took a two-tiered view of God in which the Father is relationally stable but the Son and the Spirit are not."[17] Thus, "We would be somewhat agnostic about the current state of God's being because a further change may have occurred within him, or perhaps a relational change may occur in the future."[18] If we press Rahner's Rule to its logical conclusions with respect to the Spirit's role in the Son's virgin conception and ministry,

> A view which counters both the Western and Eastern views of generation would apply: the Son is generated by the Holy Spirit with no direct relation to God the Father or to the life of God the Son. Further, the ensuing theology of relations within the Godhead would have great affinity with pantheism as God the Son is absolutely tied to history for his development.[19]

Harrower also argues that the Son's multiple receptions of the Spirit in the narrative of Luke-Acts—at the baptism (Luke 3:21–22) and at Pentecost (Acts 2:33)—create a significant "puzzle" for Rahner's Rule. If both events are read from the economy to the immanent Trinity, Harrower speculates that within God's

---

12. Ibid., 92: "Assim, o Espírito é do Pai pelo Filho (a *Patre Filioque*) como o Filho se reconhece no Pai pelo amor do Espírito (a *Patre Spirituque*)."

13. Ibid., 136, 246.

14. Thomas Weinandy, *The Father's Spirit of Sonship: Reconceiving the Trinity* (Edinburgh: T&T Clark, 1995), 81, note (n.) 44.

15. Sanders, *The Image of the Immanent Trinity*, 168; Harrower, *Trinitarian Self and Salvation*, 136–49.

16. Harrower, *Trinitarian Self and Salvation*, 154.

17. Ibid., 154.

18. Ibid.

19. Ibid.

immanent τάξις, "the nature of the relations mean the Son's first reception of the Spirit is not sufficient."[20] It "thus requires two separate acts whereby the Spirit is given over to the Son. On the other hand, the conclusion for God's inner life may be that the structure of this relational life is open to continuous change."[21] Thus, again, it is alleged that Rahner's Rule threatens the relational stability of the immanent Trinity.

3. Proposed Solutions and Their Alleged Difficulties

Before turning to Augustine, it is worth outlining some of the solutions that have been proposed to overcome the alleged difficulties raised earlier. According to Jowers, those

> who (a) identify the Holy Spirit of the anointing accounts with the third person of the eternal Trinity, (b) believe that the Holy Spirit eternally proceeds from the Father and the Son as from a single principle, (c) accept that the divine persons can effect distinct influences in the world, and (d) accept the *Grundaxiom* of Rahner's theology of the Trinity can account for the events portrayed in the gospel accounts of the anointing in at least three ways. Such persons can:
>
> 1. claim that the Spirit is in some way involved in the begetting of the Son;
> 2. argue that the anointing accounts manifest a prior occurrence in which οἰκονομία and θεολόγία correspond; or
> 3. conclude that the Spirit constitutes the Father's intra-Trinitarian gift to the Son.[22]
>
> In addition to these, those affirming the above conditions can also:
>
> 4. claim that the economic "inversions" are alternating projections of the *a Patre procedit* and *Filioque* onto the economic plane; or
> 5. suggest that we exclude certain events being read from the economy to the immanent Trinity.

We now consider how these proposed solutions have been articulated and the difficulties that ensue.

First, some, like Weinandy, seek to maintain the above-mentioned conditions and yet do justice to the Spirit's involvement in the Son's virgin conception by advocating the Spirit's involvement in the Son's generation.[23] According to Weinandy,

20. Ibid., 135.
21. Ibid.
22. Jowers, "Test of Rahner's Axiom," 434–5.
23. Weinandy lists several others who speak of the Son's generation "in the Spirit," including Durwell, Boff, Moltmann, Clément, the Church of England Doctrinal Commission, Yarnold, and Evdokimov. Weinandy, *The Father's Spirit of Sonship: Reconceiving the Trinity*, 18–19.

The actions of and roles played by the Father, the Son, and the Holy Spirit in the economy of salvation, expressed principally in functional language, illustrate the actions and roles they play within the immanent Trinity, namely that the Father begets the Son in or by the Holy Spirit, and thus that the Spirit proceeds from the Father as the one in whom the Son is begotten.[24]

Contra Harrower, there is weighty historical precedent (at least in the East) corroborating this view. It is found in several church Fathers, including Gregory of Nyssa,[25] John of Damascus,[26] and Maximus the Confessor.[27] Never does it follow that the Spirit's involvement in the Son's generation removes the direct relation between the Son and the Father, as Harrower suggests it should. Moreover, few would accuse Gregory, John, and Maximus of pantheism on the basis of suggesting the Son's being begotten in the Spirit. Jowers identifies the real issue for this proposed solution: it suggests "that Christ proceeds eternally a *Patre Spirituque*."[28] Jowers notes that the idea "that Christ *qua* divine derives his being from the Holy Spirit seems to reverse the τάξις of the Trinitarian persons revealed in the baptismal formula" of Matt 28:19.[29] In view of the decrees of the magisterium which Rahner considers irreformable and infallibly true, Jowers concludes "that Rahner cannot consistently affirm that the Son derives in any way from the Holy Spirit."[30] Thus, for Weinandy's proposal to support Rahner's Rule, this difficulty must be addressed.

Second, others, like Mühlen, argue that the anointing accounts manifest a prior occurrence in the immanent Trinity. Jesus' reception of the Spirit in the economy is congruent with the *Filioque* because the Spirit was always "in" the Son:

> For a *dogmatic* understanding of the anointing of Jesus with the Holy Spirit, it follows that one must say: Jesus had the fullness of the Spirit from the very first moment of his existence. He is himself (together with the Father) the eternal *origin* of the Holy Spirit. He remains this origin of the Holy Spirit even as the incarnate, so that the incarnate Son is never without the Holy Spirit, from the first moment of his temporal existence. The sending of the Holy Spirit into the human nature of Jesus or the anointing of Jesus with the Holy Spirit takes place for a dogmatic understanding already in this first temporal moment of the fleshly existence of the Son. The communication of the Spirit at the baptism

---

24. Ibid., 52.
25. Gregory of Nyssa, *Or. cat.* 2 (PG 45: 17).
26. John of Damascus, *Exp. Fid.* 1.7 (PG 94: 804–7).
27. Maximus the Confessor, *Quaest.* 34 (PG 90: 814).
28. Jowers, "Test of Rahner's Axiom," 438.
29. Ibid.
30. Ibid., 439.

of Jesus therefore appears more like a public promulgation of what was already there from the beginning.[31]

According to Mühlen, at the virgin conception,

> The Holy Spirit is sent into the already (in terms of logical priority) personalised human nature of Jesus! From this point of view, the outward mission of the Holy Spirit does not contain a relationship between person and *nature* like the mission of the Son, but *a relationship between person and person*, and this shows the fundamental difference between the appearance of the Holy Spirit in the history of salvation and that of the Son. (emphases in original)[32]

Mühlen is convinced that this position is corroborated by Thomas.[33] Jowers also detects patristic precedent for this position in Athanasius and Cyril of Alexandria.[34] However, according to Jowers, this position suggests that, "in the economy of salvation, the Son and the Spirit invert their intra-Trinitarian relations; the eternal giver receives, and the eternal receiver gives. Mühlen ameliorates this problem, of course, by holding that the Son anoints himself, but he does not eliminate it."[35] For

---

31. Heribert Mühlen, *Der Heilige Geist als Person: in der Trinität, bei der Inkarnation und im Gnadenbund: Ich, du, wir* (Aschendorff, 1963), §7.12, 206:

> Für ein *dogmatisches* Verständnis der Salbung Jesu mit dem Hl. Geiste ergibt sich jedenfalls, daß man sagen muß: Jesus besaß die Fülle des Geistes schon vom ersten zeitlichen Augenblick seiner Existenz an. Er ist ja selbst (mit dem Vater zusammen) der ewige *Ursprung* des Hl. Geistes. Er bleibt dieser Ursprung des Hl. Geistes auch als der Inkarnierte, so daß auch der inkarnierte Sohn nie ohne den Hl. Geist ist, und zwar vom ersten Augenblick seiner zeitlichen Existenz an. Die Sendung des Hl. Geistes in die menschliche Natur Jesu bzw. die Salbung Jesu mit dem Hl. Geiste vollzieht sich für ein dogmatisches Verständnis schon in diesem ersten zeitlichen Augenblick der fleischlichen Existenz des Sohnes. Die Geistmitteilung bei der Taufe Jesu erscheint von da her mehrals eine öffentliche Promulgation dessen, was schon von Anfang an war.

32. Ibid., 207:

> Der Hl. Geist wird in die in einem logischen Früher schon personhaft gemachte menschliche Natur Jesu gesandt! Von da her enthält die Sendung des Hl. Geistes nach außen nicht ein Verhältnis von Person zu *Natur* wie die Sendung des Sohnes, sondern ein *Verhältnis von Person zu Person,* und darin zeigt sich die fundamentale Unterschiedenheit der heilsgeschichtlichen Erscheinungsweise des Hl. Geistes von der des Sohnes.

33. Ibid.
34. Jowers, "Test of Rahner's Axiom," 442–3. See Athanasius, *C. Ar* 3.47 (PG 26:109) and Cyril of Alexandria, *Jo. Ev.* 11.10 (PG 74:549).
35. Jowers, "Test of Rahner's Axiom," 444.

Jowers, there is still a strong sense of mutuality and thus symmetry in the Son–Spirit relationship. It seems that, for Jowers, Mühlen's model has not removed the need for a *Spirituque*. For Mühlen's model to support Rahner's Rule, the *Spirituque* objection must also be attended to.

Bourassa offers a third model in which the economic relations parallel the immanent relations without introducing an inversion or reversal into the Son–Spirit relationship. He seeks to avoid an inversion by speaking of the Spirit as "the Gift of God" (*le Don de Dieu*), the Father's eternal gift to the Son. He writes:

> According to the principle that the mission is the procession of the Person, the incarnation, as the mission of the Son in the world, reveals the nature of the communications interior to the Trinity, namely that the Son himself is eternally constituted the Son of God "in the bosom of the Father," in that the Father communicates to him his fullness in the gift of the Spirit: "It is without measure that God gives the Spirit, the Father loves the Son and has given him everything" (John 3:34–35).[36]

The Son eternally receives the Spirit through generation. Bourassa recognizes that this, at first, may seem to come into conflict with the *Filioque* as expounded in DS 1301:

> By affirming that the Spirit is "Gift of God," that is to say the Gift of the Father to the Son in which the Father gives himself to him, by begetting him as his Only Begotten Son, in the outpouring of his love …, we encounter the following difficulty: If the Spirit is the gift of the Father to the Son *in generation*, then it seems that generation takes place through the Spirit or by virtue of the Spirit. The Spirit would therefore be at the beginning of the generation of the Son, while, according to the firmest data of dogma, the generation of the Son is at the beginning of the procession of the Spirit.[37]

However, this tension is only apparent. The Spirit proceeds from the Son because he is given to him from the Father in eternal generation (DS 1301). Thus, "To be Son, to be begotten of the Father, is, for the Son, to receive everything from the Father, that is to say, not only to take from the Father all that he has as a Son,

---

36. François Bourassa, "Le Don de Dieu," *Gregorianum*, vol. 50, no. 2 (1969): 217.

37. Ibid., 230:

> En affirmant que l'Esprit est « Don de Dieu », c'est-à-dire le Don du Père au Fils dans lequel le Père se donne lui-même à lui, en l'engendrant comme son Fils unique, dans l'effusion de son amour (ci-dessus, p. 218, § 6, note 35), on rencontre la difficulté suivante: Si l'Esprit est le don du Père au Fils dans la génération, il semble alors que la génération a lieu par l'Esprit ou en vertu de l'Esprit. L'Esprit serait donc au principe de la génération du Fils, alors que, selon les données les plus fermes du dogme, la génération du Fils est au principe de la procession de l'Esprit.

but to receive as a gift from the Father everything that Father has 'excepto Patris nomine.' "[38] Drawing on Thomas he argues for a distinction between the "order of origin and an order of circumincession" (*ordre d'origine et circum-incession*).[39] According to the order of origin, "The Spirit is the *third* Person of the Trinity, but according to the circumincession of the Father and the Son, the Spirit is their communion of love (koinonia), an *intermediate* between both."[40]

Jowers argues that Bourrassa "succeeds in interpreting the anointing in such a way that it undermines neither the *Grundaxiom* nor Latin Trinitarianism." It is just that he does so "at the expense of partially defunctionalizing the *Grundaxiom*."[41] Jowers argues that if we follow Bourassa's route, we find ourselves confronted with two τάξεις: Father–Son–Spirit and Father–Spirit–Son. From the existence of these "multiple τάξεις," Jowers concludes that "a methodology of Trinitarian theology that takes its data solely from the economy of salvation seems insufficient for the purpose of justifying Rahner's Filioquist doctrine of the immanent Trinity."[42] Bourassa's model cannot really support Rahner's Rule if it results in multiple τάξεις.

Balthasar presents a fourth model. For Balthasar, the problems posed by "Trinitarian inversions" are merely apparent. They are "ultimately only the projection of the immanent Trinity onto the 'economic' plane, whereby the Son's 'correspondence' to the Father is articulated as 'obedience.'"[43] For Balthasar, the Spirit's being *in* the incarnate Son is the "economic form" of the *Filioque*, while his being *over* the incarnate Son through anointing, empowering, and leading corresponds to the *a Patre procedit*.[44] It does not disrupt the order of persons in Catholic theology in favour of an Orthodox theology: "As far as the Orthodox are concerned, and the Fathers on whom they base themselves, the *diá* ("through the Son") applies to both the immanent and the economic Trinity, thus providing a point on which Orthodox and Catholic theology can agree."[45] Nevertheless, it is difficult to see how Balthasar's insistence on an "inversion" in the Son–Spirit relationship is compatible with magisterial statements on the *Filioque*. It tends

---

38. Ibid.: "Être Fils, être engendré du Père, c'est, pour le Fils, tout recevoir du Père, c'est-à dire, non seulement tenir du Père tout ce qu'il a comme Fils, mais recevoir comme don du Père tout ce qu'a le Père « excepto Patris nomine »."

39. Ibid., 233.

40. Ibid., 231–2: "Selon l'ordre d'origine, dit-il, l'Esprit est la *troisième* Personne de la Trinité, mais selon la circum-incession du Père et du Fils, l'Esprit étant leur communion d'amour (koinonia) est *intermédiaire* entre les deux leur communion d'amour (koinonia) est intermédiaire entre les deux."

41. Jowers, "Test of Rahner's Axiom," 451.

42. Ibid., 454.

43. Hans Urs von Balthasar, *Dramatis Personae: Persons in Christ*, trans. Graham Harrison, vol. 3, Theo-Drama: Theological Dramatic Theory (San Francisco: Ignatius, 1992), 191.

44. Ibid., 3: 521.

45. Ibid., 3: 190.

towards a strong sense of symmetry in the Son–Spirit relationship, such that it is difficult to avoid an appeal to a *Spirituque* to complement the *Filioque*. This, in turn, makes Balthasar's solution difficult to reconcile with Rahner's Latin Trinitarianism.

Finally, fifth, the events of the economy can be reconciled with the pronouncements of the magisterium by restricting one's application of the rule to certain events and not others. Congar reasons that, in the economy, "the Word proceeds *a Patre Spirituque* because the Spirit intervenes in all the acts or moments in the history of the *incarnate* Word. If all the *acta et passa* of the divine economy are traced back to the eternal begetting of the Word, then the Spirit has to be placed at that point."[46] Congar agrees with Barth that "to adhere, without nuance, to the principle according that the economic Trinity is the same as the immanent Trinity and vice versa would be to contradict the *Filioque*."[47] An immanent *Spirituque* would not be compatible with the *Filioque* as it places the Spirit logically prior to the Son. Congar wholeheartedly affirms the first half of Rahner's Rule but rejects the *ungekehrt* (vice versa) on the grounds that its abuse by others (e.g., Schoonenberg) challenges divine freedom by equating salvation history with God's being: "Can we *identify* the free mystery of the economy with the necessary mystery of the Triunity of God?"[48] He insists that while we can transpose some of the events of the economy of salvation into eternity, we cannot do so with all. Otherwise, "we would have to say that the Son proceeds from the Father and the Holy Spirit 'a Patre Spirituque.'"[49]

Sanders raises the obvious objection to Congar's insistence on restricting what can be transposed from economy to immanence:

> Why is this conclusion [the *Spirituque*] supposed to be necessarily inadmissible, if the economy is the source of our theological formulations? There may be good reasons for rejecting an immanent *Spirituque* extension of economic evidence, but Rahner's protest began by uncovering what he deemed very bad reasons: a

---

46. Yves Congar, *La Parole et Le Souffle* (Paris: Desclée, 1984), 151–2: "le Verbe procède « a Patre Spirituque », car l'Esprit inter vient en tous ces actes ou moments de l'histoire du Verbe *incarné*. Si l'on reporte dans la génération éternelle du Verbe ses « acta et passa » de l'Économie, on doit y placer l'Esprit."

47. Ibid., 152: "K. Barth n'a pas manqué de remarquer que cela contredirait le « Filioque » si l'on tenait sans nuance au principe selon lequel la Trinité immanente est la Trinité économique, et réciproquement."

48. Congar, *Je Crois en l'Esprit Saint: Le Fleuve de Vie Coule en Orient et en Occident*, 3: 37: "Peut-on *identifier* le mystère libre de l'Economie et le mystère nécessaire de la Tri-unité de Dieu?" Cf. Schoonenberg, "Trinität—Der Vollendete Bund," 115–17.

49. Congar, *Je Crois en l'Esprit Saint*, 3: 43: "Si l'on en transposait toutes les données dans l'éternité du Logos, il faudrait dire que le Fils pro cède a « a Patre Spirituque »."

speculatively constructed doctrine of the immanent Trinity which had become disengaged from the economy.⁵⁰

It remains unclear why Congar insists upon reading some events of the economy into the immanent relations but not others. Congar "does not undertake to explain what process of inference might be permissible for constructing an economically-based theology of the immanent Trinity, or what criteria would be in effect for determining which of the economic data are candidates for transposition into the divine life proper."⁵¹

While the difficulties associated with the solutions mentioned earlier are significant, not all of them are insurmountable. In what follows, it is demonstrated that the tight association Augustine discerns between the missions and processions offers an exegetical framework that largely avoids not only the exegetical difficulties raised concerning the Son–Spirit relationship but also the difficulties associated with some of the solutions previously mentioned. Thus, Augustine's framework also ultimately supports the application of Rahner's Rule to the Son–Spirit relationship (as well as the Father–Spirit relationship).

4. The Virgin Conception

In seeking to determine whether Augustine's treatment of the economic Son–Spirit relationship supports Rahner's Rule, we begin with his treatment of the Spirit's role in the virgin conception. Augustine is not always concerned with the particular intricacies of the Son–Spirit relationship when treating verses depicting the Spirit's involvement in the virgin conception (e.g., Matt 1:18, 20; Luke 1:35).⁵² As Barnes notes, when treating these verses, Augustine is often more interested in the fact that "pro-Nicene theology—common operations, common power, common divinity—requires him to insist that the Holy Spirit does everything that [the] Father and Son do."⁵³ Nevertheless, in other places, he deals with the Son–Spirit dynamic more acutely. Notably, this never results in a reversal of the Son–Spirit relationship. In *Trin.* 2.5.8, Augustine argues that the

---

50. Sanders, *The Image of the Immanent Trinity*, 144.

51. Ibid., 127.

52. For examples of this in his treatment of Matt 1:18 and 20, see *Cons.* 2.5.14 (CSEL 43: 95–6), 2.5.17 (CSEL 43: 104), *Serm.* 51.9 (CCSL 41Aa: 19); *Maxim.* 2.17.2 (CCSL 87A: 606). For examples of this in his treatment of Luke 1:35 see *Quaest. Hept.* 4.19 (CCSL 33: 246); *Cons.* 2.5.14 (CSEL 43: 95), 2.5.17 (CSEL 43: 102); *Tract. Ev. Jo.* 99.7 (CCSL 36: 586); *Enarrat. Ps.* 50.10 (CCSL 38: 606–7); 67.21 (CCSL 39: 884); *Serm.* 153.14 (CCSL 41Ba: 71); 214.6 (RBén 72: 17); 215.4 (RBén 68: 21); 233.4 (PL 38: 1114); 290.4 (PL 38: 1314); 291.5 (PL 38: 1319); 341.25 auctus (= Dolbeau 22, Moguntinus 55; EAA 147: 578); *corrept.* 11.30 (PL 44: 934); *Maxim.* 2.17.2 (CCSL 87A: 606).

53. Barnes, "Augustine's Last Pneumatology," 231.

Son could not be sent without the Spirit, "for it is understood that when the Father sent him, he did so of a woman, and certainly not without his Spirit."[54] He then cites the references to the Spirit in the Son's virgin birth (Luke 1:34–35; Matt 1:18) and in the sending of the Son (Isa 48:16). This discussion leads him to speculate about the Son's coactivity in his own sending.[55] Plantinga takes this as indicative of "Augustine's remorseless philosophical tendency to unify and simplify the divine life."[56] However, the inseparable operations of the three in this sending should not be mistaken for identical operations. As Gioia asserts with respect to this passage, "*inseparability—and, for that matter, equality—does not mean interchangeability*" (emphasis in original).[57] Similarly, we must not ignore Augustine's following exegetical remarks. Drawing on Scripture, Augustine clarifies that the Father "delivered up" (*tradidit eum*) the Son (Rom 8:32), the Son "delivered himself up" (*tradidit se ipsum*; Gal 2:20), and, citing Matt 1:18, the Spirit enabled the virgin to be found with child.[58] Though operating inseparably, their involvement in the Son's sending is not identical. As Gioia comments, "Divine action has to be attributed inseparably to Father, Son and Holy Spirit, but not as if it was carried out through the distribution of tasks to three equal sources of action."[59] There is a certain order and appropriation ascribed to the persons, but no reversal in any of the relations, not even when the Spirit is said to "send" the Son. In fact, Studer is able to infer the Son's peculiarity from this passage, since the Son's virgin birth inevitably reveals his eternal birth.[60] Hence, there is no conflict here between Augustine's treatment of the Spirit's role in the virgin birth and Rahner's Western Filioquism.

At one point in *Arian.*, Augustine gives the impression that the Son and Spirit possess interchangeable roles in sending one another. Comparing John 14:26 with Isa 48:12–16, Augustine states: "Here it is shown that both the Father and the Son send the Holy Spirit, as it is shown by the prophet that both the Father and the Holy Spirit sent the Son."[61] From Isa 48:16 he concludes: "Could it be clearer? Look, he himself says that he who laid the foundations of the earth and framed the heavens was sent by the Holy Spirit."[62] Augustine cites this verse to assert the divinity of

---

54. *Trin.* 2.5.8 (CCSL 50: 89): "quia intellegitur pater cum eum misit, id est fecit ex femina, wnon utique sine spiritu suo fecisse."

55. *Trin.* 2.5.9 (CCSL 50: 90–3). Augustine argues for the Son's involvement in his own sending with greater clarity in *Maxim.* 2.20.4 (CCSL 87A: 623–5).

56. Plantinga, 'The Fourth Gospel as Trinitarian Source Then and Now," 316–17.

57. Gioia, *The Theological Epistemology of Augustine's* De Trinitate, 162.

58. *Trin.* 2.5.9 (CCSL 50: 91). Augustine follows a similar line of argument in *Maxim.* 2.20.4 (CCSL 87A: 623–5).

59. Gioia, *The Theological Epistemology of Augustine's* De Trinitate, 162–3.

60. Studer, *Augustins* De Trinitate, 176.

61. *Arian.* 19.9 (CCSL 87A: 223): "Ubi ostenditur quod et Pater et Filius miserint Spiritum sanctum, sicut ostenditur per prophetam quod et Pater et Spiritus sanctus miserint Filium."

62. *Arian.* 19.9 (CCSL 87A: 224): "Quid euidentius? Ecce ipse se dicit missum ab Spiritu sancto qui fundauit terram et solidauit caelum."

the Spirit and the *inseparabilis operatio* of the three. Bonnardière suggests that this particular argument reached Augustine through Ambrose, and especially through the treatise *De spiritu sancto*.⁶³ Drawing on Isa 48:16 and 61:1 (par. Luke 4:18), Ambrose writes: "Because the Spirit is on Christ, and because the Son sent the Spirit, so the Spirit sent the Son of God."⁶⁴ This is written, Ambrose contends, to show that the Spirit is not of a "lower power" (*inferioris potestatis*).⁶⁵ While this argument may be intended to uphold the co-equality and unity of divine persons, *prima facie* it could seem to introduce a *Spirituque* into the immanent Trinity. If (1) the missions reveal the processions and (2) the Son's being sent by the Father reveals his eternal procession from the Father, surely (3) the Son's being sent by the Spirit reveals an eternal procession of the Son from the Father and the Spirit (*a Patre Spirituque*). This would appear to undermine Rahner's Rule.

However, Augustine offers an important qualification for his exegesis of Isa 48:16 in *Civ.*, where he writes:

> It was he [Jesus] who spoke as the Lord God. And yet it would not be understood that it was Jesus Christ had he not added, "And now the Lord God and his Spirit has sent me" [Isa 48:16]. For he said this referring to the form of a servant [*formam serui*], speaking of a future event using the past tense, as we read in the same prophet, "He was led as a sheep to the slaughter," [Isa 53:7]. Not, "He will be led," but the past tense is used to express the future.⁶⁶

Three important points emerge from this qualification. First, the Spirit's sending of the Son is not entirely the same as the Father's. While both certainly send the Son in *forma serui*, only the Father sends the Son in *forma dei*: "The Son is not only said to have been sent because 'the Word became flesh' [John 1:14], but he was thus sent so that the Word might become flesh, and by his bodily presence to do those things which were written."⁶⁷ The Spirit *only* sends the Son in *forma serui*. Second, the Spirit's sending of the Son differs from the Son's sending of

---

63. Bonnardière, *Recherches de chronologie Augustinienne*, 174.

64. *Spir.* 3.1.7 (CSEL 79: 152): "Quia spiritus super Christum et quia sicut filius spiritum misit, ita et filium dei spiritus misit."

65. *Spir.* 3.1.7 (CSEL 79: 152).

66. *Civ.* 20.30 (CCSL 48: 754):

> Ipse est, qui loquebatur sicut Dominus Deus; nec tamen intellegeretur Iesus Christus, nisi addidisset: et nunc dominus deus misit me et Spiritus eius. Dixit hoc enim secundum formam serui, de re futura utens praeteriti temporis uerbo, quem ad modum apud eundem prophetam legitur: sicut ouis ad immolandum ductus est. Non enim ait: "ducetur," sed pro eo, quod futurum erat, praeteriti temporis uerbum posuit.

67. *Trin.* 4.20.27 (CCSL 50: 195–6). "Secundum hoc iam potest intellegi non tantum ideo dici missus filius quia *uerbum caro factum est*, sed ideo missus ut uerbum caro fieret et

the Spirit. The Spirit sends the Son in *forma serui*, but the Son sends, gives, and pours out the Spirit as God.[68] Third, if the Spirit's "sending" only applies to the Son in *forma serui*, this sending only really commences at the virgin conception. It may also include the Spirit's driving or leading the Son into the desert wilderness (Matt 4:1; Mark 1:10; Luke 4:1)[69]—Augustine never rules this out—but certainly applies to the virgin conception and birth. According to Augustine, the Spirit's involvement in the conception cannot be said to introduce a reversal in the Son–Spirit relationship because the Son is also involved in his own conception. Again, there is no indication here that Augustine discerns a reversal in the Son–Spirit relationship that compromises Rahner's Rule.

Augustine makes similar overtures in *Serm.* 225 and 52. After affirming the Spirit's involvement (*operatus*) in bringing about the flesh of Christ in *Serm.* 225.2,[70] Augustine states:

> Christ himself, the Only Begotten Son of God brought about [*operates*] his own flesh. How do we prove this? Because Scripture says about it, "Wisdom has built a house for herself" [Prov 9:1].[71]

Similarly, in *Serm. 52*,[72] Augustine states that when "the Son emptied himself, taking the form of a servant, we see the nativity of the Son also made by the Son himself."[73] According to Augustine, the Son in *forma dei* is actively operative in the virgin birth, alongside the Father and the Spirit. If the Spirit's sending of the Son in Isa 48:16 results in an economic subordination of the Son to the Spirit, by the same logic the Son's assumption of flesh would result in an economic subordination of the Son in *forma serui* to himself in *forma dei*. Both are involved in the sending of the other. If this were not so, the inseparable operations would be compromised.

---

per praesentiam corporalem illa quae scripta sunt operaretur, id est ut non tantum homo missus intellegatur quod uerbum factum est."

68. *Trin.* 15.26.46 (CCSL 50A: 525–7).

69. Augustine is surprisingly quiet on these references, citing them in only a few places and without any comment. See *Cons.* 2.16.33 (CSEL 43: 133); *Serm.* 210.2 (PL 38: 1048).

70. Composed *c.* 400–5. For the dating, see Edmund Hill, notes on *Sermons on the New Testament (184–229Z)* by Augustine, vol. 6, The Works of Saint Augustine: A Translation for the 21st Century 3 (ed. John E. Rotelle; trans. Edmund Hill; Brooklyn: New City, 1992), 254, 259, n. 1.

71. *Serm.* 225.2 (CSEL 101: 113): "Operatus est et ipse Christus, unigenitus filius dei, carnem suam. Unde probamus? quia inde ait scriptura: Sapientia aedificavit sibi domum."

72. Composed *c.* 410–12. For the dating, see Edmund Hill, notes on *Sermons on the New Testament (51–94)* by Augustine, vol. 3, The Works of Saint Augustine: A Translation for the 21st Century 3 (ed. John E. Rotelle; trans. Edmund Hill; Brooklyn: New City, 1991), 62–3, n. 1.

73. *Serm.* 52.4.11 (CCSL 41Aa: 67): "sed quia ipse Filius semetipsum exinanivit, formam servi accipiens, videmus nativitatem Filii et ab ipso Filio factam."

However, the manner in which each one sends the other is not identical. The sending is mutual but asymmetrical. Yet again, there is no indication here that Augustine discerns a reversal in the Son–Spirit relationship that compromises Rahner's Rule.

Moreover, the Son's involvement in the assumption of flesh precedes the Spirit's. In *Trin.* 1.7.14, Augustine writes:

> Therefore, since the form of God [*forma dei*] took on the form of a servant [*formam serui*], each is God and each is man, but each is God because of God taking on, and each is man because of man taken on. Neither of them was turned or changed into the other by that assumption.[74]

It is the Son in *forma dei* that takes on the *forma serui*. According to Augustine, the Spirit is only involved in sending the Son in *forma serui*. How exactly the *inseparabilis operatio* remains intact if the Spirit does not send the Son in *forma dei* remains unanswered. However, this shows that, for Augustine, the Son's involvement in his assumption of flesh logically precedes the Spirit's involvement. Mühlen's argument is thus pre-empted by Augustine (as well as Athanasius and Cyril among others). We are then left with Jowers' objection to Mühlen's argument concerning the economic inversion of Son and Spirit, who both give to and receive from one another, an objection which may be overcome toward the end of *Trin.*

In *Trin.* book 15, Augustine offers a framework for discerning a parallel between the economic and immanent Son–Spirit relationship. In his discussion regarding the virgin birth and Pentecost, Augustine writes: "Because of this, the Lord Jesus himself not only gave the Holy Spirit as God but also received [*accepit*] him as a man."[75] As seen earlier, Augustine then states that in eternally begetting the Son, the Father *gave* him all things, including that the Spirit should proceed from him.[76] It is not difficult to discern some level of correspondence between the Son's reception of the Spirit in the immanent life and in the economy. In the economy, the Son receives the Spirit in the *forma serui* at his conception. In the immanent Trinity, the Son receives the Spirit in the *forma dei* as the *donum Dei*. As the Father begets the Son, he gives him the Spirit, or, more precisely, he gives to him that the Spirit should proceed from him. Obviously the Son's reception of the Spirit in *forma serui* is not identical with his reception of the Spirit in *forma dei*. One involves time and physical flesh; the other does not. Nevertheless, a correspondence may be discerned. Though the language of "receiving" (*accepit*) is

---

74. *Trin.* 1.7.14 (CCSL 50: 46): "Ergo quia *forma dei* accepit *formam serui*, utrumque *deus et* utrumque *homo*; sed utrumque *deus* propter accipientem deum, utrumque autem *homo* propter acceptum hominem. Neque enim illa susceptione alterum eorum in alterum conuersum atque mutatum est."

75. *Trin.* 15.26.46 (CCSL 50A: 526): "Propter hoc et dominus ipse Iesus spiritum sanctum non solum dedit ut deus sed etiam accepit ut homo."

76. For the quote in full, see p. 97.

not used in the passage mentioned earlier, it is implied by the concept of "giving" (*dedit*) and by the fact that the Spirit's proceeding jointly from the Son is "from the Father" (*de Patre*). As Kany notes, Augustine's contribution here would become the mainstay of later Latin Filioquist theology, about which the Eastern and Western churches still argue to this day.[77] More importantly for this book, we begin to see how Augustine's treatment of the virgin conception enables one to affirm Rahner's Rule and the *Filioque*.

Augustine elsewhere speaks of the Son "receiving" (*accepit*) the Spirit immanently. In one of his earlier anti-Donatist writings, *Contra epistulam Parmeniani* (*Parm.*),[78] Augustine draws a comparison between the Christian's reception of baptism and the Son's reception of the Spirit to undermine Parmenian's argument that baptism requires human mediation. This cannot be right, says Augustine,

> because, although the Son says that he received [*accepit*] from the Father and the Holy Spirit receives [*accepit*] from what is his, not as though "step by step" but as he explained when he said, "[a] All that the Father has is mine; [b] therefore I said, he shall receive [*accepit*] from what is mine [John 16:15]," yet John [the Baptist in John 3:27] himself testifies by his own example, along with so many saints before the Son of God became a man, that a person can receive something from heaven without a man's mediation.[79]

As we have already seen elsewhere, John 16:15a functions as Augustine's basis for stating that the Father gives to the Son that the Spirit proceeds from him. Now he uses the language of *accepit* used in 16:15b to explain what takes place in 16:15a: the Son "receives" (*accepit*) from the Father, just as the Spirit "receives" from the Father. Admittedly, *Parm.* is not one of Augustine's mature Trinitarian works. Still, the logic makes sense of Augustine's mature theology. Moments after the citation above, Augustine adds that "no one receives without a giver."[80] In the case of the Father "giving" the Spirit to the Son, the inverse must also be true. The giver does not give without one receiving. In this way, Augustine is able to account for the double procession of the Spirit and preserve the monarchy of the Father.

---

77. Kany, *Augustins Trinitätsdenken*, 222.

78. Composed *c.* 393–400. For the dating, see the notes by Maureen Tilley and Boniface Ramsey in *The Donatist Controversy I: general introduction and other introductions by † Maureen Tilley; translation and notes by † Maureen Tilley and Boniface Ramsey* by Augustine, ed. Boniface Ramsey and David G. Hunter, vol. 21, The Works of Saint Augustine: A Translation for the 21st Century 1 (Hyde Park, NY: New City, 2019), 265.

79. *Parm.* 2.15.34 (CSEL 51: 88): "quia, etsi dicit filius accepisse se a patre et spiritum sanctum de suo accipere, non quasi gradatim, sed sicut ipse exposuit dicens: quia omnia quae habet pater mea sunt, ideo dixi: de meo accipiet, posse tamen hominem non interposito homine diuinitus aliquid accipere exemplo suo iohannes ipse testatur et tot sancti, antequam dei filius homo fieret."

80. Ibid.: "Nemo ergo accipit sine dante."

Hence, the Son's economic reception of the Spirit in the virgin conception finds a parallel with his immanent reception of the Spirit. Just as the Son receives the Spirit from the Father immanently, so he receives the Spirit from the Father at the virgin birth. The case for Augustine's treatment of the virgin birth supporting Rahner's Rule is thus strengthening.

We now begin to see how the difficulty with Mühlen's proposal may be overcome. According to Mühlen, Jesus' reception of the Spirit in the economy is congruent with the *Filioque* because the Spirit was always "in" the Son. According to Jowers, this inverts the economic Son–Spirit relationship, thus rendering it incompatible with the *Filioque*. If this is read into the immanent Trinity, we are left with a situation in which "the eternal giver [the Son] receives, and the eternal receiver [the Spirit] gives."[81] However, in Augustine's model of the immanent Trinity, there is nothing wrong with saying that the eternal giver receives. The Son receives not just that the Spirit should proceed from him, but the Spirit himself. Moreover, he finds a way around needing to say that "the eternal receiver gives" to the Son: the Spirit is *given* to the Son. It would be surprising for one to accuse Augustine's model of requiring a *Spirituque* to complement the Spirit's joint procession from Father and Son. Augustine's fingerprints can be found all over magisterial statements on the Spirit's procession from the Son. According to DS 1300, "Since all that the Father has, the Father himself, in begetting, has given to His Only Begotten Son, with the exception of Fatherhood, the very fact that the Holy Spirit proceeds from the Son, the Son himself has from the Father eternally, by whom he was begotten also eternally." This clearly echoes what Augustine states in *Trin.* 15.26.47. Thus, Augustine overcomes the difficulty Jowers raised for Mühlen's model.

We also begin to see how the difficulty raised with Bourassa's model may be overcome. Bourassa speaks of the Father "giving" the Spirit to the Son. The difficulty with this view is that it seems to introduce two τάξεις into the immanent Trinity, an order of *origin* and an order of *circumincession*. Augustine avoids this dilemma. He preserves the monarchy of the Father and the joint procession of the Spirit by distinguishing between the Spirit's procession from the Father as *principaliter* and the Father and Son as one *principium*. The same result is likewise achieved by speaking of the Spirit (and the procession of the Spirit) as "given" to the Son. However, in not appealing to an "order of origin" and an "order of circumincession," he obviates the need to insist on multiple τάξεις in the immanent Trinity. This is not to say that Augustine evades circumincession. For the Spirit to proceed from the Son he must also indwell the Son. However, because the Spirit's procession from the Son is given to him, the one who already *is* the Son, it logically follows generation, even if this immanent "giving" and "receiving" takes place at the same "moment" as generation. We thus begin to see that what many term a relational "inversion" or "reversal" can be understood, immanently, in terms of "reception" and "procession." Just as in the virgin conception the Son receives the

---

81. Jowers, 'Test of Rahner's Axiom,' 444.

Spirit such that the Spirit should eventually be sent by him, so in eternity the Son receives that the Spirit should proceed from him. Augustine thus provides a model for the Spirit's being given to the Son in the virgin conception that parallels his model for the Spirit's being given to the Son *ad intra*.

Finally, Augustine may even push in the direction of the model adopted by Weinandy. According to Ayres:

> Augustine never discusses directly the extent to which we can speak of the Spirit having a role in the Son's generation. But because Augustine envisages the Father eternally constituting the Son through giving him his own personal and active Spirit who is love, we do seem to be able to conclude that the Son is generated *in* the Spirit. But this supposition remains just that. I suspect Augustine never discusses this question because of the lack of significant scriptural warrant, and because of his commitment to the standard taxis of Father–Son–Spirit. (emphasis in original)[82]

If Ayres' supposition is correct, Augustine's conception of the processions is also consistent with Weinandy's model. In Augustine's model, it seems that the Father's immanent giving of the Spirit logically—though obviously not temporally—follows his generation of the Son. Hence, it would seem that even here, Augustine avoids the need for a *Spirituque* to complement his account of the joint procession. Thus, Augustine's treatment of the Son–Spirit dynamic in the virgin birth seems to be consistent with his model of Trinitarian τάξις, thus corroborating Rahner's Rule.

5. The Jordan Baptism

Next, we consider how Augustine's account of the Jordan baptism further enhances Rahner's Rule. Though Augustine often refers to the Jordan baptism,[83] he usually tends to focus on the sacrament of baptism, especially in his anti-Donatist writings.[84] In a sermon from 397, Augustine explains that the Jordan baptism is significant because "an inseparable reality has been demonstrated separately."[85] That is, we see the Son in the man, the Spirit in the dove, and the Father in the voice. Consequently, as noted by Ployd in his work on the anti-Donatist sermons,

---

82. Ayres, *Augustine and the Trinity*, 265–6.

83. For example, *Ep.* 169.5 (CSEL 44: 615); *Cons.* 2.14.31 (CSEL 43: 131), 2.15.34 (CSEL 43: 131); *Trin.* 1.4.7; *Trin.* 3, proem.; *Serm.* 293B.3 (= Frangipane 8; MiAg 1: 229), 308A.4–5 (= Denis 11; MiAg 1: 45); *Arian.* 13.9 (CCSL 87A: 209), 15.9 (CCSL 87A: 214), 34.32 (CCSL 87A: 250); *Maxim.* 2.26.4 (CCSL 87A: 667–8).

84. For example, *Ep.* 89.5 (CCSL 31A: 150); *Tract. Ev. Jo.* 4–7 (CCSL 36: 31–81); *bapt.* 5.13.15 (CSEL 51: 276); *C. litt. Petil.* 2.2.5 (CSEL 52: 24).

85. *Serm.* 308A.4–5 (= Denis 11; MiAg 1: 45): "Res indiscreta discrete monstrata est."

When he preaches *Tract. Ev. Jo.* 5 and 6, Augustine already knows Christ's baptism as a Trinitarian theophany that manifests the principle of inseparable operations. Such a reading of John 1:33 allows Augustine to reorient the nature of the church founded on baptism away from the concrete historical work of the bishops and toward the eternal work of the Son who operates inseparably from the Spirit whom he gives in every baptism.[86]

In *Serm.* 52 Augustine offers an extended discussion of the Trinity with reference to the Jordan baptism, yet most of his time is taken up with the Father–Son relationship, the inseparable operations, and the psychological analogy.[87] In the previous chapter we saw that the order in which the divine three persons are mentioned does not phase Augustine, and that, when discussing this scene, he even reorders the persons to follow the Father–Son–Spirit pattern. Overall, Augustine is not particularly concerned with Trinitarian relations when treating the baptism scene, except when emphasizing that the Christ is the one who gives the Spirit.

Nevertheless, while his main interest in the baptism scene may lie elsewhere, that does not mean it has nothing to say about the Son–Spirit relationship. When addressing the Spirit's activity at the virgin conception in *Trin.* 15.26.46, Augustine turns to the Jordan baptism. He writes that "our Lord Jesus himself not only gave [*dedit*] the Holy Spirit as God [*Deus*] but also received [*accepit*] him as man [*homo*]."[88] Then he continues:

> Indeed, Christ was not only anointed with the Holy Spirit when he came down upon him as a dove at his baptism; what he was doing then was foreshadowing his body, that is his church, in which it is chiefly those who have just been baptized that receive the Holy Spirit. … We confess that he was born of the Holy Spirit and of the virgin Mary. For it is most absurd to believe that he only received [*accepisse*] the Holy Spirit when he was already thirty years old (that was the age at which he was baptized by John). Rather, just as he came to that baptism without any sin at all, so he came to it not without the Holy Spirit.[89]

---

86. Adam Ployd, *Augustine, the Trinity, and the Church: A Reading of the Anti-Donatist Sermons* (London: OUP, 2015), 154.

87. *Serm.* 52 (CCSL 41Aa: 58–80).

88. *Trin.* 15.26.46 (CCSL 50A: 526): "Propter hoc et dominus ipse Iesus spiritum sanctum non solum dedit ut deus sed etiam accepit ut homo."

89. *Trin.* 15.26.46 (CCSL 50A: 526–7)

> Nec sane tunc unctus est Christus spiritu sancto quando super eum baptizatum uelut columba descendit; tunc enim corpus suum, id est ecclesiam suam, praefigurare dignatus est in qua praecipue baptizati accipiunt spiritum sanctum. … Ob hoc eum confitemur natum de spiritu sancto et uirgine Maria. Absurdissimum est enim ut credamus eum cum iam triginta esset annorum (eius enim aetatis a Iohanne baptizatus est) accepisse spiritum sanctum, sed uenisse ad illud baptisma sicut sine ullo omnino peccato ita non sine spiritu sancto.

According to Hill, Augustine here rejects the adoptionist heresy "which declared that Jesus (a mere human being) was *adopted* as Son of God at his baptism, when the Holy Spirit came upon him."[90] This heresy is so absurd to Augustine because Christ had already been anointed and thus received the Spirit at his conception. While Christ still "receives" (*accepisse*) the Spirit at his baptism, he does so as a public announcement to his church, a foreshadowing of what they will receive. Notably, this reception of the Spirit at the baptism parallels the reception of the Spirit at the virgin birth.

As we saw earlier, immediately after Augustine discusses the Son's economic reception of the Spirit in *Trin.* 15.26.46 he turns to the Son's immanent reception of the Spirit, or, more precisely, how the Father has given to the Son that the Spirit should proceed from him (*Trin.* 15.26.47). Hence, for Augustine, the baptism theophany poses no real obstacle for Rahner's Rule. Just as the Son receives the Spirit immanently and at his conception, so he receives the Spirit (symbolically) at his baptism. For Augustine, the baptismal reception of the Spirit parallels the Son's immanent reception of the Spirit. We know that for Augustine the processions are revealed by the missions. From passages such as these we see, with Barnes, that the "repetitious character of the Spirit's *missio* is both revealed by and serves to explain the different manifestations of the Holy Spirit" such as "the dove at the Jordan."[91] The dove at the Jordan reveals the Spirit's mission which in turn reveals the Spirit's procession. Therefore, if we follow Augustine's lead, there is no need for a complementary *Spirituque*. Hence, Augustine's treatment of the baptism scene lends credence to Rahner's Rule.

6. Ministry

Similarly, Augustine's account of the Son–Spirit dynamic in Jesus' ministry parallels the immanent relationship, thus further supporting Rahner's Rule. At times this is not immediately evident. For example, in *Trin.* 1.11.22, Augustine writes that the Son

---

90. Hill continues:

> This particular heretical belief had more or less faded away by Augustine's time, and so he does not refer to it explicitly here. As a heresy, we can probably say, it only represented a hardening or freezing of an archaic understanding of the person of Jesus Christ which found expression in the story of his baptism. What seems to have happened, according to modern New Testament scholars, is that the primitive christology underlying the New Testament texts developed backward. The earliest strand saw Jesus as made or appointed Christ, Lord, Son of God by being raised from the dead (Acts 2:36; 13:33; Rom 1:4; see also Mt 28:18). (Hill, comments in *The Trinity: Introduction, Translation and Notes*, by Augustine, 560, n. 125)

91. Barnes, "Augustine's Last Pneumatology," 226.

is less than the Holy Spirit, because he himself said, "Whoever speaks blasphemy against the Son of Man, it will be forgiven him. But whoever speaks against the Holy Spirit, it will not be forgiven him" [Matt 12:32]. He also worked his deeds of power through him, as he said himself: "If I cast out demons by the Spirit of God, surely he kingdom of God has come upon you" [Matt 12:28]. And he says in Isaiah, in the reading he read in the synagogue and which he declared fulfilled in himself without a scruple of doubt, "The Spirit of the Lord is upon [*super*] me; because he has anointed me, he has sent me to preach the gospel to the poor, to proclaim release to the captives" and so on. [Isa 61:1; par. Luke 4:18]. It was precisely because the Spirit of the Lord was upon [*super*] him, he says, that he was sent to do these things.[92]

Ayres notes that Hilary had used Matt 12:28 and Luke 4:18 to argue for the Spirit's divinity.[93] Here, Augustine seems to go further, arguing that these verses seem to indicate that the Son is "less than" the Spirit since he can be blasphemed while the Spirit cannot; the Son is empowered by the Spirit; the Spirit is "upon" or "over" the Son. When read out of context, this quote gives the strong impression that Augustine discerns an inversion in the economic Son–Spirit relationship that, according to his own methodology, should be read into God's processional life.

However, when read in context, we see how Augustine avoids reaching the conclusion that the Spirit must therefore be greater than—or in some other sense "prior to"—the Son in the immanent Trinity. Immediately before the citation earlier, Augustine writes:

> According to the form of God [*formam dei*] the Son is equal to the Father, and so is the Holy Spirit, because neither of them is a creature, as we have already shown. However, in the form of a servant [*formam serui*], he is less than the Father, because he himself said, "The Father is greater than I" [John 14:28]. He is also less than himself, because it is said of him that "he emptied himself" [Phil 2:7].[94]

---

92. *Trin.* 1.11.22 (CCSL 50: 60):

> minor est spiritu sancto quia ipse ait: Qui dixerit blasphemiam in filium hominis, remittetur ei; qui autem dixerit in spiritum sanctum, non dimittetur ei. Et in ipso uirtutes operatus est dicens: Si ego in spiritu dei eicio daemonia, certe superuenit super uos regnum dei. Et apud Esaiam dicit, quam lectionem ipse in synagoga recitauit et de se completam sine scrupulo dubitationis ostendit: Spiritus, inquit, domini super me; propter quod unxit me, euangelizare pauperibus misit me, praedicare captiuis remissionem, et cetera; ad quae facienda ideo se dicit missum quia spiritus domini est super eum.

93. Ayres, *Augustine and the Trinity*, 90. Cf. Hilary, *Trin.* 8.21–24 (CCSL 62A: 333–6).

94. *Trin.* 1.11.22 (CCSL 50: 60): "Nam secundum *formam dei aequalis* est *patri* et filius et spiritus sanctus quia neuter eorum creatura est sicut iam ostendimus; secundum *formam*

As well as preventing any economic subordination of the Son to the Father being read into the immanent Trinity, Augustine's *form* rule also prevents the Son's being "less than" the Spirit being read into the immanent Trinity. The Son in *forma dei* is equal to the Father and the Spirit. He is only less in *forma serui*. Following Augustine's logic, it would also be unwise to assume that the Son's being "less than" the Spirit indicates some other kind of immanent priority of the Spirit, for the Son in *forma serui* is also "less than himself" in the *forma dei*. Hence, Augustine does not see a "reversal" in the Son–Spirit relationship any more than he sees one in the Son of Man–Son of God relationship.

This argument reflects a strategy teased out in greater detail in Augustine's written reply to Maximinus (*Maxim.*). In Augustine's earlier debate with the Homoian–Arian bishop (*Coll. Max.*), Maximinus says he knows of no biblical text that speaks of the Spirit as creator and challenges the bishop to produce such texts.[95] In *Maxim.* Augustine shifts to consider why Scripture never speaks of the Father as "greater" than the Spirit. As Barnes notes, "central to his argument is to show that by the rules of Homoian exegesis Scripture presents a hyper-pneumatology, that is, a theology in which the Son is subordinated to the Holy Spirit."[96] If silence is sufficient for a doctrinal conclusion, "then the fact is that Scripture says that the Son obeys and glorifies the Father but it says nothing about the Spirit obeying and glorifying the Son, or, for that matter, the Father. If taken seriously, the rules of Homoian exegesis actually produce a conclusion opposite to what the Homoians teach."[97] Thus, Barnes summarizes the outcome of Augustine's argument as such: "Only pro-Nicene theology can read the scriptural texts with the interpretation that corresponds to the doctrine and sense of the Church— namely, that the Holy Spirit is not 'above' or prior to the Son."[98] This will shape Augustine's approach to other texts that might seem to indicate the Spirit's being "above" or "prior to" the Son.

Augustine's interpretation of blasphemy and the Spirit in Matt 12 develops later in his career. As Hill notes, Augustine's "long and rambling" *Serm.* 71 offers "an improvement on what he says about the subject" in *Trin.*[99] He no longer argues that the Spirit is greater than the Son in *forma serui* on the basis of what Jesus says on blasphemy in Matt 12:32:

> Therefore, we ought not go along with those who give the following reason why a word spoken against the Son of Man is forgiven, while a word spoken against the Holy Spirit is not. They suppose that because Christ became the Son of Man

---

autem *serui minor* est *patre* quia ipse dixit: *Pater maior me est*; minor est se ipso quia de illo dictum est: *Semetipsum exinaniuit*."

95. *Coll. Max.* 15.21 (CCSL 87A: 455–6).
96. Barnes, "Augustine's Last Pneumatology," 230.
97. Ibid.
98. Ibid., 231.
99. Composed *c.* 417–20. Hill, *Sermons on the New Testament (51–94)*, 3:270–1, n. 1.

by taking on flesh, the Holy Spirit is certainly greater than this flesh, who by his own substance is equal to the Father and to the Only Begotten Son in his divinity, in which the Only Begotten Son is also equal to the Father and the Holy Spirit.[100]

Augustine discovers a problem with his former interpretation. "Did the Father receive the form of a servant, which the Holy Spirit could surpass in greatness? Not at all."[101] Why then is it said that only blasphemy against the Spirit cannot be forgiven and not blasphemy against the Father? Augustine must opt for a new interpretation. Thus, he arrives at what will become the classic interpretation of Matt 12:32: blasphemy against the Holy Spirit is to be equated with lifelong unrepentance and rejection of the Spirit's regenerative activity.[102] Hence, the case for *any* kind of reversal or inversion in Augustine's portrayal of the Son–Spirit relationship from this verse is destroyed. Matt 12:32 is no longer an outside threat to Rahner's Rule.

Augustine likewise develops his interpretation of Matt 12:28 in *Serm.* 71. What does it mean for Jesus to cast out demons "in the Spirit"? Augustine now seriously entertains the possibility that this verse is a case of

> the Holy Spirit given by the Father or the Son rather than by his own will, and that it's saying here, "In the Holy Spirit I cast out demons," is an instance of this. It wasn't the Spirit himself, but Christ who did this in the Spirit; so that we should understand "In the Holy Spirit I cast out demons" as meaning "I cast out by the Holy Spirit." It is common for the Scriptures to speak this way.[103]

In other words, Augustine sees the Spirit as involved instrumentally. Such a reading should not deprive the Spirit of his own proper authority and initiative,

---

100. *Serm.* 71.14.24 (CCSL 41Ab: 47):

> Proinde nec illud sentiendum est, quod quidam putant, ideo remitti uerbum quod dicitur contra Filium hominis, non remitti autem quod dicitur contra Spiritum sanctum, quia propter susceptam carnem factus est Filius hominis Christus, qua carne utique maior est Spiritus sanctus, qui substantia propria aequalis est Patri et unigenito Filio secundum eius diuinitatem, secundum quam et ipse unigenitus Filius aequalis est Patri et Spiritui sancto.

101. Ibid.: 48: "Numquidnam et Pater formam serui accepit, qua sit maior Spiritus sanctus? Non utique."

102. *Serm.* 71.12.20 (CCSL 41Ab: 42).

103. *Serm.* 71.26 (CCSL 41Ab: 50): "Hic forte quis dicat, Spiritum sanctum dari potius a Patre uel Filio quam sua uoluntate aliquid operari; et ad hoc pertinere quod dictum est *In Spiritu sancto eicio daemonia*, quod non ipse Spiritus sed Christus id faceret Spiritu: ut sic intellegatur quod dictum est *in Spiritu sancto eicio*, tamquam diceretur 'Spiritu sancto eicio.' Solent quippe ita loqui Scripturae."

citing John 3:8 and 1 Cor 12:9–11.[104] However, the activity of casting out demons no longer indicates the Spirit's being greater than the Son. As such, no "reversal" in the Son–Spirit relationship need be discerned from Matt 12:28.

The language of the Spirit being "over" the Son in Luke 4:18 (par. Isa 61:1) could cause problems for the Rule. We know that Ambrose sought to downplay such language by asserting that the Spirit is not really "over Christ" (*super Christum*) but, rather, "in Christ" (*in Christo*).[105] Ayres suggests that this "represents a distinctively Latin pro-Nicene discussion."[106] The difficulty is, of course, that the preposition *super* really does mean "over."

To his credit, Augustine affirms that there is a real sense in which the Spirit is "over" or "upon" (*super*) the Son. The key distinction is that this is so for the Son in the *forma serui*.[107] The bishop often directs attention to the mutuality in the Son–Spirit relationship to refute the Homoian–Arian claims of the Spirit's ontological subordination to the Son. In *Arian.*, Augustine writes:

> Furthermore, if they say that the Holy Spirit speaks what the Son commands, because it is written, "He will receive from what is mine and make it known to you" [John 16:14], why does the Son not also speak what the Holy Spirit commands? For the apostle says, "No one knows the things of God except the Spirit of God" [1 Cor 2:11]. And Jesus himself states that these words of scripture were fulfilled in him, "The Spirit of the Lord is over [*super*] me, because he has anointed me to preach the gospel to the poor" [Luke 4:18; par. Isa 61:1]. For if on this account he was anointed to preach the gospel to the poor, because the Spirit of the Lord was over [*super*] him, what good news did he preach to the poor but the Spirit of the Lord which he had, with whom he was filled? For this also is written of him, that he "was filled with the Holy Spirit" [Luke 4:1].[108]

Augustine is critical of his Homoian–Arian opponents for recognizing only one direction of the Son–Spirit relationship, that of the Son to the Spirit (as in John

---

104. Ibid.: 51.
105. Ambrose, *Spir.* 3.1.6 (CSEL 79: 151).
106. Ayres, *Augustine and the Trinity*, 49.
107. For example, *Enarrat. Ps.* 108.26 (CCSL 40: 1599); *Tract. Ev. Jo.* 74.3 (CCSL 36: 514); *Coll. Max.* 11 (CCSL 87A: 393–4); *Arian.* 22.18–23.19 (CCSL 87A: 229–30).
108. *Arian.* 22.18 (CCSL 87A: 229):

> Porro si Spiritum sanctum ideo "haec loqui" dicunt "quae mandat Filius," quia scriptum est: *De meo accipiet et adnuntiabit uobis*, cur non et Filius ea loquitur quae mandat Spiritus sanctus, cum dicat apostolus: *Quae Dei sunt, nemo scit nisi Spiritus Dei*, et cum ipse Iesus de seipso impletum esse confirmet, quod scriptum est: Spiritus Domini super me; propter quod unxit me euangelizare pauperibus? Si enim propter hoc unctus est euangelizare pauperibus, quia *Spiritus Domini super eum erat, quid euangelizabat pauperibus* nisi quod Spiritus Domini habebat quo repletus erat? Nam et hoc de illo scriptum est quod repletus sit Spiritu sancto.

16:14). In drawing upon Luke 4:18 and 4:1, Augustine is able to demonstrate reciprocity in the Son–Spirit relationship. The Son is anointed and filled with the Spirit who empowers his mission. While advocating mutuality in the Son–Spirit relationship, he does not insist upon a kind of identical symmetry that would pose a dilemma for the Rule.

Of course, there is still the difficulty that Luke 4:18 uses the exact language of the Spirit being "over" or "above" (*super*) the Son. However, Augustine has another strategy for managing this difficulty. In *Tract. Ev. Jo.* 74,[109] the bishop discerns a strong alignment between Luke 4:18 and John 3:34, the latter speaking of the Father giving the Spirit to the Son "without measure." Importantly, Augustine does not restrict the Father's giving the Spirit without measure to the economy. He writes:

> [A₁] But, when John the Baptist said, "For God does not give the Spirit by measure [John 3:34]," he was speaking about the Son of God himself to whom the Spirit was not given by measure because in him dwells all the "fullness of the Godhead" [*plenitudo diuinitatis*; Col 2:9]. [B₁] And neither is it without the grace of the Holy Spirit that the mediator between God and humanity is the man Jesus Christ; for he also said about himself that that word of the prophet had been fulfilled: "The Spirit of the Lord is upon [*super*] me because he has anointed me. He has sent me to bring the good news to the poor" [Luke 4:18 par. Isa 61:1]. [A₂] For that he is the Only Begotten, equal to the Father, is not of grace but of nature; [B₂] but that the man was taken up into the unity of the person of the Only Begotten is of grace not of nature.[110]

According to Augustine, John 3:34 is not only about the Father giving the Spirit to the Christ "without measure" in the economy. When Augustine says that the verse is "speaking about the Son of God himself to whom the Spirit was not given by measure," he is speaking about the Son in *forma dei*. This is strongly implied in speaking of the Son as "Son of God," a title Augustine normally uses for the Son in *forma dei*, and in the reference to the *plenitudo diuinitatis*. In *Maxim.* Augustine writes that the Father "begot one as great as he himself is, because he begot the true Son out of himself and begot him perfect in the fullness of the Godhead

---

109. Bonnardière, *Recherches de chronologie Augustinienne*, 65–87.
110. *Tract. Ev. Jo.* 74.3 (CCSL 36: 514):

> Quando autem ait iohannes baptista: *Non enim ad mensuram dat Deus Spiritum*, de ipso Dei Filio loquebatur, cui non est datus Spiritus ad mensuram; quia in illo inhabitat omnis plenitudo diuinitatis. Neque enim sine gratia Spiritus sancti est mediator Dei et hominum homo Christus Iesus; nam et ipse dicit de se fuisse propheticum illud impletum: *Spiritus Domini super me; propter quod unxit me, euangelizare pauperibus misit me*. Quod enim est unigenitus aequalis patri, non est gratiae, sed naturae; quod autem in unitatem personae unigeniti assumtus est homo, gratiae est, non naturae.

[*plenitudo diuinitatis*], not as one to be made perfect by an increase of age."[111] The *plenitudo diuitatis* dwells in the Son because the Father eternally begot him. This contrast between the Son in his divinity and humanity is further demonstrated by Augustine's contrasting divinity and humanity in those sections demarcated A_1 and B_1 above, and his contrasting nature and grace in A_2 and B_2. Thus, when Augustine writes that John "was speaking about the Son of God himself to whom the Spirit was not given by measure," he is adding exegetical support to what he writes concerning the Father "giving" the Spirit to the Son in *Trin.* 15.26.47.

The parallel drawn between John 3:34 and Luke 4:18 is telling. Augustine discerns a parallel between the giving of the Spirit to the Son in *forma dei* in A_1 with the anointing of the Spirit upon the Son in *forma serui* in B_1. Just as the Son is not without the Spirit immanently, "neither is the man Jesus Christ, the mediator of God and Man, without the grace of the Holy Spirit" in the economy. Augustine understands Jesus' possession of "the grace of the Holy Spirit" in terms of the anointing with the Spirit of Luke 4:18. Hence, the anointing is the economic analogue to the Father's immanent giving of the Spirit. Augustine's interpretation of Luke 4:18 actually supports Rahner's Rule.

Admittedly, Augustine's exegesis of John 3:34 is subject to development. In his early *De sermone domini in monte libri duo* (*Serm. Dom.*),[112] Augustine understands this verse to refer to the Father's giving of eternal and spiritual things to human subjects, as opposed to the giving of temporal things.[113] In his late *Retractionum libri duo* (*Retract.*),[114] he comments: "In another place, though I cited this text as a proof: 'For not by measure does God give the Spirit [John 3:34],' I did not yet understand that this is, more truly, to be understood in a proper sense about Christ."[115] That is, he understands the verse to refer to the Father giving the Spirit to the Christ in the economy. In a passing comment in *Tract. Ev. Jo.* 14.10, Augustine likewise speaks of "Christ" receiving the Spirit not by measure.[116] Though in his *Retract.* Augustine refutes his earlier reading of John 3:34 in *Serm. Dom.*—now arguing that it refers to the man "Christ" receiving the Spirit rather than humanity—he does not retract his reading of John 3:34 in *Tract. Ev. Jo.* 74 in which he understands the Spirit as being given to the Son in his divinity. There is no indication that Augustine does not read the verse as referring to the Son's

---

111. *Maxim.* 2.14.9 (CCSL 87A: 586): "Ac per hoc tantum genuit quantus est ipse, quia de seipso genuit uerum Filium, et perfectum genuit plenitudine diuinitatis, non perficiendum aetatis accessu."

112. Composed *c.* 393. Cf. Jos. Mizzi, "The Latin Text of Matt. V–VII in St. Augustine's « De Sermone Domini in Monte »," *Augustiniana*, vol. 4, no. 3 (1954): 453.

113. *Serm. Dom.* 1.6.17 (CCSL 35: 17).

114. Composed *c.* 427. Cf. Bogan M. Inez, *St Augustine: The Retractions*, vol. 60, The Fathers of the Church: A New Translation (Washington, DC: CUA Press, 1968), xiii.

115. *Retract.* 1.19.3 (PL 32: 615): "Alio loco quod interposui testimonium: *Non enim ad mensuram dat Deus spiritum*, nondum intellexeram de Christo proprie verius accipi."

116. *Tract. Ev. Jo.* 14.10 (CCSL 36: 148).

reception of the Spirit without measure *ad extra* and *ad intra*. This suggests that, for Augustine, such a demarcation would place a "measure" on the Father's giving of the Spirit, in contradiction of what the text says.

It is worth reiterating that, from Augustine's perspective, none of this undermines his understanding of the Spirit's joint procession from the Father and the Son. We see this most clearly in *Trin.* 15.26.47, *Tract. Ev. Jo.* 99, and *Maxim.* 2.14.1. In the latter of these, Augustine writes that the Father "begot a Son and, by begetting him, gave it to him that the Holy Spirit might proceed from him also."[117] The Spirit proceeds jointly from both precisely because the Father gives the Spirit to the Son. For Augustine, this is how the Son is able to say, "All that the Father has is mine," with reference to the Spirit. Thus, in several of the passages just cited, Augustine is able to move on quickly from texts like Matt 12:28, 12:32; Luke 4:1 and 4:18 to consider the Spirit's joint procession without a moment's hesitation.[118]

Therefore, it is not difficult to discern a strong correspondence between Augustine's teaching on the Son–Spirit relationship in Jesus' ministry and his teaching on Trinitarian τάξις. While there is a strong sense of mutuality in the Son–Spirit relationship, both *ad intra* and *ad extra*, there is also a strong sense in which this mutuality is asymmetrical for Augustine. In the immanent Trinity, the Spirit proceeds from the Son; the Son does not proceed from the Spirit. The Spirit is given to the Son; the Son is not given to the Spirit. In the economy, the Son in *forma dei* sends the Spirit; the Spirit only sends the Son in *forma serui*. The Son "gives" the Spirit; the Spirit is never said to "give" the Son. The Spirit "fills" the Son; the Son is not said to "fill" the Spirit. The Son in *forma serui* is subordinate to the Spirit who is "upon" or "over" him, but this subordination cannot be read into the immanent Trinity, just as the subordination of the Son to the Father in *forma serui* does not indicate a subordination of the Son to the Father in *forma dei*. If anything, the Spirit's being "over" or "upon" the Son as the Father anoints the Son is the economic expression of the Father immanently "giving" the Spirit to the Son (such that the Spirit then jointly proceeds from the Son). Given the asymmetry of the Son–Spirit relationship *ad intra* and *ad extra*, it is difficult to see why Augustine would need a *Spirituque*. The category of "Gift" complements his model of the double procession adequately. Thus, Augustine offers a reading strategy for interpreting those verses pertaining to the Spirit's involvement in the Son's ministry that is compatible with his own model of the immanent Son–Spirit relationship, a model foundational to Rahner's Western Filioquism. As with the virgin conception and the Jordan baptism, Augustine's framework for interpreting verses concerning the Son–Spirit relationship in Jesus' messianic ministry thus supports Rahner's Rule.

---

117. *Maxim.* 2.14.1 (CCSL 87A: 568): "qui talem Filium genuit, et gignendo ei dedit ut etiam de ipso procederet Spiritus sanctus."
118. *Serm.* 71.18.29 (CCSL 41Ab: 56); *Arian.* 23.19 (CCSL 87A: 230–1); *Maxim.* 2.17.4 (CCSL 87A: 607–8).

7. Resurrection

In his treatment of those texts referring—or potentially referring—to the Spirit's involvement in the resurrection (Rom 1:4; 8:11; 1 Tim 3:16; 1 Pet 3:18), Augustine discerns no conflict between the economic and immanent Son–Spirit relationship. His reading strategy thus supports Rahner's Rule. Though in most cases Augustine is disinterested in the Son–Spirit relationship when citing Rom 1:4,[119] this is not the case in *De praedestinatione sanctorum liber ad Prosperum et Hilarium primus* (hereafter *Praed.*).[120] Augustine comments:

> Therefore, Jesus was predestined so that he who was to be the Son of David according to the flesh should yet be in power the Son of God, according to the Spirit of sanctification, because he was born of the Holy Spirit and of the Virgin Mary. This is the unspeakably singular acceptance of man by the Word of God, so that the Son of God and the Son of Man at the same time, the Son of Man on account of the man received, and the Son of God on account of the one who receives the Only Begotten God, should be truly and properly called; lest there should be believed not a Trinity, but a quaternity.[121]

The bishop understands the reference to the Spirit in terms of his involvement in the virgin conception rather than the resurrection. As we saw earlier from *Trin.* 15.26.46–47, Augustine's interpretation of the Spirit's involvement in the virgin conception parallels the Father's giving the Son to have the Spirit proceeding from himself immanently. Thus, it seems likely that his interpretation of Rom 1:4 comports similarly. Admittedly, Augustine's interpretation of Rom 1:4 ignores the reference to the resurrection entirely, an oversight that many commentators

---

119. For example, *exp. prop. Rm.* 1 (CSEL 84: 3); *Ep. Rm. inch.* 5.2 (CSEL 84: 158); 5.4 (CSEL 84: 158); 5.5 (CSEL 84: 158); 7.2 (CSEL 84: 162); *en. Ps* 67.15 (CCSL 39: 878); *c. Fort* 19 (CSEL 25,1: 96); *Trin.* 12.6.7 (CCSL 50: 362).

120. *c.* 428/9. For the dating of *Praed.*, see Mark Vessey, "*Opus Imperfectum*: Augustine and His Readers, 426–435 A.D.," *Vigiliae Christianae*, vol. 52, no. 3 (1998): 275.

121. *Praed.* 1.15.31 (PL 44: 982):

> praedestinatus est ergo iesus, ut qui futurus erat secundum carnem filius dauid, esset tamen in uirtute filius dei secundum spiritum sanctificationis; quia natus est de spiritu sancto et uirgine maria. ipsa est illa ineffabiliter facta hominis a deo uerbo susceptio singularis, ut filius dei et filius hominis simul, filius hominis propter susceptum hominem, et filius dei propter suscipientem unigenitum deum ueraciter et proprie diceretur; ne non trinitas, sed quaternitas crederetur.

One imagines that Rahner would be relieved by Augustine's denial of divine quarternity. The phrase "a deo uerbo" may also be translated "God-Word" as distinct from "a dei uerbo," the usual phrase for "Word of God."

consider mistaken.[122] Nevertheless, it seems likely that the bishop would not find the Spirit's involvement in the resurrection incongruous with the immanent Son-Spirit relationship.

While Augustine's exegesis of Rom 8:11 often overlooks the Spirit's involvement at the resurrection,[123] we can certainly affirm that Augustine discerns no incongruity between the Son–Spirit dynamic and his model of the processions. In fact, as Studer notes, Rom 8:9 is one of Augustine's foundational texts for designating the Spirit as "Gift" (*donum*) in *Trin.* 5.11.12,[124] a reading du Roy suggests was adopted from Hilary.[125] Though Augustine does not use Rom 8:11 to describe the Spirit as the joint Gift of the Father and the Son, it is foundational to his account of the joint procession. In *Tract. Ev. Jo.* 99.6, he writes:

> Here someone may perhaps inquire whether the Holy Spirit also proceeds from the Son. For the Son is the Son of the Father only, and the Father is the Father of the Son only; but the Holy Spirit is the Spirit not of one of them, but of both. You have the Lord himself who says, "For it is not you who speak, but the Spirit of your Father who speaks in you" [Matt 10:20]. And you have the Apostle saying, "God has sent the Spirit of his Son into your hearts" [Gal 4:6]. … You have in another place the same Apostle saying, "But if the Spirit of him who raised Jesus from the dead dwells in you" [Rom 8:11]. He certainly wanted the Spirit of the Father to be understood, about whom nevertheless in another place he says, "But whoever does not have the Spirit of Christ, he is none of his" [Rom 8:9]. And there are many other testimonies by which it is clearly shown that he is the Spirit of the Father and of the Son, who in the Trinity is called the Holy Spirit.[126]

---

122. Barton, for example, argues from this verse that "Jesus was exalted to divine sonship by his resurrection, was 'designated Son of God.'" Stephen Barton, "Paul and the Resurrection: A Sociological Approach," *Religion*, vol. 14, no. 1 (January 1984): 69.

123. For example, *Ep.* 55.3 (CCSL 31: 236); 55.26 (CCSL 31: 256); 193.5 (CSEL 57: 171); *Gen. litt.* 6 (CSEL 28,1: 195); *exp. prop. Rm.* 12 (CSEL 84: 8); 43 (CSEL 84: 23); *Enarrat. Ps.* 114.8 (CCSL 40: 1651–2); 146.6 (CCSL 40: 2126); *Serm.* 155.15 (CCSL 41Ba: 128); 256.3 (PL 38: 1193); 362.24 (PL 39: 1628); *Div. quaest. LXXXIII* 66.7 (CCSL 44A: 162); *Civ.* 13.23 (CCSL 48: 406); *c. Faust.* 24.2 (CSEL 25,1: 723); *c. Spec* 10 (CSEL 25.2: 921); *Trin.* 4.3.5 (CCSL 50: 166); *Pecc. merit.* 1.4.4 (CSEL 60: 6); 1.7.7 (CSEL 60: 6); *C. du. ep. Pelag.* 1.11.24 (CSEL 60: 444); *C. Jul. op. imp.* 1.96 (CSEL 85,1:111); 4.136 (CSEL 85,2:163); 6.7 (CSEL 85,2:301).

124. Studer, *Augustins De Trinitate*, 176, n. 31.

125. Du Roy, *L'Intelligence de la Foi en la Trinité selon Saint Augustin*, 322. Cf. Hilary, *Trin.* 2.29 (CCSL 62: 64–5).

126. *Tract. Ev. Jo.* 99.6 (CCSL 36: 585–6):

> Hic aliquis forsitan quaerat utrum et a Filio procedat Spiritus sanctus. Filius enim solius Patris est Filius, et Pater solius Filii est Pater; Spiritus autem sanctus non est unius eorum Spiritus, sed amborum. Habes ipsum dominum dicentem: *non enim uos estis qui loquimini, sed Spiritus Patris uestri qui loquitur in uobis;* habes et apostolum: *Misit Deus Spiritum Filii sui in corda uestra.* … Habes alio loco

Here, Augustine reads Rom 8:9 together with 8:11 as textual support for the joint procession of the Spirit. From Rom 8:11 he deduces that the Spirit is the "Spirit of the Father." From Rom 8:9 he deduces that the Spirit is "the Spirit of the Son" since he is "the Spirit of Christ." In the larger pericope, this is used as evidence that the Spirit proceeds jointly from the Father and the Son.

Augustine makes the same point in *Maxim.* 2.14.1:

> And because he proceeds from both of them, as we have already shown, he is called the Spirit of the Father where we read, "If the Spirit of him who has raised Christ from the dead dwells in you" [Rom 8:11], and the Spirit of the Son where we read, "He who does not have the Spirit of Christ does not belong to him" [Rom 8:9].[127]

Far from inverting the Son–Spirit relationship economically, Augustine reads Rom 8:11 with 8:9 as indicative of the Spirit's joint procession. Admittedly, in both the tractate and the response to Maximinus, Augustine overlooks the Spirit's actual involvement in the resurrection. Perhaps this oversight can be excused by the fact that it is the Father, to whom the Spirit belongs, who explicitly raises the Son in this verse. However, at the very least, Augustine's interpretation demonstrates that Rom 8:11 need not be taken as an example of an inverted economic Son–Spirit relationship. It can be read, alongside Rom 8:11, as an economic foundation for the Spirit's internal joint procession.

For Augustine, the reference to the *spiritus* in 1 Pet 3:18 ("He was put to death in the flesh but made alive in the S/spirit") poses no significant threat to the Son–Spirit relationship. In *Ep.* 164 Augustine understands the reference to the *spiritus* in 1 Pet 3:18 to refer to the soul. He states that the flesh "revived when the soul returned because the flesh died when the soul departed."[128] This likely explains why Haddan, McKenna, and Hill decapitalize *spirit* when translating the 1 Pet 3:18 citation in *Trin.* 4.13.17.[129] Augustine appears to understand the reference

> eumdem apostolum dicentem: *Si autem Spiritus eius qui suscitauit Iesum ex mortuis, habitat in uobis*; hic utique Spiritum Patris intellegi uoluit, de quo tamen alio loco dicit: *Quisquis autem Spiritum Christi non habet, hic non est eius*. Et multa alia sunt testimonia quibus hoc euidenter ostenditur, et Patris et Filii esse Spiritum qui in Trinitate dicitur Spiritus sanctus.

127. *Maxim.* 2.14.1 (CCSL 87A: 569): "Et quia de utroque procedit, sicut iam ostendimus: unde et Spiritus Patris dictus est, ubi legitur: *Si autem Spiritus eius qui suscitavit Christum a mortuis, habitat in vobis*; et Spiritus Filii, ubi legitur: *Qui autem Spiritum Christi non habet, hic non est eius*."

128. *Ep.* 164.18 (CSEL 44: 537): "Ipsa enim revixit anima redeunte, quia ipsa erat mortua, anima recedente."

129. Augustine, *On the Trinity*, ed. Philip Schaff, trans. Arthur West Haddan, vol. 3, NPNF 1 (Buffalo, NY: Christian Literature, 1887), 78; Augustine, *The Trinity*, trans. Stephen McKenna, vol. 45, The Fathers of the Church: A New Translation (Washington, DC: CUA

to the *spiritus* in 1 Tim 3:16 in a similar vein.[130] To this day, there is no generally accepted consensus on whether the term (Gk.: πνεύματι) refers to *a spirit* or *the Spirit*. However, given what Augustine has said previously concerning the role of the Spirit in the economy, had he understood *spiritus* to refer to the person of the Holy Spirit, one expects that Augustine would not have found a Son–Spirit dynamic in 1 Pet 3:18 (and 1 Tim 3:16) incongruous with the immanent Son–Spirit relationship. Thus, for Augustine, none of the verses involving the Spirit (or *spirit*) in the resurrection invert the economic Son–Spirit relationship such that it becomes incongruous with his model of the immanent Son–Spirit model. Though his conception of *spiritus* in 1 Pet 3:18 may be suspect, Augustine still corroborates Rahner's Rule by avoiding the possibility of Trinitarian inversions.

8. Pentecost

Augustine's treatment of Pentecost likewise supports Rahner's Rule. Harrower detects a "reversed subordination" in the Son's reception and subsequent Pentecostal outpouring of the Spirit.[131] According to Harrower, this is something that even Augustine recognizes. He says that, in *Trin.* 15.26.46, Augustine "noted that Acts 10:38 proposed a reversal in economic relations. He believed that whereas Jesus received the Holy Spirit when he became incarnate in the womb of Mary, he then dispenses the Holy Spirit for the church. Augustine attempted (unsuccessfully) to reconcile this by the hermeneutical move of speaking separately of the distinct natures of Christ."[132] There are several issues with Harrower's interpretation of Augustine. First, it should be clarified that Augustine speaks of the Son receiving and dispensing the Spirit with reference to Acts 2:33, not 10:38. Augustine writes that when "it is written of him that 'he received the promised Holy Spirit from the Father and poured it out' [Acts 2:33], both his natures are indicated, that is to say the human and the divine. He received it as man, he poured it out as God."[133] Second, Augustine never depicts the reception and outpouring of the Spirit as a "reversal" or "inversion" in economic relations. They are simply different aspects of the Son–Spirit dynamic, aspects congruous with the immanent relation depicted in 15.26.47. Harrower has mistaken Augustine's recognition of these two aspects of the Son–Spirit relationship for a

---

Press, 1963), 151; Augustine, *The Trinity: Introduction, Translation and Notes*, trans. Hill, 202.

130. *Ep.* 199.50 (CSEL 57: 288); *Gen. litt. inp.* 5.19 (CSEL 28,1: 163); *Tract. Ev. Jo.* 72.3 (CCSL 36: 509); *Trin.* 4.20.27 (CCSL 50: 198); *cath. fr.* 24.70 (CSEL 52: 317).

131. Harrower, *Trinitarian Self and Salvation*, 145–6.

132. Ibid., 145.

133. *Trin.* 15.26.46 (CCSL 50A: 527): "In eo etiam quod de illo scriptum est, quod acceperit a patre promissionem spiritus sancti et effunderit utraque natura monstrata est, et humana scilicet et diuina. Accepit quippe ut homo, effudit ut deus."

declaration of relational inversion, or, worse, "reversed subordinations."[134] Third, while Augustine's two-nature interpretation of Acts 2:33 may lack the *exegetical* support warranted for such a firm conclusion, its theological orthodoxy can hardly be questioned. Jesus *did* receive the Spirit as a man in the economy (just as, Augustine would add, he received the Spirit immanently). The Son *did* pour out the Spirit in *forma dei*. At any rate, Augustine's reading of Acts 2:33 is less "unsuccessful" than Harrower's reading of Augustine. More to the point, his reading of the economic relationship in Acts 2:33 is congruous with his depiction of the immanent Son–Spirit dynamic portrayed in *Trin.* 15.26.47. This portrayal of their economic relationship is not incompatible with Augustine's model of the joint procession.

Harrower also suggests that Rahner's Rule cannot account for the Son's so-called "double reception" of the Spirit at his baptism and at Pentecost.[135] He even goes so far as to speculate that if both events are read from the economy to the immanent Trinity, "the nature of the relations mean the Son's first reception of the Spirit is not sufficient."[136] The Rule is thus said to expose God's relational life to "continuous change."[137] Augustine, for his part, is more committed to exploring the Son's double *giving* of the Spirit, immediately following his resurrection (John 20:22) and then at Pentecost. After citing John 20:22 in *Trin.* 15.26.46, he writes:

> This signifies that the Lord Jesus gave the Holy Spirit twice, once on earth for the love of our neighbour, and again from heaven for the love of God. If perhaps another reason may be given for the double giving of the Holy Spirit, yet it was the same Spirit given when Jesus breathed on them as he mentioned shortly afterward: "Go and baptize the nations in the name of the Father and of the Son and of the Holy Spirit" [Matt 28:19], where this Trinity is most commended to us, such that we ought not to doubt.[138]

This may not be the most convincing exegetical explanation of John 20:22. The interpretation Augustine offered earlier, in *Trin.* 4.20.29, may seem more plausible. There, as Ayres notes, "That which Christ physically breathes into the faces of the apostles cannot be the Holy Spirit and thus the action must symbolize some other

---

134. Harrower, *Trinitarian Self and Salvation*, 146.
135. Ibid., 134–5.
136. Ibid., 135.
137. Ibid.
138. *Trin.* 15.26.46 (CCSL 50A: 525–6):

> Hoc significans dominus Iesus bis dedit spiritum sanctum, semel in terra propter dilectionem proximi et iterum de caelo propter dilectionem dei. Et si forte alia ratio reddatur de bis dato spiritu sancto, eundem tamen spiritum datum cum insufflasset Iesus de quo mox ait: *Ite, baptizate gentes in nomine patris et filii et spiritus sancti*, ubi maxime commendatur haec trinitas, ambigere non debemus.

truth."[139] For Augustine, this other truth must be that the Spirit eternally proceeds from the Son:

> I cannot see what else he wished to signify when he breathed and said, "Receive the Holy Spirit" [John 20:22]. The corporeal breath that came from his body and was physically felt was not the substance of the Holy Spirit, but it was a fitting symbolic demonstration that the Holy Spirit proceeds not only from the Father but also from the Son.[140]

According to this reading from book 4, the breathing of John 20:22 symbolizes the procession whereas the sending of the Spirit in Acts is the Spirit's mission. According to Coffey, "what we have here is far from a satisfactory methodology by modern standards."[141] The bishop here "confuses, or makes no distinction between, the economic and the immanent Trinity."[142] However, though Coffey may well be correct, one can hardly deny that Augustine's interpretation is compatible with Rahner's Rule. As Coffey later admits, "In regard to the *filioque*, he [Augustine] showed that he realized that theological statements about God must be grounded in what is said directly in Scripture and also that their form is indicated from that source."[143]

Evidently, Augustine was eventually able to "see what else" the text might mean in book 15. However, even in book 15, Augustine is not troubled by the existence of two "givings," nor does he discern a hint of "relational insufficiency" from the fact that the Son gives the Spirit twice. This begs the question: would Augustine be troubled by the Son's double reception of the Spirit, and does this necessarily indicate relational instability in their relationship? Perhaps, given the Son's reception of the Spirit in his generation and virgin birth, we could stretch the question to speak of a triple or quadruple reception. Augustine's answer to this question (at least to a "triple reception") is found, again, in *Trin.* 15.26.46. Prior to the Jordan baptism, the Son receives the Spirit when "born of the Holy Spirit and the virgin Mary."[144] At the baptism he is not receiving the Spirit as one without the Spirit, as if his reception of the Spirit at his conception was insufficient. Rather, the Jordan theophany prefigures the sacrament of baptism in the church. In *Trin.* 15.26.47 Augustine implies that the Son receives the Spirit through his eternal

---

139. Ayres, *Augustine and the Trinity*, 186.

140. *Trin.* 4.20.29 (CCSL 50: 199–200): "Nec uideo quid aliud significare uoluerit cum *sufflans ait*: *Accipite spiritum sanctum*. Neque enim flatus ille corporeus cum sensu corporaliter tangendi procedens ex corpore substantia spiritus sancti fuit sed demonstratio per congruam significationem non tantum *a patre* sed *et a filio* procedere spiritum sanctum."

141. Coffey, "The Holy Spirit as the Mutual Love of the Father and the Son," 194.

142. Ibid.

143. Ibid., 195.

144. Augustine here quotes the African baptismal creed. Cf. J. N. D. Kelly, *Early Christian Creeds*, 2nd ed. (New York: David McKay, 1960), 175.

generation (though he does not use the explicit language of "reception"). From this, Augustine does not render the Son's immanent reception of the Spirit "insufficient" when he enters a new domain of existence, such that he needs a "top-up" at his conception or baptism. Rather, his reception of the Spirit at the virgin conception is more akin to a spacio-temporal re-enactment of what is received immanently. In this regard, the correspondence between the Son's economic and immanent receptions of the Spirit lends weight to Rahner's Rule.

According to Augustine, the Son's reception of the Spirit in Acts 2:33 refers to the virgin conception. One could make a strong case that this verse refers to the Son's reception of the Spirit following his ascension. However, even if we adopt Augustine's reading, the bishop has already shown us that the Son's reception of the Spirit in a new domain of existence does not necessarily render the Son's reception of the Spirit insufficient. Thus, if Acts 2:33 refers to the Son's reception of the Spirit in yet another new domain of existence—"exalted at the right hand of God" following his ascension (Acts 2:33)—it does not automatically follow that the Son's reception of the Spirit in any of the previous three events were "insufficient," nor does it follow that God's relational life is necessarily opened to "continuous change." Conversely, Augustine offers a paradigm for conceiving of the Son's reception of the Spirit that shows congruity between the dynamics of the economy and the immanent divine life. To quote Barnes again, "Augustine reads virtually all statements about the relations of Son and Spirit as also signifying aspects of their eternal relationship."[145] In this way, Augustine's reading strategy supports Rahner's Rule yet again.

9. Other Triads

In the previous chapter, we encountered the "triadic pattern" objection to Rahner's Rule. Put simply, certain biblical texts refer to each of the divine persons in an order other than Father–Son–Spirit. It is suggested that a consistent application of Rahner's Rule to these texts inevitably produces multiple τάξεις in the immanent Trinity.[146] Thus, a consistent application of Rahner's Rule cannot simultaneously comport with Scripture and the traditional Western conception of τάξις. In the previous chapter we (painstakingly) observed Augustine's strategy for interpreting those "triadic pattern" texts mentioning the Son prior to the Father. We now consider Augustine's treatment of those texts that place the Spirit prior to the Son (Father–Spirit–Son; Spirit–Father–Son; Spirit–Son–Father), following Durst's categorisation of texts.[147] This will help determine whether Augustine offers a strategy for interpreting these texts that enables Scripture to comport with the

---

145. Barnes, "Augustine's Last Pneumatology," 225.
146. Cf. Bobrinskoy, *The Mystery of the Trinity*, 65–8; Harrower, *Trinitarian Self and Salvation*, 158.
147. Durst, *Reordering the Trinity*.

traditional Western conception of τάξις. To be comprehensive, we will briefly consider Augustine's treatment of texts placing the Spirit prior to the Father (Son–Spirit–Father). The coherence of Rahner's Rule has rarely (if ever) been challenged on the basis of a possible Father–Spirit inversion. However, if this challenge was to be raised, it would likely be on the basis that the Spirit precedes the Father in various triadic passages. In what follows we will see that Augustine's treatment of texts placing the Spirit prior to the Son or the Father produces similar results to that of the previous chapter. Augustine's reading of these texts never inverts the Spirit's relationship with the Son or the Father. The bishop is completely disinterested in superficial readings of texts which focus on the order in which the divine persons are mentioned. As will be seen yet again, some of the texts citing the Spirit prior to the Father or the Son even prove to be foundational to Augustine's conception of Trinitarian τάξις.

Spirit–Son–Father and Son–Spirit–Father Texts

In the previous chapter we observed that Augustine does not draw conclusions on the nature of the Father–Son relationship from texts presenting the divine persons in the Spirit–Son–Father and Son–Spirit–Father patterns based purely on the order in which the persons are mentioned. It was asserted that texts in these formations are either irrelevant to the matter at hand (Eph 5:18–20), cited in close proximity to comments about eternal generation (1 Cor 12:4–6; 1 John 4:2), reordered to follow the Father–Son–Spirit pattern (John 15:26; Eph 4:4–6), used to defend Augustine's conception of the Father–Son relationship (John 15:26, 16:7–9, 16:13–15), or not cited at all (Acts 4:8–10).

Similar conclusions may be drawn from Augustine's treatment of the Father–Spirit and Son–Spirit relationships in these same verses. Given the extensive analysis of these texts in the previous chapter, comment here will be restricted to a few succinct observations. Augustine's citations of the above-mentioned texts are either:

1. irrelevant to his consideration of the Father–Spirit and Son–Spirit relationships (Luke 10:21; Rom 8:1–3, 15:30; 1 Cor 6:11; 2 Cor 3:3; Eph 5:18–20; Heb 10:29);[148]

---

148. For Luke 10:21, see *Serm.* 29B.2 (EAA 147: 24); 69.1 (CCSL 41Aa: 460); *Enarrat. Ps.* 117.1 (CCSL 40: 1658); *C. Jul. op. imp.* 3.106 (CSEL 85,1: 425). For Rom 8:3, see *exp. prop. Rm.* 40.48 (CSEL 83: 21); *Enarrat. Ps.* 34.2.3 (CCSL 38: 314); 67.11 (CCSL 39: 875); *Serm.* 134.3.4 (PL 38: 744); 152.1 (CCSL 41Ba: 33); 152.3 (CCSL 41Ba: 36); 152.7 (CCSL 41Ba: 41); 152.9 (CCSL 41Ba: 42); 155.9.9 (CCSL 41Ba: 120); 155.10.10 (CCSL 41Ba: 122); *Div. quaest. LXXXIII* 66.6 (CCSL 44A: 159); *Faust.* 19.2 (CSEL 25,1: 497); 19.7 (CSEL 25,1: 505); *Spir. et litt.* 19.34 (CSEL 60: 187); *C. du. ep. Pelag.* 1.10.21 (CSEL 60: 442); 3.7.20 (CSEL 60: 510); *nupt. et conc.* 1.31.36 (CSEL 42: 247); 3.7.20 (CSEL 42: 510); *Pecc. merit.* 1.27.43 (CSEL 60: 43); *Maxim.* 1.2 (CCSL 87A: 495). For Rom 15:30, see *Retract.* 1.23 (PL 32: 620); *Spec.* 30 (CSEL 12: 208). For 1 Cor 6:11, see *Serm.* 20A (CCSL 41: 274); 213 (MiAg 1: 446); 294 (PL

2. found in close proximity to his comments on the Spirit's procession from—or being "of"—the Father and the Son (John 16:13–15; 1 Cor 12:4–6; 1 John 4:2, 5:6–9);[149]
3. reordered to follow the Father–Son–Spirit pattern (Matt 3:16–17; Mark 1:22; Luke 3:22; John 1:33–34, 15:26; Acts 2:38; Eph 4:4–6);[150]
4. used to support Augustine's conception of the Father–Spirit and Son–Spirit relationships (John 15:26, 16:13–15);[151] or
5. not cited at all (Acts 4:8–10; Heb 9:14; Rev 22:17–18).

Importantly, he never discerns an inversion in either of these relationships based on the order in which the divine persons are mentioned. Thus, Augustine avoids the need to appeal to a *Spirituque* or *Patreque* clause. If Augustine's strategy for reading these texts (or the strategy we assume he would adopt for Acts 4:8–10, Heb 9:14, and Rev 22:17–18) is adopted, the fact that the Spirit is mentioned prior to the Father or the Son poses no threat to a consistent application of Rahner's Rule.

38: 1338); 335I.4 (PLS 2: 834); 351.8 (PL 39: 1545); *Ep.* 29.5 (CCSL 31: 100); 149.8 (CSEL 44: 355); *Man.* (CSEL 90: 83); *Div. quaest. LXXXIII* 76.2 (CCSL 44A: 220–1); *Praed.* 18.33 (PL 44: 986–7). For 2 Cor 3:3, see *Serm.* 155.6 (CCSL 41Ba: 114); 272B.5 (REAug 44: 199); *Ep.* 29.4 (CSEL 34,1: 115–16); *Doctr. chr.* 3.34.48 (PL 34: 85); *Spir. et litt.* 14.24 (CSEL 60: 177); 17.30 (CSEL 46: 183). For Eph 2:17–18, see *Enarrat. Ps.* 71.1 (CCSL 39: 971); 84.11 (CCSL 39: 1171); *Serm.* 112A (MiAg 1: 263); 202.1 (PL 38: 1033); 204.2 (BTT 3: 77–8); 204B.5 (CSEL 101: 71); *c. Fort.* 16 (CSEL 25: 93); *Faust.* 22.89 (CSEL 25: 696); *c. adu. leg.* 2:5 (PL 42: 640–1); *Pecc. merit.* 1.27.46 (CSEL 60: 45). For Eph 5:18–20, see *Ep.* 48.3 (CCSL 31: 210); 140.44 (CSEL 44: 192); 211 (CSEL 57: 361); *Spec.* 34 (CSEL 12: 232); *Serm.* 225.4 (CSEL 101: 118); 229B (= Guelferbytanus 8; MiAg 1: 465). For Heb 10:29, see *Spec.* 43 (CSEL 12: 258).

    149. For John 16:13–15, see *Arian.* 23.19–20 (CCSL 87A: 230); *Tract. Ev. Jo.* 107.2 (CCSL 36: 614); *Maxim.* 2.20.3 (CCSL 87A: 622). For 1 Cor 12:4–6, see *Trin.* 4.20.29 (CCSL 50: 200); 5.13.14 (CCSL 50: 221–2); *Tract. Ev. Jo.* 74.3 (CCSL 36: 514). For 1 John 4:2, see *Tract. Ep. Jo.* 6.12 (PL 35: 2027). For 1 John 5:6–9, see *Trin.* 4.20.29 (CCSL 50: 199); 9.12.18 (CCSL 50: 310); *Maxim.* 2.20.1 (CCSL 87A: 621); 2.22.3 (CCSL 87A: 638–9).

    150. For the Jordan theophany (Matt 3:16–17; Mark 1:22; Luke 3:22; John 1:33–34), see *Tract. Ev. Jo.* 6.5 (CCSL 36: 55–6). For John 15:26, see *Maxim.* 2.22.3 (CCSL 87A: 639). For John 16:7–9, see *Tract. Ev. Jo.* 94.4–5 (CCSL 36: 563–4). For Eph 4:4–6, see *Tract. Ev. Jo.* 99.6 (CCSL 36: 586). For Acts 2:38, see *Maxim.* 2.17.1 (CCSL 87A: 603).

    151. For John 15:26, see *Ep.* 170.4 (CSEL 44: 625); *Tract. Ev. Jo.* 92 (CCSL 36: 555–7), *Trin.* 2.3.5 (CCSL 50: 85); 4.20.29 (CCSL 50: 199); 5.11.12 (CCSL 50: 219); 5.14.15 (CCSL 50: 222); 12.5.5 (CCSL 50: 359); 15.26 (CCSL 50A: 525); 15.27.48 (CCSL 50A: 529); *Maxim.* 2.14.1 (CCSL 87A: 568–9). For John 16:13–15, see *Trin.* 2.3.5 (CCSL 50: 85); 4.20.28–4.20.29 (CCSL 50: 198–201); 15.27.48 (CCSL 50A: 529–30); *Tract. Ev. Jo.* 99 (CCSL 36: 581–7); 100 (CCSL 36: 588–90); *Arian.* 23.19 (CCSL 87A: 231); 23.20 (CCSL 87A: 233).

Father–Spirit–Son Texts

John 4:23 Augustine's treatment of Father–Spirit–Son texts likewise allow for a consistent application of Rahner's Rule. When treating John 4:23, the bishop remains unconcerned with the order in which the divine persons are mentioned.[152] In his tractate on John 4:1–42 (*Tract. Ev. Jo.* 15)—often considered an anti-Donatist sermon[153]—Augustine understands the Gift of God in 4:10 as a reference to the Spirit. The Spirit is a gift to humanity,[154] a gift bestowed by the Son.[155] However, when it comes to the references to the Father, the Spirit, and the Truth in 4:23, Augustine says nothing that indicates a relational inversion on the basis of the Spirit's being mentioned first.[156] Given what we know about Augustine's view of the tight association between the missions and processions, it is difficult to see how or why Augustine would infer that the divine τάξις is somehow interrupted because the divine persons are mentioned in a different order.

Acts 1:4–8 Augustine is likewise unconcerned with the order in which the divine persons are mentioned in Acts 1:4–8. Moments before quoting Acts 1:4 in *Tract. Ev. Jo.* 122.8,[157] Augustine refers to the three persons in the Father–Son–Spirit pattern and speaks of the Holy Spirit as the Spirit of both.[158] In the tenth tractate of *Tract. Ep. Jo.*,[159] Augustine likewise reorders the three persons into the Father–Son–Spirit immediately prior to citing Acts 1:6–8. In three of Augustine's Pentecost sermons, Augustine quotes Acts 1:4–8 but refers to the Son sending or giving the Spirit. No relational inversion is deduced from the order in which the persons are mentioned.[160] In other places Augustine quotes Acts 1:4–8 but does not comment on

---

152. *Ep.* 78.3 (CCSL 31A: 85); *Quaest. Hept.* 5.10 (CCSL 33: 280); *Tract. Ev. Jo.* 15.24–26 (CCSL 36: 160–1); *Serm.* 198.11 auctus (=Dolbeau 26, Moguntinus 62; EAA 147: 375).

153. Cf. Grabau, Joseph L., "Christology and Exegesis in Augustine of Hippo's XVth Tractate *In Iohannis Euangelium*," in *Studia Patristica: Papers Presented at the Seventeenth International Conference on Patristica Studies Held in Oxford 2015*, ed. Markus Vinzent, vol. 98 (Leuven: Peeters, 2017), 103. For dating, see Bonnardière, *Recherches de chronologie Augustinienne*, 61.

154. *Tract. Ev. Jo.* 15.12 (CCSL 36: 154–5).

155. *Tract. Ev. Jo.* 15.17 (CCSL 36: 156).

156. *Tract. Ev. Jo.* 15.24–26 (CCSL 36: 160–1).

157. Composed sometime after 419–20. Bonnardière, *Recherches de chronologie Augustinienne*, 65–87.

158. *Tract. Ev. Jo.* 122.8 (CCSL 36: 674).

159. Composed *c.* 407. For the complex debates over the dating of *Tract. Ep. Jo.*, refer to John W. Rettig's comments in *St Augustine: Tractates on the Gospel of John 112–24; Tractates on the First Epistle of John: Translation and Introduction by John W. Rettig*, vol. 92, The Fathers of the Church (Washington, DC: CUA Press, 1995), 97–100.

160. *Serm.* 267 (PL 38:1229–1331); 268 (PL 38: 1231–4); 378 (PL 39: 1673–4).

the Son–Spirit relationship.[161] The fact that Acts 1:4–8 presents the divine persons in the order Father–Spirit–Son is of no consequence for Augustine's understanding of the economic or immanent Son–Spirit relationship. Again, it is difficult to see why Augustine's conception of divine τάξις would change on account of the order in which the persons are mentioned.

Acts 4:24–26 Augustine only ever cites Acts 4:24–26 in *Praed.* 1.16.33.[162] He draws no attention to the order in which the three persons are mentioned. However, as we just saw, Augustine's earlier comments on the Son–Spirit relationship in *Praed.* 1.15.31 were entirely in keeping with Augustine's portrayal of their economic and immanent relationship elsewhere.[163] At the very least, we can say that the order in which the divine persons are mentioned in Acts 4:24–26 poses no obvious threat to Augustine's conception of the economic and immanent Son–Spirit relationship.

1 Cor 2:10–16 Augustine's treatment of 1 Cor 2:10–16 follows suit. In *Trin.* 1.8.18, Augustine seeks to counter the Homoian–Arian claim that the Spirit is ontologically inferior to the Son. He employs 1 Cor 2:11 as a counterexample:

> It may still seem that the reason he said, "And I will ask the Father and he will give you another advocate," suggests that the Son alone does not suffice. But in that place, it is said of him, as though it were altogether sufficient, "When he, the Spirit of truth comes, he will teach you all truth" [John 16:13]. … Let them say, then, if they like, that the Holy Spirit is greater than the Son, whom they are wont to say is inferior. Or perhaps because it does not say "he alone," or "no one but himself," he will teach you all truth, they will allow us to believe that the Son also is teaching with him? The apostle, therefore, separated the Son from knowing the things that are of God when he said, "Even so, no one knows the things of God but the Spirit of God" [1 Cor 2:11]. He said this so that these perverted people may be able to say that even the Son is only taught the things that are of God by the Holy Spirit, as an inferior by a superior.[164]

---

161. *Serm.* 268.4 (PL 38: 1234); *Ep.* 93.21 (CCSL 31A: 182–3); 102.21 (CSEL 34,2: 563); *Civ.* 18.53 (CCSL 48: 652); 22.30 (CCSL 48: 866).
162. *Praed.* 1.16.33 (PL 44: 984).
163. Cf. p. 174.
164. *Trin.* 1.8.18 (CCSL 50: 52–3):

> Sed adhuc uideri potest ideo dictum: *Et ego rogabo patrem, et alium aduocatum dabit uobis*, quasi non sufficiat solus filius. Illo autem loco ita de illo dictum est tamquam solus omnino sufficiat: *Cum uenerit ille spiritus ueritatis, docebit uos omnem ueritatem.* … Dicant ergo, si placet, maiorem esse filio spiritum sanctum quem minorem illo solent dicere. An quia non dictum est: "Ipse solus," aut: "Nemo nisi ipse" *uos docebit omnem ueritatem*, ideo permittunt ut cum illo docere credatur et filius? Apostolus ergo separauit filium ab sciendis his *quae*

Augustine entertains the possibility that 1 Cor 2:11 indicates the Son's inferiority to the Spirit. However, this is not based on the order of the divine persons, nor is this his final word. His point is not that the Son and the Spirit are unequal. Rather, Augustine argues that Jesus insists on returning to the Father because if he remained physically present he would confuse some—like the Homoian-Arians— into thinking that the Son was inferior to the Spirit, which he is not.[165] Augustine hints at the possibility of an inversion to expose the logical flaw of the Homoian-Arian argument.

When citing 1 Cor 2:11 in *Trin.* 5.14.15 and *Tract. Ev. Jo.* 32.5,[166] Augustine makes no comment about the order in which the divine persons are mentioned in the text. Nevertheless, the comments following shortly after each citation are significant for his conception of τάξις:

> If, then, he who is given also has an origin [*principium*] from which he is given, because he received the one who proceeds from him from no other origin [*principium*], it must be admitted that the Father and the Son are the origin [*principium*] of the Holy Spirit; not two origins [*principia*], but just as Father and Son are one God, and with reference to creation one Creator and one Lord, thus in relation to the Holy Spirit they are one origin [*principium*].[167]

It is difficult to imagine Augustine being concerned with the order in which the divine persons are mentioned in 1 Cor 2:10–16 when, shortly after quoting 1 Cor 2:11, he offers a statement intimately linking the Son's economic donation of the Spirit with his immanent procession. Soon after quoting the verse in *Tract. Ev. Jo.* 32, Augustine likewise speaks at length of the Son's donation of the Spirit.[168] Moreover, for Augustine, speech of the Father and the Son as one *principium* assumes an inherent asymmetry. As Lee observes, "the Son is *principium* for the procession of the Spirit only insofar as the Son is *generated* from the Father."[169] This leads one to assume that Augustine is not troubled by the order in which the three persons are mentioned in this verse. His consistent exegesis of 1 Cor 2:10–16

> *dei sunt* ubi ait: *Sic et quae dei sunt nemo scit nisi spiritus dei*! ut iam isti peruersi possint ex hoc dicere quod et filium non doceat *quae dei sunt nisi spiritus* sanctus, tamquam maior minorem.

165. *Trin.* 1.9 (CCSL 50: 53).
166. *c.* 419–421. For the dating, see Bonnardière, *Recherches de chronologie Augustinienne*, 117.
167. *Trin.* 4.14.15 (CCSL 50: 223): "Si ergo et quod datur principium habet eum a quo datur quia non aliunde accepit illud quod ab ipso procedit, fatendum est patrem et filium principium esse spiritus sancti, non duo principia, sed sicut pater et filius unus deus et ad creaturam relatiue *unus creator* et *unus dominus*, sic relatiue ad spiritum sanctum unum principium."
168. *Tract. Ev. Jo.* 32.5–9 (CCSL 36: 302–6).
169. Lee, *Gregory of Nyssa, Augustine of Hippo, and the Filioque*, 237.

elsewhere proves this point beyond doubt.[170] If anything, Augustine's reading of this passage would appear to support a consistent application of Rahner's Rule.

Gal 4:6 Augustine is likewise undeterred by the order in which the divine persons are mentioned in Gal 4:6. Previously we saw Augustine cite the verse in *Tract. Ev. Jo.* 99.6 in defence of the Spirit's double procession.[171] Augustine likewise draws upon Gal 4:6 to make the same point in *Trin.* 4.20.29, 15.26, and *Serm.* 71.29.[172] In fact, as Dunham notes, it is because of Gal 4:6 that Augustine "understands the Spirit to be from the Father and the Son."[173] Similarly, Ayres argues that Augustine's "view of the Spirit's procession is founded primarily on Scriptural statements that the Spirit is (eternally) the Spirit *of* Father and *of* Son."[174] Thus, Ayres argues that Gal 4:6 is even more important for Augustine's conception of divine τάξις than John 14:26 and 15:26. Moreover, as Iacovetti contends, "While Augustine is certainly willing to speak of the Spirit's procession from the Father *and* the Son, he clarifies this language in a way that explicitly preserves the Father's primacy and secures the Spirit's place in the trinitarian *taxis*" (emphasis in original).[175] Though in other works Augustine focuses less upon the Son–Spirit relationship when citing Gal 4:6, he never draws upon the order in which the persons are mentioned to make conclusions about their economic or immanent relation.[176] This would be unthinkable, since the Spirit is described as "the Spirit of his Son." To infer based on word order would be to miss the point of the text altogether. Augustine's interpretation of this verse most certainly—indeed, fundamentally—supports Rahner's Rule, despite the fact that the three divine persons are mentioned in the Father–Spirit–Son pattern.

Titus 3:4-6 When citing Titus 3:4-6, Augustine is usually not interested in the Son–Spirit relationship.[177] The lone exception is in his dialogue with the

---

170. For example, *Tract. Ev. Jo.* 97.1 (CCSL 36: 572); *Tract. Ev. Jo.* 102.5 (CCSL 36: 597); *Enarrat. Ps.* 52.5 (CCSL 39: 641); 71.3 (CCSL 39: 973); *Maxim.* 2.15.4 (CCSL 87A: 594); 2.17.1 (CCSL 87A: 603); 2.23.5 (CCSL 87A: 652); *Ep.* 92A (CCSL 31A: 166); 186.10 (CSEL 57: 53); 242 (CSEL 57: 564); *Quaest. Hept.* 4.18 (CCSL 33: 244–5); *Serm.* 23B.6 (EAA 147: 462); 30.3 (CCSL 41: 382); 71.30 (CCSL 41Ab: 57); 128.9.11 (PL 38: 718–19); 269.3 (PL 38: 1236); 333.6 (PL 38: 1467); 335E.6 (PLS 2: 785).

171. *Tract. Ev. Jo.* 99.6 (CCSL 36: 585–6).

172. *Trin.* 4.20.29 (CCSL 50: 200); 15.26 (CCSL 50A: 524); *Serm.* 71.18.29 (CCSL 41Ab: 56).

173. Dunham, *The Trinity and Creation in Augustine*, 146, n. 31.

174. Emphasis added. Ayres, "Spiritus Amborum," 214.

175. Christopher Iacovetti, "Filioque, Theosis, and Ecclesia: Augustine in Dialogue with Modern Orthodox Theology," *Modern Theology*, vol. 34, no. 1 (2018): 75–6.

176. *Ep.* 194.17 (CSEL 57: 189); *exp. Gal* 31 (CSEL 84: 96); *perseu.* 23.64 (PL 45: 1032); *Arian.* 25.21 (PL 42: 234);

177. *Ep.* 140.62 (CSEL 44: 208); *en. Ps* 112.6 (CCSL 40: 1633); 118.7.2 (CCSL 40: 1683); *Serm.* 312.2 (PL 38: 1420); 341.25 auctus (= Dolbeau 22, Moguntinus 55; EAA 147:573);

Homoian–Arian bishop Maximinus, the importance of which, as Barnes reminds us, "is sufficiently guaranteed by their being literally Augustine's 'last words' on Trinitarian theology."[178] Maximinus uses these verses to argue that the Spirit enlightens believers in virtue of the light received from the Son.[179] There is a movement from Son to Spirit, but not vice versa. As we saw previously, Augustine responds to his opponent by drawing attention to Luke 4:18. He states: "Christ said that the Holy Spirit was above [*super*] him, not because he is above [*super*] the Word of God, who is God, but because he is above [*super*] the man, because 'the Word became flesh' " [John 1:14].[180] For Augustine, there is a sense in which the Spirit is greater than the Son, but only in *forma serui*, just as the Son in *forma dei* is greater than the Son in *forma serui*. Even still, Augustine—like his Homoian–Arian opponent—does not reach his conclusion on the economic Son–Spirit relationship on the basis of the order in which the divine persons are mentioned in Titus 3:4–6. More significantly, elsewhere Augustine understands the movement of the Spirit in Luke 4:18 to parallel John 3:34, a text which supports his conception of the immanent τάξις.[181] In this roundabout way, Augustine's treatment of Tit 3:4–6 almost provides active support for Rahner's Rule.

1 John 4:13–14 Meanwhile, Augustine's treatment of 1 John 4:13–14 also lends itself to Rahner's Rule. The verse is only cited in *Tract. Ep. Jo.* 8 and *Trin.* book 15. In *Tract. Ep. Jo.* 8, Augustine acknowledges that the Father gives the Spirit in 4:13[182] and sends his Son in 4:14 (as the text itself indicates).[183] Earlier in the tractate Augustine mentions the Son's sending of the Spirit in passing,[184] but this dynamic is largely disconnected from his exegesis of 4:13–14. There is no hint of an inverted τάξις. In *Trin.* 15.17.31–15.19.37, 1 John 4:13 feeds into Augustine's discussion of the Spirit as Charity and Gift three times, culminating in his famous conclusion:

> And if the Charity by which the Father loves the Son and the Son loves the Father ineffably demonstrates the communion of them both, what is more

---

Pecc. merit. 1.18.23 (CSEL 60: 23); 1.27.49 (CSEL 60: 47); *C. du. ep. Pelag.* 1.9.15 (CSEL 60: 437); 1.19.37 (CSEL 60: 453); *Grat.* 5.12 (PL 44: 889).

178. Barnes, "Augustine's Last Pneumatology," 223.

179. *Coll. Max.* 6 (CCSL 87A: 388–9).

180. *Coll. Max.* 11 (CCSL 87A: 394): "Dixit autem Christus super se Spiritum sanctum, non quia super Verbum Dei est, quod est Deus, sed quia super hominem, quod *Verbum caro factum est*."

181. *Tract. Ev. Jo.* 74.3 (CCSL 36: 514).

182. *Tract. Ep. Jo.* 8.12 (PL 35: 2043).

183. *Tract. Ep. Jo.* 8.13 (PL 35: 2043–4).

184. *Tract. Ep. Jo.* 8.10 (PL 35: 2041–2).

fitting than that he should properly be called Charity who is the common Spirit of them both?[185]

The Spirit is common to the Son. He is the Spirit of both. As Gioia notes, "John's First Epistle ascribes this mutual indwelling identically to love and to the Holy Spirit, thus implying that love is indeed the property of the Holy Spirit."[186] This then leads Augustine to argue that the Spirit therefore proceeds from both the Father and the Son in *Trin.* 15.26–15.27.48. Hence, 1 John 4:13 feeds into Augustine's doctrine of the Spirit's joint procession from Father and Son. The fact that the verse mentions the Spirit prior to the Son is of no consequence. Thus, Augustine's treatment of 1 John 4:13–14 supports Rahner's Rule.

Rev 1:4–5 Augustine rarely cites or alludes to Rev 1:4–5, and when he does, the two verses are disconnected from each other.[187] Thus, in most cases, the verse is not cited in connection with the Son–Spirit relationship. In *Tract. Ev. Jo.* 122.8,[188] Augustine references the *septem spiritibus* ("sevenfold Spirit") of Isa 11:2–3 and Rev 1:4, shortly after commenting that the Holy Spirit is the Spirit of both Father and Son, a foundational concept for his understanding of the joint procession.[189] He likewise refers to the Spirit as the *septem spiritbus* in his Pentecost sermon in AD 416.[190] Unsurprisingly given the occasion, Augustine mentions Christ sending the Spirit. However, as in all other references or citations of Rev 1:4–5, he discerns no economic or immanent inversion in the Son–Spirit τάξις due to the fact that the Spirit is mentioned prior to the Son in this verse. Thus, Augustine's reading of Rev 1:4–5 is consistent with the demands of Rahner's Rule to the extent that it does not challenge such a reading. Thus, none of the Father–Spirit–Son texts challenge Rahner's Rule. The order in which the divine persons are mentioned is of no consequence to Augustine.

Spirit–Father–Son Texts

Luke 4:18 Augustine likewise provides a framework for interpreting those texts in the Spirit–Father–Son formation that is consistent with Rahner's Rule. We have

---

185. *Trin.* 15.19.37 (CCSL 50A: 513): "Et si caritas qua pater diligit filium et patrem diligit filius ineffabiliter communionem demonstrat amborum, quid conuenientius quam ut ille proprie dicatur caritas qui spiritus est communis ambobus?"

186. Gioia, *The Theological Epistemology of Augustine's* De Trinitate, 78.

187. He cites Rev 1:4 in *f. et symb.* 8.15 (CSEL 41: 17) and alludes to 1:5 in *Tract. Ev. Jo.* 122.8 (CCSL 36: 673); *Enarrat. Ps.* 150.1 (CCSL 40: 2191); *Serm.* 72A.2 (= Denis 25; CCSLAb: 109); 270.7 (PL 38: 1245).

188. This tractate was composed sometime after 419/420. Bonnardière, *Recherches de chronologie Augustinienne*, 65–87.

189. *Tract. Ev. Jo.* 122.8 (CCSL 36: 674).

190. *Serm.* 270 (PL 38: 1245).

5. The Son–Spirit Relationship

already seen how Augustine's reading of Luke 4:18 coheres with his understanding of the economic and immanent Son–Spirit relationship.[191] The analysis earlier demonstrates that, for Augustine, the fact that the Spirit is mentioned prior to the Father does not result in an economic or immanent inversion in the Father–Spirit relationship. The order in which the persons are mentioned does not affect the tight relationship Augustine envisions between the missions and processions and thus does not pose a threat to Rahner's Rule.

Acts 11:15–17 Augustine's exegesis of Acts 11:15–17 likewise demonstrates a lack of concern with the order in which the divine persons are mentioned in the text. After the only citation of these verses in Augustine's corpus (*Trin.* 15.19.35), Augustine asserts that this verse proves that "the Holy Spirit is the Gift of God, in that he is given to those who love God through him."[192] In context, Augustine is describing the Spirit as a gift given to humanity. As Gioia notes, "*The fact that charity-Holy Spirit is a gift from God means that we are saved by grace*; it means that salvation is truly divine, that only God's very self-giving can save us" (emphasis in original).[193] However, as we have noted several times already, Augustine will go on to stress that the Spirit is also given by the Father to the Son within the Godhead, such that the Spirit proceeds from both jointly, though principally from the Father. For Augustine, the fact that the Spirit is mentioned prior to the Father and the Son in Acts 11:15–17 has no bearing on the nature of the Father–Spirit and Son–Spirit relationship. Thus, his reading of this verse supports a consistent application of Rahner's Rule.

Rom 8:9 We have already seen that Rom 8:9 poses no problem for Augustine's conception of the Father–Spirit and Son–Spirit relationships. As was observed in *Tract. Ev. Jo.* 99.6 and *Maxim.* 2.14.1, Augustine reads the reference to "the Spirit of Christ" (Rom 8:9) as evidence for the Spirit's procession from the Son, and the reference to "the Spirit of him who raised Jesus from the dead" (Rom 8:11) as evidence for the Spirit's procession from the Father. It is simply unthinkable that Augustine would place any significance in the fact that the Spirit is mentioned prior to the Father and the Son for any reason other than to indicate the grammatically genitive relationship. Thus, Augustine's treatment of Rom 8:9 is consistent with Rahner's Rule.

Eph 4:30–32 When citing Eph 4:30–32, Augustine never comments directly on the Father–Spirit or Son–Spirit relationships, nor does he draw attention to the order in which the divine persons are mentioned.[194] However, shortly after citing

---

191. Cf. pp. 170–3.

192. *Trin.* 15.19.35 (CCSL 50: 512): "Donum Dei esse Spiritum Sanctum, in quantum datur eis qui per eum diligunt Deum."

193. Gioia, *The Theological Epistemology of Augustine's* De Trinitate, 138.

194. *Gen. litt.* 4.9.18 (CSEL 28: 105); *Spec.* 34 (CSEL 12: 231); *Pecc. merit.* 1.27.46 (CSEL 60: 45).

the verses in *Arian.*, he goes on to cite Gal 4:6.[195] Previously we saw that Augustine cites Gal 4:6 elsewhere in support of his doctrine of the Spirit's joint procession.[196] That he should cite Gal 4:6 in such close proximity to Eph 4:30–32 suggests that the order in which the divine persons are mentioned is inconsequential for his understanding of τάξις. At the very least, we can affirm that Augustine's reading of this verse is not inconsistent with Rahner's Rule.

Summary

Thus, a consistent picture emerges from Augustine's exegesis of those texts in which the divine persons are mentioned in the Father–Spirit–Son and Spirit–Father–Son patterns. These verses are either:

1. rearranged into the Father–Son–Spirit pattern (Acts 1:4–8);
2. cited in close proximity to statements about the Spirit's being "given" or "sent" (John 4:23; Acts 1:4–8);
3. quoted in close proximity to statements about the Spirit's joint procession from—or being "of"—the Father and the Son (Acts 4:24–26; 1 Cor 2:10–16; Rev 1:4–5);
4. used in support of the Spirit's procession from—or being "of"—the Father and the Son (Gal 4:6; John 1:4–5);
5. disconnected entirely from any comment on the Son–Spirit relationship (Acts 20:28;[197] Rom 8:16–17,[198] 14:17–18;[199] 2 Thes 2:13–14;[200] Jude 20–21[201]); or
6. not cited at all (Acts 7:55; 1 Pet 1:2; Rev 22:1).[202]

Augustine's strategy with these texts is much the same as those in the Spirit–Son–Father and Son–Spirit–Father patterns. Significantly, at no point does Augustine ever see the need to invert the economic or immanent Son–Spirit relationship purely because the Spirit is mentioned prior to the Son. Thus, Augustine offers a strategy for interpreting those biblical texts presenting the divine persons in the Father–Spirit–Son and Spirit–Father–Son patterns that is consistent with Rahner's

---

195. *Arian.* 25.21 (CCSL 87A: 234).

196. Cf. p. 186.

197. *Spec.* 29 (CSEL 12: 198).

198. *Spec.* 30 (CSEL 12: 203); *exp. prop. Rm.* 49.57 (PL 35: 31); *Div. quaest. LXXXIII* 67.2 (CCSL 44A: 165).

199. *Man.* 2.14.32 (CSEL 90: 117); *Ep.* 36.17 (CCSL 31: 141); *Spec.* 30 (CSEL 12: 207); *Adim.* 14.2 (CSEL 25,1: 150); *C. du. ep. Pelag.* 4.10.28 (CSEL 60: 558).

200. *Spec.* 36 (CSEL 12: 240).

201. Ibid.: 284.

202. Acts 7:55 is cited by pseudo-Augustine in *Liber de diuinis scripturis siue Speculum* 2 (CSEL 12: 308).

Western conception of divine τάξις. Once again, Augustine comes to the aid of Rahner's Rule.

10. Conclusion

In summary, we have observed several objections to a consistent application of Rahner's Rule to the biblical statements concerning the economic Son–Spirit relationship, stemming from the Spirit's involvement in the Son's virgin conception, baptism, ministry, death, and Pentecostal outpouring as well as from varying triadic patterns. It is claimed that these verses depict inversions or "reverse subordinations" that, when the Rule is applied, inevitably result in a *Spirituque* or *Patreque*, relational instability, and even pantheism. It is also claimed that there is no "eternal analogue" to the Son's "double reception" of the Spirit in the economy.

We then explored five proposals to overcome some of these difficulties. It can be argued that:

1. the Spirit is in some way involved in the begetting of the Son;
2. the anointing accounts manifest a prior occurrence in which οἰκονομία and θεολόγια correspond;
3. the Spirit constitutes the Father's intra-Trinitarian gift to the Son;
4. the economic "inversions" function as alternating projections of the *a Patre procedit* and *Filioque* onto the economic plane; or
5. certain events should be excluded when reading from the economy to the immanent Trinity.

Various difficulties were raised with these solutions. Can the Spirit's involvement in the Son's generation avoid a *Spirituque*? Can the "prior occurrence" model avoid the same problem? Does the τάξις of circumincession in the "gift" model require multiple τάξεις, thus rendering Rahner's Rule meaningless? Is it appropriate to speak of the Son–Spirit relationship as "inversions"? How do we pick and choose which economic events we apply the rule to and which we do not?

In turning to Augustine's exegesis, we discover a strategy that largely avoids the *Spirituque* problem that threatens the first three proposals, and the multiple τάξεις dilemma that threatens the third proposal earlier. A consistent application of Rahner's Rule does not require a *Spirituque* for balance because of the asymmetry in the economic Son–Spirit relationship. The Son in *forma dei* sends the Spirit; the Spirit only sends the Son in *forma serui*. The Son "gives" the Spirit; the Spirit is never said to "give" the Son. The Spirit "fills" the Son; the Son is not said to "fill" the Spirit. The Spirit is "upon" or "over" the Son in *forma serui*; the Son is never said to be "over" the Spirit, neither in *forma serui* nor in *forma dei*. It is inappropriate to speak of "reversed subordination" since the mutuality in the Son–Spirit relationship precludes the possibility of the Spirit's subordination to the Son. The Son is only subordinate to the Spirit in *forma serui*, just as he is subordinate to the Father and to himself in *forma dei*. Moreover, the Spirit's being "over" or "upon" the Son can also be understood as his reception of the Spirit, due to the parallel drawn between Luke 4:18 and John 3:34. While an economic subordination cannot be read into the immanent Trinity, the Son's economic reception of the Spirit can. Yes, Augustine is placing a restriction on what can and cannot be read into the immanent Trinity, as Rahner himself does when denying Subordinationism. However, this is different from Congar's model, in that Congar restricts Rahner's Rule to certain *events* and not others. Augustine's framework caters for all of the major economic events, the exception being the Spirit's involvement in the crucifixion in Luke 23:46 and Heb 9:14 (the former is irrelevant to Augustine's conception of τάξις; the latter goes uncited). The Son's reception of the Spirit in the economy—whether during his conception, baptism, ministry, or prior to the Pentecostal outpouring—mirrors his immanent reception of the Spirit, whom the Father gives to him, both to proceed from him and to have "without measure" in the fullness of deity. A *Spirituque* is not required: the Spirit is given to the Son *as* he is begotten. A *Patreque* is not required as the monarchy of the Father is preserved. There is no risk of multiple τάξεις since Augustine avoids Bourassa's unhelpful "order of origin"/"order of circumincession" dichotomy. The Son's immanent reception of the Spirit is the eternal analogue to the Son's multiple economic receptions of the Spirit. Given the congruity of the economic and immanent Son–Spirit relationship, the economic reflecting and grounded in the immanent, there is no need to fear relational instability, ontological morphing, or pantheism. Moreover, little can be gleaned from the order in which divine persons are mentioned in the various triadic texts. Thus, Augustine offers a framework that avoids the major obstacles for a consistent application of Rahner's Rule to the economic Son–Spirit relationship.

Chapter 6

CONCLUSION

This chapter concludes the book by summarizing the main findings in relation to the questions first outlined in the introduction. It will then discuss the significance and contribution of the research for contemporary theology and Augustinian studies. Then, finally, in the light of the various limitations and weaknesses pertinent to this study, recommendations for further research will be proposed.

1. Research Findings

The introductory chapter to this book outlined two problems, the first concerning Rahner's assessment of the Augustinian-Western tradition. According to Rahner, the Western tradition had cut the Trinity off from the economy of salvation, resulting in various weaknesses for the West. Rahner ultimately traces these weaknesses back to Augustine. He proposes his Rule or *Grundaxiom*—that the economic Trinity is the immanent Trinity—as the solution to re-integrating the economy and the Trinity. The Rule is supposed to return the doctrine of the Trinity to its "biblical starting point," to the "biblical statements about the economy of salvation." Yet for all of his emphasis on Scripture, the Jesuit priest offers no reading strategy for discerning how this Rule is to be applied. Significantly, he completely overlooks the various ways in which Augustine deals with the narrative particularities of the "biblical statements about the economy of salvation." This raised the first major question for our study: how does Augustine attend to the Scriptures in his doctrine of the Trinity, and how does this pre-empt and address the shortcomings noted by Rahner?

In Chapter 2, we saw that Augustine both pre-empted and addressed five of these alleged shortcomings. In contrast with the (alleged) general tendency of Western Trinitarian thought and especially that of his day, Rahner sought a doctrine of the Trinity that (1) pays close attention to Scripture and the economy; (2) does not preference the *De Deo uno* over the *De Deo trino*; (3) preserves the Son's incarnational peculiarity; (4) integrates the doctrine of the Trinity with creation and natural revelation; and (5) integrates the doctrine of the Trinity with Christian faith and piety. In this chapter, we saw, first, that Augustine's doctrine of the Trinity is closely tethered to the particularities of Scripture and the economy. Second, it was argued that through his attention to the Scriptures, Augustine's account of the Trinity was far less prone to the criticism of separating the *De Deo uno* from the *De Deo trino* than is often suggested and can even be seen to integrate the two. Third, we observed that Augustine preserved the Son's incarnational peculiarity (even through his psychological analogy) by attending to Scripture. Fourth, we saw that Augustine's doctrine of creation pays significant attention to the doctrine of creation and natural revelation, even with respect to the *vestigia*. Fifth, from start to finish, Augustine's account was seen to integrate the Trinity with the Christian's faith and piety. In each case it was argued that Augustine pays greater attention to "the biblical statements concerning the economy of salvation" than Rahner does in *Der Dreifaltige Gott*.

In Chapter 3, we saw that Augustine both pre-empted and addressed three further alleged shortcomings. In contrast with the (supposed) general tendency of Western Trinitarian thought and especially that of his day, Rahner maintained that the doctrine of the Trinity must pay heed to the Old Testament, the doctrine of salvation, and the connectedness of the missions and processions. In this chapter we saw, first, that Augustine considers in great detail the narrative particularities of the Old Testament theophanies in his presentation of the Trinity. Though his interpretation of the theophanies likely differs from Rahner's, this is because of his attention to the scriptural details. Next, we observed the bishop's penetrating integration of the doctrine of the Trinity with the doctrine of grace and the pages of Scripture. Finally, we saw that Augustine's closely tethered account of the missions and processions fundamentally supports Rahner's Rule and does so with great attention to the biblical text. From Chapters 2 and 3, we thus discerned eight ways in which Augustine's attention to "the biblical statements concerning the economy of salvation" addressed the alleged weaknesses in the Augustinian-Western tradition, thus pre-empting many of Rahner's positive proposals. Ironically, in each case Augustine provided the attention to the biblical particularities that Rahner promised but failed to deliver.

The second major question raised in the introductory chapter pertained to Augustine's exegesis and the viability of Rahner's Rule. According to Rahner's own understanding of his Rule, the intra-Trinitarian relations discerned in the "biblical statements about the economy" must correspond to the intra-Trinitarian relations of the immanent Trinity as declared in the Catholic magisterium. Modern commentators suggest that various exegetical difficulties emerge from Rahner's commitment to the Scriptures and magisterium. We observed that some allege that an even-handed application of the Rule to texts concerning the Father–Son relationship will result in Subordinationism, relational inversion, or multiple τάξεις, while in other cases—such as the Son's ascension to the Father—it is alleged that no eternal analogue can be discerned. We also noted the suggestion that a consistent application of Rahner's Rule to texts concerning the Son–Spirit relationship results in relational inversions, an immanent *Spirituque* or *Patreque* and multiple immanent τάξεις, while in other cases—such as the Son's multiple receptions of the Spirit—no immanent analogue can be found. It has also been suggested that applying Rahner's Rule to the Son–Spirit relationship could threaten the stability of the Trinitarian relations *ad intra*, potentially undermining eternal generation, and perhaps even resulting in pantheism or ontological morphing. Does Augustine's interpretation of Scripture provide a framework for overcoming these major exegetical difficulties said to emerge from a strict application of Rahner's Rule?

Chapter 4 explored how Augustine's *form* rule (from Chapter 2) and his conception of the interrelatedness of the missions and processions (from Chapter 3) offer a pathway for avoiding the difficulties in the Father–Son relationship alleged to result from Rahner's Rule. We saw, first, that Augustine's *form* rule provides a clear strategy for avoiding ontological Subordinationism when moving from the economic Trinity to the immanent Trinity. Second, we observed that Augustine's strategy for reading texts speaking of power transfer between the Father and the Son removes the risk of a reversed or inverted Father–Son relationship. A similar argument was offered, third, with texts portraying mutuality between the Father and the Son. In each case, the nature of the Father–Son dynamic in the mission parallels their processional dynamic. Fourth, Augustine demonstrated that it is possible to read biblical texts mentioning all three divine persons—in this case, those citing the Son prior to the Father—without introducing a reversing of the Father–Son relationship. Finally, Augustine offered the starting point of a strategy for discerning a parallel between the ascension and eternal generation. The bishop demonstrates that an eternal analogue for the ascension is not out of the question.

Chapter 5 considered how Augustine's exegetical strategy—following the interconnectedness of the missions and processions—both avoids and overcomes the criticisms levelled at Rahner's Rule concerning the Son–Spirit relationship (and to a lesser degree, the Father–Spirit relationship). According to Augustine, the dynamic between the Son and the Spirit in the virgin conception, Jordan baptism, desert temptation, earthly ministry, resurrection, and Pentecostal outpouring mirrors the Son's immanent reception of the Spirit, whom the Father gives to him, both to proceed from him and to have "without measure" in the fullness of deity. The Son's immanent reception of the Spirit is the eternal analogue to the Son's multiple economic receptions of the Spirit. Moreover, we saw that little can be gleaned from the order in which divine persons are mentioned in the various triadic texts. We cannot conclude that these texts reverse the Son–Spirit or Father–Spirit relationships. Thus, if we adopt Augustine's reading strategy to complement Rahner's Rule, an even-handed application of the Rule does not require a *Spirituque* since the Spirit is given to the Son *as* he is begotten. A *Patreque* is not required since the monarchy of the Father is preserved. As such, the doctrine of eternal generation is not compromised and the risk of multiple τάξεις is likewise avoided. Given the congruity of the economic and immanent Son–Spirit relationship—the economic reflecting and grounded in the immanent—there is no need to fear relational instability, ontological morphing, or pantheism. Hence, Augustine provided an alternative framework that avoids the major obstacles for applying Rahner's Rule to the economic Son–Spirit relationship (and the Father–Spirit relationship).

2. Contributions

This book offered three main contributions to scholarly discourse, the first concerning the intersection of Augustine's exegesis with Rahner's assessment of the Augustinian tradition. As was observed in the introduction, there are far fewer studies on Augustine's Trinitarian exegesis than one might expect given both the prominence of the Scriptures in the bishop's Trinitarian writings and the prominence of the bishop in the tradition more generally. Thus, it is not surprising that until now, nothing has been written specifically concerning how Augustine's exegesis intersects with Rahner's assessment of Augustine and the tradition. Though some have challenged Rahner's assessment of Augustine, these challenges have never been made with a close eye on Augustine's extensive use of Scripture. This study is the first to offer such a challenge and is one of only a few extant studies offering a sustained consideration of Augustine's use of Scripture in his Trinitarian theology.

Secondly, despite the centrality of Rahner's Rule in late twentieth-century and early twenty-first-century theology, the fourth and fifth chapters of this book offer what is probably the only sustained and detailed argument to date *for* the exegetical validity of Rahner's Rule. As was mentioned in the introductory chapter, other studies either challenge the exegetical and theological explanatory power of the Rule (Jowers and Harrower) or only touch on the validity of the Rule tangentially. Moreover, whereas the methodology of the previous studies on the exegetical validity of the Rule limited the scope to one economic event (Jowers with the Jordan baptism) or one biblical author (Harrower with Luke-Acts), limiting ourselves to Augustine's exegetical strategies allowed for a greater breadth of scriptural material to survey. Two decades into the twenty-first century, Rahner's Rule seems to have all but fallen out of vogue, while the great patristic and scholastic theologians of the Western tradition have regained a strong following, especially in Anglophone theology. By turning to Augustine's exegesis, however, it became apparent that the Rule (as articulated by Rahner) is much closer to the tradition than is often now supposed.

Thirdly, despite various calls from scholars, this book offers the only exploration into how one of the great theologians of the tradition handled the various exegetical complexities directly associated with Rahner's Rule. This study demonstrates that by returning to the great theologians of the tradition, we can address various theological challenges of the present. In other words, it demonstrates the fruitfulness of theological retrieval.

3. Recommendations for Future Research

One limitation of this study relates to the uncritical stance afforded to Augustine. That is, the book argues that Augustine's exegesis supports various aspects of Rahner's Trinitarian theology and especially his Rule. This demonstrates the possibility of alternative reading strategies that avoid or even overcome various exegetical difficulties associated with the Rule. However, this does not necessarily mean that Augustine's exegesis is always on point. One thinks of his odd Christological reading of "Beginning" in Gen 1:1, his almost sleight-of-hand exegesis of Isa 48:16, or his understanding of the word *spiritus* in 1 Pet 3:18. Given that his exegesis seems so unconvincing in some places, one may wonder why we should trust the bishop at all. Though I am not always persuaded by Augustine's exegesis of particular texts, I am convinced that stronger readings of these texts exist, readings that follow Augustine's general reading strategy, thus corroborating Rahner's Rule. For example, I see no imperative to interpret "Beginning" Christologically, and I strongly suspect that *spiritus* refers to the Holy Spirit in 1 Pet 3:18. In the latter case, I see no reason why the Spirit's involvement in the Son's resurrection could not be seen to parallel his involvement in the Son's eternal generation. I am also not convinced that the Spirit should be understood as the one who sends the Son in Isa 48:16. Rather, I find it more likely that the word "Spirit" (Heb.: רוּחַ) is a complementary object of the sending verb (Heb.: שׁלח) rather than the subject.[1] It was simply beyond the scope of this project to delve into these tangents in any depth. Further research may seek to account for the various oddities in the bishop's exegesis and offer plausible alternative interpretations with significant detail.

Another limitation of the present study concerns the narrow focus on Augustine. Given the volume and significance of Augustine's Trinitarian writings and the confines of this project, it simply was not possible to consider in detail how others might handle the various exegetical complexities. This returns us to the enquiries of Anatolios and Sanders in the introductory chapter. How might the various exegetical particularities be handled by the Cappadocians and Bonaventure whom Rahner esteems so highly? What about Athanasius, Maximus, Calvin, or Owen? Or, as Sanders ponders, what of Cyril or Thomas? How often do these theological greats refer to the equivalent of a "relational inversion" in the various texts surveyed? How does their exegesis of the various texts compare with more recent exegesis? How often do they draw major conclusions on Trinitarian τάξις based on superficial details such as the order in which the divine persons are mentioned in a text? This calls for further research.

Thirdly, over the past few decades, a strong preference has emerged to abandon the somewhat wooden language of "economic Trinity" and "immanent Trinity" for the more traditional language of "missions" and "processions" taxonomy.[2]

---

1. I suspect that the NIV captures the intended meaning of the text: "And now the Sovereign LORD has sent me, endowed with his Spirit."

2. For example, Katherine Sonderegger, *Systematic Theology: The Doctrine of the Holy Trinity: Processions and Persons*, vol. 2 (Minneapolis: 1517 Media, 2020), xx; Fred Sanders, *The Triune God*, 148–53; Emery, *The Trinity*, 177–8; Marshall, "The Unity of the Triune God," 8; Ralf Stolina, "'Ökonomische' und 'Immanente' Trinität?: Zur Problematik Einer Trinitätstheologischen Denkfigur," *Zeitschrift für Theologie und Kirche*, vol. 105, no. 2 (2008): 170–216.

Following decades of penetrating negative assessments by the likes of Schmaus, du Roy, Rahner, Gunton, and Lacugna, Augustine has re-emerged as the hero of Western theology in the English-speaking world, thanks in no small part to the seminal studies of Barnes and Ayres. In this same period, there has been a growing interest in the Trinitarian undercurrents of the Old Testament.[3] However, in Chapter 3, we observed that Augustine limits the language of "mission" to the New Testament arrival of the Son and Spirit. This raises a difficulty. If the language of "economic" and "immanent" is to be replaced with the Augustinian taxonomy of "missions" and "processions," how are we to speak of the Trinitarian undercurrents of the Old Testament? While the language of "economic Trinity" (or synonyms such as "evangelical Trinity" or Trinity "ad extra") can account for such occurrences, the traditional understanding of "missions" cannot. This leads one to wonder whether the language of "economic Trinity" (or a synonym) is still needed to complement the more traditional language. At the very least, this question warrants further attention.

Finally, at the end of Chapter 4, we saw that Augustine begins to tease out a possible way forward in discerning a parallel between the Son's ascension to the Father and his processional life *ad intra*. If pressed, we imagine that Augustine could tease this out further. The idea of an "eternal analogue" to the ascension is certainly less puzzling than some might suppose. Nevertheless, beyond Harrower's monograph, it is very difficult to find contemporary literature on the existence (or non-existence) of an eternal analogue. One wonders how theologians of ages past might have handled such complexities. How does the doctrine of circumincession (or περιχώρησις) assist in finding an analogue? This again calls for further research.

4. Summary

In summary, we have seen that in Augustine's Trinitarian exegesis of Scripture, the Augustinian-Western tradition has always had the resources at its disposal to avoid and overcome the most poignant criticisms levelled *by* and *at* Rahner. This project has made three substantial contributions to scholarly discourse. First, it contains the only sustained challenge of Rahner's assessment of Augustine with a particular view to the bishop's exegesis. Second, this book offers the only sustained argument to date for the exegetical validity of Rahner's Rule. Third, this book offers the only exploration into the complexities of the exegetical strategies of a significant theologian directly associated with Rahner's Rule. That being said, several lines of inquiry remain for further original research, particularly with respect to Augustine's exegesis, the exegetical strategies of other theological giants, the merits of certain Trinitarian taxonomies, and the eternal analogue of the Son's ascension to the Father.

---

3. One thinks particularly of Sonderegger's account of the processions in the tabernacle in *Systematic Theology*, 2: 355–484.

BIBLIOGRAPHY

1. Primary Literature

Ambrose. *De fide* in PL 16, 523–702.
Ambrose. *De Spiritu Sancto* in CSEL 79, 1–222.
Athanasius. *Orationes contra Arianos* in PG 26, 12–526.
Athanasius. *Contra gentes* in PG 25, 1–96.
Augustine. *Ad Orosium contra Priscillianistas et Origenistas* in PL 42, 669–78.
Augustine. *Arianism and Other Heresies*. Edited by John E. Rotelle, translated by Roland J. Teske, vol. 1. The Works of Saint Augustine: A Translation for the 21st Century. Hyde Park, NY: New City, 1995.
Augustine. *Collatio cum Maximino Arianorum episcopo* in CCSL 87A, 383–470.
Augustine. *Confessionum libri XIII* in CCSL 27, 1–273.
Augustine. *Contra Adimantum* in CSEL 25, 1, 115–90.
Augustine. *Contra duas epistulas Pelagianorum ad Bonifatium* in CSEL 60, 423–570.
Augustine. *Contra epistulam Manichaei quam vocant Fundamenti* in CSEL 25, 1, 193–248.
Augustine. *Contra epistulam Parmeniani* in CSEL 51, 19–141.
Augustine. *Contra Faustum* in CSEL 25, 1, 251–797.
Augustine. *Contra litteras Petiliani* in CSEL 52, 3–227.
Augustine.*Contra Maximinum Arianum* in CCSL 87A, 491–692.
Augustine. *Contra secundam Juliani responsionem imperfectum opus* in CSEL 85, 1, 3–506; CSEL 85, 2, 3–464.
Augustine. *Contra sermonem Arianorum* in CCSL 87A, 183–256.
Augustine. *De civitate Dei* in CCSL 47, 1–314; CCSL 48, 321–866.
Augustine. *De consensu evangelistarum* in CSEL 43, 1–62.
Augustine. *De diversis quaestionibus LXXXIII* in CCSL 44A, 11–249.
Augustine. *De doctrina christiana* in CCSL 32, 1–167.
Augustine. *De Genesi ad litteram* in CSEL 28, 1, 3–435.
Augustine. *De gratia et libero arbitrio* in PL 44, 881–912.
Augustine. *De moribus Manichaeorum* in CSEL 90, 3–156.
Augustine. *De peccatorum meritis et remissione* in CSEL 60, 3–151.
Augustine. *De praedestinatione sanctorum* in PL 44, 959–92.
Augustine. *De scriptura sancta speculum* in CSEL 12, 3–285.
Augustine. *De sermone Domini in monte* in CCSL 35, 1–188.
Augustine. *De spirituet littera* in CSEL 60, 155–229.
Augustine. *De Trinitate* in CCSL 50, 25–380, CCSL 50A, 381–535.
Augustine. *Eighty-Three Different Questions*, translated by David L. Mosher, vol. 70, The Fathers of the Church: A New Translation. Washington, DC: CUA Press, 1982.
Augustine. *Enarrationes in Psalmos* in CCSL 38, 1–616; CCSL 39, 623–1417; CCSL 40, 1425–2196.
Augustine. *Enchiridion de fide, spe, et caritate* in CCSL 46, 49–114.

Augustine. *Epistula 119* in PL 33, 449–52.
Augustine. *Epistula 120 (ad Dioscorum iuuenem Graecum)* in CCSL 31B, 143–59.
Augustine. *Epistula 130 (ad Probam nouercam Iulianae)* in CCSL 31B, 212–37.
Augustine. *Epistula 137 (ad Volusianum praefectum urbi proconsulemque Africae)* in CCSL 31B, 256–74.
Augustine. *Epistula 140 (ad Honoratum catechumenum Carthaginiensem)* in CSEL 44, 155–234.
Augustine. *Epistula 147 (ad Paulinam)* in CSEL 44, 274–331.
Augustine. *Epistula 148 (ad Fortunatianum episcopum Siccensem)* in CSEL 44, 332–47.
Augustine. *Epistula 149 (ad Paulinum episcopum Nolanum)* in CSEL 44, 348–80.
Augustine. *Epistula 164 (ad Euodium Uzaliensem)* in CSEL 44, 521–41.
Augustine. *Epistula 166 (ad Hieronymum)* in CSEL 44, 545–84.
Augustine. *Epistula 169 (ad Euodium Uzaliensem)* in CSEL 44, 611–21.
Augustine. *Epistula 170 (Augustinus et Alypius ad Maximum fortasse medicum Thaenensem)* in CSEL 44, 622–31.
Augustine. *Epistula 171A (ad Maximum fortasse medicum Thaenensem)* in CSEL 44, 632–5.
Augustine. *Epistula 186 (Augustinus et Alypius ad Paulinum episcopum Nolanum)* in CSEL 57, 45–80.
Augustine. *Epistula 187 (ad Dardanum praefectum praetorio Galliarum)* in CSEL 57, 81–118.
Augustine. *Epistula 193 (ad Marium Mercatorem)* in CSEL 57, 167–75.
Augustine. *Epistula 194 (ad Sixtum presbyterum [postea Sixtum I papam])* in CSEL 57, 176–214.
Augustine. *Epistula 199 (ad Hesychium episcopum Salonensem)* in CSEL 57, 243–92.
Augustine. *Epistula 211 (ad sorores)* in CSEL 57, 356–70.
Augustine. *Epistula 217 (ad Vitalem Carthaginiensem)* in CSEL 57, 403–25.
Augustine. *Epistula 238 (ad Pascentium Arianum, comitem domus regiae)* in CSEL 57, 533–56.
Augustine. *Epistula 242 (ad Elpidium Arianum)* in CSEL 57, 533–67.
Augustine. *Epistula 29 (ad Alypium episcopum Thagastenum)* in CCSL 31, 98–105.
Augustine. *Epistula 36 (ad Casulanum presbyterum)* in CCSL 31, 130–53.
Augustine. *Epistula 48 (Augustinus et fratres ad Eudoxium abbatem in Corsica et fratres)* in CCSL 31, 209–11.
Augustine. *Epistula 53 (Augustinus, Fortunatus et Alypius ad Generosum Constantinensem)* in CCSL 31, 221–5.
Augustine. *Epistula 55 (ad Ianuarium catechumenum)* in CCSL 31, 234–65.
Augustine. *Epistula 78 (ad fratres, clerum, seniores, plebem Hipponensem)* in CCSL 31A, 83–91.
Augustine. *Epistula 89 (ad Festum)* in CCSL 31A, 148–52.
Augustine. *Epistula 92 (ad Italicam uiduam Romae)* in CCSL 31A, 160–5.
Augustine. *Epistula 92A (ad Cyprianum presbyterum)* in CCSL 31A, 166.
Augustine. *Epistula 93 (ad Vincentium episcopum Cartenensis)* in CCSL 31A, 167–206.
Augustine. *Expositio in epistulam ad Galatas* in CSEL 84, 55–141.
Augustine. *In epistulam Johannis ad Parthos tractatus* in PL 35, 1977–2062.
Augustine. *In Evangelium Johannis tractatus* in CCSL 36, 1–688.

Augustine. *On the Trinity*. Edited by Philip Schaff, translated by Arthur West Haddan, vol. 3. NPNF 1. Buffalo, NY: Christian Literature, 1887.
Augustine. *Quaestiones in Heptateuchum* in CCSL 33, 1–377.
Augustine. *Retractationum libri II* in PL 32, 583–656.
Augustine. *Sermo 1* in CCSL 41, 3–6.
Augustine. *Sermo 110A* in *Vingt-Six Sermons Au Peuple d'Afrique*. Edited by Francis Dolbeau. Collection des Études Augustiniennes, Série Antiquité 147, 140–7. Paris: Institut d'Études Augustiniennes, 2009.
Augustine. *Sermo 112A* in *Sancti Augustini sermones post maurinos reperti*. Edited by Germanus Morin. Miscellanea Agostiniana 1, 256–64. Rome: Tipografia Poliglotta Vaticana, 1930–1.
Augustine. *Sermo 114* in RBén 73 (1963), 23–8.
Augustine. *Sermo 117* in RBén 124 (2014), 227–53.
Augustine. *Sermo 118* in PL 38, 671–3.
Augustine. *Sermo 128* in PL 38, 713–20.
Augustine. *Sermo 134* in PL 38, 742–6.
Augustine. *Sermo 135* in PL 38, 746–50.
Augustine. *Sermo 136* in PL 38, 750–4.
Augustine. *Sermo 143* in PL 38, 784–7.
Augustine. *Sermo 144* in PL 38, 787–90.
Augustine. *Sermo 152* in CCSL 41Ba, 33–46.
Augustine. *Sermo 153* in CCSL 41Ba, 49–52.
Augustine. *Sermo 155* in CCSL 41Ba, 105–31.
Augustine. *Sermo 16A* in CCSL 41, 218–29.
Augustine. *Sermo 175* in CCSL 41Bb, 526–36.
Augustine. *Sermo 18* in CCSL 41, 245–50.
Augustine. *Sermo 184* in SPM 1 (1950), 74–7.
Augustine. *Sermo 185* in PL 38, 997–9.
Augustine. *Sermo 19* in CCSL 41, 252–8.
Augustine. *Sermo 192* in PL 38, 1011–13.
Augustine. *Sermo 198 auctus* in *Vingt-Six Sermons au Peuple d'Afrique*. Edited by Francis Dolbeau. Collection des Études Augustiniennes, Série Antiquité 147, 366–417. Paris: Institut d'Études Augustiniennes, 2009.
Augustine. *Sermo 200* in PL 38, 1028–31.
Augustine. *Sermo 202* in PL 38, 1033–5.
Augustine. *Sermo 204* in Bonnardière. Edited by Anne-Marie la Bonnardière, *Saint Augustin et la Bible*, vol. 3, 3 vols. Bible de tous les Temps, 77–9. Paris: Beauchesne, 1986.
Augustine. *Sermo 204B* in CSEL 101, 67–72.
Augustine. *Sermo 20A* in CCSL 41, 269–74.
Augustine. *Sermo 210* in PL 38, 1047–54.
Augustine. *Sermo 211* in SC 116 (1966), 154–72.
Augustine. *Sermo 213* in *Sancti Augustini sermones post maurinos reperti*. Edited by Germanus Morin. Miscellanea Agostiniana 1, 441–50. Rome: Tipografia Poliglotta Vaticana, 1930–1.
Augustine. *Sermo 214* in RBén 72 (1962), 14–21.
Augustine. *Sermo 215* in RBén 68 (1958), 18–25.
Augustine. *Sermo 225* in CSEL 101, 1098–9.
Augustine. *Sermo 227* in SC 116 (1966), 234–42.

Augustine. *Sermo 228B* in *Sancti Augustini sermones post maurinos reperti*. Edited by Germanus Morin. Miscellanea Agostiniana 1, 18–20. Rome: Tipografia Poliglotta Vaticana, 1930–1.

Augustine. *Sermo 229 auctus* in *Sancti Augustini sermones post maurinos reperti*. Edited by Germanus Morin. Miscellanea Agostiniana 1, 29–32. Rome: Tipografia Poliglotta Vaticana, 1930–1.

Augustine. *Sermo 229B* in *Sancti Augustini sermones post maurinos reperti*. Edited by Germanus Morin. Miscellanea Agostiniana 1, 464–6. Rome: Tipografia Poliglotta Vaticana, 1930–1.

Augustine. *Sermo 229E* in in *Sancti Augustini sermones post maurinos reperti*. Edited by Germanus Morin. Miscellanea Agostiniana 1, 466–71. Rome: Tipografia Poliglotta Vaticana, 1930–1.

Augustine. *Sermo 229H* in in *Sancti Augustini sermones post maurinos reperti*. Edited by Germanus Morin. Miscellanea Agostiniana 1, 479–83. Rome: Tipografia Poliglotta Vaticana, 1930–1.

Augustine. *Sermo 229L* in *Sancti Augustini sermones post maurinos reperti*. Edited by Germanus Morin. Miscellanea Agostiniana 1, 485–8. Rome: Tipografia Poliglotta Vaticana, 1930–1.

Augustine. *Sermo 233* in PL 38, 1112–15.

Augustine. *Sermo 23B* in *Vingt-Six Sermons Au Peuple d'Afrique*. Edited by Francis Dolbeau. Collection des Études Augustiniennes, Série Antiquité 147, 459–68. Paris: Institut d'Études Augustiniennes, 2009.

Augustine. *Sermo 246* in SC 116 (1966), 294–306.

Augustine. *Sermo 252A* in *Sancti Augustini sermones post maurinos reperti*. Edited by Germanus Morin. Miscellanea Agostiniana 1, 712–15. Rome: Tipografia Poliglotta Vaticana, 1930–1.

Augustine. *Sermo 256* in PL 38, 1190–3.

Augustine. *Sermo 263* in *Sancti Augustini sermones post maurinos reperti*. Edited by Germanus Morin. Miscellanea Agostiniana 1, 507–9. Rome: Tipografia Poliglotta Vaticana, 1930–1.

Augustine. *Sermo 265A* in *Sancti Augustini sermones post maurinos reperti*. Edited by Germanus Morin. Miscellanea Agostiniana 1, 391–5. Rome: Tipografia Poliglotta Vaticana, 1930–1.

Augustine. *Sermo 265D* in *Sancti Augustini sermones post maurinos reperti*. Edited by Germanus Morin. Miscellanea Agostiniana 1, 659–64. Rome: Tipografia Poliglotta Vaticana, 1930–1.

Augustine. *Sermo 267* in PL 38, 1229–31.

Augustine. *Sermo 268* in PL 38, 1231–4.

Augustine. *Sermo 269* in PL 38, 1234–7.

Augustine. *Sermo 270* in PL 38, 1237–45.

Augustine. *Sermo 272B* in REAug 44, 380–5.

Augustine. *Sermo 29* in CCSL 41, 373–6.

Augustine. *Sermo 290* in PL 38, 1312–16.

Augustine. *Sermo 291* in PL 38, 1316–19.

Augustine. *Sermo 293B* in *Sancti Augustini sermones post maurinos reperti*. Edited by Germanus Morin. Miscellanea Agostiniana 1, 227–31. Rome: Tipografia Poliglotta Vaticana, 1930–1.

Augustine. *Sermo 294* in PL 38, 1335–48.
Augustine. *Sermo 29B* in *Vingt-Six Sermons au Peuple d'Afrique*. Edited by Francis Dolbeau. Collection des Études Augustiniennes, Série Antiquité 147, 244–9. Paris: Institut d'Études Augustiniennes, 2009.
Augustine. *Sermo 30* in CCSL 41, 382–9.
Augustine. *Sermo 306A* in *Vingt-Six Sermons au Peuple d'Afrique*. Edited by Francis Dolbeau. Collection des Études Augustiniennes, Série Antiquité 147, 645–6. Paris: Institut d'Études Augustiniennes, 2009.
Augustine. *Sermo 308A* in *Vingt-Six Sermons au Peuple d'Afrique*. Edited by Francis Dolbeau. Collection des Études Augustiniennes, Série Antiquité 147, 43–50. Paris: Institut d'Études Augustiniennes, 2009.
Augustine. *Sermo 312* in PL 38, 1420–3.
Augustine. *Sermo 315* in PL 38, 1426–31.
Augustine. *Sermo 316* in PL 38, 1431–4.
Augustine. *Sermo 317* in PL 38, 1435–7.
Augustine. *Sermo 319* in PL 38, 1440–2.
Augustine. *Sermo 330* in PL 38, 1456–9.
Augustine. *Sermo 333* in PL 38, 1463–7.
Augustine. *Sermo 335E* in PLS 2, 781–5.
Augustine. *Sermo 335I* in PLS 2, 832–4.
Augustine. *Sermo 341 auctus* in *Vingt-Six Sermons au Peuple d'Afrique*. Edited by Francis Dolbeau. Collection des Études Augustiniennes, Série Antiquité 147, 171–96. Paris: Institut d'Études Augustiniennes, 2009.
Augustine. *Sermo 352* in RBén 129 (2019), 35–64.
Augustine. *Sermo 360A* in *Vingt-Six Sermons au Peuple d'Afrique*. Edited by Francis Dolbeau. Collection des Études Augustiniennes, Série Antiquité 147, 232–42. Paris: Institut d'Études Augustiniennes, 2009.
Augustine. *Sermo 360B* in *Vingt-Six Sermons au Peuple d'Afrique*. Edited by Francis Dolbeau. Collection des Études Augustiniennes, Série Antiquité 147, 248–67. Paris: Institut d'Études Augustiniennes, 2009.
Augustine. *Sermo 369* in RBén 79 (1969), 124–8.
Augustine. *Sermo 378* in PL 39, 1673–4.
Augustine. *Sermo 51* in CCSL 41Aa, 9–50.
Augustine. *Sermo 52* in CCSL 41Aa, 58–81.
Augustine. *Sermo 53* in CCSL 41Aa, 88–104.
Augustine. *Sermo 53A* in CCSL 41Aa, 111–31.
Augustine. *Sermo 60A* in CCSL 41Aa, 253–7.
Augustine. *Sermo 68 auctus* in CCSL 41Aa, 437–53.
Augustine. *Sermo 69* in CCSL 41Aa, 460–4.
Augustine. *Sermo 71* in CCSL 41Ab, 14–70.
Augustine. *Sermo 72A* in CCSL 41Ab, 108–19.
Augustine. *Sermo 76* in CCSL 41Ab, 180–8.
Augustine. *Sermo 77* in CCSL 41Ab, 198–212.
Augustine. *Sermo 94A* in *Sancti Augustini sermones post maurinos reperti*. Edited by Germanus Morin. Miscellanea Agostiniana 1, 252–5. Rome: Tipografia Poliglotta Vaticana, 1930–1.
Augustine. *Sermons on the New Testament (51–94)*. Edited by John E. Rotelle, translation and notes by Edmund Hill, vol. 3. The Works of Saint Augustine: A Translation for the 21st Century 3. Brooklyn: New City, 1991.

Augustine. *Sermons on the New Testament (148–183)*. Edited by John E. Rotelle, translation and notes by Edmund Hill, vol. 5. The Works of Saint Augustine: A Translation for the 21st Century 3. Brooklyn: New City, 1992.

Augustine. *Sermons on the New Testament (184–229Z)*. Edited by John E. Rotelle, translation and notes by Edmund Hill, vol. 6. The Works of Saint Augustine: A Translation for the 21st Century 3. Brooklyn: New City, 1992.

Augustine. *Sermons on the New Testament (306–340A)*. Edited by John E. Rotelle, translation and notes by Edmund Hill, vol. 9. The Works of Saint Augustine: A Translation for the 21st Century 3. Brooklyn: New City, 1994.

Augustine. *The Donatist Controversy I: General Introduction and Other Introductions by † Maureen Tilley; Translation and Notes by † Maureen Tilley and Boniface Ramsay*. Edited by Boniface Ramsey and David G. Hunter, vol. 21. The Works of Saint Augustine: A Translation for the 21st Century 1. Hyde Park, NY: New City, 2019.

Augustine. *The Trinity: Introduction, Translation and Notes*. Edited by John E. Rotelle, translated by Edmund Hill, vol. 5. The Works of Saint Augustine: A Translation for the 21st Century 1. Brooklyn: New City, 1991.

Augustine. *The Trinity*. Translated by Stephen McKenna, vol. 45. The Fathers of the Church: A New Translation. Washington, DC: CUA Press, 1963.

Augustine. *Tractates on the Gospel of John 112–24; Tractates on the First Epistle of John*. Translation and Introduction by John W. Rettig, vol. 92. The Fathers of the Church. Washington, DC: CUA Press, 1995.

Basil of Caesarea. *Contra Eunomium* in PG 29, 468–774.

Basil of Caesarea. *Epistula 168* in PG 32, 683–94.

Bonaventure. *Breviloquium: Introduction*. Translation and Notes by Dominic V. Monti, O.F.M, edited by Robert J. Karris, vol. 9. Text in Translation Series. St. Bonaventure, NY: Franciscan Institute, 2005.

Clement of Alexandria. *Paedagogus* in PG 8, 247–684.

Cyril of Alexandria. *In Joannis Evangelium* in PG 74, 9–756.

Cyril of Jerusalem. *Catecheses* in PG 33, 331–1064.

Didymus. *De Trinitate* in PG 39, 269–992.

Epiphanius. *Expositio Fide* in PG 42, 773–832.

Gregory of Nyssa. *Refutatio Confessionis Eunomii* in GNO 2, 296–389.

Gregory of Nyssa. *Oratio catechetica magna* in PG 45, 9–106.

Hilary. *De synodis* in PL 10, 471–546.

Hilary. *De Trinitate* in CCSL 62, 1–310; CCSL 62A, 311–627.

Irenaeus. *Adversus haereses* in PG 7, 433–1118.

John of Damascus. *Expositio Fidei orthodoxae* in PG 94, 790–1228.

Justin. *Dialogus cum Tryphone* in PG 6, 471–800.

Maximus the Confessor. *Quaestiones et Dubia* in PG 90, 786–856.

Novatian. *Liber de Trinitate* in PL 3, 883–952.

Origen. *Homiliae in Genesim* in PG 12, 145–263.

Origen. *De principiis (Peri archōn)* in PG 11, 115–414.

Theophilus. *Ad Autolycum* in PG 6, 1023–68.

Tertullian. *Adversus Praxean* in PL 2, 153–96.

2. Secondary Literature

Ables, Travis E. *Incarnational Realism: Trinity and the Spirit in Augustine and Barth.* London: Bloomsbury, 2013.
Altaner, Berthold, and Alfred Stuiber. *Patrologie: Leben, Schriften Und Lehre Der Kirchenväter.* Freiburg im Breisgau: Herder, 1938.
Anatolios, Khaled. *Retrieving Nicaea: The Development and Meaning of Trinitarian Doctrine.* Grand Rapids: Baker, 2011.
Arnold, Johannes. "Begriff und heilsökonomische Bedeutung der göttlichen Sendungen in Augustinus' *De Trinitate*." *Recherches Augustiniennes et Patristiques*, vol. 25, no. 1 (1991): 3–69.
Ayres, Lewis. *Augustine and the Trinity.* Cambridge: CUP, 2010.
Ayres, Lewis. "The Fundamental Grammar of Augustine's Trinitarian Theology," in *Augustine and His Critics*, edited by Robert Dodaro and George Lawless, 51–76. New York: Routledge, 2005.
Ayres, Lewis. *Nicaea and Its Legacy: An Approach to Fourth-Century Trinitarian Theology.* Oxford: OUP, 2004.
Ayres, Lewis. "Spiritus Amborum: Augustine and Pro-Nicene Pneumatology." *Augustinian Studies*, vol. 39, no. 2 (2008): 207–21.
Bailleux, Emile. "La Sotériologie de Saint Augustin dans le *De Trinitate*." *Mélanges de Science Religieuse*, vol. 23 (1966): 149–73.
Balthasar, Hans Urs von. *The Action*, vol. 4. Theo-Drama: Theological Dramatic Theory. San Francisco: Ignatius, 1994. Translation of *Die Handlung*, vol. 3. Theodramatik. Einsiedeln: Johannes, 1981.
Balthasar, Hans Urs von. *Dramatis Personae: Persons in Christ.* Translated by Graham Harrison, vol. 3. Theo-Drama: Theological Dramatic Theory. San Francisco: Ignatius, 1992. Translation of *Die Personen Des Spiels: Die Personen in Christus*, vol. 2, pt 2. Theodramatik. Einsiedeln: Johannes, 1978.
Bardy, Gustave, J.-A. Beackaert, and J. Boutet, eds. *Œervres de Saint Augustin.* Bibliothèque Augustinienne 10. Paris: Desclée de Brouwer, 1952.
Barnes, Michel. "De Régnon Reconsidered." *Augustinian Studies*, vol. 26, no. 2 (1995): 51–79.
Barnes, Michel R. "The Arians of Book V, and the Genre of 'De Trinitate.'" *Journal of Theological Studies*, vol. 44, no. 1 (1993): 185–95.
Barnes, Michel R. "Augustine in Contemporary Trinitarian Theology." *Theological Studies*, vol. 56, no. 2 (1995): 237–50.
Barnes, Michel R. "Augustine's Last Pneumatology." *Augustinian Studies*, vol. 39, no. 2 (2008): 223–34.
Barnes, Michel R. "Exegesis and Polemic in Augustine's *De Trinitate* I." *Augustinian Studies*, vol. 30 (1999): 43–52.
Barnes, Michel R. "The Visible Christ and the Invisible Trinity: Mt. 5:8 in Augustine's Trinitarian Theology of 400." *Modern Theology*, vol. 19, no. 3 (2003): 329–55.
Barrett, C. K. *The Gospel According to St. John.* Philadelphia: Westminster, 1978.
Barton, Stephen. "Paul and the Resurrection: A Sociological Approach." *Religion*, vol. 14, no. 1 (January 1984): 67–75.
Beasley-Murray, George R. *John.* 2nd ed., vol. 36. Word Biblical Commentary. Nashville: Thomas Nelson, 1999.

Behr, John. "Calling Upon God as Father: Augustine and the Legacy of Nicaea," in *Orthodox Readings of Augustine*, edited by George E. Demacopoulos and Aristotle Papanikolaou, 153–65. New York: St Vladimir's Seminary Press, 2008.
Benner, Drayton C. "Augustine and Karl Rahner on the Relationship between the Immanent Trinity and the Economic Trinity." *International Journal of Systematic Theology*, vol. 9, no. 1 (2007): 24–38.
Berrouard, Marie-François. "'Introduction' in Augustine," in *Homélies Sur l'Evangile de Saint Jean XVII–XXXIII*, by Augustine, vol. 72. Bibliothèque Augustinienne. Paris: Desclée de Brouwer, 1977.
Bobrinskoy, Boris. *The Mystery of the Trinity: Trinitarian Experience and Vision in the Biblical and Patristic Tradition*. Translated by Anthony P. Gythiel. Crestwood, NY: St Vladimir's Seminary Press, 1999. Translation of *Le Mystère de La Trinité, Cours de Théologie Orthodoxe*. Paris: Cerf, 1996.
Bochet, Isabelle. « *Le firmament de l'Ecriture* »: *L'herméneutique Augustinienne*. Paris: Institut d'Études Augustiniennes, 2004.
Boff, Leonardo. *A Santíssima Trindade é a Melhor Comunidade*. Petrópolis: Vozes, 1988.
Bogan M. Inez. *St Augustine: The Retractions*, vol. 60. The Fathers of the Church: A New Translation. Washington, DC: CUA Press, 1968.
Bonnardière, Anne-Marie la. *Bible de tous les temps: Saint Augustin et la Bible*. Paris: Beauchesne, 1986.
Bonnardière, Anne-Marie la. *Recherches de chronologie Augustinienne*. Paris: Études Augustiniennes, 1965.
Bonnardière, Anne-Marie la. "Recherche sur la structure du *De Trinitate* de saint Augustin." *Annuaires de l'École pratique des hautes études*, no. 82 (1973): 293–7.
Boulnois, Marie-Odile. "Le *De Trinitate* de Saint Augustin: Exégèse, logique et noétique," in *"Le De Trinitate de Saint Augustin"*: *Exégèse, logique et noétique*, edited by Emmanuel Bermon and Gerald O'Daly, 35–66. Paris: Institut d'Études Augustiniennes, 2012.
Bourassa, François. "Le Don de Dieu." *Gregorianum*, vol. 50, no. 2 (1969): 201–37.
Bourassa, François. "Sur le Traité de la Trinité." *Gregorianum*, vol. 47, no. 2 (1966): 254–85.
Bourassa, François. "Théologie Trinitaire chez Saint Augustin." *Gregorianum*, vol. 58, no. 4 (1977): 675–718.
Bourassa, François. "Theologie Trinitaire de Saint Augustin." *Gregorianum*, vol. 59, no. 2 (1978): 375–412.
Canale, Fernando L. "Doctrine of God," in *Handbook of Seventh-Day Adventist Theology*, edited by Raoul Dederen, 125–82. Seventh-Day Adventist Bible Commentary Reference Series 12. Hagerstown, MD: Review and Herald, 2001.
Carson, D. A. *The Gospel According to John*. Grand Rapids: Eerdmans, 1990.
Cary, Phillip. "On Behalf of Classical Trinitarianism: A Critique of Rahner on the Trinity." *The Thomist: A Speculative Quarterly Review*, vol. 56, no. 3 (1992): 365–405.
Cavadini, John C. *Visioning Augustine*. Oxford: John Wiley & Sons, 2019.
Cipriani, Nello. *La teologia di sant'Agostino: introduzione generale e riflessione trinitaria*. Kindle ed. Rome: Institutum Patristicum Augustinianum, 2015.
Clark, Mary A. "*De Trinitate*," in *The Cambridge Companion to Augustine*, edited by Norman Kretzmann and Eleonore Stump, 91–102. Cambridge: CUP, 2001.
Coffey, David. "The Holy Spirit as the Mutual Love of the Father and the Son." *Theological Studies*, vol. 51, no. 2 (1990): 193–229.
Coffey, David. "The Roman 'Clarification' of the Doctrine of the Filioque." *International Journal of Systematic Theology*, vol. 5, no. 1 (2003): 3–21.

Congar, Yves. *Je Crois en l'Esprit Saint: Le Fleuve de Vie Coule en Orient et en Occident*, vol. 3. Paris: Cerf, 1980.
Congar, Yves. *La Parole et Le Souffle*. Paris: Desclée, 1984.
Daley, Brian E. "The Giant's Twin Substances: Ambrose and the Christology of Augustine's Contra Sermonem Arianorum," in *Augustine: Presbyter Factus Sum*, edited by J. T. Lienhard, E. C. Muller, and R. J. Teske, 477–95. New York: Peter Lang, 1993.
Denzinger, H., and A.Schönmetzer, eds. *Enchiridion Symbolorum, Definitionum et Declarationum de Rebus Fidei et Morum*, 35th ed. Rome, 1973.
Du Roy, Olivier. *L'Intelligence de la Foi en la Trinité selon Saint Augustin*. Paris: Études Augustiniennes, 1966.
Dukeman, Jeffrey A. *Mutual Hierarchy: A New Approach to Social Trinitarianism*. Eugene, OR: Wipf & Stock, 2019.
Dunham, Scott A. *The Trinity and Creation in Augustine: An Ecological Analysis*. Albany: SUNY Press, 2008.
Durst, Rodrick. *Reordering the Trinity: Six Movements of God in the New Testament*. Grand Rapids: Kregel Academic & Professional, 2015.
Erickson, Millard J. *God in Three Persons: A Contemporary Interpretation of the Trinity*. Grand Rapids: Baker, 1995.
Emery, Gilles. *The Trinity: An Introduction to Catholic Doctrine on the Triune God*. Translated by Matthew Levering. Washington, DC: CUA Press, 2011. Translation of *Introduction Théologique à la doctrine catholique sur Dieu Trinité*. Paris: Cerf, 2009.
Evdokimov, Paul. *L'Esprit Saint dans la tradition orthodoxe*. Paris: Les Éditions du Cerf, 1969.
Fee, Gordon D. *God's Empowering Presence: The Holy Spirit in the Letters of Paul*. Peabody, MA: Hendrickson, 1994.
Ferri, Riccardo. "Il *De Trinitate* di Agostino d'Ippona: Commento al Libro Primo." *Lateranum*, vol. 78, no. 3 (2012): 549–70.
Ferri, Riccardo. "Le Missioni Divine nel *De Trinitate* di Agostino d'Ippona: Commento ai libri II–IV." *Lateranum*, vol. 82, no. 1 (2016): 55–75.
Gangauf, Theodor. *Des Heiligen Augustinus speculative Lehre von Gott dem Dreieinigen*. Augsburg: Schmid, 1865.
Giles, Kevin. *Jesus and the Father: Modern Evangelicals Reinvent the Doctrine of the Trinity*. Grand Rapids: Zondervan, 2009.
Gioia, Luigi. *The Theological Epistemology of Augustine's* De Trinitate. Oxford: OUP, 2008.
Godet, Frédéric Louis. *Commentary on the Gospel of John: With an Historical and Critical Introduction*, vol. 2. New York: Funk & Wagnalls, 1886.
Grabau, Joseph L. "Christology and Exegesis in Augustine of Hippo's XVth Tractate *In Iohannis Euangelium*," in *Studia Patristica: Papers Presented at the Seventeenth International Conference on Patristic Studies Held in Oxford 2015*, edited by Markus Vinzent, vol. 98, 103–8. Leuven: Peeters, 2017.
Green, Bradley G. *Colin Gunton and the Failure of Augustine: The Theology of Colin Gunton in Light of Augustine*. Eugene, OR: Pickwick, 2011.
Green, Bradley G. "The Protomodern Augustine? Colin Gunton and the Failure of Augustine." *International Journal of Systematic Theology*, vol. 9, no. 3 (2007): 328–41.
Grudem, Wayne. *Evangelical Feminism and Biblical Truth: An Analysis of More Than 100 Disputed Questions*. Wheaton: Crossway, 2012.
Gruenler, Royce G. *The Trinity in the Gospel of John: A Thematic Commentary on the Fourth Gospel*. Eugene, OR: Wipf & Stock, 2004.

Harnack, Adolf von. *Lehrbuch der dogmengeschichte*, 3rd ed., vol. 2. Freiburg im Brisgau: Mohr, 1894.
Harrower, Scott. "Bruce Ware's Trinitarian Methodology," in *Trinity without Hierarchy: Reclaiming Nicene Orthodoxy in Evangelical Theology*, edited by Harrower Scott and Michael F. Bird, 307–30. Grand Rapids: Kregel, 2019.
Harrower, Scott. *Trinitarian Self and Salvation: An Evangelical Engagement with Rahner's Rule*. Eugene, OR: Wipf & Stock, 2012.
Hendrikx, Ephraem. "La date de composition du *De Trinitate*," in *La Trinité I: Le Mystere*, 557–66. Bibliothèque Augustinienne 15. Paris: Desclée de Brouwer, 1955.
Hennessy, Kristin. "An Answer to de Régnon's Accusers: Why We Should Not Speak of 'His' Paradigm." *Harvard Theological Review*, vol. 100, no. 2 (2007): 179–97.
Hill, Edmund. "Karl Rahner's 'Remarks on the Dogmatic Treatise *De Trinitate* and St. Augustine.'" *Augustinian Studies*, vol. 2 (1971): 67–80.
Hombert, P. M. *Nouvelles Recherches de Chronologie Augustinienne*. Paris: Institut d'Études Augustiniennes, 2000.
Iacovetti, Christopher. "*Filioque, Theosis,* and *Ecclesia*: Augustine in Dialogue with Modern Orthodox Theology." *Modern Theology*, vol. 34, no. 1 (2018): 70–81.
Jowers, Dennis W. "An Exposition and Critique of Karl Rahner's Axiom: 'The Economic Trinity *is* the Immanent Trinity and Vice Versa.'" *Mid-America Journal of Theology*, vol. 15 (2004): 165–200.
Jowers, Dennis W. "A Test of Karl Rahner's Axiom, 'The Economic Trinity *is* the Immanent Trinity and Vice Versa.'" *Thomist: A Speculative Quarterly Review*, vol. 70, no. 3 (2006): 421–55.
Jowers, Dennis W. *The Trinitarian Axiom of Karl Rahner: The Economic Trinity is the Immanent Trinity and Vice Versa*. Lewiston: Edwin Mellen, 2006.
Kany, Roland. *Augustins Trinitätsdenken: Bilanz, Kritik und Weiterführung der modernen Forschung zu "De trinitate."* Studien und Texte zu Antike und Christentum/Studies and Texts in Antiquity and Christianity 22. Tübingen: Mohr, 2007.
Kärkkäinen, Veli-matti. "Is the Spirit Still the Dividing Line between the Christian East and West? Revisiting an Ancient Problem of *Filioque* with a Hope for an Ecumenical Rapprochement." *Perichoresis*, vol. 9, no. 2 (2011): 125–42.
Kelly, J. N. D. *Early Christian Creeds*, 2nd ed. New York: David McKay, 1960.
Kloos, Kari. *Christ, Creation, and the Vision of God: Augustine's Transformation of Early Christian Theophany Interpretation*. Leiden: Brill, 2011.
Kloos, Kari. "Seeing the Invisible God: Augustine's Reconfiguration of Theophany Narrative Exegesis." *Augustinian Studies*, vol. 36, no. 2 (2005): 397–420.
Lacugna, Catherine M. *God for Us: The Trinity and Christian Life*. San Francisco: HarperCollins, 1993.
Lee, Chungman. *Gregory of Nyssa, Augustine of Hippo, and the Filioque*, 169. Leiden: Brill, 2021.
Letham, Robert. *The Holy Trinity: In Scripture, History, Theology, and Worship*. Phillipsburg: P&R, 2004.
Letham, Robert. "The Trinity between East and West." *Journal of Reformed Theology*, vol. 3, no. 1 (2009): 42–56.
Levering, Matthew. *The Theology of Augustine: An Introductory Guide to His Most Important Works*. Grand Rapids: Baker, 2013.
Mansini, Guy. *The Word Has Dwelt among Us: Explorations in Theology*. Ave Maria, FL: Sapientia, 2008.

Marmion, Declan, and Rik van Nieuwenhove. *An Introduction to the Trinity*. Cambridge: CUP, 2011.

Marshall, Bruce D. "The Unity of the Triune God: Reviving an Ancient Question." *The Thomist: A Speculative Quarterly Review*, vol. 74, no. 1 (2010): 1–32.

Mizzi, Jos. "The Latin Text of Matt. V–VII in St. Augustine's « De Sermone Domini in Monte »." *Augustiniana*, vol. 4, no. 3 (1954): 450–94.

Molnar, Paul D. *Divine Freedom and the Doctrine of the Immanent Trinity: In Dialogue with Karl Barth and Contemporary Theology*, 2nd ed. New York: T&T Clark, 2017.

Moltmann, Jürgen. *Trinität und Reich Gottes: Zur Gotteslehre*. Munich: Kaiser, 1980.

Mühlen, Heribert. *Der Heilige Geist als Person: in der Trinität, bei der Inkarnation und im Gnadenbund: Ich, du, wir*. Münster: Aschendorff, 1963.

Ormerod, Neil. *The Trinity: Retrieving the Western Tradition*. Milwaukee: Marquette University Press, 2005.

Ormerod, Neil. "Wrestling with Rahner on the Trinity." *Irish Theological Quarterly*, vol. 68, no. 3 (2003): 213–27.

Pannenberg, Wolfhart. *Systematic Theology*. Translated by Geoffrey W. Bromiley, vol. 1. 3 vols. London: T&T Clark, 1992. Translated from *Systematische Theologie*, vol. 1. Göttingen: Vandenhoeck & Ruprecht, 1988.

Pecknold, C. C. "How Augustine Used the Trinity: Functionalism and the Development of Doctrine." *Anglican Theological Review*, vol. 85, no. 1 (2003): 127–41.

Pelikan, Jaroslav. "Canonica Regula: The Trinitarian Hermeneutics of Augustine," in *Collectanea Augustiniana: Augustine: "Second Founder of the Faith*," edited by Joseph C. Schnaubelt and Frederick van Fleteren, 329–43. New York: Peter Lang, 1990.

Peterson, Brandon R. *Being Salvation: Atonement and Soteriology in the Theology of Karl Rahner*. Minneapolis: Fortress Press, 2017.

Plantinga, Cornelius. "The Fourth Gospel as Trinitarian Source Then and Now," in *Biblical Hermeneutics in Historical Perspective: Studies in Honor of Karlfried Froelich on His Sixtieth Birthday*, edited by Mark S. Burrows and Oaul Rorem, 303–21. Grand Rapids: Eerdmans, 1991.

Ployd, Adam. *Augustine, the Trinity, and the Church: A Reading of the Anti-Donatist Sermons*. London: OUP, 2015.

Rahner, Karl. "Bemerkungen zum Dogmatischen Traktat 'De Trinitate,'" in *Schriften zur Theologie*, 4, 103–33. Einsiedeln: Benziger, 1960.

Rahner, Karl. "Buch Gottes–Buch der Menschen," in *Schriften zur Theologie*, vol. 16. Einsiedeln: Benziger, 1984.

Rahner, Karl. "Der Dreifaltige Gott als Transzendenter Urgrund der Heilsgeschichte," in *Sämtliche Werke*, edited by Peter Walter and Michael Hauber, 22/1b, 512–628. Freiburg im Brisgau: Herder, 2013.

Rahner, Karl. "Dogmatische Fragen zur Osterfrömmigkeit," in *Schriften zur Theologie*, 4, 157–68. Einsiedeln: Benziger, 1960.

Rahner, Karl. "E latere Christi: Der Ursprung der Kirche als zweiter Eva aus der Seite Christi des zweiten Adam; Eine Untersuchung über den typologischen Sinn von Joh 19,34.51," in *Sämtliche Werke*, 3, 3–84. Zürich: Benziger, 1999.

Rahner, Karl. "Exegese und Dogmatik," in *Schriften zur Theologie*, 5, 82–111. Zürich: Benziger, 1962.

Rahner, Karl. "Fragen der Kontroverstheologie über die Rechtfertigung," in *Schriften zur Theologie*, 4, 237–71. Einsiedeln: Benziger, 1960.

Rahner, Karl. "Fragen zur Unbegreiflichkeit Gottes nach Thomas von Aquin," in *Sämtliche Werke*, edited by Peter Walter and Michael Hauber, 22/1b, 306–19. Freiburg im Brisgau: Herder, 2013.
Rahner, Karl. "Geschichtlichkeit der Theologie," in *Schriften zur Theologie*, 8, 72–92. Zürich: Benziger, 1967.
Rahner, Karl. *Grundkurs des Glaubens: Einführung in den Begriff des Christentums.* Freiburg im Breisgau: Herder, 1976.
Rahner, Karl. "Jungfräulichkeit Marias," in *Schriften zur Theologie*, 13, 361–77. Zürich: Benziger, 1978.
Rahner, Karl. "Kirchliche Christologie zwischen Exegese und Dogmatik," in *Schriften zur Theologie*, vol. 9, 197–226. Einsiedeln: Benziger, 1970.
Rahner, Karl. "Kleine Anmerkungen zur Systematischen Christologie Heute," in *Schriften zur Theologie*, vol. 15, 225–35. Zürich: Benziger, 1983.
Rahner, Karl. "Natur und Gnade," in *Schriften zur Theologie*, vol. 4, 209–36. Einsiedeln: Benziger, 1960.
Rahner, Karl. "Probleme der Christologie von Heute," in *Sämtliche Werke*, vol. 12, 261–301. Freiburg im Brisgau: Herder, 2005.
Rahner, Karl. "Theologisches zum Monogenismus." *Zeitschrift für Katholische Theologie*, vol. 76, no. 2 (1954): 187–223.
Rahner, Karl. "Theos im Neuen Testament." *Bijdragen*, vol. 11, no. 3 (1950): 212–36.
Rahner, Karl. *The Trinity*. Translated by Joseph Donceel. New York: Herder, 1970. Translated from "Der Dreifaltige Gott als Transzendenter Urgrund der Heilsgeschichte," 317–47, in *Mysterium Salutis*, edited by Johannes Feiner and Magnus Löhrer. Einsiedeln: Benziger, 1967.
Rahner, Karl. "Trinität," in *Sacramentum Mundi: Theologisches Lexikon für die Praxis*, edited by Karl Rahner, vol. 4, 1005–21. Freiburg im Breisgau: Herder, 1969.
Rahner, Karl. "Trinitätstheologie," in *Sacramentum Mundi: Theologisches Lexikon für die Praxis*, edited by Karl Rahner, vol. 4, 1022–31. Freiburg im Breisgau: Herder, 1969.
Rahner, Karl. "Über das Geheimnis der Dreifaltigkeit," in *Sämtliche Werke*, edited by Peter Walter and Michael Hauber, vol. 22/2, 833–44. Freiburg im Brisgau: Herder, 2013.
Rahner, Karl. "Über den Begriff des Geheimnisses in der Katholischen Theologie," in *Schriften zur Theologie*, vol. 4, 51–99. Einsiedeln: Benziger, 1960.
Rahner, Karl. "Über die Verborgenheit Gottes," in *Schriften zur Theologie*, edited by Karl H. Neufeld, vol. 12, 285–305. Zürich: Benziger, 1975.
Rahner, Karl. "Überlegungen zur Methode der Theologie," in *Schriften zur Theologie*, vol. 9, 79–126. Zürich: Benziger, 1970.
Rahner, Karl. "Was Ist Eine Dogmatische Aussage?," in *Schriften zur Theologie*, vol. 5, 54–81. Zürich: Benziger, 1962.
Rahner, Karl. "Zur Theologie der Menschwerdung," in *Schriften zur Theologie*, vol. 4, 137–56. Einsiedeln: Benziger, 1960.
Rahner, Karl. "Zur Theologie des Symbols," in *Schriften zur Theologie*, vol. 4, 275–311. Einsiedeln: Benziger, 1960.
Ratzinger, Joseph. "The Holy Spirit as Communio: Concerning the Relationship of Pneumatology and Spirituality in Augustine." *Communio: International Catholic Review*, vol. 25 (1998): 324–37.
Régnon, Theodore de. *Études de Théologie Positive sur la Sainte Trinité*, vol. 1, 3 vols. Paris: Victor Retaux, 1892.

Régnon, Theodore de. *Études de Théologie Positive sur la Sainte Trinité*, vol. 3, 3 vols. Paris: Victor Retaux, 1898.
Ridderbos, Herman. *The Gospel of John: A Theological Commentary*. Translated by John Vriend. Grand Rapids: Eerdmans, 1997. Translated from the two volumes of *Het Evangelie naar Johannes. Proeve van een theologische Exegese*. Kampen: Uitgeversmaatschappij J. H. Kok, 1987, 1992.
Sanders, Fred. Foreword to *Trinitarian Self and Salvation: An Evangelical Engagement with Rahner's Rule*, by Scott Harrower. Eugene, OR: Wipf & Stock, 2012.
Sanders, Fred. *The Image of the Immanent Trinity: Rahner's Rule and the Theological Interpretation of Scripture*. New York: International Academic, 2004.
Sanders, Fred. *The Triune God*. Grand Rapids: Zondervan Academic, 2016.
Scheffczyk, Leo. "Lehramtliche Formulierungen und Dogmengeschichte der Trinitätslehre," in *Mysterium salutis*, edited by Johannes Feiner and Magnus Löhrer, vol. 2, 146–220. Einsiedeln: Benziger, 1967.
Schierse, Franz Josef. "Die Neutestamentliche Trinitätsoffenbarung," in *Mysterium Salutis*, edited by Johannes Feiner and Magnus Löhrer, 82–131. Einsiedeln: Benziger, 1967.
Schindler, Alfred. *Wort und Analogie in Augustins Trinitätslehre*. Tübingen: Mohr, 1965.
Schmaus, Michael. *Die psychologische Trinitätslehre des heiligen Augustinus*. Münster: Aschendorff, 1927.
Schmaus, Michael. "Die Spannung von Metaphysik und Heilsgeschicte in der Trinitätslehre Augustins," in *Studia Patristica*, edited by F. L. Cross, vol. 6, 503–18. Berlin: Akademie-Verlag, 1962.
Schoonenberg, Piet. "Trinität—Der Vollendete Bund: Thesen zur Lehre vom Dreipersonlichen Gott: 115–17." *Orientierung*, vol. 37 (1973): 115–17.
Schulte, Raphael. "Die Selbsterschliessung des Dreifaltigen Gottes," in *Mysterium Salutis*, edited by Johannes Feiner and Magnus Löhrer, 49–84. Einsiedeln: Benziger, 1967.
Sonderegger, Katherine. *Systematic Theology: The Doctrine of the Holy Trinity: Processions and Persons*, vol. 2. Minneapolis: 1517 Media, 2020.
Starke, John. "Augustine and His Interpreters," in *One God in Three Persons: Unity of Essence, Distinction of Persons, Implications for Life*, edited by Bruce A. Ware and John Starke, 155–73. Wheaton: Crossway, 2015.
Stolina, Ralf. "'Ökonomische' und 'Immanente' Trinität?: Zur Problematik Einer Trinitätstheologischen Denkfigur." *Zeitschrift für Theologie und Kirche*, vol. 105, no. 2 (2008): 170–216.
Strauss, Gerhard. *Schriftgebrauch, Schriftauslegung und Schriftbeweis bei Augustin*. BGBH 1. Tübingen: Mohr, 1957.
Studer, Basil. *Augustins* De Trinitate: *eine Einführung*. Paderborn: Ferdinand Schöningh, 2005.
Studer, Basil. "Theologia—Oikonomia: Zu einem traditionellen Thema in Augustins De Trinitate," in *Patrimonium fidei*, edited by Magnus Löhrer and Pius-Ramon Tragan, 575–600. Studia Anselmiana 124. Rome: Pontificio Ateneo S. Anselmo, 1997.
Studer, Basil. "Zur Bedeutung der Heiligen Schrift in Augustin's De Trinitate." *Augustinianum*, vol. 42, no. 1 (2002): 127–47.
Tinkham, Matthew L. "Neo-Subordinationism: The Alien Argumentation in the Gender Debate." *Andrews University Seminary Studies*, vol. 55, no. 2 (2017): 237–90.
Torrance, Thomas F. "Toward an Ecumenical Consensus on the Trinity," in *Trinitarian Perspectives: Toward Doctrinal Agreement*, 77–102. Edinburgh: T&T Clark, 1994.

Van Fleteren, Frederick. "Principles of Augustine's Hermeneutic: An Overview," in *Augustine: Biblical Exegete*, edited by Frederick Van Fleteren and Joseph C. Schnaubelt, 1–32. New York: Peter Lang, 2004.

Vass, George. *Understanding Karl Rahner: The Atonement and Mankind's Salvation*, vol. 4. A Pattern of Doctrines. London: Bloomsbury, 1998.

Vessey, Mark. "*Opus Imperfectum*: Augustine and His Readers, 426–435 A.D." *Vigiliae Christianae*, vol. 52, no. 3 (1998): 264–85.

Wainwright, Arthur William. *The Trinity in the New Testament*. London: SPCK, 1962.

Ware, Bruce. "Equal in Essence, Distinct in Roles: Eternal Functional Authority and Submission among the Essentially Equal Divine Persons of the Godhead." *JBMW*, vol. 13, no. 2 (2008): 43–58.

Weinandy, Thomas. *The Father's Spirit of Sonship: Reconceiving the Trinity*. Edinburgh: T&T Clark, 1995.

Wilken, Robert Louis. "The Resurrection of Jesus and the Doctrine of the Trinity." *Word & World*, vol. 2, no. 1 (1982): 17–28.

Williams, Rowan. *On Augustine*. London: Bloomsbury, 2016.

Wilson, Andrew. "The Walls of Carthage and the Date of Augustine's *De Trinitate*." *Journal of Theological Studies*, vol. 70, no. 2 (2019): 680–705.

Wisse, Maarten. *Trinitarian Theology beyond Participation: Augustine's* De Trinitate *and Contemporary Theology*. London: Bloomsbury, 2011.

Zizioulas, John D. "One Single Source: An Orthodox Response to the Clarification on the Filioque." Orthodox Research Institute, 2017. http://www.orthodoxresearchinstitute.org/articles/dogmatics/john_zizioulas_single_source.html (accessed February 10, 2021).

ANCIENT SOURCE INDEX

Ambrose
  Fid.
    1.13.79-84   67
    2. pro. 2   132
    3.11.89   125
  Spir.
    1.12.131   39
    3.1.6   170
    3.1.7   159
Athanasius
  C. Ar.
    3.13–14   67
Augustine
  Adim.
    9   68
    14.2   190
  Arian.
    4   131
    4.4   132, 137
    6.6   28, 92
    8.6   29, 31
    9.7   28, 29, 78, 79, 148
    11.9   30
    13.9   164
    15.9   164
    16.9   49
    19.9   158
    22.18   28, 170
    22.18–23.19   170
    22.18–23.20   30
    23.19   173, 182
    23.19–20   113, 182
    23.20   182
    25.21   58, 186, 190
    34.32   164
    37   30
  C. du. ep. Pelag.
    1.8.13   140
    1.9.15   187
    1.10.21   181
    1.11.24   175
    4.10.28   190
  Civ.
    2.26   81
    8   84
    8.6   83
    8.7   83
    8.8   83, 84
    11   52
    13.23   82, 175
    18.34   30, 114
    18.49   110
    18.50   141
    18.53   184
    20.21   79
    20.30   159
    22.18   116
  C. Jul. op. imp.
    1.96   175
    3.106   140, 181
    6.37   116
  C. litt. Petil.
    2.2.5   164
    2.32.76   140
    2.92.202   116
  Coll. Max.
    2.25–26   69
    2.26   70
    6   187
    11   28, 170, 187
    12   29
    13   29, 30
    14.17   31
    14.19   30
    15.2   29
    15.16   114
    15.18   30
    15.21   168
    15.24   124
    15.26   30, 49
  Conf.
    7.20.26   83

7.21.27	82	89.5	140
9.4.9	116, 129, 130	92.4	78
10.42.67	81	92A	186
11–13	52	93.21	184
11.13.15	114	120	85
Cons.		137.12	78
2.5.14	115, 157	140.6	92
2.14.31	164	140.52	58
2.16.33	160	140.62	186
2.33.80	140	164.10	116
3.4.13	58	164.18	176
3.18.55	148	166.7.21	82
3.25.79	115	169.5	140
Div. quaest. LXXXIII		170.4	93, 182
66.6	181	174	32
66.7	175	187.16	57
67.2	190	189.6–8	39
69.1–10	110	194.17	186
69.6	110	199.50	177
69.10	116	217.6	57
76.2	140, 182	238.28	126
Doctr. chr.		Exp. Gal.	
3.34.48	140, 182	31	58
Enarrat. Ps.		Faust.	
3.5	122	11.8	140
30.1.6	148	18.6	134
34.2.3	181	19.2	181
39.14	140	22.69	141
44.18	116	22.89	140, 182
50.10	157	Fund.	
52.5	181	6	130
54.14	57	9	140
71.1	140, 181	Gen. litt.	
108.26	170	1	52
109.9	116, 141	4.9.18	189
114.8	175	5.19	177
117.1	181	6	175
146.6	175	Grat.	
150.1	188	5.12	187
Enchir.		Man.	
14.49	114	2.14.32	190
Ep.		Maxim.	
29.4	140, 182	1.2	135, 181
29.5	140, 182	1.5	31
36.17	190	1.7	29
48.3	138, 140, 182	1.8	30
53.7	81	1.19	30, 110
55.3	175	2.2	29
78.3	183	2.9	135

2.9.2	113, 138	*Retract.*	
2.12.2	79	1.19.3	172
2.13	58	1.23	181
2.14.1	96, 136, 173, 176, 182, 189	*Serm.*	
		1.1	57
2.14.1.	99	51.1	33
2.14.2	139	51.6.9	28
2.14.9	172	52.1	28
2.15.4	186	52.2–16	33
2.16.1	29	52.4.9	28
2.16.2	115	52.17–23	33
2.17.1	134, 182	71	168
2.17.2	28, 157	71.17.28	58
2.17.4	173	71.29	186
2.18.6	30	143	30
2.20.1	182	265A	29
2.20.3	29, 182	*Serm. Dom.*	
2.20.4	29, 158	1.6.17	172
2.21.2	74	2.4.15	57
2.22.3	28, 136, 182	3.14	58
2.25	29	*Spec.*	
2.26.1–12	66	25	57
2.26.2	71	29	190
2.26.2–3	49	30	181, 190
2.26.4	164	34	182, 189
2.26.5–8	73	36	190
2.26.11	74	43	182
2.26.14	130	*Spir. et litt.*	
Parm.		14.24	140, 182
2.15.34	162	19.34	181
Pecc. merit.		25.14	140
1.4.4	175	*Tract. Ep. Jo.*	
1.18.23	187	2.3	129
1.27.43	181	6.12	182
1.27.46	140, 182, 189	7.11	132
Praed.		8.10	187
1.15.31	174, 184	8.12	187
1.16.33	184	8.13	187
8.33	140	*Tract. Ev. Jo.*	
18.33	182	1.1	36
18.35–36	116	1–3	52
Priscill.		1.7	30, 79
7.8	115	2.15–16	28
Quaest. Hept.		3.2	92
2.55	58	3.3	29
4.18	186	3.18–3.20	85
4.19	157	4–7	164
5.10	183	4.12	28
5.55	124	4.16	132

5	165	45.12	29
6	132, 165	46.4.2	30
6.3	30	47	123
6.5	28, 132, 182	47.3	121
7.23	29	47.7	122, 123
8.10	187	47.14	124
8.12	187	48.10	126
8.13	187	49.8	113
9.4	29	49.14	141
9.10	31	55.3	115
10.11	29	62.4	29
12.6	29	63.3	119
12.11	28	68.3	79
12.12	28	69.2	29
14	122, 130	70	125
14.9	130	70.1	126
14.10	172	72.3	177
14.11	116, 123	74	130, 171, 172
15	183	74.1	29
15.12	183	74.3	28, 130, 138, 170,
15.17	183		171, 182, 187
15.24–26	183	77.1	131
16.4	29	77.2	29
16.6	28	78	143
16.7	78	78.1	144
17.3	29	79	124
17.16	57	79.2	124
18.9	123	92	136, 182
19.5	30	92.1–2	29
19.11–15	91	94	137
19.15	112	94.4	30
19.15–19.16	30	94.4–5	182
19.18	30	97.1	186
20.1–20.8	44	99	129, 137–139,
20.3	44, 48		173, 182
20.7	91	99.2	129, 138
20.8	44, 91	99.4	95
20.13	93	99.6	175, 182, 186, 189
21.3	57	99.6.1	139
23.9	91	99.6–8	98
25.2	110	99.7	28, 96, 129, 157
31.4	93, 121	99.8	98
32	185	99.9	99
32.5	185	100	138
32.5–9	185	100.4	113
34.9	30	100.4.1	112
41.1	134	101.6	140
42.8	94	102	142
43.14	117	102.5	186

102.6	142	1.13.29	29
103	142	1.13.29–1.13.30	30
103.2	142	1.13.30	30, 78
104.1	113	1.13.31	30, 78
105.1	118	2.1.2–2.4.6	132
105.3	118	2.1.3	30, 37, 43, 44
105.7	118	2.1.3–2.3.5	30
106.3	119	2.3.5	29, 30, 112, 136, 137, 182
106.6	119		
106.7	119	2.4.6	117
107.2	113, 182	2.5.7	29
108.3–4	135	2.5.8	28, 92, 157, 158
108.4	135	2.5.8–2.5.9	38
110.4	126	2.5.9	28, 29, 38, 92, 158
121.3	29	2.5.10	28, 30
122.8	183, 188	2.6.11	28
Trin.		2.7.12	28, 38, 92
1.1.1	25, 55	2.7.13	63, 64, 67, 78
1.1.2	25, 55	2.10.17	71
1.1.3	29, 56	2.10.18	72, 132
1.2.4	26, 27, 36, 38, 56	2.10.19	72
1.3.5	56	2.10.19–2.12.22	72
1.3.6	57	2.12.22	73
1.4.7	27, 36, 44, 164	2.13.23	30, 73
1.5	39	2.15.25	74
1.6.9	26, 28, 38, 47, 48	2.15.26	74
1.6.10	38	2.17	30
1.6.12	30, 48	2.17.30	29
1.7.14	28, 30, 41, 42, 49, 78, 161	2.17.31	29
		2.17.32	74
1.8.15–1.10.20	30	2.18.33	30, 75, 114
1.8.15–1.13.31	110	3	164
1.8.16	30, 37, 58, 78	3.1.4	28
1.8.16–1.8.17	58	3.7.12	74
1.8.17	30, 58, 59, 78, 79	3.10.20	29
1.8.17–1.8.18	37	3.11.22	75, 141
1.8.18	29, 30, 143, 184	3.11.22–3.11.27	76
1.8.19	29	3.11.26	78
1.9	29, 143, 185	3.proem.3	28, 67, 92
1.9.19	130	4.1.2	79
1.10.20	30, 78	4.1.2–4.2.4	79
1.10.21	29, 30	4.1.2–4.18.24	78
1.11.22	28–30, 92, 107, 166, 167	4.1.3	38
		4.2.4	28, 79
1.12.21	137	4.2.4–4.12	80
1.12.23	29	4.3.5	80, 175
1.12.25	29, 37, 131, 137	4.3.6	29
1.12.26	43	4.4.7	80
1.13.28	29, 30, 78	4.7.11	28, 81, 92

4.10.13	81	13.10.13	78
4.12.15	81, 82	13.17.22	28, 29
4.13.16	122	13.18.23	78, 82
4.13.17	82, 176	13.19.24	28, 83
4.14.15	185	14.2.4	30
4.15.20	83	14.17.23	30
4.15.20–4.18.24	82	14.18.24	28
4.16.21	83	14.19.25	30
4.17.23	83	15.3.5	33, 36
4.18.24	83	15.6.10	122
4.19.25	88	15.8.14	30
4.19.25–4.20.30	28	15.10.19	38
4.19.26	38, 89, 92	15.11.20	28, 46, 48
4.20.27	28, 89, 92, 159, 177	15.11.21	30
		15.13	30, 57
4.20.28	28, 92	15.17.27	122
4.20.28–4.20.29	182	15.17.29	98
4.20.29	29, 43, 94, 96, 129, 131, 135, 136, 138, 178, 179, 182, 186	15.17.31	122
		15.17.31–15.19.37	187
		15.19.35	189
4.20.29–4.21.31	94	15.19.37	122, 188
4.20.30	92	15.21.40	30
4.proem.1	79	15.23.44–15.24	30
5.11.12	29, 136, 175, 182	15.25	78
5.13.14	138, 182	15.26	29, 38, 182
5.14.15	97, 182, 185	15.26–15.27.48	188
6.1.1	38	15.26.46	28, 160, 161, 165, 166, 177–9
6.2.3	38		
6.5.7	122, 139	15.26.46–47	174
6.10.12	51	15.26.47	97, 163, 166, 172, 173, 178, 179
7.1.1	38		
7.3.4	28, 38, 45, 119, 120	15.27.48	182
		15.27.49	57
7.3.6	122	15.28.51	28, 29, 38, 92
7.5	28		
7.6.12	49, 50	Basil	
8.1.2	28	*Eun.*	
8.4.6	30	2.18	67
8.7.11	122	Bonaventure	
8.8.12	122	*Brev.*	
9.1.1	30, 122	1.2.5	53
9.12.18	182	1.9.7	53
11.1.1	50	2.1.2	53
12.5.5	182	2.4.1–2.12.5	53
12.6.6–7	49	2.6.3	53
12.6.7	174	2.9.1	53
12.14.22	30	2.9.3	53
13	85	2.12.1–2.12.4	53
13.9.12	28, 45	7.1.2	53

Clement of Alexandria
  Paed.
    1.7   67
Cyril of Alexandria
  Ev. Jo.
    11.10   153
Cyril of Jerusalem
  Catech.
    12.16   67

Didymus
  Trin.
    1.19   68

Epiphanius
  Exp. Fid.
    14   69

Gregory of Nyssa
  Or. cat
    1   39
    2   152
  Ref. Eun.
    193–194   68

Hilary
  Syn.
    50   67
  Trin.
    2.29   175
    4.15   67
    6.37   132
    7.17–18   39

    8.21–24   167
    8.52   125

Irenaeus
  Haer.
    4.11-42   67

John of Damascus
  Exp. Fid.
    1.7   152
Justin
    60   67

Maximus the Confessor
  Quaest.
    34   152

Novatian
  Trin.
    18–19   67

Origen
  Hom. Gen.
    4.5   67
  Princ.
    1.2.6   139

Tertullian
  Prax.
    14   67
Theophilus
  Autol.
    1.2   67

Scripture Index

Old Testament

Dan
7	75
7:13	80
7:13–14	30, 109, 114

Eccl
17:1	80

Exod
3:6	73
19:18	74
20:11	80
31:17	80
31:18	74
33:20	69

Gen
1:1	197
1:1–2	53
1–3	52–3
1:4–5	80
1:5	80
1:26	33, 47, 49–51, 54
1:26–27	80
2:1–2	80
9:6	80
12:7	72
18:1	72
18:3–5	72
18:22	72
19:1	72
19:18	72

Hab
2:4	58

Isa
6	68
7:14	80
11:2–3	188
48:12–16	158
48:16	158–60, 197
53:7	159
61:1	149, 159, 167, 170, 171

Psalms
2:7	72, 114
2:9	109, 116
8:6	110
36:10	120
56:7	80
104:4	56
110:1	72

Wis
7:25	92
7:26	92
7:27	93

Zech
12:10	29

New Testament

Acts
1:4	183
1:4–5	128, 140
1:4–8	183–4, 190
1:6–8	183
1:8	98
2:1	74
2:1–4	30
2:32–33	127, 128, 140
2:33	15, 150, 177, 178, 180
2:38	128, 134, 182
4:8	128
4:8–10	140, 181, 182
4:24–26	184, 190

7:30	76	4:4	139
7:55	190	4:4–6	98, 127, 128, 139,
10:38	126, 149, 177		181, 182
11:15–17	127, 189	4:12	80
15:9	58, 79	4:23	80
20:28	190	4:30–32	189–90
28:25–26	68, 72	5:1	50
		5:8	80
Col		5:18–20	128, 140–1, 181,
2:9	171		182
2:15	82		
3:10	50	Gal	
		2:20	29, 37, 158
1 Cor		3:19	76
1:24	38, 45, 120	4:4	28, 38, 42, 92, 107
2:2	29	4:4–6	38
2:8	29	4:6	58, 98, 175, 186, 190
2:10–16	184, 185, 190		
2:11	170, 184, 185	Heb	
6:11	128, 140, 181	1:3	76
8:5	72	2:3–4	128, 141
12:4	138	3:1–7	128, 141
12:4–6	127, 128, 138, 181,	9:14	128, 140, 148, 149,
	182		182, 192
12:6	138	10:12–13	109, 116
12:9–11	170	10:12–15	128, 141
13:12	30, 51	10:29	128, 181
15:21	82	10:29–31	140
15:24–28	30, 37, 109–11, 114		
15:27	109, 110, 114	John	
15:27a	110	1:1	38, 80
15:27b	110	1:3	33, 42, 47–9,
			54, 91, 92
2 Cor		1:4–5	190
3:3	128, 140, 181, 182	1:12–13	46
3:17	72	1:14	28, 46, 80, 92,
3:18	80		159, 187
4:6	80	1:18	121
4:16	80	1:32	19
11:14	81	1:32–33	28, 149
13:14	127, 128, 133, 140	1:33	132, 165
		1:33–34	128, 132, 182
Eph		2:19–20	80
1:4	118	2:19–21	80
1:10	109, 116	3:8	170
1:20–22	109, 116	3:14	29
2:17–18	140, 182	3:27	162
2:17–19	128	3:34	128, 130, 171, 172,
2:21–22	128, 140		187, 192

3:34–35	154	16:15a	112, 113, 162
3:35	109, 116, 122, 123	16:15b	112, 162
4:1–42	183	16:28	142
4:2	181	16:32	142
4:23	183, 190	17:1	117, 118
4:27–28	143	17:1–5	116
5:19	43, 91	17:3	59, 118
5:19–30	109	17:4	117, 118
5:20	116, 122, 123	17:5	117
5:22	30, 111–13	17:6–8	119
5:26	42, 43, 91, 97, 111–12, 120, 124, 125	17:8	119
		17:10	113
5:27	30, 113	17:19	37
6:38	42, 107	17:23	116, 117, 126
7:16	98	17:24	122
7:27	121	19:14	80
7:28	93	19:41	80
7:29	93, 94, 121	20:17	29
8:42	94	20:22	96, 98, 178, 179
10:15	116, 121	20:28	29
10:17	116, 122, 123	27:46	80
10:18	124	27:50	80
10:30	37, 42, 96		
10:36	37	1 John	
10:38	116, 117	3:2	58
12:41	68	3:8	80
13:3	109, 115	4:2	128, 139–40, 182
13:31–32	116, 119	4:7	122
14:7–10	125	4:8	122
14:10	59, 116, 117, 125, 126	4:13	187, 188
14:15–17	29, 130	4:13–14	187, 188
14:16	128, 130–1	4:16	122
14–16	29	5:6–9	128, 135, 182
14:25–26	128, 131, 137	5:7	96
14:26	29, 96, 129, 134, 158, 186	5:8	135
14:28	42, 107, 143, 167	Jude	
14:31	116, 122, 124	20–21	190
15:26	29, 96–9, 128, 129, 136, 181, 182, 186	Luke	
16:7	30, 131, 137	1:31	80
16:7–9	128, 137, 181, 182	1:32	109, 115
16:13	95, 138, 184	1:34–35	98, 158
16:13–14	30	1:35	28, 149, 157
16:13–15	98, 137–8, 181, 182	1:80	149
16:14	117, 170	2:40	149
16:14–15	128	3:21–22	15, 28, 149, 150
16:15	109, 112–13, 131, 162	3:22	19, 132, 149, 182
		3:32	128

4:1	149, 160, 170, 171, 173	26:38	107
		26:39	29
4:14	149	26:61	80
4:18	28, 149, 167, 170–3, 187–9, 192	27:40	80
		27:45–46	80
6:19	98	27:60	80
8:46	98	28:18	109, 114–15
10:21	128, 140, 181	28:19	127, 132–4, 136, 152, 178
10:22	116, 119–21		
11:13	128		
11:20	74	1 Pet	
13:11–13	80	1:2	190
13:16	80	3:18	149, 174, 176, 177, 197, 198
23:46	148, 192		
23:52	80	3:22	109, 116
24:26	29		
24:39	29	2 Pet	
24:49	98	1:4	79
24:49–50	128, 129		
		Phil	
Mark		2:6–7	30, 41, 42
1:10	18, 160	2:7	42, 80, 107, 167
1:10–11	28, 128, 132	2:8	29, 107
1:11	18	2:9	29, 109, 111–13
1:12	149		
1:22	182	Rev	
14:58	80	1:4–5	188, 190
15:25	80	1:7	29
15:33–37	80	2:27	109, 116
15:46	80	22:1	190
		22:17–18	128, 140, 182
Matt			
1:17	80	Rom	
1:18	28, 37, 157, 158	1:14	149, 174
1:20	149, 157	1:20	47, 51, 54, 73, 83
1:21	80	5:8–9	79
3:14–17	33	5:13	80
3:16	18, 149	6:14	80
3:16–17	28, 128, 132, 182	7:4–6	128, 140
3:17	133	8:1–3	127, 128, 134–5, 181
4:1	160		
5:8	30, 58, 59, 78	8:3	181
6:9	57	8:9	136, 175, 176, 189
10:20	98, 175	8:9–11	98
11:27	45, 116, 119	8:10	80
12:28	74, 149, 167, 169, 170, 173	8:11	174–6, 189
		8:15	58
12:32	167–9, 173	8:16–17	190
12:40	80	8:31	79

8:32	29, 37, 158	2 Thess	
9:5	73	2:9	81
11:33–36	53	2:13–14	190
12:2	50		
14:17–18	190	Titus	
15:12–13	128, 140	3:4–6	186–7
15:30	128, 181	3:5–7	80

SUBJECT INDEX

agapē love 116–17
Ambrose of Milan 67, 125, 132, 159, 170
Anatolios, Khaled 18, 19, 197
Anselm of Canterbury 5, 40
Aquinas, Thomas 19
Arnold, Johannes 17, 40, 91
ascension 14, 21, 28, 29, 36, 105, 141–2
   parallel end point 143–4
   parallel starting point 142–3
Athanasius 67, 79, 153, 161
Augustinian-Western tradition 2, 3, 5, 7, 11, 15–18, 21, 23, 24, 63, 76, 100, 193, 194, 198
Ayres, Lewis 16, 18, 38, 41–3, 89, 95, 107, 108, 117, 120, 125, 126, 129–32, 136, 164, 167, 170, 178, 179, 186, 198

Bailleux, Emile 17, 18
Balthasar, Hans Urs von 14, 15, 149, 155, 156
baptism 14, 15, 21, 28, 33, 36, 60, 132–4, 148–50, 152, 162, 164–6, 173, 178–80, 191, 192, 195, 196
Barnes, Michel R. 16, 18, 59, 122, 129, 143, 148, 157, 166, 168, 180, 187, 198
Basil of Caesarea 67
Behr, John 12, 38
Benner, Drayton C. 13, 16, 17, 40, 84–5, 106
Bobrinskoy, Boris 14, 127, 141, 149, 150
Boff, Leonardo 150
Bonaventure 4, 6, 11, 47, 51, 53–4, 60
Bonnardiere, Anne-Marie la 159, 171
Bourassa, François 14, 17, 59, 60, 154, 155, 163, 192

Cappadocians 7, 24, 35, 69, 197
Cary, Phillip 102
christological peculiarity 3–7, 10, 17, 20, 37, 41–7, 60, 66, 76, 88, 90, 95, 158, 193, 194

Christology 39–41
Clement of Alexandria 67
Coffey, David 98, 122, 179
Congar, Yves 14, 15, 156, 157
creation
   doctrine of 6–7, 47–54
   inseparabilis operatio 7, 37, 40, 43–4, 47–8, 131, 159, 161
   psychological analogy 1–2, 4, 6–8, 20, 24, 31–3, 35–6, 41, 46–51, 53, 55, 56, 59, 60, 77, 86, 165, 194
   Trinitarian reading 52–3
   vestigia 20, 47, 51, 53, 194
   Western tradition 6–7, 47
crucifixion 14, 27, 28, 36, 148, 192
Cyril of Alexandria 19, 153
Cyril of Jerusalem 67

De Deo uno and *De Deo trino* 3, 7, 17, 20, 23
   Augustine's integration of 35–7
   God the Father 37–9
   inseparabilis operatio 37
   Trinity 37–39
   Western tradition 34–5
de Régnon, Theodore 10, 18, 24, 34, 35, 40, 68, 69
desert temptation 21, 82, 149, 160, 195
Devil 81–2
Didymus the Blind 68–70, 72
Die psychologische Trinitateslehre (Schmaus) 9, 24, 35, 41, 66, 70, 90, 113, 131
doctrine of salvation 61, 63, 76–86, 194
du Roy, Oliver 25, 55, 175, 198
Durst, Rodrick 127, 128, 135, 180

earthly ministry 21, 195
economic/immanent taxonomy 11, 12, 198

economic Trinity 2, 10, 12, 13, 17, 19, 21, 66, 84, 87, 88, 100, 102–4, 144, 155, 156, 193, 195, 197, 198
economy of salvation 2, 3, 6–9, 15, 17, 19–21, 23–7, 31, 33, 37, 39, 47, 51–5, 60, 61, 63, 64, 71, 78, 80, 82, 84–6, 94, 98, 100–2, 104, 131, 147, 152, 153, 155, 156, 193, 194
Epiphanius of Salamis 68–70
Erickson, Millard J. 116, 117, 125, 119
eternal generation 15, 21, 22, 42–4, 93, 97, 106, 108–15, 118–21, 123–7, 129, 130, 132, 135, 138–140, 144, 145, 148, 154, 181, 195, 197
Evdokimov, Paul 149
exegetical difficulties with Rule 11–15, 104–5, 149–51

faith
  end of 58–9
  praying to the Father 57–8
  and psychological analogy 59–60
  starting point of 55–7
  Trinity 57–8
  Western tradition 54–5
Father–Son relationship 2, 13–14, 19, 21, 101–45, 183–8, 194–5
Ferri, Riccardo 32, 55, 90, 91, 112
Filioque 12, 14, 17, 97, 98, 104, 147–52, 154–6, 162, 163, 179, 191

Giles, Kevin 106
Gioia, Luigi 110, 112, 125, 131, 137, 139, 158, 188, 189
God the Father 37–9, 46, 73–5, 114, 120, 121, 141, 150
grace, doctrine of 5–6, 21, 76–8
Green, Bradley G. 18
Gregory of Nazianzus 69, 72
Gregory of Nyssa 68–70, 152
Gregory XIII 13, 148
Grundaxiom 2, 19, 20, 42, 66, 102, 147, 151, 155, 193
Gunton, Colin 18, 198

Harnack, Adolf von 24, 31, 54
Harrower, Scott 14, 15, 18, 19, 109, 116, 119, 127, 141, 144, 149, 150, 152, 177, 178, 196, 198

Hilary of Poitiers 41, 67, 125, 132, 167, 175
Hill, Edmund 2, 16, 17, 23, 35, 36, 40, 45, 56, 60, 78, 95, 166, 168, 176
Holy Spirit 2, 5, 8, 13–15, 18, 19, 21, 23, 26, 27, 29, 36–8, 40, 43–6, 49, 52, 53, 57, 60, 63–5, 67–9, 72, 74, 75, 86, 87, 90, 94–9, 102–5, 107, 112, 113, 115, 117, 122, 125, 127–40, 147–92

Ignatius of Loyola 3
immanent Trinity 2, 12, 14, 15, 17, 19, 21, 42, 86, 87, 100, 102–5, 107, 116, 128, 133, 141, 144, 145, 150–2, 155–7, 159, 161, 163, 167, 168, 173, 178–80, 191–5, 197
incarnation 3–6, 9, 12, 14, 28, 39, 41–3, 46, 59, 60, 69, 76, 80, 84, 90, 93, 94, 106, 154
inseparabilis operatio 7, 37, 40, 47–8, 131, 159, 161
interchangeability 13, 105, 109, 110, 158
Irenaeus 67

Jesus 5, 10, 14, 27, 40, 59, 68, 80, 85–6, 93, 106, 108, 114, 116, 121, 134, 137, 141–3, 149, 152–3, 159, 161, 163, 165–6, 168–75, 177–8, 185, 189
Jesus' ministry 21, 28, 148–50, 166–73, 191–2, 195
John of Damascus 152
Jowers, Dennis W. 14, 18–19, 101–4, 149, 151–5, 161, 163, 196
Justin 67, 68

Kany, Roland 15, 16, 18, 26, 33, 133, 162
Kärkkäinen, Veli-matti 35
Kloos, Kari 16, 68, 70

Lacugna, Catherine M. 5, 12, 40, 103, 198
Lee, Chungman 136, 145, 156, 185
Levering, Matthew 83, 84
Logos 4–6, 11, 39–42, 45, 46, 59, 156

Maximinus 69, 70, 114, 168, 176, 187
Maximus the Confessor 152, 197
ministry *see* Jesus' ministry

missions 10–11, 101, 105, 108, 116, 127, 128, 130, 131, 135, 136, 138–140, 142–5, 147, 151, 153–4, 157, 159, 166, 171, 179, 183, 189, 194–5, 197–8
  Augustine's approach to 88–89
  correspondence of the Son's 89–92
  correspondence of the Spirit 94–5
  exegetical support for correspondence of Son's 92–4
  exegetical support for correspondence of Spirit's 96–9
  Rahner's approach to 86–8
Modalism 106
Moltmann, Jürgen 103
Mühlen, Heribert 14, 152–4, 161, 163
mutuality 14, 21, 154, 161, 170–1, 173, 179, 188, 191, 195
  glorification 105, 117–19, 126, 144
  indwelling 105, 125–6, 144
  knowledge and revelation 105, 119–22, 126, 144
  love 105, 122–6, 144
  reversibility, problem of 105, 116–17, 126, 144

Neo-Scholastic theology 34
New Testament 8, 11, 12, 37, 65, 67–9, 72, 77, 78, 99, 110, 127, 128, 140–1, 198
Novatian 67

Old Testament 3, 8–10, 21, 40, 41, 59, 61
  Augustine's approach to 66–7
  mediation 75–76
  Rahner's approach to 63–6
Origen 67
Ormerod, Neil 17, 50, 51

Patre procedit 151, 155, 191
Patreque 14, 22, 150, 182, 191, 192, 194, 195
patristic exegesis 19–20
Pelikan, Jaroslav 16
Pentecost 15, 21, 27, 28, 36, 74, 96, 148, 150, 161, 177–80, 183, 188, 191–2
Pentecostal outpouring of Spirit 14, 21, 177–80, 191–2, 195

piety 3–5, 17, 20, 23, 49, 54, 55, 57, 59, 60, 63, 193, 194
processions *see* missions
psychological analogy 4, 6, 7, 20, 24, 36, 41, 47
  biblical backdrop of 31–3
  christological peculiarity 46–7
  faith 59–60
  Gen 1:26 49–51
  John 1:3 48–9

Rahner, Karl 1, 2
  assessment of West 15–18
  biblical defence of 18–19
  christological peculiarity 4–5
  De Deo trino 7
  De Deo uno 7
  difficulties for Rule 104–5
  doctrine of creation 6–7
  doctrine of grace 5–6
  economy of salvation 8–9
  exegetical criticisms of 11–13
  Father–Son relationship 13–14
  missions and processions 10–11, 86–8
  Old Testament 9–10, 64–6
  patristic exegesis 19–20
  religious piety 3–4
  salvation 76–8
  Scriptures 8–9, 101–2
  Son–Spirit relationship 14–15
  Trinity 76–8
Rahner's Rule 2, 11–14
  alleged difficulties for 104–5, 149–151
  biblical defence of 18–19
  definition of 102–4
Ratzinger, Joseph 142
resurrection 14, 21, 28, 29, 36, 80, 83, 118, 148, 149, 174–7, 195
reversibility
  mutuality 116–26
  transfer of authority 109–15
  triadic patterns 127–40, 180–91

salvation
  Augustine's argument 78
  exegetical backdrop 78–0
  inadequacy of philosophy 82–4
  mediation, Christ, and Devil 81–2

mediation, the one, and the many 80–1
    Rahner's approach to 76–8
Sanders, Fred 11–14, 19, 106, 109, 111, 141, 144, 150, 156, 157, 197
Scheffczyk, Leo 10, 25, 40, 66
Schierse, Franz Josef 8
Schindler, Alfred 41, 90
Schmaus, Michael 9, 10, 24, 31, 35, 41, 54, 57, 66, 69, 70, 90–2, 125, 131, 198
Schoonenberg, Piet 103, 156
Schulte, Raphael 8, 10
Son–Spirit relationship 14–15, 147–8
    alleged difficulties 151–7
    Jesus' ministry 166–73
    Jordan baptism 164–6
    Pentecost 177–80
    Rahner's Rule 149–51
    resurrection 174–7
    virgin conception 157–64
soteriology 6, 18, 23, 76, 85
Spirituque 14, 15, 21, 148–50, 152, 154, 156, 159, 163, 164, 166, 173, 182, 191, 192, 194, 195
Studer, Basil 16–18, 110, 158, 175
subordination 13, 14, 17, 42, 70, 90, 104, 105, 107–9, 111–17, 119, 120, 122–5, 127, 149, 160, 168, 170, 173, 177, 191, 192
Subordinationism 13, 21, 26, 36, 43, 105–8
    Augustine's strategy for preventing 107–8
    problem of 106

τάξις 2, 15, 17, 18, 21, 105, 106, 127–9, 131–9, 145, 147, 148, 150, 151, 180, 181, 183–8, 190–2, 197
Tertullian 67
theophanies 9, 10, 16, 21, 41
    Abraham theophanies 72–3
    Augustine's approach to 66–7
    Daniel theophany 75
    Eden theophany 71–2
    Exodus theophany 73–4
Theophilus 67
transfiguration 28, 36
triadic patterns
    Father–Son–Spirit 105, 127–9, 131, 133, 135–6, 140, 145, 159, 164, 165, 180–3
    Father–Spirit–Son 127, 155, 160, 183–8
    reversibility, the problem of 127–9
    Son–Father–Spirit pattern 105, 128–32, 181–2
    Son–Spirit–Father pattern 105, 126, 132–6, 181–2, 190
    Spirit–Father–Son pattern 188–90
    Spirit–Son–Father pattern 105, 128, 136–40, 181–2, 190
Trinity
    and Christology 39–47
    and creation 47–54
    De Deo uno and *De Deo trino* 37–9
    and faith 54–60
    missions and processions 86–99
    psychological analogy 31–3
    salvation 76–84
    and Scripture 23–33
Tritheism 106

vestigia 20, 47, 51, 53, 194
virgin conception 21, 148, 150, 151, 153, 157–65, 173, 174, 180, 191, 195
von Harnack, Adolf 24, 54

Weinandy, Thomas 14, 15, 150–2, 164
Western tradition
    Christology 39–47
    De Deo trino 34–5
    De Deo uno 34–5
    faith 54–5
    separation of Scripture and Trinity 23–5
Williams, Rowan 38

Zizioulas, John D. 98

www.ingramcontent.com/pod-product-compliance
Lightning Source LLC
Chambersburg PA
CBHW051520230426
43668CB00012B/1684